Writing Well

BOOKS BY DONALD HALL

Books of Poetry

Exiles and Marriages, 1955
The Dark Houses, 1958
A Roof of Tiger Lilies, 1964
The Alligator Bride: Poems New and Selected, 1969
The Yellow Room: Love Poems, 1971
The Town of Hill, 1975
Kicking the Leaves, 1978

Books of Prose

String Too Short to Be Saved, 1961
Henry Moore, 1966
Writing Well, 1973, 1976, 1979
Playing Around (with G. McCauley et al.), 1974
Dock Ellis in the Country of Baseball, 1976
Goatfoot Milktongue Twinbird, 1978
Remembering Poets, 1978

Edited Works

New Poets of England and America (with R. Pack and
    L. Simpson), 1957
The Poetry Sampler, 1961
New Poets of England and America (Second Selection) (with
    R. Pack), 1962
Contemporary American Poets, 1962; Second Edition, 1971
*A Concise Encyclopedia of English and American Poetry and
    Poets* (with Stephen Spender), 1963
Poetry in English, 1963; Second Edition, 1970 (with Warren
    Taylor)
The Faber Book of Modern Verse (New Edition with Supplement),
    1965
The Modern Stylists, 1968
A Choice of Whitman's Verse, 1968
Man and Boy, 1968
American Poetry, 1970
A Writer's Reader (with D. L. Emblen), 1976, 1979

Writing Well

Third Edition

Donald Hall

Little, Brown and Company

Boston   Toronto

ACKNOWLEDGMENTS

James Agee. Quotation on page 118 from "Southeast of the Island: Travel Notes." Reprinted from *The Collected Short Prose of James Agee* by permission of Houghton Mifflin Company and Calder & Boyars Ltd., London. Copyright © 1968, 1969 by The James Agee Trust.

The Ann Arbor News. Quotation on pages 240–241 from "Highways Are for Everyone, Not Just Studded Tire Users," the editorial page of *The Ann Arbor News,* July 4, 1972. Reprinted by permission.

James David Barber. Quotation on pages 255–256 from *The Presidential Character* by James David Barber. Copyright © 1972 by James David Barber. Published by Prentice-Hall, Inc., Englewood Cliffs, New Jersey. Reprinted by permission.

R. P. Blackmur. Quotation on page 275 from "New Thresholds, New Anatomies" in *The Double Agent* by Richard Blackmur. Copyright 1935 by Richard Blackmur. Reprinted by permission of Peter Smith Publisher, Inc.

(Acknowledgments continued on page 398)

To Gerard McCauley

Author's Note

The people from whom I derived my ideas of style are the writers whose work I have loved. I quote many of them here, so that they may speak in their own voices, and need not depend upon the articulation of an admirer. I do not quote them all. I owe my sense of style, as well as some ideas of it, especially to the modern writers I read and imitated when I was young: Ernest Hemingway, Ezra Pound, Marianne Moore, George Orwell, Gertrude Stein, James Joyce. I do not mean that I may call myself a pupil.

In earlier editions of *Writing Well*, I benefited from the help of many people, and mentioned their help in my notes. Because their assistance persists in this third edition, I want at least to list their names again. At Little, Brown, I was greatly aided by Margaret Zusky, David Lynch, and Rab Bertelsen. I used editorial help by Lawrence Russ and Rosemary Yaco. Some of the teachers whose suggestions informed the second edition were Donald Butler, Terrence Collins, Steven V. Daniels, H. Ramsey Fowler, Neita Gleiker, Frederick Goff, Richard Larson, Thomas Lux, Russell J. Meyer, Marcia Stubbs, M. Elisabeth Susman, Barbara Wicks, and Peter T. Zoller.

In the third edition, I am indebted to Jan B. Welch at Little, Brown, who has been in charge of production, and to Dale Anderson, my copy editor. I am grateful to Elizabeth Philipps for ten thousand things. I learned much from the students to whom I taught Freshman English at Colby-Sawyer College in New London, New Hampshire; special thanks to Sandy Bielunis. Traveling around the country, I have profited from many conversations with teachers of Freshman English, and with directors of writing programs. I think particularly of visits to Ball State University, to Oakland University in Michigan, to the University of Wisconsin at Stevens Point, to the University of Vermont, to Syracuse University, and to Orange Coast College. I cannot list the names of everyone with whom I have conversed — and from whom I have taken instruction — but here are a few: Thomas Carnicelli, Peter De Blois, William Hiss, Frederick Bromberger, Joann Mercer, Diana Anderson, Charles Berger, Muriel Allingham-Dale; and Sandra Donaldson, who spoke by letter.

I am also grateful for the many suggestions from Linda Albright, Robert Aldridge, Nell Altizer, Maureen Andrews, Barry Bakorsky, Richard Bausch, May Brown, Carl Brucker, Ingrid Brunner, Harriet Carr, T. L. Clark, Steve Connolly, Marion Copeland, David Dawson, Anne Elam, Michele Giannusa, Norman Hane, Joyce Hicks, Walter Isle, Sighle Kennedy, Sharon King, Jim Ledford, Silvine Marbury, Doreen Maronde, Timothy Materer, Michael Martin, Sr. Jean Milhaupt, C. R. Moyer, Helen Naugle, Kenneth Newman, George Pittman, Martha Rainbolt, Kenneth Requa, Robert Spiegle, Sandra Stancey, Diane Stege, Sharon Stuut, Kathleen Sullivan, J. C. Taylor, Ricki Wadsworth, Louis Williams, Thomas Wilson, and George Wymer.

Students who mailed completed questionnaires to Little, Brown helped me revise this text for future students. On both the second and the third editions, I have been helped by Clayton Hudnall of the University of Hartford, who has for the third edition improved the excellent Instructor's Manual that he made for the second. He has constructed a Master Key, which I believe will help all of us who use this book, allowing us to indicate where in *Writing Well* a student can look to correct his faults.

In all editions, I am greatly indebted to Richard Beal, of Boston University, who has supplied strengths in the areas of my own weakness, who has been tireless and good-natured and relentless and kind. In all editions, I am most grateful to my editor at Little, Brown, Charles Christensen, who is intelligent, efficient, diligent, demanding, and rewarding.

Contents

5

PARAGRAPHS   185

6

EXPOSITION, ARGUMENT, DESCRIPTION, NARRATIVE   227

7

AUTOBIOGRAPHY, FICTION, CRITICISM, RESEARCH   263

8

A BRIEF REVIEW OF GRAMMAR, PUNCTUATION, AND MECHANICS   305

1

Writing, and Writing Well

WRITING TO DISCOVER AND MAKE CONTACT

Students write papers and answer questions on tests, scientists write reports on their work, teachers write evaluations of their students, people make lists to remember what they must do, some of us keep diaries to remember what we have done, salesmen write messages from the field to the office, and we write notes and letters to keep in touch with relatives and friends. There are practical reasons for literacy. The reasons for writing *well* are practical also.

But not at first. First, comes the message: "I want milk." Even earlier, "Mmm," to the mother's ear, can mean "I want milk." As our brains grow, our messages become more complicated. We make our verbal messages emphatic by gesture and facial expression, as a guitar may borrow some of its rhythmic drive from a drum. Learning to write well is harder than learning to talk, but it can bring pleasures deeper than the satisfaction of immediate needs. It can bring us the pleasures of discovery; writing well, we must think clearly; writing well, we must understand our feelings.

A good writer uses words to *discover*, and to bring that discovery to other people. He writes so that his prose is a pleasure that carries knowledge with it. That pleasure-carrying knowledge comes from self-understanding, and becomes understanding in the minds of other people. It makes the difference between writing and writing well.

Here is a passage from a student essay about registering for freshman courses:

> I got nothing but hangups all over the gym, bad vibes and it got worse and a bad way to begin anything as important like college.

This writer has problems in mechanics, in levels of diction, and in generality of language. A message comes through, but inferior writing garbles the faint sound of complaint. Later in the term, the student rewrote the passage.

> There were long lines at every table, during registration at the gym. It took me one hour to find out that a class was closed and I could not take it. Some teachers didn't know the rules for their own departments. After half a day of feeling frustrated, I went back home and told my mother I wasn't sure about going to college after all.

This version gains clarity through detail, and through improved mechanics. Any reader will respond to stories of institutional incompetence. A short version could have read:

> Registration took a long time and accomplished nothing. I felt frustrated.

This version is brief and correct, better than the first version, but not good enough. Because it only *tells* us a feeling, but does not *show* us anything, it will not create the feeling in the reader. It tells its message abstractly, making a message purified of character and feeling, like a slice of bread purified of nutrition or taste.

When we write, we make a contract: *my words are addressed to the outside world; I construct sentences in order to reach someone else.* Too often we write as if we ourselves were our only reader. If we leave out punctuation or use a cliché, then, it does not matter — *we* know what *we* mean. But neither the first version with its errors and its vagueness, nor the third version with its meagerness, tell enough to *someone besides the writer.* The second version, on the contrary, is sociable: it enters the world of other people, and by using detail and conventional mechanics, it speaks to an audience.

Writing well means making contact with an audience. Every piece of advice this book offers — about argumentation and about commas, about paragraph structure and about spelling, about avoiding clichés and about inventing transitions — helps the writer make contact with the reader.

HONEST AND DISHONEST FEELING

The phrase "honest feeling" implies an opposite, dishonest feeling, which no one admits to, but which we sometimes see clearly in others. We all know that many feelings are falsely expressed. We have grown up on the false laughter of television, the fake enthusiasm of advertising, the commercial jollity and condolences of greeting cards, and the lying assertions of politicians. If some falsity has not entered our prose, we are made of aluminum.

We can be false in a thousand ways. We do it with handshakes and we do it with grunts. We do it by saying outright lies and we do it by keeping silent. But in these examples we understand our own falsity. When we fool *ourselves* — which we do frequently — we are in more trouble. We fool ourselves with words that can mean almost anything. How much have we said when we call someone "liberal"? We fool ourselves when we avoid blame by using a passive (the table was knocked over and broke) or by using personification (the glass fell off the table). We fool ourselves by using clichés, trite expressions that have become meaningless substitutes for feeling and thought.

> It's not black and white.
> The situation is very complicated.
> That's more or less what I had in mind.

Clichés are little cinder blocks of crushed and reprocessed experience. When we use them in writing, we make false contact with the reader; they are familiar, and seem to mean something, but really they are meaningless from overuse. Clichés prevent true contact, by making false contact in its place.

Every profession — medicine, law, theater, business — has its own clichés. We call the clichés that belong to a particular profession *jargon*. One set of clichés appears especially at graduations, from primary school through graduate school.

> The future belongs to you.
> The challenge of new . . .
> The most exciting generation of . . .
> Responsibility, good citizenship, service to the community, . . .

The university, in fact, is one of the great sources of jargon. Here are two paragraphs from a letter addressed by a newly elected college president to his faculty.

Dear Members of the State College Community:

I am deeply honored and challenged by the opportunity to join State College as its seventh president. The hospitality and spontaneous warmth of everyone we have met has made both Barbara and me feel very welcome. We look forward to making State our home as quickly as we can arrange an orderly transition from our current responsibilities.

State College is rich in tradition: it is an institution with a past, and, more importantly, it is a College with a future. Building on its heritage, and maximizing its resources, State College can continue to achieve distinction by providing educational opportunities for young men and women.

Not all college presidents write this sort of thing; many do. It is the sort of language we expect from officials — from politicians and bureaucrats, from the presidents of colleges and the presidents of corporations. It says nothing, and it says it with maximum pomposity. It took this man years to learn the trick of empty jargon, the style of interlocking cliché. Every phrase is trite, and the phrases are stuck together with mortar like "is" and "and" and "with." The edifice is reprocessed garbage.

deeply honored
challenged by the opportunity
spontaneous warmth
making . . . our home
orderly transition
current responsibilities
rich in tradition
Building on its heritage
maximizing its resources
achieve distinction
providing educational opportunities

One should mention as well the trite and meaningless contrast between the past, as in "heritage" — a word as hokey as "home" — and "a college with a future." The contrast says nothing. Unless the collegiate doors are closing tomorrow, of course it has "a future." The word "future" — like "heritage" and "home" — carries with it vaguely positive connotations. A candidate for president of the United States once used as a slogan, "The future lies before us," trying to associate himself with this positive connotation; no one found the slogan offensive, but he lost.

In the college president's letter, the smoothness of the masonry is exceptional, but the passage is without content and without feeling. The paragraphs are "insincere" because they do not represent a person's feelings. Of course the author did not *intend* insincerity, nor did he feel that he was lying. He felt, we can presume, that he was using the language expected of him.

We must look closely at the notion of sincerity, or we can use it to justify its opposite. The worst liars sincerely say — to themselves and to the world — that they are the most honest. Yet sincerity can be a valuable idea, if we think clearly about it, and sincerity has everything to do with the reasons for writing well. Peter Elbow, quoted in Ken Macrorie's book *Uptaught,* says:

> I warn against defining sincerity, as telling true things about one self. It is more accurate to define it functionally as the sound of a writer's voice or self on paper — a general sound of authenticity in words. The point is that self-revelation . . . is an easy route in our culture and therefore can be used as an evasion: it can be functionally insincere even if substantially true and intimate. To be precise, *sincerity is the absence of "noise" or static — the ability or courage not to hide the real message.*

The static is the distance between what the words say and what we sense lies behind them. The person with a pose of sincerity fixes us with his eyes, saying, "I am going to be wholly honest with you. I am a bastard. I cheat on my girlfriend and I fink on my roommate. I hate my father because he gave me a car. I hit a blind man once when nobody was looking." The real message: "Love me, I'm so *honest.*"

The distance between the meaning (the apparently stated) and the expression (the really implied) ruins the statement, and prevents real communication between people. In the college president's letter, the meaning has something to do with expressing pleasure in a new task; the expression is an exhibition of academic smoothness; it is a little dance, performed by a well-trained educationist seal. It says, "Look at me. Admit me to your ranks. I am one of you."

We cannot accept sincerity as a standard if we are going to take the writer's word for it. We can take it seriously if we listen to his *words* for it. Sincerity is *functional* (Elbow's word) if we believe it, if we hear the voice of a real person speaking forth in the prose — whether of speech or of the written word. The reader must feel that the prose is sincere. And functional (maybe we should call it "convincing") sincerity comes from the self-knowledge we earn by self-exploration. It is not easy. It requires self-examination, and hard thinking or analysis. It is worth it. Socrates made the commitment: the unexamined life is not worth living.

EXAMINING THE LIFE

By learning to write well, we learn methods of self-discovery and techniques for self-examination. Understanding the self allows us to move outside the self, to read, to analyze, to define. Writing well can be a starting point for all thinking. Self-discovery and self-examination are separate things, though they can happen at the same time. Self-examination finds what we have inside us that is our own. Of course we are stuffed with clichés — we have been exposed to them all our lives — but clichés are not "our own." We have swallowed everything that has ever happened to us: we dropped the bottle to the floor, at the age of eight weeks, and cried for the loss of it; the telephone did not ring last week, and we cried for the loss of it; the toy shines under the tree, the toy rusts behind the garage; the smell of bacon, the smell of roses, the smell of kittens that have been careless; the flowers and the beer cans emerging from the snow. Everything that ever happened to us remains on file in our heads. As a professor at M.I.T. put it: the human brain is a big computer made of meat.

If the brain is a computer, we are all engaged in learning how to operate it. For the college president quoted above, the task of writing was simple; he was programmed to write that kind of prose; he pushed the right keys and his brain computer turned out preassembled units of academic jargon. The commencement speaker, or the student writing home for money, presses other keys for printouts of ready-made pseudothoughts and pseudofeelings. But let us suppose that we are interested in something genuine, the voice without static, the utterance in which expression and meaning are the same. We must learn new ways to use the accumulation of words, sense impressions, and ideas that we keep in the disc-packs of the brain.

Confucius told us to "Make it new." "It" was thinking, feeling, expressing, writing. Only by making it new, each time we speak or write, can we make it true. To make it new does not mean to make it merely novel. One can leave out capitals, change typography, create new rules of spelling — and still write with clichés or other static. Really to make it new, we must avoid the worn roads of conventional association; we must find what is uniquely our own voice out of our own experience. Then our words will not make rows of identical houses like the subdivision prose of cliché. "New" is fresh, genuine, ourselves, our own experience. Making it new, we make contact with the reader.

It is not, however, the inevitable result of spontaneity. Spontaneous writing is a good way to start to learn how to write, and a good way to uncover material you didn't know was in you. One important computer key is a sense of freedom in writing. But then there is the second half of genuine expression, the half that applies the map-maker's self-examination to the new country of self-exploration. This self-examination, leading to revision, allows the writer to communicate knowledge to other human beings. Revising the map, we think of the reader; we revise to make contact with the reader.

REVISING THE MAP

Almost all writers, almost all the time, need to revise. We need to revise because spontaneity is never adequate. Writing that is merely emotional release for the writer becomes emotional chaos for the reader. Even when we write as quickly as our hand can move, we slide into emotional falsity, into cliché or other static. And we make leaps by private association that leave our prose unclear. And we often omit steps in thinking, or use a step that we later recognize as bad logic. Sometimes we overexplain something obvious. Or we include irrelevant detail. First drafts remain first drafts. They are the material that we must shape, a marble block that the critical brain chisels into form. We must shape this material in order to pass it from mind to mind; we shape our material into a form that allows other people to receive it.

Good writing is an intricate interweaving of inspiration and discipline. A student may need one strand more than the other. Most of us continually need to remember both sides of writing: *we must invent, and we must revise.* And in these double acts, invention and revision, we are inventing and revising not just our prose style but our knowledge of ourselves and of the people around us. When Confucius recommended "Make it new," he told us to live what Plato called "the examined life." It was a moral position. By our language, we shall know ourselves — not once and for all, by a breakthrough, but continually, all our lives. Therefore the necessity to write well arises from the need to understand and to discriminate, to be genuine and to avoid what is not genuine, in ourselves and in others. By understanding what our words reveal, we can understand ourselves; by changing these words until we arrive at our own voices, we change ourselves; by arriving at our own voices, we are able to speak to others and be heard.

THEMES AND REVISIONS

On the first day of class, the assignment was to write for twenty minutes under the heading, "How I Came to College." Here is an impromptu theme by Jim Beck.

> Education is of paramount importance to today's youth. No one can underestimate the importance of higher education. It makes us well-rounded individuals and we must realize that all work and no play is not the way to go about it, but studies is the most important part, without a doubt. Therefore I decided when I was young that I would go to college and applied myself to studies in high school so that I would be admitted. I was admitted last winter and my family was very happy as was I. Coming here has been a disappointment so far because people are not very friendly to freshmen and everyone has their own clique and the whole place is too big. But I expect that it will get better soon and I will achieve my goal of a higher education and being a well-rounded person.

Repetition at the end of the impromptu gives it some unity. When Jim Beck says that "people are not very friendly to freshmen," the reader glimpses Jim Beck and his feelings. But through most of the paragraph, the writer is not being himself. You can tell that he is not being himself because he is sounding like so many other people. Jim Beck is assembling an impromptu from the cliché collection in the why-I-want-to-go-to-college box. When he says "paramount importance," does he really know what "paramount" means? Does he mean that "today's youth" is genuinely different from yesterday's or tomorrow's? And how far into history does "today" extend? What does "well-rounded" mean? Why say "individual" instead of "person" or "people"? "Importance" is vague, and saying it twice makes it vaguer. In the sentence of complaint, where the reader briefly senses an actual writer, Jim Beck would have done better to *show* his loneliness in an anecdote, instead of just *telling* us about it. Showing makes contact; telling avoids it.

Later in the term, when he had a free theme, Jim Beck wrote an essay which was not so much a revision of his impromptu as a new start, and which *really* told how he came to college.

The Race to College
Jim Beck

It's horrible now, and I don't know if it will get any better. The only people who pay attention to me are the people who are trying to beat me out for the track team. My roommate is stoned all day and gets A's on his papers anyway. I hate him because he hates me because I'm a jock. My classes are boring lectures and the sections are taught by graduate students who pick on the students because the professors pick on them.

But I remember wanting to come here so bad! Nobody from Hammerton named Beck had ever been to college. Everybody knew the Becks were stupid. This went for my father, who never got through high school, and for my grandfather, who died before I was born, and who was the town drunk. It went for my two older brothers who went bad, as they say in Hammerton. Steve got a dishonorable discharge from the Marines and he works on a farm outside town and gets drunk on Fridays and Saturdays. Curt stole a car and did time at Jackson and nobody has heard from him since. My sister had a three-month baby and the town liked to talk about that.

I was different. Everybody told me I was. My mother told me I wasn't a Beck. My father told me I was going to bring back the family's good name. (I never knew it had one.) In grammar school the teachers all told me how much better I was than my brothers. By the time I was in sixth grade my father and the school Principal were talking about the University.

My father isn't really dumb. Sometimes people look dumb because it's expected of them. He's worked at the same grocery for twenty years, I guess. Now that I made it to the University, he wants to be called Manager, because he's the only man there besides Mr. Roberts who owns it. (The rest of the help are — is? — kids who bag and an old lady cashier.) When I went back for a weekend everybody treated me as if I won the Olympics.

I said the Principal and my father were talking about my going to the University. All through junior high I said I didn't want to go. I was scared. No Beck could do that. Bad things kept happening to my family. My father had an accident and totalled the car and lost his license and for a year we didn't have a car at all. He had to walk home two miles every night pushing a basket of groceries. When I said I would quit school and get a job, everybody jumped on me.

It wasn't that I was an A student. It was just that I tried hard at everything I did. I got B's mostly. Now with B's, the counsellors kept telling me, I could be admitted to the University, but I wouldn't get a scholarship. I needed mostly A's for that, and then when I got to the University I would lose the scholarship if I couldn't keep the grades up. Then my brother Steve, who was a pretty good athlete once, suggested athletics.

I was too skinny for football, too short for basketball, I could barely swim and my school didn't have a swimming team anyway. There is one sport you can practice with no money and no equipment. I started to run when I was in my last year of junior high. It felt good right away. I ran to and from school. I went over to the high school and did laps. The high school coach noticed me and asked me to go out the next year. Running long distances hurts a lot. Sometimes you get a stitch in your left side and suddenly it shifts to your right side. I didn't exactly mind the pain. I studied it. I studied it in order to go to the University, the way I studied everything else.

In my Senior year I was all-state and held two high-school records (600 and half-mile) and I had an athletic scholarship to the University. Now I am here, the first Beck to make it. I don't know why I'm here or why I ran so hard or where I go from here. Now that I am here, the race to get here seems pointless. Nothing in my classes interests me. I study, just as I did before, in order to pass the course or even get a good grade. I run to win, but what am I running for? I will never be a great runner. Sometimes when I cannot sleep I imagine packing my bags and going back to Hammerton. But I can't do that. They would say, "He's a Beck, all right.

Jim Beck's essay has the two most important features of good writing: it has unity, which means the focus, the point, the coming together of many details; and it has the voice of a real person speaking out of his own experience, using his own language, with a minimum of tired phrases, of borrowed clothing. It has discipline, and it has feeling. Although Jim Beck is discouraged and feels aimless and melancholy, his mind has made an enormous stride toward knowing and being able to present itself. Self-knowledge may feel uncomfortable, but in the end it is more satisfying than self-delusion. He revised, using his own experience in his own language. *And* he was disciplined; he used tighter sentence structure and he found unity in his experience. He learned about himself while learning to write prose.

The same assignment brought forth this theme from Marian Hart:

I always wanted to go to the University because my Dad went here.

I remember how it got started. I had a job as a car-hop in a drive in, an A & W in Flint where I make my home. Business was slack because it was about 3:30 Saturday afternoon so I was talking away with Barb and Karen who were working there too and I knew them from school of course. We had to wear these very tight stretch pants because Boss said it was good for business. A car came in and because it was my turn I picked up a pad and started out for it, then I saw it was my Dad. He jumped out of the car and hugged me. I knew what it was and so did Barb because we were all waiting to hear about admissions. I told him he could open it and he did and that's why he drove out, to tell me. Barb had to wait until she got off, the Boss wouldn't let her go and there was nobody at home to call up.

So! We got here three days ago, in the same car, only loaded to the roof with my stuff. I was petrified with fear. My Dad kept telling me what to do, and then he kept saying he knew it had changed a lot in 25 years. I wished he'd be quiet. My Mom cried. We couldn't find the dorm. Everybody we asked didn't know either. The boys all had long hair and beards and looked exactly the way I expected them too. My Dad hated it. Then when we found my dorm and we found my room my Dad was all out of breath, and mad, and he just pushed the door open with his shoulder and busted in. There was a naked girl standing there, with no clothes on, my roommate (whose very nice, named Terri, but I didn't know that yet) and he made a funny noise and dropped the suitcase and ran back out into the hall.

The theme needs only revision; it needs focusing, understanding, thinking, and care. When you look over a first draft, trying to find ways to clarify it and bring it together, ask yourself, "What is this *really* about?" and see if you can come up with an answer. Jim Beck's first paper was about nothing at all — or about what he imagined the institution wanted to hear. His second paper was about social class, and trying to escape a family social pattern, and the empty feeling of success. Marian Hart's paper is mostly a playful account of her feelings for her father and his for her, with evidence of some jealousy and flirtation.

"I always wanted to go to the University because my Dad went here."

The word "because" begs questions. Probably thousands of high-school graduates *don't* want to go to some university precisely because their dad went there. And this one-sentence paragraph does not really introduce the reader to the action. It does not set up what follows in an intelligible or unifying way. Of course at the same time it is exactly what Marian Hart had to say, and thus is the first clue to the paper's real content. It *was* true that she wanted to go to the University because her dad went there. But because she has not yet examined the implications of her prose — the literal illogic, and the emotional truth, of her first sentence — she is not ready to write or think with coherence.

Some of the writing is bad. "Where I make my home" is a euphemism for "where I live." (Euphemisms are fancy words for simple things, or soft words for harsh things, like "pass away" for "die." See pp. 65–67 for more about euphemism.) Barb and Karen are useless details; they add nothing and are there only because they were part of the landscape in the opening anecdote. The story becomes truer when they are omitted, because its outlines become clearer as the mists of futile detail recede. Another detail, about the tight stretch pants, might seem to be irrelevant also, but, unintentionally, this detail is a prelude to her father's arrival. The beards and long hair of the boys, and her father's irritation, could also seem irrelevant, if you didn't understand that her father is as fond of her as she is of him, and therefore jealous of young male rivals. The chance discovery of a naked roommate provides the writer with the perfect, comic moment, in which the embarrassed father drops the suitcases. The materials are abundant, and this is the place to stop. In her first account she ran out of time here, or she would have gone on to have them eating supper at a German restaurant with a dressed Terri, and then waving goodbye as her parents drove off to U.S. 23. The clock saved her from going on too long.

The week after she wrote the impromptu, Marian Hart rewrote the theme for unity and focus. As she learned more about writing and about herself, she returned to it occasionally and rewrote a passage as part of an exercise. Finally, feeling bored with the theme but also determined to finish it once and for all, she rewrote it as a free theme near the end of term.

My Father's Place
Marian Hart

It is about an hour and a quarter from my house in Flint to the dormitory in Ann Arbor. All the way, as we drove here last August to move in, my Dad was talking about the class of 1939. I tried to listen. I had heard him talk about the University since I was a little girl, and since I was a little girl I had wanted to come here to college. But in the car I was shy and frightened. I was going to meet a roommate named Terri who was from Detroit. She would be sophisticated and have long hair. All the boys would be crazy about her. I would be the invisible frump from Flint. My Dad was talking about *fraternities* and *dances!* My God.

I tried to think about happy things. I tried to think about how happy I was, as I sat there feeling stupid and ugly. I remembered how happy I was to be accepted. It was a Saturday last Spring when I was working at the A & W, being a car hop in the stretch pants that the boss made us wear "because it's good for business."

It was a slack time of day, and suddenly a car rolled up, parking across two parking places, and rocking with the brakes put on too fast. I picked up an order pad and headed out, and then I saw that it was our car and that my Dad was jumping out at me waving an envelope and grinning. He didn't have to say anything. We hugged and he called me his sweetheart. The three of us went out to dinner that night and celebrated.

Now my mother was sobbing and my teeth were chattering and my father was talking about *corsages!* I groaned a little, and he said — for the twelfth time — that of course he knew that everything was different now, with student rights and politics and ecology and (he gagged a little) co-ed dormitories. But . . . and he was off again. He was as nervous as I was.

When we drove into town my Dad's composure fell apart completely. He didn't know where he was. We asked directions but everyone else was as lost as we were. The whole place had changed, he said; none of the old landmarks were there. And he obviously hated the new landmarks. Girls with overalls and no bras and bare feet and long hair were throwing frisbees with boys with blue jeans and no shirts and bare feet and long hair and beards. My father's jaw went tight, and from the back seat I could see the tenseness of his neck that happened when he was worried or angry.

We found the dorm. My father carried the four suitcases. I carried a portable stereo and a box of indispensable records. My mother had three garment bags full of clothes which I knew I would never wear. Of course my room was on the third floor. Every time we passed a boy in the hallway my father's neck, which was red with carrying four suitcases, got tenser.

When we got to the door of my room, he didn't set down the suitcases to knock. Puffing and snorting, he pushed open the door with his shoulder and strode in, me and my mother close behind.

> Then he dropped all four suitcases, crash, and made a weird little
> noise. I thought: My God, he's having a heart attack. Then I looked
> past him and saw a girl standing facing him with her mouth
> flopped open in surprise — Terri, I thought, even then, and she's
> *not* too beautiful — and stark naked.

Notice how Marian Hart has brought in the essentials of the A & W
scene, but kept her unity by judicious repetition: car / car; affection /
affection; college / college. Because of these connections, the flashback
is not mechanical but organic; it grows naturally out of the scene. The
structure seems to take form spontaneously from its material, the way
a wildflower grows from a crack in the cement. Of course this writer
worked hard, as all writers must, to seem effortless.

Both of these student writers revised their work by improving
their understanding of themselves and their material; and Marian Hart
improved hers by unifying her anecdote, cutting unnecessary detail
and arranging the rest to give her story dramatic point.

SOME PROFESSIONAL WRITING

These essays were impromptu, and the revisions printed here
came two months later. Professional writers often take longer still,
and struggle with the same enemies, disunity and evasion. The professional writer differs from the beginner in many ways: he knows that
he is likely to fail at first, and why; he is patient, he is adamant, and
he expects his writing to be hard work. Comparing professional models
and freshman examples is unfair, of course, but we do not compare
them to emphasize the distance between the two. We bring in the
models to give an idea of a goal, to exemplify and make concrete the
standards we can otherwise only talk about; to show and not just to
tell.

A good way to learn to write well is to read good prose. Gradually
we acquire the manners that make the good writing we admire. It is
like learning a foreign language by living with a family that speaks it,
by shopping in it, and by listening to television shows with dialogue
in it. Take this paragraph of exposition, which begins a *Scientific
American* article:

> In medieval Europe wood was utilized not only in many types of
> construction but also in most domestic and industrial heating.
> Then in Britain in the second half of the 16th century coal came
> into widespread use as a substitute for wood as fuel. The earliest
> coal-burning economy the world has known was established first

in England and then in Scotland between about 1550 and 1700. This transition from woodcutting to coal mining as the main source of heat was part of an early British economic revolution. The first energy crisis, which has much to do with the crisis we now face, was a crisis of deforestation. The adoption of coal changed the economic history of Britain, then of the rest of Europe and finally of the world. It led to the Industrial Revolution, which got under way in Britain in the last two decades of the 18th century. The substitution of coal for wood between 1550 and 1700 led to new methods of manufacturing, to the expansion of existing industries and to the exploitation of untapped natural resources.

The author introduces us to a subject, and leads us step by step through a summary of historical change. The article's title, "An Early Energy Crisis and Its Consequence," makes an implicit comparison that the paragraph begins to explore; "deforestation" must make a parallel to the present depletion of oil reserves. Clearly the import of the closing sentences is optimistic. Yet the author, strolling us past considerable information, allows the analogy to rise out of the material presented; we are not bludgeoned by bullying interpretation.

Or take this expository paragraph from a book about an Arctic explorer.

In the nineteenth century, Arctic exploration captured man's imagination just as space exploration has captured it today. The coldness and indifference of the Arctic, its beauty and terror, the unknown riches and dangers that lay in its unexplored vastness — all these appealed to man's capacity for wonder and his desire for challenge. The Victorian reading public followed the preparations of an expedition to the North with the same avid attention modern television viewers give to a space flight. Newspaper readers learned of iron sheathing on ships, experimental screw propellers, and ingenious methods of heating cabins, just as today we learn of nose cones, solid fuels, and oxygen support systems. Increasingly in the nineteenth century, the expeditions became a matter of national enterprise. The controversies aroused and the questions asked are familiar: Could not money and energy be better spent in more practical and humane ways? Was this purely a national enterprise, or was it the culmination of the work of many nations? Was science perhaps becoming too arrogant? Should such exploration be under military control, or was it best kept in the "private sector"?

Chauncey C. Loomis, *Weird and Tragic Shores*

Again, a writer explains the past by analogy to the present. Here, the writer touches the reader's imagination; we become educated in our feelings, which are invoked and summoned by the writer's skilled use of parallel and analogous detail. These details grant image and flesh to the stated comparison: Arctic exploration is the nineteenth century's equivalent to contemporary space travel.

Or take another example, from fiction this time. One of the models of prose style in contemporary literature is Ernest Hemingway, who worked carefully on rhythm and sound. When he was young especially, he studied style and practiced and revised, to learn the way to his own voice. A short story called "In Another Country," about some wounded soldiers in a hospital in Italy during World War I, opens with this paragraph:

> In the fall the war was always there, but we did not go to it any more. It was cold in the fall in Milan and the dark came very early. Then the electric lights came on, and it was pleasant along the streets looking in the windows. There was much game hanging outside the shops, and the snow powdered on the fur of the foxes and the wind blew their tails. The deer hung stiff and heavy and empty, and small birds blew in the wind and the wind turned their feathers. It was a cold fall and the wind came down from the mountains.

Such a simple style! And if you try to imitate it, you are likely to lace one shoe to the other. The grammar is simple, yet the length of sentence and clause — the units of rhythm — varies continually. The vocabulary is simple — the fall, cold, and wind repeated, wind four times in the last five lines — yet expressive. The effect of the whole is hypnotic or dreamy; the war is around us but "we" are not in it. Then the paragraph ends with the corpses of animals, described with a loving detail. Look at the word "pleasant"; normally, we might find this word too general, and want to ask *how*, exactly, did you feel? But here, in the emotions of the paragraph, the vagueness is an accurate understatement; it embodies the emotional restraint in this removal from war, the tentative acceptance that "we" are alive, unlike the animals outside the shops and the unmentioned combatants among whom "we" used to count ourselves.

DISORGANIZED WRITING, POMPOUS WRITING

For a perverse sort of fun, let us rewrite the Hemingway passage in a couple of bad versions. First, a parody (an imitation of a style, for the sake of mockery) of the disorganized writing that most of us start out with.

September through December, in the fall, at any rate, the war still went on, but we ourselves weren't doing the fighting by this time. It got chilly then in the Italian city of Milan. It started to get dark earlier in the day. When it got dark they turned on the lights. It was nice to look in the windows of stores. There were a lot of dead wild animals outside of the stores. When it snowed it snowed on the animals' fur too. There was a lot of wind and it blew the animals' fur and it even blew the little ones around. It was really cold because the wind was coming down from the mountains, which were cold.

Actually, this parody is better than the prose most of us write at first, because the writer observes real things. Most bad writing omits anything that might be interesting and expressive. The whole paragraph might be reduced to:

It was fall in Milan, Italy, one year during World War I. It got colder and the days got shorter.

But the short version omits all feeling. In the real paragraph, details of image and action carry the scene to the reader. You cannot reduce *War and Peace* to a telegram.

Or we could try it in Pompous Institutional Moderne.

During the autumn, the hostilities continued to ensue, but we no longer engaged in them ourselves. The daily temperature declined in Milan as the autumn continued, and the hours of daylight gradually contracted. When darkness ensued, lights were illuminated. It was altogether agreeable to promenade and investigate the contents of shop windows. There was considerable unrationed meat available at this time, by reason of the prevalence of slaughtered wild animals. Precipitation in the form of snow, as the months progressed, accumulated on the fur of these slaughtered beasts, and the cold breeze that accompanied the snow caused the tails of the animals to wave. Venison was available, as was small fowl. The extreme cold of this autumn is attributable to the fact that the prevailing winds came from the direction of the mountains which, because of their elevation and the snow which had already accumulated thereon, were lower in temperature than the temperature which normally prevailed in the city.

This last writer, if he existed, might be elected chairman of the board, but he would never excite our feelings, or understand his own.

We learn to write well, if we learn, for good reason. Few of us will ever write with Hemingway's skill. We don't need to, unless we are writers. But we need to move toward this skill. If we write with the chaos of the first parody, or with the pomposity of the second, we are in trouble in our heads and our hearts, not just in our writing. If we learn to write well, we will sharpen our wits on the one hand, and point our imagination on the other — both together, or neither at all.

LEARNING TO WRITE WELL

How then do we learn to write well? We can do three things, at least. First, we can read well, which helps slowly, but keeps on helping; second, we can study writing and think about it and discuss it with others; third, and most important, we can write, and rewrite, and rewrite. Because rewriting our own work is most useful, we must have writing to rewrite. Keep a notebook. Keep a journal. Keep your old themes. Keep copies of papers or exams you write for other courses. In this collection of your own prose, you will find ideas for expanding and rewriting. You may notice, the tenth time you reread something, that you have written in order to hide something from yourself instead of to discover. After thinking about clichés or paragraph organization or passive verbs, you will find examples in your own prose, and you will see how to revise them.

DAILY WRITING

While you are learning to write, it is a good idea to write something every day. Continually applying pen to paper will ease the work of writing, and will give you a collection of words and sentences in which to look for ideas to develop and for work to revise. Writing is a skill, like an athletic skill, which comes more naturally to some people than to others, but which improves with practice for everyone. Practice is a necessity. Maybe the best method is to write daily dated entries in a notebook. This notebook sounds like a journal, but for most people a journal is like a diary, and records merely the day's events:

> Had pancakes for breakfast. 9 o'clock boring . . .

Little entries that set out our daily schedule do not help us. Better are memories, whole anecdotes, ideas, and queries. Or it may help to concentrate on the world outside the self.

Doing daily writing means writing a page or two a day, every day, seven days a week, working rapidly and without trying to impose a direction on it, without conscious control or focus. Nor should a daily entry be continuous, necessarily. Some days one has apparently unrelated flashes of thought or memory. Some days one seems to have no ideas at all. On such a day, you may let your hand flow over the page with disconnected words and phrases. When Henry Moore, the great English sculptor, sits in front of the television set at night, sometimes he lets his hand wander over a page, "sketching" while he pays little attention; and sometimes ideas start, in this way, which later (with direction, control, focus, and attention to mechanics) become works of art.

Many professional writers keep notebooks. Theodore Roethke, the American poet, left two hundred and seventy-seven notebooks behind when he died. Some entries were lines and images for poems; some were used, some were not. Others were prose notes to himself about writing poetry, and might have been seeds for unwritten essays.

> Get down where your obsessions are. For Christ's sake, shake it loose. Make like a dream, but not a dreamy poem. The past is asking. You can't go dibble dabble in your tears. The fungi will come running; the mould will begin all over the noble lineaments of the soul. Remember: a fake compassion covers up many a sore. . . .

At other times, he made a more conventional journal entry.

> Today, or tonight, I realized finally at the age of 40, for the first time, that it is really possible for me to think, and even get pleasure from the process. Not that my efforts — or effects — are spectacular. Perhaps four consecutive related thoughts at present is the absolute top of my form — and that only just before falling asleep, or just after eating a fine breakfast, when I'm too lazy to write anything down. But still, even this is a beginning. And such excitement!

F. Scott Fitzgerald kept a notebook in which he recorded situations, observations, jokes, and anything else.

> Widely separated family inherit a house and have to live there together.
>
> . . .
>
> Girl and giraffe.
>
> . . .
>
> Family quarrels are bitter things. They don't go according to any rules. They're not like aches or wounds; they're more like splits in the skin that won't heal because there's not enough material.
>
> . . .

Jules had dark circles under his eyes. Yesterday he had closed out the greatest problem of his life by settling with his ex-wife for two hundred thousand dollars. He had married too young, and the former slavey from the Quebec slums had taken to drugs upon her failure to rise with him. Yesterday, in the presence of lawyers, her final gesture had been to smash his finger with the base of a telephone.

. . .

Hearing Hitler's speech while going down Sunset Boulevard in a car.

. . .

Run like an old athlete.

Daily writing can loosen minds. Our minds are muscle-bound, not by intellect, but by formulas of thought, by clichés both of phrase and of organization. Our minds do not need to remain restricted. An economics student wrote this entry in a notebook:

Blue clouds in Arizona. I was hitchhiking last August, at the edge of the desert waiting for a ride that would take me across state. A little tree, a little shade. Sun so hot it melted turtles. Blue clouds of Arizona. Because there were no clouds at all, just blue glaring and turning white toward the sun. Like an egg only a lot brighter and hotter. Got a ride with a truck driver. "Never went to college myself. The war came along and then I had kids, you know. My daughter's at State." Jiggle. Oil. Hot. We had cheeseburgers in an airconditioned diner and I never felt so good in my whole life as when that ice-air hit me. Then the heat outside. Walking into the oven. (cliché.)

There is no point to his story, or maybe no story. No one said he had to make a point. All he had to do was write a page. He was practicing.

Practice was the first thing for him, sheer practice in putting pen to paper, letting the words follow each other across the page; if the habit of writing remains alien to us, we will never learn to write with any naturalness. Second, he was learning to loosen up. No one was going to correct his spelling, or argue with his logic, or tell him that his clauses were not parallel; he felt free to let the images follow each other loosely by association. Until the last phrase, his loosened mind provided fresh images. But if he had written a string of clichés, nobody was going to bother him about it. Earlier in his notebook, before he trusted himself to loosen up, his prose had been rigid and trite.

Beginning a notebook of daily writing, almost everyone is shy and stiff, as if this private writing were a public performance. One student began her notebook:

> I am not "an emotionalist," if such a word exists. I feel as if I'm taking a step forward in saying that I tend not to be sincere in my writing. From this point forward I shall try to do so. I feel that I'm honest with myself, but when I know that others will read my work I unconsciously become dishonest as I write.
>
> If I were to write a short essay on any topic and hand it to a person to read, I wouldn't stay in the same room while the person read my work. Whether this is because of shyness or embarrassment, or both, I don't know.

Two months later, her prose was less self-conscious and more relaxed, and she seemed to enjoy herself more.

> They try to give something special every week. When I read eggrolls listed on the menu, I thought, great, my favorite thing in the world. But to my dismay, I was shocked at what the Stockwell Cafeteria had done. How could they destroy *my* eggrolls? I bit into one of them and I noticed *black*, inside my eggroll. Shortly later, I discover that *raisons* had been planted in the eggrolls! Raisons! How could they! It seemed that they just sat around saying, "What can we put in the eggrolls to make them terrible? We can't lose our image!" Of all the stupid things. That's enough to start a new war with China!

Nobody leaned over her shoulder, drew a red circle around "raisons," and wrote "raisins" in the margin. Over the term her writing improved, perhaps because she wrote ninety-two pages of daily writing; her spelling stayed about the same.

Everybody who starts daily writing at first fears running out of material. Really, we have enough memory packed away, by the age of eighteen, to keep us writing until we are seventy. We gradually discover tricks that keep the pages coming. We should stop writing while we still have something to say; it is even wise to make an arbitrary rule: stop at the bottom of a full page, even in the middle of a sentence, and write nothing more until the next day. The next day, you will not have to sit and wait for the words to start.

Many students find that they work best with large categories of reminiscence, writing many pages — weeks of daily writing — on one general subject: my six best friends and their families; fishing trips with my mother; Christmas vacation; jobs I have had; my teacher in grammar school; pets; relatives; the Little League; 4–H clubs; fights with my brother; learning to repair my ten-speed bike; my favorite meals; and my favorite jokes (one student remembered forty pages of jokes!) Some students interested in science and technology try to write about science in a language that nonscientists can understand — a difficult and useful kind of writing.

Daily writing is a means and not an end, however. Unless the writing becomes directed and shaped toward an end, it does not help us when we want to write for another person. Unity, clarity, and the discipline of the sentence and paragraph — all are necessary to move the message from the writer to the reader. Once we have found an idea or an image or a secret lode of language, then we must learn to shape and control in order to communicate.

We need to learn all about language — choosing words, inventing metaphors, phrases, clauses, and sentences, and constructing paragraphs — before we can establish control over our writing. But of course we must try to make whole shapes, like the revisions by Jim Beck and Marian Hart, from the very beginning, even before we have learned the names of what we do. It makes sense, before we begin to study words, to look at what happens when we write a paper.

___ **EXERCISES** _____

1. Write a brief impromptu essay on the events of your first few days in college. Use specific examples or anecdotes. Find some unity or focus to hold your writing together.

2. Write a paper about the English courses you took in high school. What did you do? What did you learn? What did you feel was emphasized? What did you feel was not emphasized enough? Find some unity or focus to hold your writing together.

3. We discover ourselves by the language we use. Write a dialogue, or a conversation, in which two people reveal their characters by their language.

4. Analyze in class the language in this theme. Try revising the first paragraph.

My Big Moment

In my humble opinion, after all is said and done, opportunities for people to show what they are made of are conspicuous by their absence at this university. Because of this sad truth, the day I gave my report stuck out like a sore thumb. It was a red letter day. I had spent the entire year at college burning the midnight oil and leading a precarious existence earning my tuition working for a professor who was a veritable mine of information. I was very much interested in the finer things of life. My hope to do things that would make me stand out from the crowd were usually doomed to disappointment. As I wended my way from class to class each day, and then to the job where I put my nose to the grindstone, I often thought that the events in my life at which I could point with pride were few and far between. But today would be different.

Today I, a rank outsider, would be the center of attention. People would realize that I was smart as a whip. They would listen with bated breath. At ten o'clock I stood as scared as a rabbit before the class. Although I was hungry as a bear because I had not eaten breakfast, I was calm and collected. I stood before them and I told the unvarnished truth about Man's mistreatment of Mother Nature. I explained that the powers that be must sit up and take notice of the fast and furious pace of pollution, and that there was a crying need for immediate action. I viewed with alarm the future of society when the purity of the very air we breathe hangs in the balance. When I concluded my few remarks, there was thunderous applause. I could tell I had hit the nail on the head. I was tired but happy. I had hit one out of the ballpark.

5. In *The Atlantic Monthly* a writer discussed some schools he disapproved of. In one paragraph, he wrote:

> In such places students are taught clichés. In one college a test consisted of stories with blank spaces to be filled with adjectives, the "correct" answers arcane or phony words used by *Time* magazine during the era of Henry Luce (but no longer used even by *Time*). In another college the blanks to be filled were the most hackneyed phrases, so that fires were always "raging," heavy rains always "torrential downpours," and recriminations always "bitter."
>
> Ben H. Bagdikian,
> "Woodstein U.: Notes on the Mass Production
> and Questionable Education of Journalists"

Make a short paragraph in which you leave blanks for parts of clichés — usually an adjective or an adverb. Read it aloud in class, to see if other students can fill in the "correct" clichés.

6. (a) In the paragraph from the *Scientific American*, on pages 14–15, try omitting any sentence after the first, and see if the passage needs the missing information. Try reordering any two sentences, and decide if any other organization of the information is possible. (b) In the paragraph comparing Arctic exploration with space travel, on page 15, cross out any details that the passage can

do without. Does the greater brevity improve or impoverish the paragraph?

7. Read this passage carefully. Try to decide what makes it good writing. Point out how the author achieves her effects.

> For many people moving is one kind of thing and travel is something very different. Travel means going away from home and staying away from home; it is an antidote to the humdrum activities of everyday life, a prelude to a holiday one is entitled to enjoy after months of dullness. Moving means breaking up a home, sadly or joyfully breaking with the past; a happy venture or a hardship, something to be endured with good or ill grace.
>
> For me, moving and staying at home, traveling and arriving, are all of the piece. The world is full of homes in which I have lived for a day, a month, a year, or much longer. How much I care about a home is not measured by the length of time I have lived there. One night in a room with a leaping fire may mean more to me than many months in a room without a fireplace, a room in which my life has been paced less excitingly.
>
> Margaret Mead, *Blackberry Winter*

8. Here is another "How I Came to College" impromptu. (a) Criticize it, for language and for structure. (b) Edit it. Rearrange, and rewrite.

> I looked for work waitressing or anything last summer. Not finding anything school seemed like the best thing. Besides my family wants me to go. Learn a trade or skill I guess. So thats how come I am sitting here writing this!
>
> My girlfriend had already gotten in here and so she told me how to do it. I sign up and they tell me what I had to do. Just before I started classes I got the job I was looking for! But my father says you go to school. That's life.
>
> I can't tell yet how I like it or not. But I had a hard time getting here every morning because I don't have a car and, my mother doesn't drive and my father needs it except on Thursdays. My girlfriend has a car, she drives me here MWF. Tuesday I take buses for one hour or so.

9. Here is a better example. (a) What makes it better? (b) In what ways could this student learn to improve her writing? Pay attention to mechanics, to focus, and to word choice.

> All my life I have known that I would, some day, go off to school. By the end of my senior year in High School I knew where and when I'd be leaving and spent the summer getting used to the idea. But getting used to the idea was all I did — I did not begin to think or worry about what college was really going to be like. I did not spend hours contemplating the importance of "going off into the big wide

world." I did not even speculate what things would be like, what if I hated my roommate, what if the work was too hard, what if I'm unhappy. I did not think about specifics, I had told myself that I would have time to get psyched the week before I left.

But a week before the day I had planned to leave, before I had prepared myself I got a phone call from my father. He had to give a lecture at a convention on the west coast in five days. For him to make it we had to leave that day and he would drop me off in Michigan on his way to California. I had one hour to pack. One hour to collect all my belongings and somehow fit them into a car that looked like it could not hold half the things I wanted to take. It happened so fast I did not have time to think, I did not even have time to say goodby to my mother who was out shopping. We left in a hurry leaving behind many things I had forgotten to pack and a small note to my mother that simply said good-by.

If I had more time I'm sure my goodbye to my mother and friends would have been a long, emotional scene. Driving through my town I had no time to look at my Elementary School, my High School, the house of my best friend and get sentimental. It was pouring and concentrating on the driving was all I could do.

The eleven hour drive also left no time for thought. I drove most of the way so that my father could prepare his speech. Every so often he would read parts to me to try them out. Our talk consisted of whether injection-lasers was a hyphenated word or not. (I still don't know.)

Then I was here, in the dorm, with my roommate, in my classes. It seemed as if I had been here all my life and the trauma of leaving home was over. I did not even have time to think about it until later and then I could not even remember how it felt to leave home.

10. Write a page in a notebook, every day, for the rest of the term. Bring your notebook to conferences for your instructor to inspect, but not to correct. Bring it to class, if your instructor asks you to, with a page or a paragraph marked to read aloud. Discuss in class the problems and rewards of daily writing, giving each other suggestions for subjects.

2

Writing a Paper

"Students write papers and answer questions on tests. . . ." So I began this book, naming an immediate and practical necessity for the student writer. Then I talked about emotional honesty and self-discovery, matters essential to good writing, and matters that good writing leads to. But in most composition courses the student is asked to write a complete paper at the very beginning, and to write additional complete papers every week or two throughout the term. It is time for some practical advice on writing a paper.

We have looked a little at the complete papers written by Jim Beck and Marian Hart, and have spoken about focus and unity. Now we must investigate how a paper comes to be written, and how it comes to achieve focus and unity. For these two students, doubtless their daily writing increased their fluency, and fluency helped them to revise their papers. But daily writing — spontaneous and undirected and uncorrected — is a means to an end, and not an end in itself. The end is good writing, and the occasion for good writing in a composition class is the paper. The paper is *controlled, disciplined, and directed* by the student writer — and generally corrected by a teacher. Both Jim Beck and Marian Hart learned to write papers, something quite different from daily writing.

A paper has a purpose. A paper *shows* its purpose, both in its shape and in its statement, or the paper fails. In beginning a paper, we *find* that purpose; in writing the paper, we make that purpose *clear* to the outside world.

A paper must support its purpose by detail; it must have sufficient detail, and yet it must not have too much. It must set details into an order that expresses purpose. If we are writing three hundred words, we must find a purpose small enough to be supported adequately in two pages of writing. Our first necessity, when we begin a paper, is to narrow the subject down.

To accumulate detail, we can use the dreamlike spontaneity we cultivate in daily writing. But to cut and to shape, to narrow and to focus, we need to cultivate other qualities of mind. We must develop a sense for order and shape, a sense by which we understand the whole paper as several units organized to become one larger unit, and controlled by a purpose to an end.

We must also understand that our whole paper — from our choice of words for the opening paragraph to our choice of detail for the concluding paragraph — directs itself to the eyes and ears of other people. We do not write for ourselves only. We need to persuade, to inform, to please, to convince, to charm, to arouse, to impress *other people.*

Once we understand that writing is directed elsewhere — and not inward, where we can be sure that a generous interpretation will accept our intentions — then we can understand the function good style fills. We avoid clichés, or extraneous information, or misleading abstractions, or dangling modifiers, or incomplete arguments, *for one reason:* all these flaws, errors, or imperfections block the passage between the writer and the reader.

In later chapters, I will look into the choice of words, the making of sentences, and the construction of paragraphs, and at the different types of writing a student may undertake. But first we must investigate how the whole paper is made. We must look into the process that will be the student's classroom task throughout the term: writing papers single in purpose, whole and adequate in shape, and clear to an audience.

GETTING IDEAS

Many beginning writers find that getting started is the hardest work in writing. How do you find a starting point for a paper?

It depends on what you are doing. It also depends on the agility of your mind. But however spry or stiff you feel, you can learn to become *more* agile, *more* open, *more* prolific with ideas. If you have been doing daily writing, you have a warehouse of possibilities on the pages that you have accumulated. If you are writing a free theme, you can consult your daily writing for a thought or an anecdote that is apt for expansion. If you are assigned a theme to demonstrate a technique of writing — a type of argument, for instance — you can find a starting point in your daily writing to develop and use.

If you are assigned to write a paper on Sino-Soviet relations, or on why you want to go to law school, or on a novel, your daily writing will not help you to find an idea. You must accumulate detail, allow ideas to grow from other ideas, and then shape the whole. I will speak more of this shaping later.

If you have no daily writing, and you are assigned a free theme, you have numerous ways of looking for subject matter. Topics come from your own life. For some papers, you can write anecdotal reminiscence. But even when you are not writing a free theme, even when you write exposition, or argument, the subject can come from your own life. If you wish to write an argument, think of recent conversations. Almost everyone gets involved in controversy from time to time. Choose a position to attack or defend, out of something in your own experience. Newspaper articles leave us feeling angry or approving — and are another source of topics for argument. Supreme Court decisions, presidential speeches, international conferences. Still lacking ideas, look over letters from home, or remember an argument you had with your parents.

But argument or advocacy are not necessary to make an essay. You may want simply to investigate something. Hearing about how state lotteries proliferate, you may want to do research on them and set forth the information in a paper. You may want to write exposition on the safest way to ride a motorcycle, or how to organize a rent strike. Books, television, talk shows, and everything we see in our daily lives — from movies to the way customers and shop clerks behave — can provide a topic for exposition. We must keep our eyes open. When we need to get an idea, we must let our inward eyes move freely over our experiences recent and past. A million topics wait for us.

One January, an instructor at the University of Michigan assigned a short theme, to be written outside class, as the second paper of the term. Students were to write two hundred and fifty to three hundred words of comparison and contrast, taking their subject at least partly from university life. For instance, the instructor suggested, they could compare living at home to living in a dormitory. But perhaps this subject would prove too large, too vague, and too inclusive. Maybe they could narrow the topic, and compare sleeping at home with sleeping in the dormitory, or home cooking with dormitory food. Or they could contrast two things at the university; resident students could compare living in a dormitory with living in an apartment; residents and nonresidents could compare riding a bicycle on campus with driving a car; all students could compare lecture courses taught by professors with recitations taught by graduate students or part-time instructors.

The instructor asked for questions. Yes, they could write about something they didn't have direct knowledge of — like living in an apartment — provided the comparison was not too distant; don't compare walking to class with hiking in Switzerland. No, he didn't think a comparison of two beers sounded like a promising paper. Could the student compare tastes so that his audience could tell the difference? Maybe he could compare two bars?

Sharon Rustig returned to her room without a subject. Going over her daily writing, she noticed that on an earlier page she had mentioned her ten-speed bicycle, which she had left home because she feared that it would be stolen if she brought it to Ann Arbor. Now she wished she had brought it anyway. Maybe she could compare having a bicycle with not having one.

ACCUMULATING DETAIL

Normally, an idea comes to us with a few bits of detail attached. For safety, the motorcyclist must wear a helmet and keep his equipment in good repair. During the Easter vacation when we went to Washington, the buses broke down and the cherry trees failed to bloom, Alice Notley had hepatitis, and Mrs. Reade disappeared for two days. A state lottery must distribute x percent of its earnings or people will not support it.

We must do two contrary things with detail. We must accumulate a great deal of it; and we must cut it down to what is essential and useful. First, let us look at ways of accumulating detail; if the next section of this chapter tells us how to cut and to shape, this section should tell us how to gather the material for shaping and cutting.

Paper-writing for most of us goes through many stages. First, we take notes at random, not trying to think in an orderly way, but simply to gather as much possibly useful material as we can. We should *brainstorm*, letting our minds float freely and writing down the memories and associations that swim around us. We should take notes even if we think we will probably never use them. Writing about lotteries, we might associate them with bingo at the church, or with dog racing. Writing about motorcycle safety, we might think of the air bags proposed for automobiles. Probably both ideas will be cut out in the third stage of composition, when we shape the paper. But when we brainstorm, we censor nothing; at this stage, it is impossible to be certain what will fit our paper's shape, because we do not have the shape.

You can write notes freely and loosely, secure in the knowledge that no one but you need ever *read* your notes. Training in daily writing is useful at this stage. Write down what may be silly and what may be pompous; just write. Follow the train of thought even when you have no idea of its destination. Stop, put the notes away, and come back to them later. When you return, you will usually discover that some secret part of your head has been doing homework in the meantime; you will discover a fresh flow of details.

I have been describing the kind of paper that comes from your memory, your thought, and your imagination. Some papers properly take you to the library, or to an interview. You will need facts and figures to talk about state lotteries. You will be doing research, which is another matter. But before you begin research, before you look at your first index, you should brainstorm; you can accumulate speculative notes about what to look for and where to look.

When you have accumulated detail by floating freely, you may find that you can create more detail by scrutinizing what you have written down. Perhaps this scrutiny could be called another stage in writing the paper. Looking over your brief notes, *think* about each one, asking yourself if the one bit of information implies anything you had not thought of. If Mrs. Reade was missing for two days, what were the other teachers on the trip up to? The cherry trees did not bloom; was there any other vegetation? color? smell? By scrutiny and self-questioning — apparently opposite mental acts from the dreamy note-taking of the first stage — you can acquire more detail.

Sharon Rustig began to take notes in her spiral notebook, lining up two columns about bicycles.

Advantages	Disadvantages
quickness/save time	get stolen
fun	have to take inside
keep in shape	winter

She ran out of ideas quickly, and felt disappointed. She couldn't get a hundred words out of *that,* much less two hundred and fifty. Besides — she thought, looking at her list — who's going to care about "fun"? What could she write to *show* the fun?

She started to think of other topics, and then she remembered that one of her instructor's suggestions had been the comparison of bicycle with car. Sharon had never considered bringing an automobile to campus, because of the expense. But the expense would be something to talk about, another item on a list. Quickly, she began another two columns, this time about cars.

Advantages	Disadvantages
distance	ecol.
bad weather	money
	insurance
	gas
	parking
	trouble parking

As the list of disadvantages grew, she realized that she had found her topic. She would compare and contrast the advantages of bikes and cars on campus. Bikes were going to win.

A day later, Sharon began to write, in order to see what her ideas looked like when they turned into sentences.

Bicycles or Cars?

At first sight, a car seems as if it ought to be a better deal when you are going to college. Because it's bigger and you can go longer in it. Also because of bad weather. But really bicycles are better because of the ecology and the price of everything. Automobile insurance costs an incredible amount of $. So does gas, and its going up, when the oil producing nations raise the price again next fall. Parking here is expensive also but worse than that its impossible to find any. A friend of mine got his car towed because he had parked it next to a hospital place and paid $30 to buy it back from the garage that the police towed it away.

The trouble with bikes is that they get stolen all the time. If you are careful you can usually prevent this from happening to you. You get a good lock and you make sure that you get it looped through the rear wheel and the chain and you get it locked to something really solid. Also you take it inside although that's a lot of trouble.

All in all, because of money and ecology, it's better to have a bike than a car.

Sharon wrote her first draft late at night. When she read it in the morning, she crunched it into a ball and threw it at the wastebasket. It missed. Then she picked it up, flattened it out, read it, and made notes in the margin, criticizing herself. "What's 'a better deal' mean?" she wrote after the first sentence; "mixes up two things," she wrote beside her sentence combining ecology and money. Then she took notes from her paper, arranged them in order, and began again.

> If a student could have either a car or a bicycle at college, she should have a bicycle. There are many reasons for this. First I will tell the advantages of cars and the disadvantages of bicycles, and then I will do vice versa.

She crossed out the paragraph and started again.

> Bikes are better than cars, at least on this campus. Although cars give you protection in winter, and take you greater distances, they cannot compare to bikes for practical daily use.

She had found her beginning.

When Jim Beck wrote "The Race to College" he consulted his daily writing. From the term's beginning, his daily writing had frequently been about his family, and his real feelings about coming to college.

> September 20. I don't know what to write about except I got an E on my class theme about coming to college. God I hate everything about this place and I want to go home so bad I can taste it but if I go home now they'd laugh at me and my parents will want to kill themselves. So I stick it out, right? The trouble with getting so many congratulations on going to college — you have to go to

college! I can't remember why they wanted me/I wanted me to go
so much . . .

He wrote a page a day, and kept circling back to this subject. Later, he
spent five pages talking about his brothers and their failures, and several pages talking about his father's job, interrupted by recollections of
a fishing trip, and recollections, too, of his father watching him win a
race in a state track meet. Without knowing that he was doing it, Jim
Beck was accumulating detail the way many writers do.

Although some writers are able to plan their work ahead, and
even outline before they write, most writers have to proceed like Jim;
they must write rapidly and without much control, *at first,* in order to
accumulate detail, in order to find out what they want to write about.
Then they must cut, shape, organize, and control.

SHAPING THE PAPER

To write a good paper, you have to organize details in the best
order, and you must leave out any details, however attractive, which
do not contribute to the whole. The idea of focus, in the first chapter,
is perhaps the most important *structural* idea in making a paper.

Purpose

For focus we need *purpose.* When he came finally to make "The
Race to College," Jim Beck understood his purpose: to make clear the
connection between his background and his drive to go to college, and
the troubles that this connection made for him. Sharon Rustig's purpose gradually became clear to her as she accumulated detail, and as
she thought about what she accumulated. She would show that bicycles were preferable to cars. Clarity would require details set in opposition. Her paper had to show contrast by its form. Beginning with the
daily practicality of bicycles, she continued her first paragraph by listing more advantages of bicycles.

> You can pedal to class, lock up outside the door, and carry your
> books upstairs in ten minutes. If you have an hour between classes,
> you can go back to your room, if you have a bike. Or you can run
> downtown to shop and run back again.

She decided that it was time for some contrast, and that the contrast
would turn on a paragraph break.

> But with a car, you would get to class later, because you would spend all your time looking for a place to park. When you do park, you have to pay for it, and if you park illegally, sometimes you have to pay a *lot* for it. A friend of mine who's car got towed had to buy it back for thirty dollars.

For the development of the rest of her list of ideas, she went back to her notes. Her next paragraph began,

> But parking isn't the only thing that's expensive about a car . . .

Then in the next paragraph she returned to her favorite vehicle.

> And bikes are not only quick and cheap. They give you exercise . . .

She had one negative thing to say: you had to worry about your bike getting stolen. She didn't see how to work it in, so she made a note to herself in the margin of her draft — "Say about getting stolen" — to remind her when she wrote her final draft.

Selecting Detail

Professional writers often find that they do most of their revision by cutting. They cut details that are irrelevant to their point, they cut details that repeat feelings or information that other details have already carried, and they cut explanations of the obvious. Revision is more than omission, but learning what to omit is much of learning how to *finish* a piece of writing. Probably we are more troubled with irrelevant detail when we write out of our own lives than when we write from any other source. Ezra Pound talks about his experience in writing a poem, and what he says of poetry is also good advice on what we must do continually in prose.

> Three years ago in Paris I got out of a "metro" train at La Concorde, and saw suddenly a beautiful face, and then another and another, and then a beautiful child's face, and then another beautiful woman, and I tried all that day to find words for what this had meant to me, and I could not find any words that seemed to me worthy, or as lovely as that sudden emotion. . . . I wrote a thirty-line poem, and destroyed it because it was what we call work "of second intensity." Six months later I made a poem half that length; a year later I made the following *hokku*-like sentence: —
>
> "The apparition of these faces in the crowd;
> Petals on a wet, black bough."

Writing is acquiring material (the floating on memory, the rapid daily writing) and it is ordering and cutting that material. The writer must be a paradoxical combination of opposites: the big spender and the miser, the nymphomaniac and the virgin. Cutting can take place when we organize our notes before writing, or it can come later. When we start to write, it is often hard to know which details are going to prove relevant. Many writers consciously write too much in their first drafts, knowing they do not yet know what will be useful, and knowing that they will later cut for focus and form.

Suppose you describe a particular day. At the end of a vacation, you had a perfect (or perfectly horrible) day. On that Thursday, when you woke up, it was 8:35. You ate scrambled eggs with catsup. These details could be relevant, or they could be mere padding. Cut what does not contribute to the whole. But first, you must have a whole. The point of your paper could be the triviality of your day; a dog barked, the mail was junk, nobody was home when you telephoned your friends. The point is to have a point. Find one — or even make one up. The truth we want is truth-to-feeling; we are not under oath in a court. If we are remembering a sequence of events — A, B, C, and D — we can rearrange the sequence to make a piece of writing more true to the feeling we want the whole to give. If event B happened second, but we see in retrospect that it was the emotional climax, we can *lie* a little, in order to tell the emotional truth. We can use C, A, and D in that order, and save B for last. We are still writing out of our own life. We are telling the truth in the serious sense. Within the limits set by credibility, we can even combine different events into one, or different people into the same character. Suppose in a family anecdote two uncles move in and out of a story, doing approximately the same things. In telling the anecdote, it might well be more shapely and pointed — and just as true — to turn them into one person.

To make a point, and to give our writing a shape, we must limit our material. Here we are back to unity. If we try to write about a whole summer, we are most likely to write disjointed paragraphs, and be boring and superficial. We should find one event, or one unifying device (a place, a person, an automobile, a time of day, a kind of food) to tie together different details. Contrast can make a glue as adhesive as similarity. We must find the detail and form that combined will embody the summer's spirit.

At one point in her note-taking, Sharon described her own bicycle, its make and size, and began to tell how she had acquired it. Wisely she crossed out these notes. This subject gave her more detail — and her instructor liked details — but it was irrelevant to the shape of her paper.

When Jim Beck decided to make a theme out of his drive to attend college, he knew that he had accumulated detail in his daily writing. In fact, he had too much detail. At first, when he looked over thirty-six pages of undisciplined writing, he felt elated because he had so much to write about; then he felt depressed because he had too much to write about.

Should he tell about his father's parents? The story of their troubles was background to his father's diffidence. Should he tell about his brother Steve's dishonorable discharge? In two pages of daily writing he had told only half the story, but he suspected that Steve's life story contributed to local opinion of the Becks. In a way, it belonged.

Of course *everything* belongs. Everything that ever happened to us contributes to how we are, how we act, and how we feel at this moment. But because Jim Beck had to condense his idea into three pages, he had to narrow his topic. He had to focus on his purpose, to seek out the proper order for his thoughts. The idea of focus helped him begin to narrow. In this paper, the topic was his personal feelings; he realized that he must concentrate on himself and keep his family at the side, mentioning his parents and his brothers only so far as details about them promoted his purpose.

Right away, he could cut thirty-six pages down to eight or ten. The rest of the cutting came when he chose details that would be most felt by a reader. He decided that accounts of races by which he won his athletic scholarship would mean little to a reader. He decided with regret to omit an anecdote about a vice principal.

Beginnings

Beginnings of papers, for inexperienced writers, can turn into shapeless horrors. Experienced writers learn to pay special attention to beginnings. One professional says that if he can "find" the first sentence — as if a piece of paper were lying around on a dark shelf of the brain, with the right words on it — the rest of the essay is simple; the door opens, and he finds it easy to invent the house of the essay. But, he says, sometimes it takes him months to find the key.

Most of the time, we lack the months. Some hints about beginnings may help.

We usually overexplain, at the beginning of a paper, and begin too far back. Trying to talk about something that we did last weekend, we realize that it resembled something we did last summer; then we realize that last summer's feelings were like the feelings we had at age five when we started kindergarten, or at age three, when we moved to a new town. All these details may be valid, but to include them all would destroy the paper's shape. The bridge into the country of last weekend would be longer than the country itself. With enough self-questioning, we could begin every autobiographical paper with "I was born," or, "My grandparents emigrated from Lithuania in 1905," or, "Life for my peasant ancestors in medieval Turkey must have been difficult." Too much detail prevents the reader from perceiving the shape of thought. This malady of origins and causes might be called the house-that-Jack-built syndrome.

Long bridges curse not only autobiography; the same malady can afflict all writing. In discussing how World War II began, we can begin with the fall of the Roman Empire. In making up a short story, we can supply causes from our imagination as prolifically as we can supply them from memory in writing autobiography. In assembling a research paper, we can go backward in time, or laterally in comparisons. Wanting to write about ecology, we may pick the disappearing whale as our topic; we can begin the paper with the general topic of man's destroying his environment, narrow it to his destroying animal species, narrow it to his destroying whales, and then narrow it to the decline in the population of one type of whale. The last category is the paper's focus, but if we are not careful we can spend three-quarters of our paper walking the bridge to our topic.

The good, sharp beginning narrows the topic. When we understand our writing's purpose, we can begin with reference to that purpose, or with a thesis we propose to explain. We can begin with something that arrests the reader, and points to the main topic. Reference back (or laterally) can follow if it is necessary, and it can be brief.

> Last weekend I broke up with Ed. I have not felt so lonesome since I moved to a new town when I was four, leaving the friends of my whole life behind me, and knowing no one at all.
>
> I know other people besides Ed, but I feel as if I didn't. The break-up had been coming for weeks. . . .

Or we can begin *without* an immediate lateral glance.

> Humpbacks are mammals, as all whales are; they breathe into
> huge lungs, bear live young, which they nurse for the better part of
> a year, and have vestiges of hair. . . .

In this research paper, the author catches our attention immediately
with facts that will interest almost anyone, probably because they
interested her and she shows it: "huge lungs," "for the better part of a
year."

Editors of magazines sometimes refer to "zingers," beginnings (or
"leads") to articles constructed to grab the reader by the hair. *Time* is
good at zingers. Here are three opening sentences from one issue.

> The United States was founded on a complaint.

> When the young Chinese woman heard a mysterious voice ask-
> ing, "What's under your pillow?" she felt sure that the answer was
> a "biological radio apparatus" put there by a special agent who
> suspected her of crimes against the state.

> Professor Jürgen Zerche was lecturing on political science one
> day this spring when a band of some 70 young leftists barged into
> his classroom at the Free University of Berlin and began shouting
> curses at him.

All immediately involve our interest, and none has a preamble. One
begins with a startling short sentence, the other two with arresting
anecdotes.

Much serious writing begins with what we might call a quiet
zinger, something exciting or intriguing and at the same time relevant
to the material that follows. When Homer begins the *Iliad*, which is
about the anger of Achilles and its consequences, the first word in the
long poem means "rage." Here are the beginnings of three books.

> On top of everything, the cancer wing was Number 13.
> > Alexander Solzhenitsyn, *Cancer Ward*

> My bandana is rolled on the diagonal and retains water fairly
> well.
> > John McPhee, *Coming into the Country*[1]

> Harold Ross died December 6, 1951, exactly one month after his
> fifty-ninth birthday. In November of the following year the *New
> Yorker* entertained the editors of *Punch* and some of its outstand-

ing artists and writers. I was in Bermuda and missed the party, but weeks later met Rowland Emett for lunch at the Algonquin. "I'm sorry you didn't get to meet Ross," I began as we sat down. "Oh, but I did," he said. "He was all over the place. Nobody talked about anybody else."

James Thurber, *The Years with Ross*

In this last example, the first sentence is a conventional way to introduce a biographical memoir. Then Thurber shifts abruptly to anecdote, showing (not telling) in his first paragraph how important and fascinating Ross was to his staff. This showing points to the book's focus.

At other times and in other kinds of books, a definition of the subject may be essential before we can begin.

In its widest possible extension the title of this book — *Adventures of Ideas* — might be taken as a synonym for The History of the Human Race. . . .

A. N. Whitehead, *Adventures of Ideas*

Whitehead builds a swift bridge into his topic.

Purpose and context determine the kind of beginning. But in any piece of writing, the beginning focuses our writing; it requires special attention, and it requires brevity and incisiveness. Some information we need quickly; information which may be pertinent but not wholly necessary should be suppressed; information which is both pertinent and necessary, but which might make a tedious beginning, can often be put off until later in the essay, when its relevance becomes obvious and it ceases to seem tedious.

One kind of opener is often boring, the overt announcement of what is to be done: "I am going to show that the government of the United States is split into three branches, the executive, the legislative, and the judicial." Papers may be constructed analytically, by delineating parts, but they should show and not tell. The paper that begins with the sentence above will probably take a paragraph each for the three branches, and end, as boringly as it began, "I have shown that the government of the United States is comprised of the executive, the legislative, and the judicial branches." It is essay structure for people who have difficulty following the story line of a Disney movie.

We already saw Sharon Rustig starting her paper. Jim Beck, once he had discarded the thought of beginning with his grandparents, tried several opening sentences.

When I was daydreaming about college it scared me, but I didn't have any idea how I would hate it. I thought that it might be too hard but I never suspected that it would be horrible. It's horrible now, and I don't know if it will get any better. . . .

Since I first came to the university, I haven't slept more than four hours in a row. . . .

When I arrived in this town for orientation at the end of August, the first thing I saw was a bunch of Hare Krishnas. . . .

Giving up on getting the beginning right in his first draft, he went on to the rest of his paper. When he looked at his draft the next day, he decided to start with the third sentence of his first attempt.

It's horrible now, and I don't know if it will get any better.

principally because he thought it would arouse curiosity; it was a bit of a zinger.

Middles: Development

Beginnings and endings are important points of attention when we concentrate on shape, on narrowing, and on focus. But obviously, the passage from beginning to ending must create an order that is lucid and expressive. Revising her theme, Marian Hart achieved unity and shape by omitting unnecessary details and ordering the necessary ones.

Remarks on unity, sequence, and coherence in the chapter on paragraphs give standards for the mini-essay, the paragraph, that also apply to the maxi-paragraph, the essay. Remarks in that chapter on transition within the paragraph apply to transition *between* paragraphs also, and therefore to the flowing development of the whole essay. For further attention to developing the paper, see Coherence in the Paragraph, pages 193–201, and Development in the Paragraph, pages 202–216.

The middle is the matter. *The shape we give the essay, like the motion in the paragraph, is the structure formed by our thought.* Our matter determines our manner — or it ought to. An anecdote or a historical summary or an exposition of a process must use chronological order. In an argument that advances a thesis, the essay's order seldom depends on chronology. Instead, it is an order of persuasion — accumulating detail, proceeding by logic, and using various forms of persuasion or argument.

Focus itself depends on order or development. A different order of ideas can make a different statement, even when the ideas or details remain the same. In a reminiscence, if we begin with pleasant associations and move to horrid ones, we leave the reader with a negative impression; if we move from horrid to pleasant, we leave the reader feeling positive. We could accumulate identical details for each paper, but make a different impression by our organization. There are "insides" to the order we give details, as there are to words and syntax. One student wrote, in a history paper:

> The rainfall in the Southern provinces is approximately two inches a year. On the average. What this means is that most years the country people starve in a drought; one year in five, they drown in a flood. However, the combination of a surviving Indian ritual, and a local brand of Roman Catholicism, keeps the people remarkably cheerful and content.

For the same assignment, writing from the same source, another wrote:

> Indian rituals which still survive, combined with a peculiar indigenous Catholicism, keep the natives of the South apparently contented. However, the climatic conditions are deplorable. The rainfall averages two inches a year. This means that the peasants parch for several years in drought, and are drowned in floods the next one.

Both students' notes for this passage were, approximately:

> Catholicism and Indian stuff
> happy
> infant mortality
> rainfall
> floods
> starvation, drought

The two students were heading in different directions — the first toward an expository essay on daily life in the tribe, the second toward an argument for public works such as irrigation and flood control — but they started from the same information, which they organized or pointed in different ways.

Notice that neither student used the detail about infant mortality. It was not directly related to religion, or to the economy of water. Because it was not part of the movement of the passage, it was irrelevant and was cut. When we shape into our paper the details we have accumulated, we will find that we have to cut many of them.

We wish to make an order that is lucid and expressive. Too often, middles lack lucidity because they lack an orderly development, one sentence leading into another, and leading the reader to follow the track of thought. Lucidity and expression carry our thought, writer to reader; we are not expressive if our message is garbled by repetition, by lack of transition, or by afterthought. We need orderly progress of middles as we need order in all our writing — in order to engage the reader. We must always address a reader incapable of knowing our intentions, but capable of understanding good sentences.

The development in Jim Beck's paper is deceptively simple. He started with a paragraph telling us how much he hated college, with details to make sure the reader understood the feeling.

> It's horrible now, and I don't know if it will get any better. The only people who pay attention to me are the people who are trying to beat me out for the track team. My roommate is stoned all day and gets A's on his papers anyway. I hate him because he hates me because I'm a jock. My classes are boring lectures and the sections are taught by graduate students who pick on the students because the professors pick on them.

But this would not be news. Lots of people are unhappy in college. He then constructed his second paragraph to make a contrast to the first. He not only told us how much he wanted to come to college, but gave us reasons why.

> But I remember wanting to come here so bad! Nobody from Hammerton named Beck had ever been to college. Everybody knew the Becks were stupid. This went for my father, who never got through high school, and for my grandfather, who died before I was born, and who was the town drunk. It went for my two older brothers who went bad, as they say in Hammerton. Steve got a dishonorable discharge from the Marines and he works on a farm outside town and gets drunk on Fridays and Saturdays. Curt stole a car and did time at Jackson and nobody has heard from him since. My sister had a three-month baby and the town liked to talk about that

In the third, fourth, and fifth paragraphs, his writing made us understand his separateness from the rest of his family, and from his home town, and then the easy and appropriate order of chronology began to organize the paper. Jim Beck began a paragraph speaking of athletics in general, to move on to his own ambitions as a runner, and he carried us with him — right up to the paper's conclusion — with ease and clarity.

I was different. Everybody told me I was. My mother told me I wasn't a Beck. My father told me I was going to bring back the family's good name. (I never knew it had one.) In grammar school the teachers all told me how much better I was than my brothers. By the time I was in sixth grade my father and the school Principal were talking about the University.

My father isn't really dumb. Sometimes people look dumb because it's expected of them. He's worked at the same grocery for twenty years, I guess. Now that I made it to the University, he wants to be called Manager, because he's the only man there besides Mr. Roberts who owns it. (The rest of the help are — is? — kids who bag and an old lady cashier.) When I went back for a weekend everybody treated me as if I won the Olympics.

I said the Principal and my father were talking about my going to the University. All through junior high I said I didn't want to go. I was scared. No Beck could do that. Bad things kept happening to my family. My father had an accident and totalled the car and lost his license and for a year we didn't have a car at all. He had to walk home two miles every night pushing a basket of groceries. When I said I would quit school and get a job, everybody jumped on me.

It wasn't that I was an A student. It was just that I tried hard at everything I did. I got B's mostly. Now with B's, the counsellors kept telling me, I could be admitted to the University, but I wouldn't get a scholarship. I needed mostly A's for that, and then when I got to the University I would lose the scholarship if I couldn't keep the grades up. Then my brother Steve, who was a pretty good athlete once, suggested athletics.

I was too skinny for football, too short for basketball, I could barely swim and my school didn't have a swimming team anyway. There is one sport you can practice with no money and no equipment. I started to run when I was in my last year of junior high. It felt good right away. I ran to and from school. I went over to the high school and did laps. The high school coach noticed me and asked me to go out the next year. Running long distances hurts a lot. Sometimes you get a stitch in your left side and suddenly it shifts to your right side. I didn't exactly mind the pain. I studied it. I studied it in order to go to the University, the way I studied everything else.

Endings

Endings are nearly as important as beginnings, and the same cautions apply. We often make them too long, summarize facts that are already obvious, reargue a point already established, say abstractly what we have shown concretely — and by all these methods dilute the intensity our conclusion should have. Our endings often drag and decline into blank space, dwindling instead of concluding. This diminishment is bad organization. Usually the dwindling can be cut, just as most bridges at the beginning can be removed. If the dwindling qualifies the conclusion, the qualification can come before the conclusion.

There are exceptions. In a long and complicated argument, we may be pleased to find at the end a succinct summary of the author's argument. It is like seeing an aerial photograph of country we have just walked through. But the short paper — the kind in which we are most interested in this book — rarely profits from summary, and often withers by it. We should point the whole essay toward the last sentence, and when we have written it, stop writing. Often we conclude an essay and then continue writing. The essay writer must develop the confidence to let facts and arguments stand by themselves without epilogue. People who moralize at the end of a story, or summarize at the end of an argument, are the same people who kill jokes by explaining them. In a short paper about an experience she had while babysitting, a student concluded:

> After that third phone call, the breathing, and the hanging-up, I sat huddled in a big chair and shaking, waiting for the Bakers to come back. For a while I turned out the lights, thinking that a dark house might not seem so inviting to any fiend prowling around. But the darkness scared me.
>
> It was about three-quarters of an hour before they came back. In that time, I thought through everything I could do if I was attacked. I could scream — but the neighbors were all away. I could run — but then I was leaving Connie. My mind went over and over everything. I even started to wonder which dress I ought to be buried in.
>
> When I heard the car stop I was petrified. But then I heard Mrs. Baker saying something when she opened the garage door. My heart slowed down. When they came in, I told them all about the phone calls, my parents being out of town, the houses dark next door. I guess I thought they'd give me a medal.
>
> Instead, they looked puzzled.
>
> "Why didn't you call *us?*" said Mrs. Baker.

> Then I realized that I had been dumb to sit there scared in the dark, waiting for the breather to knock down the door, with the telephone number written on the pad beside the phone. While the phone had rung three times, I had simply become more and more panicked, and I had never thought of the easiest thing to do. I must have been too scared. Well, I thought, that's one mistake I won't make again.

Here, the essay dwindles like an explained joke. She might have ended it,

> "Why didn't you call *us?*" said Mrs. Baker.

Or, if she had wanted to add another idea, and a detail, she might have extended it for one sentence.

> I began to wonder if I had enjoyed my fear so much that I forgot the pad of paper beside the telephone which had a phone number on it.

At any rate, her paper would have improved if she had crossed out her last paragraph.

Usually we should conclude a topic without seeming to draw attention to the conclusion. Part of the paper's unity is the resolution it comes to, all details organized toward an end, a coda felt by the reader. Paradoxically, this resolution can be violated by obviousness. Anything that feels tacked on destroys a sense of unity.

Joan Didion, in an essay called "On Going Home," writes about the fragmentation of American family life. Visiting her parents in the house where she grew up, she encounters familiar details of her old life. She feels that she was "born into the last generation to carry the burden of 'home,' " and clearly finds a value in the burden. Her feelings are complex, and she ends her essay not by summarizing her feelings or reducing them to abstraction, but by turning to her own small child and enacting her ambivalence.

> It is time for the baby's birthday party: a white cake, strawberry-marshmallow ice cream, a bottle of champagne saved from another party. In the evening, after she has gone to sleep, I kneel beside the crib and touch her face, where it is pressed against the slats, with mine. She is an open and trusting child, unprepared for and unaccustomed to the ambushes of family life, and perhaps it is just as well that I can offer her little of that life. I would like to give her more. I would like to promise her that she will grow up with a sense of her cousins and of rivers and of her great-grandmother's

teacups, would like to pledge her a picnic on a river with fried chicken and her hair uncombed, would like to give her *home* for her birthday, but we live differently now and I can promise her nothing like that. I give her a xylophone and a sundress from Madeira, and promise to tell her a funny story.

Joan Didion, in *Slouching Towards Bethlehem*

When Jim Beck first drafted his paper, he had no title and he had no ending. His last paragraph trailed off.

Sometimes when I cannot sleep I think about going back to Hammerton but I can't do that. Sometimes I think about getting a gold medal in the Olympics. Both of them are happy dreams except that I *know* I'm not Olympic class and if I went home it would be a disgrace to everybody. So all I am doing is sticking it out and hating every minute of it and hoping that things will get better some time.

Then he saw that he had a title by turning his actual running into a metaphor for his drive to get to college. Next he saw that by cutting and shaping his original last paragraph, he could make the paper's ending strike the reader, and refer back to the beginning without being obvious about it.

In my Senior year I was all-state and held two high-school records (600 and half-mile) and I had an athletic scholarship to the University. Now I am here, the first Beck to make it. I don't know why I'm here or why I ran so hard or where I go from here. Now that I am here, the race to get here seems pointless. Nothing in my classes interests me. I study, just as I did before, in order to pass the course or even get a good grade. I run to win, but what am I running for? I will never be a great runner. Sometimes when I cannot sleep I imagine packing my bags and going back to Hammerton. But I can't do that. They would say, "He's a Beck, all right."

When Sharon Kustig had finished blaming cars for being expensive and impractical while praising bikes for being cheap and efficient and healthy, she had one major topic left over. She had saved her best for last, where she could compare the ecological values of car and bicycle. Starting with convenience had led her to the problem of parking, which had led her to the expense of cars: the ecological argument was delayed to the end — which was lucky, because it allowed her to end strongly by using her best reason.

She drafted her final paragraph, and slept on the paper, and on the evening before it was due, wrote her final draft. She turned a personal anecdote into a generalization, because she thought it made better argument. She looked for the right word instead of the approximate one. She checked punctuation and spelling. She even found a place to mention bicycles being stolen. She typed it up, proofread it — and this is the theme she handed in:

Two Wheels Are Better Than Four
Sharon Rustig

Bikes are better than cars, at least on this campus. Although cars protect you against bad weather, and take you on long trips, they cannot compare with bikes for practical daily use. You can pedal from dorm to class, lock up outside the door, and backpack your books upstairs — ten minutes from bed to classroom! If you have an hour's break between classes, you can go back to your room instead of wasting your time hanging around the hallways. Or you can zip downtown and do an errand and zip back to your next class.

But with a car, you would get to class half an hour late, because you couldn't find a place to park. If you park legally, you feed a meter. If you park illegally, you feed more than that. If your car is towed away from a no-parking area, you may pay as much as thirty dollars to get it back again. And not only parking is expensive, in connection with cars. Automobile insurance if you are student age will cost you about two hundred dollars a year. Gasoline has become expensive and is liable to get more so by the end of the year.

Bikes are better, not only because they are more efficient in getting you from place to place, and not only because they are cheaper, but because they're good for your body. They give you good exercise, especially if you live on a hill. Most students don't do much exercise, and just sit around getting flabby, so a bike is good for your health as well as everything else. The only bad things about bikes are their habit of getting stolen, but this works out for health too. You toughen up your neck muscles by riding around with a ten pound bike chain for a necklace.

But I haven't said the most important reason that bikes are better than cars. Cars use up petroleum which is in short supply. Bikes use up nothing but the bike riders' excess fat. Car exhaust pollutes the atmosphere and causes respiratory diseases. Bicycles exhaust nobody except the rider. Ecology makes the final reason why a bike is better than a car.

Sharon had written her three hundred words.

Of course it's impossible to use Sharon's experience as a model for everyone. We are all different, and we need to find our own ways to write well. The only rules to make for someone writing a paper are abstract ones: clarity, coherence, wholeness, development, and adequacy. Whether we write autobiography like Jim Beck, or exposition like Sharon Rustig — or whatever else — these general standards must apply. Each paper we write is a separate, personal attempt to reach these goals.

Our goals change, as we learn more about writing. We become more demanding on ourselves; we learn new demands. Sharon's instructor marked her paper with a C+, and made marginal notes criticizing her diction for excessive informality, and her sentence structure for lack of variety and for occasional awkwardness. At the end of the term, her instructor offered the class an opportunity to raise grades by rewriting any two old papers. "Don't merely correct the errors noted in the margins," she said. "Find papers you can improve as a whole." Working for a B or better, Sharon looked through "Two Wheels Are Better than Four" and decided to start over again. She kept to the same general organization, but worked on vocabulary and sentence structure — during the term she had done exercises in variety of sentence structure and her daily writing had improved her available vocabulary — she had developed an idea of audience other than her instructor. On the last day of class, she handed in this paper.

Two Wheels Are Better Than Four — Number Two
Sharon Rustig

On a large residential campus, like the University of Michigan's, bicycles suit the needs of students more than automobiles do. Buicks and Chevrolets are useful for long trips, or as protection against bad weather, but the daily advantages of Schwinn or Raleigh are far greater. Bicycles save students time; from dormitory to classroom, bike rack to bike rack, will take only five or ten minutes. If students have an hour between classes, they can pedal to the library, lock up, and spend forty minutes in a book on Library Reserve. Or they can do an errand at a nearby store, and return to the classroom in time for the next lecture.

On the other hand, if students were driving an automobile, these alternatives would not be available. Parking makes the difference. Starting out for class, they would need to allow an extra half hour to look for a parking space. They would need to walk to the library or the store, because they would not be able to count on finding a second or a third parking space. On this campus, cars parked illegally are ticketed and towed, which wastes the student not only time but money. The bicycle, which saves the student parking fines, saves the cost of gasoline as well, and the immense expense of insurance. The practicality of bicycles includes the economy of student finance, as well as the economy of student time.

There is also the economy of student health. Most students work hard at their books, and relax by sitting with their friends at taverns. The student body gets no exercise at all. But the bicyclist uses muscles otherwise unused, and adds to health while subtracting the waste of money and time. The only waste connected with bicycle riding is the epidemic of bicycle thievery; a stout chain prevents theft — and, worn around the neck, contributes to the health of the rider's neck muscles.

Finally, automobiles are detrimental to the health, not only of the sedentary student, but of everyone in the community. It is clear that bicycles are preferable to cars on this campus for purely practical or utilitarian reasons. But we should always ride bicycles, or walk, whenever we can, if an automobile can be avoided. Not only is the world's supply of energy diminishing, requiring us all to conserve what energy we can, but the expense of that energy in car exhaust is a present danger to everyone alive. Pollution from carbon monoxide causes respiratory disease. Conservation and ecological danger makes it imperative that all of us make use of two wheels rather than four.

___ **EXERCISES** _____

1. In class, imitate collectively how we choose a subject and narrow a topic. Narrow these general subjects into topics.

the arms race	funding social security
the plight of the aged	alternate energy sources
the Saturday-night special	women's athletic programs
wiretapping	legalization of marijuana

Some topics are broader than others but all can be narrowed further.

2. (a) On your own, work up an idea that might be developed into a theme. (b) Accumulate details. (c) Organize details, eliminating those that seem irrelevant. (d) Bring all material to class. One student at a time can read his material for general discussion. Or the instructor may want to collect the material and mimeograph some of it to use in the next class meeting.

3. In class, brainstorm details for a paper on a recent local controversy (housing rules? parking regulations? faculty unionization? women's studies?). Then try to organize the details, using the blackboard. Or take the details home and elaborate and organize them for the next class.

4. Analyze these passages for the order and relevance of the details used.

a. But the Dolphin House was not grand. Hermione and I settled in, for what we thought would be a weekend, and developed, in fact, to be eighteen months, with the occasional relief of a day in the city. The head waiter, who had been born in Constantinople, actually carried our bags. Dinner that first night was exquisite. We bathed in the cool glow of a '45 Château Lafite-Rothschild which I had all but forgotten. The quarters, however, were shabby.

A walk on the beach, after lunch the next day, revealed that we had unknowingly chosen a coast that resembled, in uncanny ways, our native Dalmatia. Sigurd was to join us in a fortnight. How pleased he would be!

Hermione and I played jacks until tea, a lively American game which we had picked up during a visiting lectureship in Seattle. Tea was mediocre, as breakfast had been. We noticed that Americans were good at the more obvious things, but lacked expertise at the small ones. When did we ever see toast cut with elegance, in all this wide land?

Hermann von Kreicke, The Migrant Swan

b. In a rather pathetic attempt to keep her home, Scott had sent her Compton Mackenzie's book *Plasher's Mead* to read. But she didn't like it: "Nothing annoys me more than having the most trivial action analyzed and explained." She said the heroine was "ATROCIOUSLY uninteresting" and maybe she'd save the book and try to read it again in rainy weather. But she also tipped her hand more than she may have intended, for in the same letter she told him, "People seldom interest me except in their relations to things, and I like men to be just incidents in books so I can imagine their characters — " Everything, it seemed, had to revolve around her, her perceptions, her games, or she was not interested and refused to play. Certainly that letter carried a note of warning about herself, if Fitzgerald had been in any condition to receive it. But he was not. He knew the terms, they were remarkably like his own, and that exquisite egotism drew him even more completely to her.

But what he did not fully perceive, perhaps because Zelda did not, was the uncertainty within his girl. For, as worldly as she loved to seem to be, as reckless and ebullient as she was, Zelda knew nothing first hand of any world other than the protected Southern one of provincial towns and families who knew one another and were kin. For all her banter, New York, chic and fabulous, must have seemed as remote to her as the Orient.

Nancy Milford, *Zelda*

5. Revise the beginning:

Every Easter we drove to my great Aunt's house in Troy to eat a ham for Easter dinner. Even when my father was little boy, they had gone to Troy for Easter. Sometimes it would snow and we would be late. Once we blew a tire about half way, and the spare was soft, and we took at least an hour and a half to get it fixed.

Last year was my Senior year in high school, and my great aunt thought graduating from high school was a big deal, so I knew I would get a lot of attention when I got there. We have to pack because we actually stay over Friday and Saturday nights. Fortunately, for some reason, I packed my tennis shoes and my jeans. If I hadn't, I wouldn't have been able to play touch football decently, I wouldn't have wound up in the emergency ward, and I wouldn't have met Linda.

6. Which of these beginnings are interesting, and which seem potentially boring? Why?

a. When the United Nations met in September, its members were already agitated, anxious, and almost apoplectic.

b. The origins of the missile crisis are already well-known to the informed reading public.

c. Bang!

d. When I was born I lived in Cleveland. Then my family moved to Akron when I was two years old. After that we moved to Muncie, Indiana. . . .

e. The goat had three eyes.

7. Here is a small article from *The New Yorker*'s "Talk of the Town." What do you think of the beginning, details, development, shape, and ending?

A lot was wrong with Elvis Presley's first-ever New York appearance, at Madison Square Garden last weekend. Somebody in the Presley organization misjudged the desires of the crowd, and as a result Elvis was preceded by a standup comedian called Jackie Kahane. No doubt Mr. Kahane's patter knocks 'em dead in Vegas, but New York is not Vegas and the Garden is not a night club. "Kids today . . ." said Mr. Kahane gamely, and lamely, as the audience clapped in unison. "I have a kid. Everything this kid eats turns to hair." He was finally booed off the stage. There was fault to find with Elvis's own performance as well. Instead of a rhythm section to back him up, he had a twenty-three-piece orchestra, a six-man rock band, and an eight-member chorus — a bit too much insurance, even for the Garden. The program was rigidly arranged and planned, allowing for little in the way of spontaneity, and it consisted largely of romantic ballads and sugary, easy-listening songs. The classics that most of the audience had come to hear — "Heartbreak Hotel," "Don't Be Cruel," "Hound Dog" — occupied only fifteen minutes of a fifty-minute program. The blandness was conceptual as well as musical, as when Elvis sang a non-controversial medley of "Dixie," "All My Trials," and the "Battle Hymn of the Republic." The gyrations that made the man famous were seldom in evidence. Instead, he offered a repertoire of stereotyped actions and heroic poses.

Oddly, none of this made any difference. The audience was ecstatic throughout. (It would have been ecstatic even if Elvis had sung nothing but Gregorian chants.) During the intermission before Elvis's appearance, our companion, a young woman who still has her Elvis scrapbook packed away in a trunk somewhere, told us a story that made it all quite comprehensible. "When I was twelve years old," she said, "I was riding in the car with my mother and brother, and a song called 'I Want You, I Need You, I Love You' came on the radio. I immediately felt a certain twinge. My mother said, 'This is that Elvis Presley they're all talking about. I don't see what all the fuss is about.' My brother said the same thing. I just sat on the back seat and didn't say anything. You see, I *did* know what all the fuss was about."

The lights went down, the orchestra struck up what used to be called "Thus Spake Zarathustra" and is now called "The Theme from '2001,'" the audience began a full-throated scream, and Elvis appeared. He looked magnificent. His coal-black hair was fuller and drier than in days of old, and he wore a fantastical white costume studded with silver. He strolled back and forth on the stage, accepting the plaudits of the crowd like a Roman emperor. He looked like an apparition, and this was appropriate, because he has been a figure of fantasy for seventeen years. As the performance went on, it became impossible to avoid the conclusion that he is a consummate professional. He never cut loose, but he did not have to. The slightest gesture of his hand, the smallest inclination of his head set off waves of screams from the favored direction. The greatest ovation, except for the one that attended his initial appearance, came when he went into the first of his old songs, "Love Me." "Treat me like a fool," he sang. "Treat me mean an' cruel, but love me."

Throughout, Elvis maintained a certain ironic distance from it all, sometimes engaging in a bit of self-parody. At the beginning of "Hound Dog," for example, he posed dramatically on one knee, said, "Oh, excuse me," and switched to the other knee. But he manifestly enjoyed the audience's enjoyment, even as he indicated with a smile here and a gesture there that it all had less to do with him than with their idea of him. On our way out, we asked our companion if she had liked the show. "It was bliss," she said, "I haven't felt so intensely *thirteen* since — well, since I was thirteen."

8. Here are some exercises and questions about Sharon Rustig's papers. (a) Go through her first complete draft (on pages 32–33) and correct it, as if you were the teacher and this paper were submitted to you. (b) On page 33, Sharon tries two beginnings. What is wrong with the first one? Why is the second one better? (c) Notice the changes between the first draft and the next (on page 48). Are the changes improvements? Why? (d) Look at the diction, mechanics, and organization of this version. Make marginal comments as if you were her instructor. (e) Looking at Sharon's end-of-term paper (pages 49–50), decide what she has learned in the weeks between this and the second. Is anything in the earlier version superior to the later? Make marginal comments, and grade her paper. How can she further improve her writing?

9. Here is another comparison and contrast theme.

Night and Day

There is a small ski area about five miles away from my home town of Easthampton, Massachusetts, called the Mt. Tom Ski Area. Besides its excellent slopes and trails, Mt. Tom is the only ski resort in my neighborhood that offers both night and day skiing. Although night skiing is convenient and fun, there are many advantages to skiing during the day.

One annoying problem that can be avoided by skiing during the day is the large crowds. In the daytime, most people are in school or working and therefore, aren't able to go skiing. That means the parking facilities are less crowded and the lift lines are shorter, giving you more time on the ski slopes. Usually the conditions of the mountain are best during the daytime. The surface powder is still deep and fluffy. At night, the slopes often become icy because the deep powder has been worn away.

Also, feeling the sun's warmth as you glide down the slopes makes daytime skiing quite enjoyable. When the sun is warm, you can shed some of those layers of clothing. Who knows, maybe you'll even get a suntan!

With all that daytime skiing has to offer, there are still some disadvantages. For example, because your friends are either in school or working, you have to ski alone. Skiing just isn't as much fun unless you have a friend to fall down and look like a fool with! The view when riding the chairlift is much more glamorous at night than in the day. The bluegreen and white lights you see from above look like the flashing eyes of some Hollywood monster!

However, I still haven't mentioned safety, the most important advantage to skiing during the day. In the daytime, the trails are much more visible. At night, they are dimly lit and can be dangerous if you're not careful. In case of injury, it is much easier to locate an emergency telephone than it is at night. For these reasons alone, I feel that daytime skiing is best.

(a) Could the organization of this paper be improved, to clarify comparison and contrast? (b) Find sentences that need reworking. Revise them. (c) Where has the author attempted colorful writing? Are these attempts successful? See if you can rewrite for liveliness. (d) Would more detail help this paper? Where does it seem lacking?

3

Words

THE INSIDES OF WORDS

Words Themselves

It may seem difficult, at first, to think of words apart from contexts; "salt" does not stand alone; it is part of "salt and pepper," or "please pass the salt." Words seem like drops of water in a stream that has its own wholeness and its own motion. But when you write well, each word is accurate and honest and exact in itself, and contributes its special history to the wholeness of the stream of meaning.

The writer must be able to feel words intimately, one at a time. He must also be able to step back, inside his head, and see the flowing sentence. But he starts with the single word. He starts with tens of thousands of these units, and he picks among them. He may end by writing a passage like this account of man's first sleep on the moon:

> It was almost three-thirty in the morning when the astronauts finally prepared for sleep. They pulled down the shades and Aldrin stretched out on the floor, his nose near the moon dust. Armstrong sat on the cover of the ascent engine, his back leaning against one of the walls, his legs supported in a strap he had tied around a vertical bar. In front of his face was the eyepiece of the telescope. The earth was in its field of view, and the earth "like a big blue

eyeball" stared back at him. They could not sleep. Like the eye of
a victim just murdered, the earth stared back at him.

> Norman Mailer, *Of a Fire on the Moon*

Until the end, this exposition seems simple and straightforward. Simple and straightforward it is, with the power of visual exactness, "his nose near the moon dust," and the unexpected detail, "a strap he had tied around a vertical bar." Mailer cements each word in place exactly and inevitably, with the help of rhythm and sentence structure. For now, just look at how he prepares for the last, emotional image with related words.

This passage, and much of Mailer's book, is about man and machine. The machinery is sophisticated, complex, overwhelming. Men are frail in comparison. The language begins to embody this idea, by repeating the names of parts of the body: "nose," "back," "legs," "face." We have become accustomed to the jerking motions of the puffed-up spacesuits, as if we were watching robots. Now suddenly we see "nose" and "face." We might be a mother looking at a sleeping child. From "face" we move to the most vulnerable and necessary of sense organs, the "eye," first by way of a telescope's "eyepiece," then by a visual comparison, easy to follow, of the earth to a "big blue eyeball," which stares. We have departed from the astronauts' bodies, and moved onto metaphorical bodies. Then, because the eyeball stares, we can leap to the emotional crux: the earth is dead, murdered by the astronauts who leave it behind for another planet, beginning the exploration outward, into the stars. Mailer makes his point not by telling us about it overtly, but by his control of language, his understanding of the insides of words, so that the movement from "nose" to "face" to "eyepiece" and "view" to "victim just murdered" has an inner and emotional necessity.

> All the warm night the secret snow fell so adhesively that every twig in the woods about their little rented house supported a tall slice of white, an upward projection which in the shadowless gloom of early morning lifted depth from the scene, made it seem Chinese, calligraphic, a stiff tapestry hung from the gray sky, a shield of lace interwoven with black thread.
>
> John Updike

These sentences begin a short story called "The Crow in the Wood." Updike exercises the possibilities of our language in rhythm, in variety of sentence structure, and in observation that is dreamy and precise at the same time. He does it with words. Instead of looking at everything he does, let us look at two words that stand out. "Adhesively" is a word we all know, from the noun or adjective "adhesive," as a longer way of saying "glue" or "sticky." Here the snow "fell . . . adhesively." Snow really cannot fall like glue, and so we have something apparently inaccurate; yet it is right, because the context prepares us. It is a "warm night"; the snow will be damp. And using "adhesively" rather than "stickily" shows that the snow is not gooey to the fingers, but will actively adhere to something. "Adhesively" by its unusualness draws the right attention to itself.

Then look at the word "slice," "every twig . . . supported a tall slice of white." Most of us would have said something about snow "piling" or "accumulating" on branches. But "a tall slice of white," besides being pleasing to the ear, is a brilliant image; the sharpness of "slice," together with the image of whiteness, nearly dazzles the eye. With the word "slice" is an unspoken knife, just out of sight. And I think we have a moment's vision of an upright piece of white-frosted cake.

We could pick many more words for praise in the passages from Mailer and Updike, and maybe for blame as well (we will do that later). But the excellence here is perhaps like all excellence. These writers are *original, as if seeing a thing no one has seen;* yet they report their vision in a *language that reaches the rest of us.* Here, again, we find the opposites we must combine. For the first quality the writer needs imagination; for the second he needs skill. Without both qualities, he could not write the passage. Imagination without skill makes a lively chaos; skill without imagination, a deadly order.

No Synonyms

To appreciate the word — the "eyepiece," the "eyeball," the "slice," the "adhesively" — the writer and the reader must first realize that no words can be synonyms. Some words are close to each other in meaning, close enough to reveal that they are not the same. The writer must know not just the surface definitions of words; he must go deeper, and realize the families of contexts into which words have extended their associations — like "slice" with "knife" and even "cake." These families are the connotations of the word and the asso-

ciations we make with its denotation; "pepper" is not a connotation
of "salt" but an association of it. Since the writer uses the whole
family, it does not matter that he discriminates connotation from association. But he must know the insides of words; he must be a friend
of the family.

The verbs "to emulate," "to imitate," "to copy," and "to ape" are
synonyms, by definition — but when we use them in a sentence they
carry slight differences in meaning. "To emulate" sounds fancy; also
it usually implies that the imitation involves self-improvement. "To
imitate" is neutral, except that everyone knows that an imitation is
not the real thing; inferiority shadows the word. "To copy" is to repro-
duce exactly; like "to imitate" it states a lack of originality. "To ape"
is to mimic, and to be comical or mocking about it. If you wanted to
say that a young pianist imitated a famous virtuoso, but you carelessly
used "ape" instead of "imitate," you would grant his style the grace of
a gorilla. Context is all; the inside of a word must reinforce or continue
the force built by the context. When a sportswriter wrote that one
middle linebacker aped another middle linebacker, he was being witty.

Dictionaries of synonyms and other books, especially *Roget's
Thesaurus*, list words that resemble each other. The experienced
writer can sometimes use a thesaurus to joggle his brain, to find not a
"synonym" but the *right* word. He will be aware of the insides of the
words he discovers. The thesaurus can be useful, not for supplying
words never heard before (we know words only when we have met
them in sentences; some dictionaries supply examples of words in use)
but to remind the writer of words known in the past, but not remembered when needed.

Sometimes an unsophisticated writer finds disaster in such a
book. A thesaurus supplies us with words that *resemble* each other,
but we must recognize the *differences* between them. When I look up
"imitation," in my pocket *Roget*, I find under Verbs:

> imitate, copy, mirror, reflect, reproduce, repeat; do like, echo,
> re-echo, catch, match, parallel; forge, counterfeit.

> mimic, ape, simulate, impersonate, act, etc. (*drama*), 599; repre-
> sent, etc., 554; parody, travesty, caricature, burlesque, take off,
> mock, borrow.

> follow in the steps (or wake) of, take pattern by, follow suit
> [colloq.], follow the example of, walk in the shoes of, take after,
> model after, emulate.

The editors separate the verbs into three categories, which ought to help the cautious writer, but it is difficult sometimes to defend their sorting out. Why does "forge" or "counterfeit" belong among the closer synonyms in the first group, and "emulate" among the phrases in the third group? Why is "represent" among the comic or belittling words? Putting "ape" with "travesty" and "parody," however, reminds us of the comic insides of "ape." The beginning writer should certainly be wary of a thesaurus, because if he believes in synonyms he could produce a prose that means something wholly different from what he intends.

> I walked in the flowers that bordered the garden, sniffing the sweet airs of spring.

could become,

> I peregrinated in the flowerets that flounced the orangery, sniffing the saccharine ventilation of the vernal equinox.

Spoken by W. C. Fields, the second version could be perfect for its context, but as an example of how people misuse a thesaurus, it is exaggerated.

Using dictionary synonyms, you can test your sensitivity to the insides of words. Put the adjectives "false," "fake," "phoney," and "insincere" with the noun "laugh." Everyone has heard laughs that were unreal, laughs for the sake of flattery, laughs that express the laugher's nervousness, or laughs at jokes that are not funny. If we wrote a description of such a laugh, we might want to write, "His laugh was false," or "His laugh was fake," or "His laugh was phoney," or "His laugh was insincere." Each time the exact meaning differs. "His laugh was false" sounds direct and serious, a stern and objective judgment. "His laugh was fake" sounds harsher, a strong indictment of the laugher; it implies that the falseness was deliberate. "His laugh was phoney" tells us more about whoever wrote the phrase. The choice of "phoney" over "false" or "fake" or "insincere" makes the speaker imply something like, "I am relaxed enough to be slangy." On the other hand, "His laugh was insincere" sounds pompous in its moral judgement — partly pompous, partly naïve.

These attempts to name the associations that words gather, without seeing the context that story or essay bestows, are speculation; but, whatever the context, the words would all be different. Slightly, but genuinely, different. Katherine Anne Porter announced in 1961 that she had discovered "a law" that she put into "a little axiom":

> There is no such thing as an exact synonym and no such thing as an unmixed motive.

Literalness and Metaphor

Another way to become sensitive to the insides of words is to take them as literally as you can. When you read, "Fog enveloped the city," try seeing a gigantic gray-brown envelope enclosing Los Angeles. You can see some silliness in literal images — but it is a silliness that can increase your sensitivity to words. Puns help too, working through the ear. Literal-mindedness, like all exercises that can improve your writing, can improve your reading as well.

Literal-mindedness exposes mixed metaphors, careless phrases comparing things that are comic or gross or inappropriate when brought together. Metaphors usually become mixed when a writer uses the kind of clichés called dead metaphors without noticing their original meanings. Sometimes people write, "The door yawned open"; the would-be comparison of door to mouth is dead from overuse. Sometimes people write, "The door beckoned," and the dead metaphor has the door turn into a hand that gestures an invitation. Once a student wrote in a paper, "The door yawned and beckoned." Two clichés make a mixed metaphor, if we are reading the insides of words: first the door is a huge, gaping mouth; suddenly an arm materializes between rows of teeth, and motions us to enter. Seeing the silliness in some mixed metaphors, you can invent situations to explain them. If you read, in a newspaper headline, that A GOLDEN OPPORTUNITY GOES DOWN THE DRAIN you can translate the sentence, "Somebody dropped the lemon jello down the disposal."

When we take words literally, we respond to metaphor. We see the fog *compared* to an envelope. A metaphor is a comparison made without being stated. We *state* a comparison as a simile — "like a big blue eyeball" — and we *make* a comparison when we leave out "like" or "as." Hamlet in his soliloquy wonders if he should "take arms against a sea of troubles." It is futile to fight with the ocean. The futility is what Shakespeare had in mind. If you take the words literally, you can see an armored knight wading into the surf and slashing at the waves with his sword. The image shows an emotion that the abstract word (futility) would only name. The picture — which we receive by literal reading — gives us the emotion, without losing the idea of futility that the picture expresses.

Sense Words

Words that carry feeling most strongly are pictures and smells and touches and tastes and noises. Images are details of sense. The more sensuous words are, the more they reach us and move us. Updike embodies feelings of cozy shelter, and of precise observation of the outside world, by using images, not by using words that *tell* us how to feel (like "cozy") or that abstract ideas from actions (like "observations"). Mailer gives us an exact visual image of the astronauts trying to sleep on the moon. We feel the astronauts' cramp and discomfort because of the images; he need not say "cramp" and "discomfort." In the next paragraph, Mailer writes about the failure to sleep, and he writes ideas, but he uses images as well.

> It used to be said that men in the hour of their triumph knew the sleep of the just, but a modern view might argue that men sleep in order to dream, sleep in order to involve that mysterious theater where regions of the unconscious reach into communication with one another, and charts and portraits of the soul and the world outside are subtly retouched from the experience of the day.

"Theater," "charts," "portraits . . . retouched" — Mailer uses images to make his concept clear by a comparison. Not all writing can be sensuous and figurative, but most writing can be. Of course it is always possible to be safe and boring by stating only the facts, without images and feelings. Mailer could have said that the astronauts arranged themselves to go to sleep but couldn't, perhaps because so much had happened that day. Updike could have said that when his characters woke up, they discovered that it had snowed while they slept.

Sense words carry feeling, and they fulfill purposes appropriate to different kinds of writing: for Mailer, the sense words embody a speculation; for Updike, they convey sensation that will soon body forth fiction to the reader's imagination. For Jane Addams, in this passage from *Twenty Years at Hull House*, images explain a scene at the same time as they express outrage over poverty in Victorian London:

> . . . On Mile End Road, from the top of an omnibus which paused at the end of a dingy street lighted by only occasional flares of gas,

we saw two huge masses of ill-clad people clamoring around two hucksters' carts. They were bidding their farthings and ha'pennies for a vegetable held up by the auctioneer, which he at last scornfully flung, with a gibe for its cheapness, to the successful bidder. In the momentary pause only one man detached himself from the groups. He had bidden on a cabbage, and when it struck his hand, he instantly sat down on the curb, tore it with his teeth, and hastily devoured it, unwashed and uncooked as it was. He and his fellows . . . were huddled into ill-fitting, cast-off clothing, the ragged finery which one sees only in East London. Their pale faces were dominated by that most unlovely of human expressions, the cunning and shrewdness of the bargain-hunter who starves if he cannot make a successful trade, and yet the final impression was not of ragged, tawdry clothing nor of pinched and sallow faces, but of myriads of hands, empty, pathetic, nerveless and workworn, showing white in the uncertain light of the street, and clutching forward for food which was already unfit to eat. . . .

Notice that our sense of outrage, almost without exception, comes from the images chosen; we are not *told*, except when she writes "that most unlovely of human expressions"; we are *shown*. If Jane Addams used only abstractions like "degradation" and "extreme poverty," we could forget them easily; we do not forget the man who devours the cabbage "unwashed and uncooked," or the hands clutching at inedible food.

Misusing the Insides of Words

Just as we can learn to embody feelings by being aware of a word's whole family and by using language that appeals to the senses, so we can misuse words to fool ourselves and other people. The poet W. B. Yeats wrote, "The rhetorician would deceive his neighbors, / The sentimentalist himself." Sentimentality means faked or exaggerated feeling, emotion that is not genuine. Usually, the rhetorician who wishes to deceive others must first become a sentimentalist who deceives himself. In the advertising business, it is common wisdom that you have to *believe* in your product; so that grown people ride the commuter trains believing that Hotz is superior to all other cold breakfasts. To con others, you begin by conning yourself, or you end that way.

Some propagandists deceive by will. The conscious manipulator sets out to change minds by slanting words to *seem* objective and yet to carry a disguised subjective content. Newsmagazines (*Time, News-week, U.S. News and World Report*) often convey subtle editorial comment within their reporting. Newspapers do the same, though editors try to keep the editorials editorial, and the news objective. But even when you appear objective, you can select with bias. One photograph of candidate Y looks flattering; another makes him look like an ass.

We will never destroy bias, but we can learn to see bias, and not be deceived by reporting that is really editorializing. A few years back, one newsmagazine blatantly supported one presidential candidate. It openly supported him editorially. And in its "news" stories it supported him subtly, using the associations of words. Candidate A, they said, "in his rumpled suit slouched into the gleaming limousine." Candidate B, on the other hand, "strode smiling into his black sedan."

Now a sedan may sound expensive, but it may also seem to suit the dignity required of a candidate for high office. "Gleaming limousine" is more lavish, more gloatingly rich. "Rumpled suit" and "smiling" are obvious contrasts. The most telling use of the loaded word is the contrast between "strode" and "slouched." Who would vote for a man who slouched when he could pick one who strode instead? Yet in all fairness, can we say that the *news* in each sentence is different? In Dick-and-Jane language, the sentence would read, "The man got in the car." The rhetoricians of the newsmagazine, playing upon the separation between meaning and expression, flash us the sign: "Vote for B!" Because they pretend to objectivity, their use of sense words to influence opinion is dishonest and underhanded.

They seem to be doing it consciously, though no one can ever be sure of someone else's consciousness. More dangerous, for anyone who wishes to be honest, are the loaded words we kid ourselves with. We use euphemism to persuade ourselves that one thing is really another; a janitor cleans floors, but it sounds more lofty to call him a custodian. When we say that someone is "wealthy," we avoid the plainer word "rich," which has acquired overtones of vulgarity. If a real estate agent shows you a two-room shack converted from a chicken coop, he does not call it a "house," he calls it a "home." A Cadillac is never a "used car"; it is "previously owned."

Often, a euphemism is more abstract or general than the plain word. The euphemism not only sounds fancier (mortician / undertaker; route salesman / milkman) but it has less color or imagery. Apparently,

Americans are especially prone to euphemism. H. L. Mencken, in *The American Language,* gave some historical background.

> The tendency to engaud lowly vocations with names presumably dignified goes back to the Revolution, and has been frequently noted by English travelers, beginning with Thomas Anburey in 1779. In 1784 John Ferdinand Dalziel Smyth observed that the smallest American shopkeepers were calling their establishments *stores,* which indicated a large place to an Englishman. "The different distinct branches of manufacturers," he said, "such as *hosiers, haberdashers, clothiers, linen drapers, grocers, stationers,* etc., are not known here; they are all comprehended in the single name and occupation of *merchant* or *storekeeper.*" By 1846 the American barbershop had begun to be a *shaving salon* and by 1850 a photographer was a *daguerrian artist.* By 1875 barbers were *tonsorial artists* or *tonsorialists,* and in the early 80s presentable saloonkeepers became *restauranters* or *restauranteurs.* By 1901 the *Police Gazette* was carrying on a campaign for the abandonment of the lowly *bartender* and the adoption of either *bar clerk* or *mixologist.* . . .

But euphemism is not only comical. We employ euphemism, frequently, when we want to conceal something painful. When we have a tomcat castrated, we hesitate to admit that we have cut off his testicles, or even that we have castrated him; we have had him "altered." We have a tooth "extracted"; it would be more painful to have it "pulled."

Politics and political acts of destruction always bring forth the worst in our prose, as we struggle to justify ourselves. Hitler euphemistically labeled his genocide of Jews "the final solution." One of the finest essays on style is George Orwell's "Politics and the English Language," written in the forties. He says:

> Millions of peasants are robbed of their farms and sent trudging along the roads with no more than they can carry: this is called *transfer of population* or *rectification of frontiers.* People are imprisoned for years without trial, or shot in the back of the neck or sent to die of scurvy in Arctic lumber camps; this is called *elimination of undesirable elements.* Such phraseology is needed if we want to name things without calling up mental pictures of them. Consider for instance some comfortable English professor defending Russian totalitarianism. [George Orwell was British, and was writing after Stalin's execution of the Kulaks and the mass murders of the Soviet purges of the late thirties.] He cannot say outright, "I

believe in killing off your opponents when you can get good results
by doing so." Probably, therefore, he will say something like this:

"While freely conceding that the Soviet regime exhibits certain
features which the humanitarian may be inclined to deplore, we
must, I think, agree that a certain curtailment of the right to political opposition is an unavoidable concomitant of transitional periods, and that the rigors which the Russian people have been
called upon to undergo have been amply justified in the sphere of
concrete achievement."

Meanwhile, the bullet enters the back of the head. Always be suspi-
cious — as Orwell advises — when the words do not call up a picture.
"Terminate with extreme prejudice" does not call to mind the prisoner
bound, blindfolded, kneeling, the pistol at the back of his head, the
sound, the rush of the body forward, the splatter of brains and blood.

Avoiding Self-Deceit

Sometimes, then, we use abstractions or euphemisms to avoid or
suppress feeling. And sometimes we use sense words in dishonest
ways, not so much to evade feeling as to twist it. "Slouched" and
"strode" are both verbs of action that make us see. We must decide, by
using our brains and our sensitivity, whether the difference between
two images is literal description or an emotional nudge disguising
itself as objective description. We do not complain that emotions
show; we complain that the emotions are *disguised*. We do not object
to laughter or to anger. We object to laughter that hides anger, expressing gaiety while it means hostility. We can learn to sense the falseness
in language — our own or others' — as we learn to sense falseness in a
gesture or a facial expression.

If we ourselves have strong opinions or biases, we must try to
correct for the veer of our own wind, both in reading and writing. If we
react instantly to a cliché like "the military-industrial complex," we
are not thinking about it, and we can manipulate ourselves or be ma-
nipulated by others. We must become aware of our habits of opinion.
We need not alter our convictions; we need only open them to the
air — and to our own conscious minds. When we hear a phrase like
"iron-curtain countries," we must not respond like an automaton to a
pressed button, but like a human being, and decide what the phrase
means, if it means anything, in its current context.

The more intense our convictions, the more vulnerable we are to self-deceit. Knowing ourselves comes first: if we understand our feel-ings, we are forewarned of our vulnerability.

Collecting Words

We must watch our words to see if we are using them with re-spect for honest expression. It helps to love words, and a love of words is something that we can develop. The growing writer finds pleasure in becoming a word collector, picking up, examining, and keeping new words (or familiar words seen suddenly, as if for the first time) like seashells or driftwood. Think of the richness in "hogwash," or the exact strength in "rasp." English is thick with short, strong words. You can collect words from books, of course, but you can also find them in speech; a sense of lively speech adds energy to the best writing. A writer listens to speech — others' and even his own — with a greedy ear. Primitive people and children love words as things in themselves and collect them as ornaments. To become a better writer, rediscover some of the pleasure from words-as-things that you had in your child-hood but have probably lost along the way. Patrol the miles of speech looking for words like "flotsam."

Dictionaries can help, too. A thesaurus or a list of synonyms has the limitations mentioned earlier (pages 60–61). Brief dictionaries have brief definitions, and though they may light up a dark patch in our reading, they often give such a limited definition for the word, so void of context, that we may misuse the word when we try to say it in a sentence. Good-sized college dictionaries carry more information, and can be a pleasure to read. The more information, the better. The big-gest dictionary in the language rewards investigation. Some time, when you are in the library, take down from the shelves one of the thirteen volumes of the *Oxford English Dictionary* and browse a little. The English poet and novelist Robert Graves says only one book is indispensable to the writer's library: the OED. In the thirteen volumes, the editors collect almost all the words you are likely to come across, except for new words, and words that at the time of publication were considered unprintable. Currently, new editors are making a supple-ment that includes new words, and old words newly printable. Now the publishers have photographically reduced all the pages of the dic-tionary, making a two-volume set out of the original thirteen. The price of the two-volume set puts this great dictionary within many people's reach.

It is not the OED's completeness that makes it so valuable; it is the context given — the editors try to supply a context for the earliest example of each shade of meaning for every word. Suppose we look up the word "vegetable." More than three columns of small print chronicle the life of the word, which began as an adjective meaning "having the vegetating properties of plants; living and growing as a plant or organism endowed with the lowest form of life." The earliest example is from 1400. The poet John Lydgate, a couple of decades later, wrote of the wind (spelling modernized): ". . . that is so comfortable / For to nourish things vegetable." When Andrew Marvell wrote "To His Coy Mistress" two and a half centuries later (1687), he used the adjective in the same way: "My vegetable love should grow / Vaster than empires and more slow." Six examples (complete with small context) come between Lydgate and Marvell.

Meanwhile, the noun "vegetable" got started in 1582, when an author named J. Hester spoke of "the Hidden Vertues of sondrie Vegitables, Animalles, and Mineralles." The reader can discover thirty-six contexts for the word vegetable as a noun from 1582 to modern times — and many shades of meaning. If you take pleasure in words, you will find your sensitivity to the insides of words increasing the more you know the history of words. So much of our history, external and internal, global and psychic, is coded into our words. The more you know, the more you respect the integrity of the word; integrity means wholeness; a word's wholeness includes all its possibilities: its family, its insides.

Words as Blanks

A frequent failure in our language, spoken or written, is our use of words that can mean anything the context requires. These words are like blanks for the reader or listener to fill in. Words of vague praise or blame—"lovely" and "terrible"—are frequent blanks. "Great." "Terrific." What does "lovely hair" look like? Is it red or blonde or white or black or brown? Long or short? Liveliness is specificity. Vogue words are usually blanks also. "Dig," "heavy," "cool." "Fink" was popular a few years ago as a vogue word of contempt, no more precise than the "jerk" or "creep" of earlier generations. Yet once "fink" meant something exact: a man employed to join a labor union and spy for bosses. Words of complex history suddenly come into fashion and lose all color. "Funky" and "uptight" are words that moved from black American speech into the television set — and no longer have anything to say.

Words and Associations

Words used as blanks get in the way of writing and thinking and feeling. Words mean things only by our agreement. If we start using "April" to mean "sunset" or "anything pleasant." it will not be of use to us any more. Our agreements about words are coded into dictionaries, which of course change, as the words shift gradually in meaning because of historical change and the literary genius that adapts old words to new conditions. Our agreements about words are also coded into the dictionary from which we really make our sentences — the dictionary (the computer) of the brain. This mental collection is even more complicated and useful, for our writing, than the dictionary on the shelf. The thirty thousand associations of the word "April" are stored in it, waiting to be used in the right way at the right time. The inside of a word is a huge room of possibilities, limited — because "April" does not include "August" or "catsup" for most of us — but multiple: flowers and showers, Easter, spring, seeds, vacation from school, Chaucer and Browning and Eliot for readers of poetry, ploughing or manure-spreading for farmers.

Someone might associate April with catsup or cats or soup or a girl in the first grade called April. These associations are private; the few phrases I listed at the end of the last paragraph are public or general. A moment's thought will usually reveal to the writer, at least in revision, whether he is using a word privately or generally. "Tulips like catsup" would be a grotesque and inappropriate simile for most of us — despite the real color — though it might be a spontaneous expression of the writer who privately associated April with catsup. A writer must learn to suppress the highly private, because writing must get through to an audience; you are talking to someone besides yourself; you have climbed out of the pure autism of the crib, and are trying to make human contact.

Words and Audience

But we must also remember, in choosing words, that an audience is not "everyone." The larger the audience we try to reach, the fewer associations we can take for granted, and the more circumscribed our room of possibilities. If we are writing for a big newspaper, we probably do not assume that most of our readers associate April with Chaucer, Browning, and Eliot. An idea of the audience is crucial to our choice of words. Everyone makes this sort of choice in conversation: we use words with our best friend that we do not use with our grandmother; if we hitch a ride with a white-haired man wearing a blue suit, our words differ from those we would use if the driver wore sunglasses, bell-bottoms, and long hair. If our vocabulary stays the same, chances are that we are being hostile in the sacred name of honesty.

In writing we make the same choices. If we write a letter to the college newspaper, we choose the words from a pool different from the one we choose from when we write a thank-you letter to an aunt. The term paper in business administration requires a vocabulary different from the one for a term paper in literature.

The difficult, necessary task is to adjust your vocabulary to your audience with tact, humility, and appropriateness — but without hypocrisy, without being false. Sometimes it is merely a matter of common sense. If you are writing for an audience from the southern hemisphere, you must remember that April connotes autumn and leaves falling, not green and seeds sprouting. But common sense is easy, compared to the difficulties of learning the difference between appropriate tact and gross hypocrisy. When Jim Beck wrote his first essay, the one about "well-rounded individuals" and so on (on page 8), he was writing *for* an assumed audience, and *against* himself. Probably at that moment he did not believe that he could write with honesty for an audience that was a teacher. Probably Jim Beck had no vocabularies to fall back on at that moment but that of high-minded hypocrisy, and that of the boys in the locker room or the dorm, which can be just as hypocritical and one-sided as graduation oratory. By learning to write with more respect for himself, for his own feelings told in his own words, he learned to write with honesty, and to face things with honesty. By becoming aware of the insides of words, he learned a lot about the insides of Jim Beck; and he learned to make the inside outside — to *write*.

EXERCISES

1. Here are three lists of words similar in meaning. Discuss the varieties of meaning within each list.

> ostentatious, showy, conspicuous, exhibitionistic;
> preserve, maintain, keep up, support;
> disease, illness, sickness, infirmity, disorder, indisposition, debility.

2. Using a thesaurus, rewrite this passage by substituting a "synonym" for each of the words in italics. See the example on page 61.

> I *remember sitting* with my *foot* up on *pillows* on the edge of my *bed* in my *room, gazing* at my *freckled face* in a *hand mirror.* My *face embarrassed* me most of the time and I couldn't *get* a *comb* through my *mass* of *unruly, tangled red hair.*
>
> Shirley MacLaine, *Don't Fall off the Mountain*

3. Look past these thesaurus words, and find the proverb:

  a. It requires an entirety of species to fabricate a cosmos.

  b. Precipitousness occasions depletion.

  c. The sum total of matter which scintillates is not necessarily bullion.

4. Here are some headlines or sentences quoted from daily newspapers. Try the tests of "Literalness and Metaphor," pages 62–63.

  a. Unmasked as a faceless automaton, he toyed with her affections, and a stormy argument ensued.

  b. Auto Show Fans Bask in Cream of City's Crop

  c. A gush of poetic language cushions these pivotal events until they are nearly — but not quite — camouflaged.

  d. Mushrooming insurance and energy costs represent a double-barreled shotgun pointed at New England ski areas.

  e. PTA Opens Fire on TV Violence.

5. Make up new euphemisms for the following professions, events, or actions.

> goaltender in hockey, food server in a cafeteria, bookseller;
> final exams, Mother's Day, Veterans Day;
> tackling a quarterback from the blind side, cheating on a quiz,
> asking for money.

6. When prose gets out of control, there is often more than one thing wrong with it. In the following passages of bad prose, find words used as blanks and as euphemisms. If you notice other faults, name them.

  a. Thank you for the information you recently provided in connection with your request for Gulf Travel Cards. The information contained in your communication, along with other data developed has enabled us to reverse our previous decision regarding your Travel Card application.

b. We will be experiencing a development of shower activity

c. The purpose of this program is to provide opportunities for teachers at undergraduate colleges and universities and at junior and community colleges to work in their areas of interest with distinguished scholars in their fields and to have access to libraries suitable for advanced study.

. . .

Because of the short duration of the seminars, and because the principal value of the seminar for the college teachers is the close association with the seminar director, it would be disadvantageous for a seminar to have more than a single director, except in special cases, or for the director to share the work of the seminar with large numbers of visitors or associates. Since we seek to balance the final list of seminars by topic and discipline in order to serve the needs of college teachers having a wide variety of teaching and research specializations, grants awarded under the program ought not to be considered simply as recognitions of the seminar directors' merits and accomplishments.

d. The evidence developed was not corroborative of the allegation on which it was predicated.

7. In these paragraphs, underline the words that the author uses most brilliantly — the way John Updike uses "adhesively" and "slice" — and defend your choices in class.

a. As the waves roll in toward Lands End on the westernmost tip of England they bring the feel of the distant places of the Atlantic. Moving shoreward above the steeply rising floor of the deep sea, from dark blue water into troubled green, they pass the edge of "soundings" and roll up over the continental shelf in confused ripplings and turbulence. Over the shoaling bottom they sweep landward, breaking on the Seven Stones of the channel between the Scilly Isles and Lands End, coming in over the sunken ledges and the rocks that roll out their glistening backs at low water.
Rachel Carson, *The Sea Around Us*

b. The top of the hill, pasture for one straggly cow, was clear of brush except for patches of dark juniper, in spreading flat circles ten feet across. Around the tumbled stone walls tall pines and maples held off an advancing army of small gray birch. At one side, by the bouldery path that had once been a town road, a little family graveyard lay on slightly tilted ground. A deer trail ran right through it, bright and twisting between the slate stones, and a birch had fallen and rotted out of its bark, leaving a print like a white hand.
Thomas Williams, *Town Burning*

8. Underline the sense words in this passage from a magazine article. How effective are they? Does the author have the insides of words under control?

> A blinding splendor sparkling in lazy rhythm to the whine of retarding jet engines welcomes you to Mexico City. The surreal glow seems to extend to the end of the world and it's not hard to believe some ten million persons are rising for the day, hustling in the brilliant carpet of light below.
>
> Before the plane has touched the runway, dawn explodes. Sentry volcanoes glisten in rainbow hues — imperfect cones turned upside down, slowly shifting their color from black, to grey, to crystalline sugar frost. Below them, smog clouds — modern mad children of our times — begin to drift in peaceful motion as a soft light invades the aircraft and stirs its sleepy passengers.
>
> Sergio Ortiz, "Mexico" (Playgirl)

9. Underline examples of euphemism in these passages from a speech about the public relations business:

> So confident were we that a breakthrough was imminent that it became popular to think of changing our name from public relations specialists to communications specialists.
>
> . . .
>
> What is new is the role the public relations consultant is beginning to play in relation to the social crises which no one foresaw 10 or 20 years ago. In these new assignments — which represent a small but rapidly growing part of his business — he is no longer primarily a communicator: he is a sort of moderator whose job it is to try to prevent the crisis from getting out of hand. He may still use the same tools, but the measure of his performance is not how effectively he gets his clients' message across, but how successful he is in avoiding a flare-up which can stop the machinery of his clients' business, how he can help his clients conduct their business in a way that is responsive to the new demands made by concerned scientists, environmentalists, consumerists, minority leaders, underprivileged segments of the community, the young generation.
>
> David Finn, "Modifying Opinions in the New
Human Climate" (Public Relations Quarterly)

10. Disregarding your own convictions, look in these passages for loaded language, euphemism — the use and misuse of language in general. Underline whatever seems underhanded, and discuss in class.

> a. During 1974, expenditures for industrial air and water pollution control at GM facilities totaled $74 million, not excluding expenditures for research and development and operating costs. Because of

recent E.P.A. rules promulgated as part of the water and air pollution control and solid waste disposal laws, GM and industry in general may be faced with additional substantial capital expenditures over the next three to five years. There is concern that some mandated time schedules may be unachievable, and that some requirements for control systems may be questionable on a cost / benefit relationship. GM will actively pursue its stated goal of compliance with all applicable pollution control laws — but at the same time will do what it can to ensure that such control is economically justifiable in relation to the anticipated benefits.

> "1974 General Motors Report
> on Programs of Public Interest"

b. The Great Lakes, which hold one-fifth of all the fresh water on the surface of the earth, have become heavily contaminated. Hundreds of millions of gallons of industrial pollutants are discharged into Lake Superior and flow on into Lake Huron. Lake Michigan drains a huge complex of industries. Lake Erie is described as a "chemical sink." Most of the lake's fish, once a rich harvest, have been killed. In the slow-moving lake water, contaminants have settled to the bottom. Thus, although clean-up efforts are now beginning, experts are far from sure that the lakes can be reclaimed even if further pollution can be halted.

> John Perry, *Our Polluted World*

c. The coal companies propose to extract North Dakota's lignite over the next few decades by strip-mining — the environmentally notorious method of removing all the earth from atop the seam rather than removing the coal from under the earth via tunnels. They are offering to sign coal-mining leases at royalty rates that have drawn the interest of prosperous farmers.

> Ben A. Franklin, "What Price Coal?"
> (*The New York Times Magazine*)

d. The world needs nuclear energy. The fossil fuels — coal, oil and natural gas — are being consumed at an alarming rate. Many experts believe that by the end of this century half of the world's supply of electric power will come from nuclear stations.

Nuclear fuels are highly concentrated. Operation of a coal-fueled Fermi-2 would require about 3,650,000 tons of coal a year. As a nuclear plant it will consume about 1.25 tons of nuclear fuel annually.

The basic difference between a nuclear and a fossil-fueled power plant is the heat source and method of generating steam. From there on the process is similar to conventional plants: Steam goes to the turbine which spins the rotor of the electric generator. The spent steam is condensed back into feed-water which goes back to the reactor where it is again turned into steam.

Another difference is the very large investment in control, safety and environmental protection systems. If one system fails there is another, and yet another, to take charge and correct the situation. Every effort is made to design, fabricate and construct nuclear plant facilities to the highest quality standards. No other industry has a safety record to match nuclear power.

> The Nuclear Way, "Building Fermi-2"
> (from a publication by Detroit Edison)

e. We also learned from fallout, how little was known about the risks incurred by large populations exposed to radiation or toxic substances. Before the advent of nuclear energy, medical experience with the internal effects of radiation was very limited, based largely on the fate of several hundred unfortunate women who in the 1920's had used their lips to point up brushes for applying radium-containing luminous paint on watch dials. Standards of radiation exposure were set on the assumption that, at some minimal level, the body would experience no harm at all from radiation, and the AEC used these standards in order to support their claim that fallout was "harmless" to the population as a whole. Later, when it was realized that unlike industrial workers, the general population is unable to escape exposure (for example, by quitting a job) and includes especially susceptible individuals such as children and the aged, the "acceptable" limits were reduced to about three percent of their original value. Finally, experiments show that *every* exposure to radiation, however small, carries with it *some* risk, in the form of genetic damage or cancer.

> Barry Commoner, *The Closing Circle*

f. *How large is the risk from normal radioactive discharges?* As explained in Sections 2, 3, and 4, the allowable exposure to the general public from nuclear power plants is limited by Federal regulations to less than one mrem / year. The effects of radiation resulting from nuclear power plants are undetectable. However, making very conservative estimates based on the effects of large doses of radiation, the public risk from allowable exposure limits (which are greater than actual exposures) is less than one in 10 million persons per year.

> The American Nuclear Society,
> *Nuclear Power and the Environment: Questions and Answers*

VERBS

Action, and the Choice of Style

Verbs act. Verbs move. Verbs do. Verbs strike, soothe, grin, cry, exasperate, decline, fly, hurt, and heal. Verbs make writing go, and they matter more to our language than any other part of speech.

Verbs give energy, if we use them with energy. I could have said, "Verbs are action. Verbs are motion. Verbs are doing." But if I had written the sentences this second way, I would have written dull prose. I could have gone even further into dullness, and written, "Verbs are words that are characterized by action."

Try to use verbs that act. Yet sometimes you will need to write verbs that are less than active. Just as there are no synonyms, there are no two sentences that mean the same thing but are different only in style. A change in style, however slight, is always a change in meaning, however slight. Is it, therefore, possible to make a stylistic generalization at all?

I think that the generalization remains possible, with explanation and with room for exception. Both explanations and exceptions will follow in the sections on verbs and nouns, but let us start with a general explanation. Most of the time passives and weak verbs evade precision and commitment. Examples follow, in which weak verbs add static to statement, and in which passives avoid being wrong by evading definite statement. These habits fuzz our prose with bad brain fuzz. To recommend that we use active forms of active verbs, is to recommend energy and clarity, definite statement and commitment.

Verbs with Nouns and Adjectives

Usually, a single verb is stronger and better than a strung out verb-and-adjective or verb-and-noun combination. People say, "I am aware of this fact," or, "I am cognizant of this situation," when they could have said, "I know it." In these examples, we have a weak verb and adjective followed by a noun that means little, but appears to end the sentence, to give the verb an object. The phrases mean something different from "I know it," but the difference is mere pomposity. "I am aware of the fact" differs from "I know it" because it shows us that the speaker thinks well of himself; he sounds like a professor trying to put down another professor who has tried to put him down. "I am cognizant of the situation" is so pompous it may sound ironic; it would usually fall from the lips, or leak from the pen, of someone nervous about his intellectual status, like a television executive.

Look out for the verbs be / is / are and has / have combined with nouns and adjectives. See if you do not gain by using the verb itself, clear and clean. "He looked outside and became aware of the fact that it was raining" revises easily into "He looked outside and saw that it was raining" or, more simply, "He looked outside. It was raining." Instead of "We had a meeting," try "We met." The meaning is different, slightly, but if the second phrase is accurate, it is better — we save three syllables and add energy to our prose; when we cut to the essential motion, we add vitality. Instead of "They were decisive about the question of . . . ," try "They decided to. . . ."

Now "to be decisive" — if we look at the insides of words — means something quite different from "to decide." The person who "is decisive" has vigor and intellectual intensity; he cuts through the uncertainties that surround a question, and makes a choice firmly and quickly. If you are describing a committee meeting in which, after long discussion, the members reached a consensus or took a vote and decided to do something, "they decided" is the clearest phrase to use. "They reached a decision" wastes words, probably; it does imply that it took some work "to arrive at the decision," which by itself would imply more ease, and less struggle, than "reached." If you feel that the meaning requires "reached" or "arrived," use the accurate word. But, certainly, in writing about the committee meeting described above, "they were decisive about . . ." would be misuse of words. They weren't decisive at all. They decided. Most of the time, when we use a wordy noun / adjective-verb phrase, we are merely trying to *sound* more complicated. Most of the time, the shade of meaning in "reached" or "arrived" is not needed. We use the longer phrase just to *seem* to be considering fine points. The sensible rule: use the shorter, more direct verb ("they decided") except when the longer variation has a precision that your meaning requires. "They talked for two days about lowering the voting age, without coming to a conclusion. Then Senator Jensen returned from a junket. He spoke briefly. He was decisive. The measure carried by a two-thirds majority."

Verbs with Participles

The same advice applies to phrases that use verb forms ending in -ing (present participles). "They were meeting to discuss" can often become "They met to discuss," and "He is clearing his throat" becomes "He clears his throat." But the participle is different in meaning — it marks a different sort of time — and therefore it can be useful when that difference is important. "She'll be comin' 'round the mountain" has more continuous motion in it than "She'll come 'round the mountain." Participles imply continuing action. But be sure that you *intend* the difference, and are not just lazy. Apparently the mind finds it easier to be pale than to be colorful. Or maybe the mind finds it easier to avoid the extra vocabulary of verbs, sticking to "be" and "has" with nouns and adjectives. Whatever the reason, when we add little words like "is" and "has" to participles, adjectives, and nouns, usually we thin our prose into invisibility.

The Passive Voice

When writers use the passive, they usually subtract meaning from their prose. We say, "a message was received," instead of "they" (or "I" or "you" or "he" or "she") "received a message." We suppress identity, which is a particular, and we put hazy distance between implied subject and definite action. The passive voice avoids responsibility, as we sometimes claim that "a dish was dropped in the kitchen," rather than name the dropper. It diminishes a sentence by omitting a doer. It can be politically useful: "Napalm was dropped yesterday on structures in a fire-free zone near the DMZ." Sometimes we use the passive from diffidence, or modesty, or false modesty, or all three. It waters the soup. We sound as if we wrote labels for medicine bottles. "Doses may be administered three times daily. Dosage recommended for adults is. . . . ." So a depressed writer might say, making an argument: "It can be assumed that someone in college is fairly mature. It might be objected that. . . ." Here, passives make invisible dialogue, a pale argument between people who are not there. Scientific prose uses the passive by convention, establishing an impersonal tone. Sometimes writers on nonscientific subjects achieve a pseudoscientific tone by using the passive.

Occasionally the passive is right, or unavoidable. Passives are used in a textbook whose author advises against passives.

> The author uses passives in the text.
> The text uses passives.
> Passives are used in the text.

In some contexts, the third sentence is best. The second is most terse, but it involves a metaphor — the text must be compared to a person, if it "uses" something — which may weaken it. The first correctly says that the author does the using, but it would be intrusive in some contexts to state the subject when the subject is perfectly obvious; it would be overexplained, and wordy. It might be better to use the passive to avoid these other troubles, choosing it as the least of three evils.

Sometimes the passive is useful because we do not know the identity of the doer. The passive (especially if we use it sparingly) can imply this ignorance, which may be part of the meaning of the sentence. Suppose this were the start of a story:

> He walked into his bedroom. Clothes lay in heaps on the floor. Dresser drawers lay upside down on the rug, their contents scattered.

This describes a scene, mostly in the active voice, with inanimate objects (clothes, dresser drawers) doing active things (lay, lay upside down). It is terse, but it implies no reason for the scene, and no response to it. The active voice in this passage is less meaningful than the passive would be:

> He walked into the room. Clothes were heaped on the floor. Dresser drawers were dumped on the rug, and their contents had been scattered.

The scene is the same. We still don't know who did it. But the passives (after the first sentence, which is active) imply that someone else, unknown, has done the damage. They only *imply* it, they do not *state* it, but the implication is real, and further implies shock. The second and third sentences suggest what happens in his mind as he enters the room: "I've been robbed!" To make this last sentence active would sound artificial: "Someone has robbed me!" The writer would be taking as absolute the advice to avoid the passive, which is only a sensible, general rule.

Good writers use the passive for variety in sentence structure, too. Rarely, but they do. In a paragraph about two groups taking opposite sides on an issue, in which all sentences have the active voice, the author looking for stylistic variety might insert the sentence, "Arguments were put forward, on both sides, which would make a goat blush." When you use a passive for variety, be certain that you are not using it for any of the reasons that make passives bad: diffidence, false modesty, evading responsibility, or imitating scientific respectability.

Particular Verbs

I have been writing all along as if there were two classes of verbs: strong ones and weak ones. Of course language is more complicated than that, and not only because weak is sometimes better than strong, as I have argued. Some strong verbs are stronger than others. "He moved" is stronger than "he was in motion." But in a context that admits it, we might say with greater strength, "he crept," or "he slid," or "he hurtled." We would almost always want to say "he crept" rather than "he moved, creeping." (A difference of meaning might, once, make the second phrase useful.) The first verbs I listed in the paragraph that starts this section are general verbs: do, move, act. The second series is particular, and more colorful. Energy lies often in small shades of difference, rather than in opposites like "she was in motion" and "she slithered."

Invisible Verbs

In the prospectus for a dissertation, a Ph.D. candidate wrote this sentence in which he misused verbs; in fact, he managed to write almost *without verbs.*

> Illustrative of what Kornhauser means by constraint imposed on professionals in organizations are the findings of Leo Meltzer in a survey of 3,084 physiologists in the United States.

The sentence has no strong and active verbs. "Means" is the closest. "Illustrative" is an adjective substituted for a verb. "Imposed" is a past participle that suppresses responsibility. "Are" is boring.

To rewrite the sentence in a language not far from the original, but with more vigor and clarity, we can simply cut and rearrange.

> Leo Meltzer questioned 3,084 physiologists in the United States; his findings illustrate Kornhauser's contention that organizations constrain professionals.

Maybe "surveyed" is more accurate than "questioned," but "surveyed" smells of jargon.

The last phrase of this revision may not mean what the original author had in mind. Did he mean that the institution imposed the constraint, or that something else, unnamed, chose professionals in organizations, rather than others, to impose restraint on? The ambiguity in the original passage is real, and serves no function; it is merely unclear. The second version is clearer, though without context it still raises questions. What is this constraint? What desires are held back? Does the author mean "constraint" as restraint or as compulsion?

Does he mean all organizations — like YMCAs, universities, corporations, fraternities, bridge clubs, and nations — or specifically professional ones, like the American Association of University Professors, the Modern Language Association, or the American Medical Association? Clarity comes from vigor combined with detail. Verbs are the most vigorous parts of speech; by particularity, they add to detail.

False Color in Verbs

The search for particularity and color can become obvious, and the prose look silly. In the examples that follow, the faults do not lie in the verbs alone, but in the whole style. Verbs are at the center of the action in our prose, however, for good or for ill. In the play, *The Owl and the Pussycat,* a would-be novelist reads the first page of his manuscript to the girl who has invaded his apartment. When he starts by saying the sun "spat" on his protagonist, she flies into a rage. So should we. Men's action magazines are full of Methedrine prose, violence done to language in the name of violence. In a recent thriller called *A Clash of Hawks,* the author's second sentence reads,

> The 200-foot-high derrick was a black, latticed steel phallus raping the hot, virginal blue sky.

Tough writing is not the only kind of bad overwriting. Maybe pretty writing is worse. It is Liberace prose, and it can rely on verbs for its nasty work, too.

> Songbirds trilled out my window, vines curled at the eaves, and Spring drenched the day with gladness.

Often a beginning writer tries to make the verbs describing dialogue too specific: "he whimpered," "she snapped." Almost always it looks too strenuous. We should use "said," or nothing at all, most of the time. The emotion should be in the dialogue itself, in the speaker's words; if the reader has to be told, the emotion is not there. The trick is energy with appropriateness. We may need to learn to do too much before we can learn to do the right amount. Newly wakened to verbs, one student wrote this passage in his next theme:

> The train slammed to a stop in the station. Steam vomited from all apertures. Passengers gushed through the barriers and hurtled into the night.

It was a useful exercise, because the student was searching through his mental dictionary for energetic verbs. The color was more vivid than the actions colored, like photographs in advertisements for food. Steam gushing out at the base of an engine is not like vomiting; "vomiting" is too sick and unpleasant and bad smelling a word; the writer used it only for its power, and not for what it contributed to the picture. Though the general advice — choose color over pallor, energy over lethargy — holds true, one matter overrides all others, in any discussion of style, and that is appropriateness: context is all.

Fancy Verbs

Some verbs are too fancy for normal use. Writers use them when they think their prose ought to wear fancy clothes. "Depict" is usually inferior to "paint" or "draw" or "describe." "He depicted a scene of unparalleled magnitude." (W. C. Fields / thesaurus talk again.) Maybe that means "he painted a big picture," or "he told a good story," or half a dozen other things, but its real meaning is its would-be fanciness. It is a sentence admiring itself in the mirror. "Emulate" would usually be fancy for "copy," "ascertain" for "make sure," and "endeavor" for "try."

Made-Up Verbs

Then there are the made-up words, neologisms, which sound fancy to the people who use them. When we are tempted to say "finalize," we would do better to say "end" or "finish." In general, we should avoid verbs made of an adjective and an -ize; "personalize" is another. Advertising and politics have created many crude verbs, sometimes using nouns as bases instead of adjectives. Some good old English verbs end in -ize. "Scrutinize," deriving from the noun "scrutiny," is a useful verb "Finalize," on the other hand, is used to sound fancier than "finish" or "end," to give false complexity to a simple act. Therefore it is bad style, pretending to be something that it isn't, a form of euphemism. The writer should search the language for the simplest and most direct way of saying and expressing, not make up a new word when an old one will do.

EXERCISES

1. Underline the weak verbs (verb-noun or verb-adjective or verb-participle combinations, invisible verbs, verbs lacking partic-

ularity) in these sentences. See if you can substitute strong verbs for those underlined. When you make a substitution, does the meaning of the sentence vary? Can you think of reasons for preferring the weaker verb combinations in any of the sentences?

a. She made the observation that German had been her minor in college.

b. We have endeavored to reach a conclusion that will be satisfactory.

c. We were just starting to sing when the door opened.

d. The committee has been meeting every day for a month.

e. I am trying to be healthy so that I will be playing tennis when I have arrived at eighty.

f. We had gotten around to the subject of getting good grades and got into an argument.

g. A different way of expressing the same idea is that having no commitment to activity we are engaged upon a course of activity lacking purpose.

h. We were in action right away, moving out into the field on our stomachs until we got to the river.

2. These five sentences contain passives. Underline the passive verbs, and then consider if any are necessary or useful. When the passive is objectionable, figure out why, and revise the sentence so that passive becomes active.

a. Arabella was understood by her neighbors to have cornered the market in soybean futures.

b. People committed to excellence are sought after in the business community.

c. At the picketing sites on North Campus, GEO members were not allowed to use the restrooms.

d. My canoe tipped over, I was thrown out into the water, and I saw the MacDonalds ahead of me.

e. Remembering August with Emily in Poughkeepsie, and rereading her letter which arrived this morning, I gradually realized that I had been deceived.

3. Here are some fancy verbs. Find simpler verbs that would usually do better.

masticate	permeate
cogitate	imbue
commence	disseminate
expectorate	substantiate
perspire	estimate

4. Here is a list of verbs chosen for varieties of tone and degrees of color. With each of them, find alternatives, near synonyms, which might work better in a specific context. For an example, remember the differences between emulate / imitate / copy / ape discussed on pages 60–61. Make up a context for five of the verbs — listed and discovered — in which the verb feels appropriate.

clutch	communicate
exterminate	rasp
rattle	split
cook	decide
act	recommend

5. Look through your own writing — old themes or daily writing — and find a paragraph that can be improved by strengthening the verbs. Copy out the old version, and revise it. (You will probably change other words as well as verbs; but pay closest attention to verbs.)

6. Here are five passages of prose. Underline the verbs, and in class discuss their quality.

a. John was the son of a prostitute and a naval officer. He lived with his mother until he was six, when he was transferred to his father's care. He was transported into a completely different world. His father, who had not married, sent him to a public school where he did well until, unexpectedly, he failed his university entrance exam. Thereupon he was drafted into the Navy, but failed to become an officer. His father, who was a very exacting man, had been somewhat upset by his son's failure at university level, but was much more upset by his failure to become an officer, and it drew from him the remark that he did not think he could be his son at all. When, in the next few months, John disgraced himself as a sailor in a number of ways, his father told him plainly that he was not his son any more, and that he now knew he never had been. He formally disowned him.

During his early months in the Navy, John was noted to get into states of anxiety, and it was on the grounds of anxiety neurosis that he had been turned down as an officer. Subsequently, however, his behaviour earned the label of psychopathic delinquent, and it was out of keeping with his "character" hitherto. When his father disowned him his deviance escalated to what was called an acute manic psychosis. His basic premise had become: *he could be anyone he wanted, merely by snapping his fingers.*

R. D. Laing, *Self and Others*

b. When it comes to the actual methods of consumption, asparagus eaters seem to be roughly divided into two groups. There are those who assume a crouching position and attack the vegetable with knives and forks. Lined up against this faction are those who believe the only way to eat asparagus is to throw back the head, grasp the stalk between thumb and forefinger and lower it slowly into the mouth, chewing steadily.

Diane White, "The Noble Asparagus"
(The Boston Globe)

c. A machine gun lashed at him from across the river, and he ducked in his hole. In the darkness, it spat a vindictive white light like an acetylene torch, and its sound was terrifying. Croft was holding himself together by the force of his will. He pressed the trigger of his gun and it leaped and bucked under his hand. The tracers spewed wildly into the jungle on the other side of the river.

Norman Mailer, The Naked and the Dead

d. The service shall be delivered in the following manner: Immediately before commencing to serve, the Server shall stand with both feet at rest behind the base line, and within the imaginary continuation of the center mark and side line of the singles court. The Receiver may stand wherever he pleases behind the service line on his own side of the net. The server shall then throw the ball into the air and strike it with his racket before it hits the ground. Delivery shall be deemed complete at the moment the racket strikes the ball.

"How Service is Delivered," Official Tennis Rules

e. Weighing the half-pounds of flour, excluding the scoop, and depositing them dust-free into the thin paper sacks held a simple kind of adventure for me. I developed an eye for measuring how full a silver-looking ladle of flour, mash, meal, sugar or corn had to be to push the scale indicator over to eight ounces or one pound. When I was absolutely accurate our appreciative customers used to admire: "Sister Henderson sure got some smart grandchildrens." If I was off in the Store's favor, the eagle-eyed women would say, "Put some more in that sack, child. Don't you try to make your profit offa me."

Maya Angelou, I Know Why the Caged Bird Sings

NOUNS

Particularity and Choosing a Style

Nouns are the simplest parts of speech, the words least tricky to use. Nouns are the names of things, "things" in the broadest sense: table, elm, Nancy, rain, noun, Centerville, nation, hunger, nine o'clock. If verbs supply the energy that makes prose go, nouns are the body of prose. Without nouns, nothing would be doing the going.

Many of the generalizations that apply to verbs apply to nouns also. We prefer as a rule the specific, the sensuous, the strong, the simple, and the colorful over the abstract, the general, the polysyllabic, and the fancy. We prefer "elm" to "tree," "Nancy" to "girl," and "nine o'clock" to "evening." The more particular the noun, the clearer the pictures we make, and the more accurately we can represent feelings. When a student wrote,

> I remembered a group of flowers that grew on some land near a relative's house . . .

he changed it to,

> I remembered a patch of daisies that grew on a meadow near my Cousin Annie's farm . . .

and the particularity is all gain. The first example was not bad style, but it was pale prose. The second by comparison is vivid.

But we generalize, and we must express reservations. Sometimes the more general noun is more accurate and honest than the specific one. From a distance, you see "a man" or "a woman," not "a sophomore" or "a mechanic." "Town" may be more appropriate, in the right context, than "Centerville," though it is less specific. We must keep in mind the advice to be specific; but, as ever, we must be wary that our rules do not lead us into absurdity. A student revised some daily writing into,

> On Tuesday afternoon, October thirteenth, I read a sentence half-way down the first page of *War and Peace* which . . .

Maybe in a particular context, such extreme specificity would be useful, but usually it would sound overly precise.

Also, we must remember again that the advice to cultivate one kind of style, at the expense of another, means thinking or seeing things in special ways. *A change in style, however slight, is always a change in meaning, however slight.* For some types of writing, like a scientific summary, or a paper in philosophy, an injunction to "Be particular!" and "Avoid abstraction!" is worse than useless; it is destructive.

> At first cats would not seem to offer a likely clue to human history. Yet when one considers that the writing of adequate histories of human populations began scarcely 200 years ago, that writing itself dates back only about 6,000 years and that for many populations historical, linguistic and cultural records are inadequate or nonexistent, cats appear in a different light. They have been associated with human beings for a long time, but they have never had any

economic significance and only rarely have they had much social significance. Genetically they, unlike other domesticated animals, have been left largely to themselves. The study of the population genetics of cats is therefore rewarding not only for what it reveals about the evolution of cats but also for what it suggests about the movements of human populations.

Neil B. Todd, "Cats and Commerce"
(Scientific American)

Todd writes a vigorous expository prose, which must be abstract and concrete by turns, where each level of diction is appropriate. So must books about prose style, for that matter.

The wise advice is simply to be as particular as the context allows us. Too often, we are vague and general, when we would say much more by discovering the concrete. Instead of saying,

> When it got cold the animals looked for shelter.

we could convey much more by a particularity.

> In October there was frost; the sheep huddled in one corner of the barn for warmth, the cattle in another.

Abstract and Particular

Degrees of difference separate the noun at an extreme of abstraction from the noun at an extreme of particularity. S. I. Hayakawa, in his book *Language in Thought and Action*, speaks of moving up a ladder of abstraction, climbing from the most particular level, gradually discarding particularities, and arriving into the thin air around the highest abstraction. His example is clear.

> 1. The cow known to science ultimately consists of atoms, electrons, etc., according to present-day scientific inference. Characteristics . . . are infinite at this level and ever changing. This is the *process level.*
> 2. The cow we perceive is not the word, but the object of experience, that which our nervous system abstracts (selects) from the totality that constitutes the process-cow. Many of the characteristics of the process-cow are left out.
> 3. The word "Bessie" . . . is the *name* we give to the object of perception of level 2. The name *is not* the object; it merely *stands for* the object and omits references to many of the characteristics of the object.
> 4. The word "cow" stands for the characteristics we have ab-

stracted as common to cow$_1$, cow$_2$, cow$_3$, . . . , cow$_n$. Characteristics peculiar to specific cows are left out.

5. When Bessie is referred to as "livestock," only those characteristics she has in common with pigs, chickens, goats, etc., are referred to.

6. When Bessie is included among "farm assets" reference is made only to what she has in common with all other saleable items on the farm.

7. When Bessie is referred to as an "asset," still more of her characteristics are left out.

8. The word "wealth" is at an extremely high level of abstraction, omitting *almost* all reference to the characteristics of Bessie.

The number of rungs on this ladder is limited only by our ingenuity, but I think we can most usefully distinguish three main degrees — the abstract, the general, and the particular. These notions can always be expanded. Within "the particular," we can subdivide into greater or lesser particularity. Take "animal, dog, spaniel." One might go further into particularity by adding a proper noun, or age, or color, or by naming a breed of spaniel — with the greater particularity always requiring more words. One might go higher in generality to "organism" or sideways into scientific classification with "quadruped." And these threesomes are quite relative. We can list three words which are all abstract but which become more nearly specific: "emotion, love, lust." The writer could use "lust" not as one of the seven deadly sins, but as an embodiment of the general "love"; he might have said "desire" or "eros," but "lust" seemed clearer.

The more abstract a noun, the more difficult it is to use well. Words like "emotion" (or "love," for that matter) or "courage" or "hatred" or "responsibility." To make these nouns work, you must provide a context with anecdote or analogy; you must put flesh on the bones. Usually an adjective in front of an abstraction does not do the work. The abstraction is lazy, retrieved by the writer from the attic of Big Ideas, and the adjective strives to do all the work; but adjectives themselves often are weak, and so we have two weaklings failing to budge the door that one strong noun could burst open. "Love" is thin and airy; it is pretty, but what is it about? Our affection for a pet salamander? The feeling of a grandfather for his grandaughter? Bert's obsession with the character of Charles Dickens? Mark and Nancy in the Oldsmobile? Married affection? "Love" is a grab bag of possibilities, only a bit less abstract than "emotion" or "feeling." If we modify it with the adjective "intense," we narrow its possibilities a little, but we do not really localize it. If we speak of "young love," we are more particular — and yet we move toward cliché. Many clichés are adjective-noun combinations in which the adjective is a desperate, though habitual, attempt to rescue a bland abstraction; "blind faith," for example.

Abstractions are usually lazy. The writer finds it easier to label the general category of a feeling than to search out the particulars that embody the feeling. Sight, taste, smell, touch, and hearing carry feeling from writer to reader — concepts don't. (And most writers using abstractions, we notice instantly, are not using concepts with the precision of a philosopher but vaguely and inaccurately.) Usually, we talk best about "love" when we do not use the word at all. If we use "Nancy," and "Centerville," and "a 1969 Pontiac," and "rain," and "nine o'clock," and connect them with strong verbs, the reader may know what we mean by the big hazy word "love" — in this time and in this place.

"Time" and "place" are abstractions. Are they used appropriately here? Sometimes the abstract affords a setting for the concrete, as a black velvet background shows up diamonds. In other contexts, instead of "time" and "place" we would want to use more specific words — steering wheel, September, elm, Long Lake Road.

Abstractions: Beginnings and Endings

An abstraction can be explained by context, an analogy or an anecdote. Some abstraction or generalization is necessary to any conceptual or argumentative writing. Only fiction, poetry, and autobiography can be free of it, and they do not always stay free. When we revise an essay, we should look most carefully to eliminate abstractions at two points — beginnings and endings. Frequently, we introduce a subject with an abstraction, "I am going to tell a story that illustrates inequality," and then we tell a story that illustrates inequality. If the illustration is clear, the introductory abstraction was unnecessary; what is more, it was probably distracting. When you announce that you are going to tell a funny joke before you tell it, you take the humor away. Let the idea of inequality arise in the reader's mind — by name or not — from your anecdote, and it will be much more powerful. Telling the reader the meaning of what he is going to hear bullies him; he is likely to resist.

Similarly, we often write anecdotes that trail off with an abstraction. Having told a perfectly clear story, we end, "which is an illustration of the inequality so prevalent today." Don't nudge your reader in the ribs, saying, "In case you didn't get it, this is what I mean." We summarize abstractly because we lack confidence in our own writing, and in the reader's intelligence. Of course some stories need interpreting; that usually makes them less valuable. If the road is clear, do not put up road markers; they are good only for stumbling over.

Invisible Nouns

So far, we have been talking about degrees of particularity and color, and we have admitted that some prose needs abstractions. The Preacher could not have said, "All is vanity," if there had been an enforced commandment against abstractions. But some nouns are almost always useless. These nouns are invisible. When someone says, "The snow is gray in color," what is the phrase "in color" doing? It doesn't do anything for meaning or particularity. It tells us more about the speaker, though not on the snow. Maybe it contains a message informing us that the speaker is precise, academic, and pompous.

Words like "nature" and "character," which have perfectly good uses, turn up invisibly in pale prose. Probably the snow was gray in color because of the urban nature of the environment, and the frigid character of the weather.

We use invisible nouns with adjectives — much as we use invisible verbs like "be" and "do" and "has" with adjectives or nouns — to make a sentence *sound* grander than it really is, or because we lack the vocabulary. Whatever the reason, we abuse the language. Some other nouns we render invisible: "sense," "kind," "action," "situation," "respect," "regard," "case," and "element." Look at this piece of prose from the annual report of a large corporation:

> The President is pleased to report that, despite the unusual nature of the fiscal situation in the past twelve months, earnings have risen substantially above the margin foreseen by the Treasurer's Report of March, 1971. In a marketing sense, the profitable character of the corporation proved itself under trying circumstances.

"Circumstances" is another invisible noun — at least as it is used here.

Making Bad Nouns from Verbs

The sensible writer chooses the plain noun, if it is adequate, over the fancy one, and he chooses the old noun rather than making up a new one. On page 83 I mentioned the verb "finalize," which had been wrenched out of an adjective: it has been wrenched further into a noun: now and then we run across "finalization," when "end" or "finish" or maybe "finality" would do. Bad stylists know no limits. "Scrutiny" is a fine noun; "scrutinize" is a necessary and traditional verb. But recently a young man wrote on an application form that he submitted documents "for your scrutinization." The word means nothing more than "scrutiny"; it must have sounded more respectable to this writer.

Or maybe his vocabulary failed him. He remembered the verb "scrutinize" but forgot the noun "scrutiny." So he made up a new noun out of the verb. When you are tempted to make a new noun from a verb, go to the dictionary first. You know "unify"; when tempted to create "unifization," go to the dictionary and you will find "unity" and "unification" — and clarity, and a more eloquent prose.

Fancy Nouns

Reading bad prose, we find thousands of examples of pomposity or fanciness, either neologisms like "scrutinization," or polysyllabic alternatives to simple words, like "domicile" for "house" or "cessation" for "end." These words parallel verbs like "masticate," substituted for "chew." The fanciness may arise from diffidence or ignorance or pretension or whatever. The result is the same; fanciness separates the thing described and the mental act of perceiving it. Feelings are kept at a distance. Fancy abstractions and clichés enable Orwell's Communist professor to discuss without feelings the murder of innocent people.

Revising Nouns

In revising, we should look for the lazy abstraction, as well as the invisible noun, the neologism, and the merely fancy noun, and remove them when we find them. Removing one of these leaves a hole, which we can fill with another noun, or a phrase, to specify and bring down to earth the airy word we started with. Lazy abstractions are like clichés and jargon — and the three are usually discovered together — because they are instantly available to the tongue; they lie heaped together with clichés and jargon in the foreroom of the brain; we do not have to search for them with our intelligence, or dream for them with our imaginations. Here is a passage from a paper.

> Financial problems were coming to a head in my family last spring and we didn't know if my sister and I could have the benefit of higher education. Then my grandfather got the surprise of his life when a large amount of money came his way when he least expected it. He got a sum from the VA which he didn't know was coming him. Through his generosity, we were enabled to arrange payment for tuition.

As usual with faulty prose, the faults do not lie in one part of speech alone. Some hunks of cliché are ready-made — "financial problems," "coming to a head," "benefit of higher education," "surprise of his life," "when he least expected it," "arrange payment" — and combine with a dozen other signs of lazy thinking and evasion of feeling. Think of the emotional reality — the anxiety, the jubilation in a family — these phrases obscure with their familiar haze. Instead of "financial problems," let us forget euphemism and talk about being in debt, or having no money, or losing a job, or payments coming due; *anything* more particular. The ultimate particularity would probably sound as cold as a balance sheet (outstanding indebtedness $27,429.31; assets . . .), but we know a median lies between the bland, evasive euphemism of "financial problems" and the sterile figures. The median is actual circumstances and anecdotes; the median is stronger than the extremes.

Certainly "go to college" or "go on in school" is preferable to "have the benefit of higher education." Then instead of speaking generally of "surprise" — an abstraction that takes the surprise out of surprise — why not show it happening? Describe the grandfather opening the envelope, or picking up the telephone. Use dialogue. Or use some new analogy to express his feelings, instead of a useless cliché. He could be as surprised as someone who finds a pearl in his clam chowder. How much is "a large amount of money" or "a sum"? Both seem genteel evasions for saying a specific figure, like "a check for $5,000." But perhaps it seems crass to the writer to name the figure. Then at least some phrase could give a better idea of numbers, so that the reader can place the figure between five hundred and five million dollars, or judge the amount of money by what it can do: "received a check for enough money to send us both through school."

The phrase "through his generosity" includes an unnecessary, labeling abstraction. We do not need to be told that he is generous. When we are bullied with the notion, we resist it. Maybe the old man just wants to boast that his grandchildren go to college. Finally, the last part of the paragraph has a pair of general nouns and a fancy verb in place of simpler and more natural language. It is pretentious to write "we were enabled to arrange payment for tuition" when we could write, "we were able to pay for college."

The student, in fact, revised the passage into:

> My family was so far in debt last spring that we didn't think my sister and I could go to college. My father had borrowed money to get a fish and chips franchise, and lost it all in six months. My sister and I both took jobs in the summer. I was working twelve hours a day in the mill, and when I came home at night I was so mad and tired I just drank beer and watched the box. Then my grandfather telephoned my father and I saw my father suddenly start crying. The VA had just sent my grandfather a check he didn't know was coming, and it was enough to pay for us both. That night, we bought a bottle of Four Roses.

He changed verbs and other parts of speech, but the revision of his nouns is most useful of all.

_____ EXERCISES _____

1. Write a paragraph with a highly abstract title — "love," "idealism," "education," "boredom," "naïveté," "courage" — which does not contain the title word, but which describes a particular occasion that embodies the word. Read your paragraph aloud in class, and see if the class recognizes the abstraction.

2. Take each of these nouns and find two other words to go with it, one more general and one more specific. If you can't find a word, use a short phrase.

rodent	cat
student	butter
lily	book
day	spaghetti
business	sports car

3. Collect four or five clichés that combine an abstract noun with an adjective, like "blind faith," "basic need," and "conflicting desires." See how many alternatives you can find, always realizing that a different context will require a different substitute for each of these filler phrases. Thus, "basic needs" in seven contexts might well be revised into seven distinct phrases. Provide brief contexts, if you need them for clarity.

4. In these sentences, underline the nouns that fail by invisibility, imprecision, fanciness, neologism, or over-abstraction. Invent substitutes that improve the sentences.

    a. I chewed the food without swallowing it.

    b. What is the nature of your complaint?

    c. Religion, says Harvey Cox, has undergone privatization.

    d. When I think about my high school, I remember the love I felt for my Spanish teacher and the other feelings I felt for other people.

    e. Precipitation in the form of a thunderstorm situation is expected.

    f. Different aspects of the case of migrant laborers need discussion.

    g. Relationships are a matter of togetherness.

5. Underline the nouns in these passages, and label each as abstract or general or particular, according to the context. In class, compare your judgments with those of other students. Be prepared to argue. These distinctions are often tenuous, but discussing the distinctions will sharpen your eye for the insides of words.

    a. Cultures, likewise, are more than the sum of their traits. We may know all about the distribution of a tribe's form of marriage, ritual dances, and puberty initiations, and yet understand nothing of the culture as a whole which has used these elements to its own purpose. This purpose selects from among the possible traits in the surrounding regions those which it can use, and discards those which it cannot. Other traits it recasts into conformity with its demands. The process of course need never be conscious during its whole course, but to overlook it in the study of the patternings of human behaviour is to renounce the possibility of intelligent interpretation.

                            Ruth Benedict, *Patterns of Culture*

    b. It was formerly the custom in our village, when a poor debtor came out of jail, for his acquaintances to salute him, looking through their fingers, which were crossed to represent the grating of a jail window. "How do you do?" My neighbors did not thus salute me, but looked first at me, and then at one another, as if I had returned from a long journey.

                            Henry David Thoreau,
                    "On the Duty of Civil Disobedience"

    c. At 15,000 feet, its best operating height, the Kittyhawk IA could fly at a maximum speed of only 354 mph and climb to that height in 8.3 minutes, a longer time than the AGM2 Zero took to reach 20,000 feet. Empty weight was 6,350 pounds, normal loaded weight 8,280 pounds, which was the load carried into combat without drop tank or bombs, and maximum permissible weight was 9,200 pounds. Service ceiling was 29,000 feet. The IA climbed best at lower altitudes, but its best rate was only about 2,100 feet per minute at 5,000 feet.

                            John Vader, *Pacific Hawk*

d. One Hundredth Street was dark, filled with life. I turned off Second Avenue into the street, searching for Number 321. I passed the people, and they were dark too, as seemed appropriate for those who lived in this block. For a moment I imagined that if white men lived here very long, they too would turn dark, by laws as irrefutable as the one that would make them dark if they lived on the beach in Florida — except that here the darkness would not be caused by the sun but by the lack of it.

I passed the dark scar of a vacant lot, blistered with refuse, and came to a building that looked like most of the others. The number was 321. I pushed through the door that was patched with raw board where glass once was, and started up the steps. There were voices, in Spanish, and sounds of frying. An odor like dead cats possessed the stairway. On the third floor I knocked at the door of the front apartment, and one of the girls greeted me.

Dan Wakefield, Island in the City

e. It is a very small office, most of it taken up by a desk. The desk is placed smack in front of the window — not that it could have been placed anywhere else; this window looks out on the daylight landscape of Bergman's movies. It was gray and glaring the first day I was there, dry and fiery. Leaves kept falling from the trees, each silent descent bringing a little closer the long, dark, Swedish winter. The forest Bergman's characters are always traversing is outside this window and the ominous carriage from which they have yet to escape is still among the properties. I realized, with a small shock, that the landscape of Bergman's mind was simply the landscape in which he had grown up.

James Baldwin, Nobody Knows My Name

6. In the passages just quoted: (a) Discuss each author's use of verbs, and how it suits the nouns he uses. (b) Can you find places that might be improved? Try improving one phrase in each passage.

ADJECTIVES AND ADVERBS AND OTHER MODIFIERS

Qualities and Choosing a Style

Modifiers — adjectives, adverbs, participles, and sometimes other words — give quality to nouns and verbs. "The *huge, green* lion"; "leapt *slowly.*" Adjectives and adverbs *modify* nouns and verbs. Participles, and sometimes nouns, work in the same way: "the *grinning* lifeboat," "the hypothesis constructed on Thursday," "*rock candy mountain*," "*mouse* music." Used well, modifiers create distinctions in meaning, and add particularity to the particular. They discriminate and add precision.

But modifiers give us the greatest trouble of all parts of speech. A writer using clichés assembles prepackaged combinations of nouns and adjectives. A beginning writer, when he tries to write colorfully, may stuff his style into obesity with a diet of fat adjectives.

Overuse or misuse of adjectives and adverbs makes prose weak and lethargic. Because they are qualities rather than actions or things, adjectives and adverbs are inherently weaker parts of speech. Yet once more, choosing a style *means* something. A *change in style, however slight, is a change in meaning, however slight.*

To choose vigor in writing is usually to work with fewer modifiers. A few great writers, like Faulkner, use as many adjectives as any beginner — but use them well, and with great originality. Most of the best writers use them sparingly and then make them count. We are not saying that adjectives are unimportant to writing. They are important. But verbs and nouns carry the sentence; if they take charge properly, they liberate adjectives, adverbs, and other modifiers to do their proper work, to make the exact final discriminations necessary to honesty and fullness.

Using Modifiers Well

Ernest Hemingway is known for using adjectives and adverbs sparingly. Let us look once more at the passage that begins "In Another Country."

> In the fall the war was always there, but we did not go to it any more. It was cold in the fall in Milan and the dark came very early. Then the electric lights came on, and it was pleasant along the streets looking in the windows. There was much game hanging outside the shops, and the snow powdered on the fur of the foxes and the wind blew their tails. The deer hung stiff and heavy and empty, and small birds blew in the wind and the wind turned their feathers. It was a cold fall and the wind came down from the mountains.

Hemingway says, "the war," not "the long war" or "the distant war" or "the bloody, maiming, killing, useless, horrid, revolting war." He uses "always" and "any more" as adverbs in his simple predicates.

"Cold" is an adjective in the second sentence; "electric" is necessary to lights, at a time when electric lights were new — in a country at war they seemed especially unwarlike; "pleasant" is an adjective as restrained as the verbs "was" and "go." Then the eye of the paragraph turns away from restrained thoughts of war, and looks at the dead animals that substitute for dead soldiers; right away the verbs and nouns become stronger and more particular: "game," "shops," "powdered." Then the adjectives, exact and strong, come marching in: "stiff and heavy and empty." The last is especially vigorous. The adjectives used sparingly are used strongly and well.

Let us apply the same standards to the passage quoted before from a story by John Updike.

> All the warm night the secret snow fell so adhesively that every twig in the woods about their little rented house supported a tall slice of white, an upward projection which in the shadowless gloom of early morning lifted depth from the scene, made it seem Chinese, calligraphic, a stiff tapestry hung from the gray sky, a shield of lace interwoven with black thread.

Updike is sometimes condemned by critics for overwriting, for self-indulgence in description, for too much prettiness. Can you find anything here to back up such a charge? We can admire a writer, or a passage of his writing, and still find flaws.

What good does the word "secret" do us? It adds a little to the meaning — a kind of coziness — but to me the word seems there mostly to be pretty. I would like the line better if it read, "all the warm night the snow fell so adhesively. . . ." "Warm" is connected to "adhesively," but "warm" would be stronger if as an adjective it were more isolated, if the next noun, "snow," did not carry its adjective also. Then later, in one phrase after another, each noun takes one adjective, and although each adjective is defensible in itself, the effect is monotonously pretty: "tall slice," "upward projection," "shadowless gloom" "early morning." The mixture tastes too sweet. Rearranging clauses, putting an adjective after a noun instead of before it, putting two adjectives with one noun and none with the next — any number of minor reworkings could improve the passage.

The modifier in exposition or argument can help you or hurt you, just as in poetry and fiction. E. B. White, in a brief essay on schools, says that he always went to public ones; by contrast, he says, "my wife was unacquainted with public schools, never having been exposed (in early life) to anything more public than the washroom of Miss Winsor's." The sentence includes several modifiers — "unacquainted," "public," "exposed," "early," and "public" again — and yet it has vigor and clarity. The words express light disdain for the snobbism that White associates with private schools. The verb phrase "was unacquainted with" is preferable to alternatives like "knew nothing about" because "acquainted" is a word we use in social contexts: "No, I am not acquainted with that person." In the small world of White's sentence, the past participle wears a monocle and looks down at the peasants. "Exposed (in early life)" suggests that public schools are a contagious disease, like measles. And the parenthesis "(in early life)" has a mock formality that agrees with the medical metaphor.

But the adjective with which White plays the best trick is "public," which he uses twice: first with "schools," and then in the phrase "anything more public than the washroom of Miss Winsor's." "Public" then becomes associated with public lavatories; we wrinkle our nose in disdain. At "Miss Winsor's" — the name sounds snobbish — of course the lavatory would be spotless and relatively private. What's more, it would not be a lavatory, john, W.C., or even bathroom; it would be a "washroom." By a *turn* on the adjective "public" — from describing schools to implying lavatories — White makes his point most clearly.

In expository prose, adjectives usually narrow a noun's generality, to make the statement more specific. But if we do not watch ourselves carefully we'll let the adjective drift into one of its characteristic errors. Here is a passage of exposition from a student theme.

> If you approach the shore of a rocky island, in your kayak, you
> must paddle slowly and cautiously. Even a gentle breeze may crush
> the kayak against a sharp rock, and sink the traveler, his vehicle,
> and all his very precious equipment.

Let us examine the modifiers. "Rocky" is necessary. "Slowly and cautiously" might become only "cautiously," because "slowly" seems included in the idea of caution. "Sharp" is useful, to make the threat more particular. But "very precious" is not so useful; is the equipment any more precious by being called so? Does "very" do anything at all? The sentence would end more vigorously as three nouns in a series: ". . . the traveler, his vehicle, and his equipment."

One adjective in the piece makes a palpable cliché, "gentle breeze." Yet the writer clearly wants, and needs, to tell us that the winds that can cause this accident need not be gale force. "Why not use 'gentle breeze' " says the beginning writer, "since 'gentle breeze' is exactly what I mean?" But the problem is not "what I mean," but "what gets through"; the problem is communication. "Gentle" together with "breeze" simply repeats a commonplace, and the reader is unmoved. We would do better simply to alter the expectation slightly, and speak of a "faint breeze," "slight breeze," or "tiny breeze."

Take another passage, this time by a professional writer.

> The November meeting at the Union League Club was widely reported in the press, which saw evidence of high enthusiasm and sober purpose in the proceedings. A period of feverish activity now ensued. Legal documents were drawn and redrawn (mostly by Choate), potential trustees were sounded out, and advice was solicited. On January 31, 1870, the first board of trustees was elected. The ingredients of this twenty-seven-man founding board were predictable — a pomposity of businessmen and financiers, a clutch of lawyers, a nod of city officials, and a scintillation of writers and architects; less predictable, perhaps, was the inclusion of four practicing artists — the painters John F. Kensett, Frederick E. Church, and Eastman Johnson, and the sculptor J. Q. A. Ward.
>
> Calvin Tomkins, *Merchants and Masterpieces*

Usually a careful writer, Tomkins sounds fatigued. Commonplace combinations of adverb and verb, or adjective and noun, make much of the prose tedious, wordy, and wasteful: "widely reported," "high enthusiasm," and "feverish activity." The clichés of color are there too: the "ingredients" of the "board" were "predictable." Other modifiers are decent qualifications, like "*November* meeting," and "*legal* documents." The author moves into color and vivacity at the end through strong nouns, "a pomposity of businessmen and financiers, a clutch of lawyers, a nod of city officials, and a scintillation of writers and architects."

The Adjective and the Cliché

Beginning writers often misuse modifiers, especially as portions of clichés. In our minds we associate adjectives and nouns in pairs. Our minds are not only computer dictionaries, they are junkyards of cliché. If we think "grass," we probably think "green." We move in worn tracks. If we think "snow," we think "white." These weary associations are not really thinking; they are automatic responses to stimuli.

The more we can be ourselves, the less we will resemble a machine. If we remember more closely the grass and the snow we are describing, we will describe it precisely, out of our own memories, not out of the sad memory bank of other people's words. We might find an unexpected adjective for grass that is accurate for the grass at that place and that time. We might think of "harsh grass." Or we might not describe the grass at all, or we might describe it in a clause or in a whole sentence. But we must avoid the description that repeats familiar associations. Only the distinct particular takes our attention. Green snow is news.

Other nouns summon their cousin adjectives by bookish associations. The word "sentinel," for many of us, carries with it the adjective "lonely"; "the lonely sentinel" is a cliché. Some of these combinations become comical from overuse or inherent absurdity, like "inscrutable Oriental." Others have sources not so bookish: "responsible citizen," "gracious living." Whenever you use an adjective that sounds habitual to its noun, try omitting the adjective, or recasting the phrase. In avoiding cliché, we have to *think*. We have to decide what we mean by a phrase like "fundamental truth."

The Modifier That Weakens the Noun

An adjective gives us the noun's quality or type: *white* snow. An adverb relates to a verb in the same way: he grinned *happily*. But each of these examples would be bad style in most contexts. In each, the modifier diminishes the word it should strengthen. "Snow" is whiter than "white snow." "Snow" is white in the brain's computer-diction ary, so why color it, unless to suggest its opposite? To say "white snow" brings to mind snow that is gray with dirt. This suggestion might be just what the writer wanted: "White snow fell, that morning, on the trash of the old city." The contrast is part of the meaning; "white" takes its place, modifying "snow," because of the later words "trash" and "city." But most of the time, when a writer adds "white" to "snow," he subtracts from his sentence. He adds "white" in an uneasy search for particularity; he lacks confidence in the insides of "snow." The adjective overinsists on a quality already firm in the word.

If we know that the character grinned, must we be told that he "grinned happily"? It can only bring to mind that he *might* have grinned unhappily, which is a nasty thought; the author reassures us that this supposition is not so, but without the reassurance, there would have been no supposition.

A beginning writer often goes through stages with adjectives, and different people have different problems with them. With some beginners, all adjectives are predictable.

> It was a long trip from the high mountains of the frozen north to the desert wastes of sunny Arizona, but it was highly educational and well worth while.

Or remember Jim Beck's original theme on going to college.

> Education is of paramount importance to today's youth. No one can underestimate the importance of higher education. It makes us well-rounded individuals and . . .

The problem is not primarily adjectives and adverbs, but thinking (or not thinking) in the old tracks.

Modifiers as Weak Intensives

We misuse adjectives and adverbs as weak intensifiers. We say "she moved gracefully" when we might say with more gusto that "she danced" or "she swept" or "she glided." We use vague adjectives in place of specific ones or in place of clauses that could add color and precision. We say "a tremendous amount," when "amount" is vague and "tremendous" is a weak and unspecific intensifier, or "really huge," when we might say "ten million" or "as long as a supertanker." Here the specific number or the comparison carries color; the accuracy is one of feeling, not of dimensions.

Automatic Adjectives

Another misuse of adjectives and adverbs, a more advanced or sophisticated misuse, appears in writers when they suddenly appreciate bright colors in writing, and appears frequently when we begin to write stories and poems. In this misuse, the symptom is not cliché but multiplicity. Nearly every noun carries its adjective, like a tote bag, and every verb wears an adverb for a cape. The style is flashy and overdressed. Here is part of a poem written by a student in a creative writing class.

> I woke suddenly from a ghost-ridden dream
> of old women, to find myself wandering vaguely
> on the far edges of the raw city where white skulls tipped crazily
> in the western sky, and dirty children ran by
> to the cave shelters of abandoned cars . . .

The lines are improved by mechanically stripping them of modifiers. Should any be kept? Yes. "Abandoned" is necessary to the emotion in "abandoned cars." If it is merely "cars" that are "shelters," they could be comfortable, middle-class vehicles in which one drives to the supermarket with one's mother. The "abandoned" makes the children take "shelter" in something like a dump.

Certainly "old women" is different from "women." The phrase is altered by leaving out the adjective; perhaps we should restore "old." But the other modifiers are well exterminated. "Suddenly" does nothing but make the line move less quickly. "Ghost-ridden" does little to intensify "dream," and what little it does, the later image of the skulls does better; also, hyphenated adjectives are usually bad — John Heath-Stubbs, an English poet, says that one should always be cautious of hyphenated names: it means that the lineage of one of the families is not too sound. In "ghost-ridden," what does "ridden" mean? Is the author really using the inside of the word? Does he know what the inside *is?*

"Wandering" includes "vaguely" the way "snow" includes "white." "Edges" are necessarily "far." "Raw" seems to add something to city, and perhaps the author would want to keep it, but the word adds little to the poem except a harshness that is better expressed elsewhere (in "skulls tipped" and "children ran by to the shelters of abandoned cars"). And it adds a metaphor that connects with nothing else in the poem. When you call a city "raw," you are making a metaphor; since cities are not culinary objects, they are in reality neither "raw" nor "cooked." When we call a city raw we are comparing it to a steak or a carrot or an egg, "uncooked" is an inevitable inside of the word "raw." But nothing else in the poem comes from the kitchen. The metaphor in "raw" is not followed through, unused because the author was unaware that he was using a metaphor. He was using "raw" conventionally, as in "raw deal" and "raw material" — without paying attention to its insides. In a poem, the experienced reader absorbs the insides, and is disturbed by the dead and unfulfilled metaphor. Let us omit the adjective "raw."

"Skulls" are "white" enough without calling them so. If skulls are tipping in the sky, we don't need an elbow in our ribs commenting "crazily." This adverb appears to specify the action "tipped" — but would you be able to distinguish between a skull that was tipping crazily and one that was tipping sanely? Really, "crazily" describes nothing; it unecessarily testifies to craziness in an image that is already crazy.

"Western" in this context adds nothing to speak of. West is sunset and death, perhaps, but here it is mostly a pretty noise and a useless specificity. "Dirty" does nothing for "children" that is not done better by verbs and nouns (and by the "abandoned" modifier in the spare version). "By" together with "to" is overly prepositional, wordy. And "cave" adds an image or a metaphor that clutters the final line. It is harsh and moving to find that "shelters" for these children are "abandoned cars." This juxtaposition elicits the emotion. To compare (by way of an adjective) the shelters to caves is to confuse the feeling, and to drag in another world of comparisions: cavemen, Neanderthals, and fur clothing.

The general noun "shelter" seems to me to work better than the more specific noun "cave," which is used as an adjective. But a good argument could support choosing "cave" over "shelter," making the last line, "to the caves of abandoned cars." We could argue that the associations of "cave" include darkness, and that the primitive world (cavemen) makes a strong contrast with the automobile. Whichever word you prefer, "cave" or "shelter," one thing seems clear: either word by itself is better than the two words together. The modifier belongs to the same world as the noun — caves are like shelters are like caves — and so adds nothing but the slight confusion of its difference. The noun alone is preferable, here as everywhere in poetry and prose, unless the modifier adds something to a noun that is already precise.

The poet was at a stage in his writing when he used a modifier automatically with every noun and verb. The modifiers were not predictable; the author was past the stage of clichés, or, more accurately, he was at a stage where he could cut them out before he brought his work to class. But he was diffident about his nouns and his verbs. His nouns and his verbs were doing their jobs well, but he lacked confidence in them. And so, to protect the poor things, he sent each of them to kindergarten with an adjective holding its hand.

When he revised it, the poem read:

I woke from a dream
of old women, to find myself wandering
on the edges of the city
where skulls tipped
in the sky, and children ran
to the shelters of abandoned cars . . .

Here only two modifiers remain from the thirteen in the original version. Certainly the spare revision is better writing, and it was accomplished wholly by deleting modifiers.

Nouns as Modifiers

In the phrase "cave shelter," "cave" was a noun used as a modifier. Writers use participles and nouns as modifiers — "sheltering cave," as well as "cave shelter" — with the same dangers, and the same opportunities, which attend plain adjectives. Use them with the same cautions in mind.

It is an advantage of the English language that its grammar is not rigid. In some languages, a noun would have to undergo respelling before it could be used as an adjective. English has a reputation among languages for adaptability and looseness. It can accept change. And because it accepts change, in speech and writing, the writer or the speaker can make shades of meaning more precise. Using nouns as modifiers, we can say "house party," "religion committee," "death wish."

We can also say "this type grammar," or — as in Bergen Evans's example of tediously multiplied nouns-as-modifiers — ". . . he absconded with the River Street fire house Christmas Eve party funds." Because English lacks rigidity, it is subject to chaos and disorganization. "Type" is frequently a filler-noun, and when we use it as a modifier we make even less sense with it than we normally do. With Bergen Evans's example, as with too many sentences that are seriously intended, the proliferation of nouns as modifiers creates heaviness and awkwardness.

Be careful when you use nouns as modifiers. Sociologists are guiltiest of abusing this device. One hears of the "city group research effort." By the time one reaches the third of these noun-modifiers, one begins to feel afloat in a sea of possibilities. What will go with what? It is as if one were suddenly cast adrift in a Chinese sentence, with no inflections, and with no connectives, and with no tense or number. Instead, confine yourself to one or two noun-modifiers in a row.

Revising Modifiers

When you revise your prose, question the need for every adjective and adverb. Can I do without these modifiers? Does the noun (like "postulate" in "basic postulate") or the verb (like "run" in "run quickly") do the job without the modifier? Or can I find an exact noun or verb to do the job in one word? Do I avoid a succession of adjective-noun combinations, the monotonous pairs? Do I fall into cliché by joining two words that are commonly used together? Do I, on the other hand, use the modifier when I need it, to make the discrimination, or to add the color, which makes the sentence expressive?

____ EXERCISES _____

1. Here are five simple nouns and five simple verbs. Make up ten sentences, using one of the words in each, in which you use an adverb or adjective that would not be a normal association. But let your context make the modifier work. If "snow" were the word, you might speak of "warm snow" as Updike does, and make it work by a word like "adhesively."

cut	sand
scramble	humility
search	concern
waver	hut
bask	scholar

2. In these sentences from student themes, underline adjectives and adverbs that are useless, either because they are redundant (like "white snow" or "basic postulate") or because they are vague intensives (like "very cold").

a. The cat slinks quietly into the room, its sharp claws ready for instant combat.

b. It was a very long examination, with huge one-hour questions to answer completely, and I didn't have the slightest idea how to prepare for it.

c. Whenever a large supertanker approaches a coastal port, concerned environmentalists take special notice.

d. We got to know each other real soon and she is real nice.

e. The forthcoming encounter between these two great teams promises to add luster to the annual classic.

f. It was a spooky horror movie, and we were awfully happy when it finally ended and we could go back home.

3. In these passages from student themes, underline all modifiers. Then see if you can improve the passages by cutting some of them, or by substituting other modifiers.

a. Traveling is a great way to learn history. After seeing important places like Bunker Hill and the Smithsonian Institute, national history takes on new and significant meaning.

b. Twenty-four separate and distinct pieces of glass in a metal frame make windows that open outward and dull the landscape with layers of dirt. The factory metal window frame is rusting through the yellow, chipped, peeling paint.

c. Side by side, the swimmers skimmed across the water like swift hydroplanes. The crowd was frantic as it cheered the racing swimmers on.

d. It was a perfect day for skiing, except that the snow was so bright and shiny that it hurt my eyes.

e. Social security is a regressive tax, harming the old and the poor as much as it helps them.

f. George Washington crossed the Delaware in a rowboat.

4. Underline adverbs and adjectives in these passages of published prose. Can you criticize the authors' use of modifiers?

a. After the age when hunting was done by males and the gathering of vegetables and small animal food by females — always with close cooperation between men and women — the discovery of planting and herding and then of the animal-drawn plow assured a steadier food supply, which underwrote male enterprises: conquest, the building of cities, trade, and *the stratification of society*. But woman's role continued to be circumscribed by childbearing; whatever a woman did, she had to do near home.

> Margaret Mead, "Needed: Full Partnership for Women"
> (*Saturday Review*)

b. Far out along the autumn plain, beneath the sloping light, an immense drove of cattle moved eastward. They went at a walk, not very fast, but faster than they could imaginably enjoy. Those in front were compelled by those behind; those at the rear, with few exceptions, did their best to keep up; those who were locked within the herd could no more help moving than the particles inside a falling rock.

James Agee, "A Mother's Tale," Collected Poems

c. The needs of a society determine its ethics, and in the Black American ghettos the hero is that man who is offered only the crumbs from his country's table but by ingenuity and courage is able to take for himself a Lucullan feast. Hence the janitor who lives in one room but sports a robin's-egg-blue Cadillac is not laughed at but admired, and the domestic who buys forty-dollar shoes is not criticized but is appreciated. We know that they have put to use their full mental and physical powers. Each single gain feeds into the gains of the body collective.

Maya Angelou, "Mr. Red Leg"

d. Nick looked at the burned-over stretch of hillside, where he had expected to find the scattered houses of the town, and then walked down the railroad track to the bridge over the river. The river was there. It swirled against the log spiles of the bridge. Nick looked down into the clear, brown water, colored from the bubbly bottom, and watched the trout keeping themselves steady in the current with wavering fins. As he watched them they changed their positions by quick angles, only to hold steady in the fast water again. Nick watched them a long time.

Ernest Hemingway, "Big Two-Hearted River"

e. Personal consideration of various and sundry matters of considerable importance have led numerous observers to ultimately conclude that the final end of Western civilization is certainly closer to a realistic possibility than might earlier have been tentatively assumed.

Warner Gillespie, Autobiography

f. All girls in this period of American Victorianism suffered in an environment that utterly discouraged the healthy development of their emotional lives. However, at least some enterprising girls with a full measure of curiosity were less ignorant — perhaps less virginal — than the popular mythology supposed.

Cynthia Griffin Wolff, A Feast of Words

g. We were camping in the oasis. My companions were asleep. The tall, white figure of an Arab passed by; he had been seeing to the camels and was on his way to his own sleeping place.

I threw myself on my back in the grass; I tried to fall asleep; I could not; a jackal howled in the distance; I sat up again. And what had been so far away was all at once quite near. Jackals were swarming round me, eyes gleaming dull gold and vanishing again, lithe bodies moving nimbly and rhythmically, as if at the crack of a whip.

Franz Kafka, "Jackals and Arabs"

h. Braggioni sits heaped upon the edge of a straight-backed chair much too small for him, and sings to Laura in a furry, mournful voice. Laura has begun to find reasons for avoiding her own house until the latest possible moment, for Braggioni is there almost every night. No matter how late she is, he will be sitting there with a surly, waiting expression, pulling at his kinky yellow hair, thumbing the strings of his guitar, snarling a tune under his breath. Lupe the Indian maid meets Laura at the door, and says with a flicker of a glance towards the upper room, "He waits."

Katherine Anne Porter, "Flowering Judas"

5. You might make more exercises out of the eight examples above. Here are some possibilities. (a) Discuss in class the modifiers in each passage. (b) In each passage, look at the verbs and nouns. Are they used well? (c) In example d, put an adjective with every noun that lacks one, and an adverb with every verb. Make the additions as apt as you can, and see what you have done. (d) Try to rewrite passage a or b, omitting adverbs and adjectives. How much, and what, do you lose?

ORIGINAL WORDS: COMPARISONS

The Need for Originality

When we put words together — adjective with noun, noun with verb, verb with object — we start to talk to each other. We begin to show our original selves, or we show a dull copy of someone else's original. Originality is clarity and vigor. A source of originality in language is comparison — simile, metaphor, and analogy. In order to talk about metaphoric writing and originality, we must go over some old ground again.

Formulas or clichés or trite expressions substitute for the originality that each of us can master. A girl who was mourning the death of her grandfather wrote, starting her first theme of the term, "A tragedy recently occurred at my ancestral home." In a conference with her instructor, the girl wept over the death, she was pale, her hands shook. Her body showed her wretchedness, but her prose showed her reading of a weekly country newspaper. No grief was in her phrasing, only the set phrases of headlines or lead sentences in obituaries. Perhaps the formulas came to her pen so that she might avoid the pain that comes with real feeling. Or perhaps they came because she did not know the difference, in words, between the formula that communicates nothing, and the originality that communicates feeling. No feeling reaches her reader. "A tragedy occurred" is a formula that denies the tragic. Compare "a catastrophe was averted" and "a blessed event took place"; they all communicate a journalistic source; but also they all deny feeling, not only by being familiar (the newspaper phrase reminds us of so many similar stories) but by being passive or fancy.

A phrase becomes a formula or a cliché not just because it is used commonly, but because it prevents feeling. The phrase "rain fell" is more common than "a tragedy occurred," yet we do not think of it as a formula because we do not use it to keep feelings down. A psychiatrist described clichés as "the lies we tell ourselves, that we *want* to hear." When the student wrote, "A tragedy recently occurred at my ancestral home," she was not lying overtly, or intending to lie. It was not like saying that she did not chop down a cherry tree when she really did. The lie was internal, the lie of using language to avoid difficult reality, the lie of euphemism.

Overhearing Your Original Self

Listen to yourself as you daydream, or think idly. Are you reciting newspaper formulas or greeting card verse? If you overhear yourself, in your own head, thinking trite sentimentality about your love, something is wrong with your loving.

In general, trying to *overhear* yourself is a good idea. On some days, you can listen to the dreaming voice easily; on other days that voice seems mute; it is more likely that you are deaf. The dreaming language is clichés sometimes, sometimes puns or phrases with crazy originality. Sometimes the voice hums the tune from a song; when you remember the lyrics a coded message is there. You may hear "Eleanor Rigby" when you are feeling lonely or abandoned, or when something inside you feels that you will be lonely soon. The puns and crazy phrases are codes too. Look at them closely. They have information for you. They are spoken by your original self, looking for attention from your conventional self, the self trained by parents and school and television to think like a train on a track. The crazier the phrase, the more devious the pun, the deeper the source in the self. When the dreaming voice talks in cliché, the train track is getting in the way of the real voice, because the real voice would tell us the truth we would find painful.

Overhear yourself to know yourself. Then you can farm your daydreams for original verbal images that express feeling. The crazy image and the pun do not make good writing in themselves — though often they can be the leaping-off point in daily writing — but they do give clues to feelings that the conscious mind can follow. Here is an unrevised passage from a student's daily writing.

> I was taking out the garbage this morning and I heard (in my head) Fanny Davis's voice talking. She has a funny way of talking, Englishy but not really, and I knew it was her. She was saying, "I like to use the word 'to intimate' without any regard for its actual meaning." I kept stuffing the garbage bags into the cans, wondering why I made that up, and why I chose Fanny's voice. It's always sounded affected to me. But that wasn't the sort of thing she says. She talks about her family and the home on the lake up North and going skiing in Switzerland. I was feeling blue. Bob had gone to New York and I knew that Sally was there, his old girl friend, and I worried about that. Then I started laughing, right at the garbage, because I saw that "to intimate" and "too intimate" are close, but "to intimate" is a long way from the meaning of "too intimate." I was blue because I was too close to Bob, and I could get hurt. I think I chose Fanny because she always seemed totally sexless.

The girl had uncovered something — which she almost knew already — by overhearing a daydream pun and by figuring it out. We may start dreaming; we end up thinking. Now she might be ready to examine her feelings about Bob, or her feelings about her feelings

Looking for Original Images

We can try to activate the daydreaming mind. We will not always succeed. The girl who wrote the paper beginning "A tragedy occurred" was never fully able to write about her grandfather. But her writing and her self-knowledge improved. In her daily writing she returned to the subject many times. The week after her initial theme, she wrote, "A month ago my grandfather died," and went on for a few rather dry sentences. Though the prose was colorless, it was much more honest than tragedies occurring at ancestral homes. Still, it had no images, no pieces of *sense*.

Later, thinking about things she could associate with her grand-father, she wrote about "farm implements" that were "unused" and "hanging on the wall of the barn." Then she changed "farm imple-ments" to "rake and hoe." Then she revised the sentence again and added an image that could come only from the imagination extending itself into the unseen by the probable. "His hoes and rakes hang from pegs in the barn. Spiders will spin webs there while the iron turns red with rust." She had farmed the dreaming part of her self, which imag-ined the barn, with a selective intelligence, and wrote two sentences that, in their detail and their associations, began to embody her mel-ancholy and loss.

Simile and Metaphor

Images are groups of words that give an impression to the senses. Most images are visual, but we can also make images of taste, touch, hearing, and smell. Images communicate feelings and locate them firmly, really making contact between writer to reader. Comparisons in simile and metaphor mostly use images, and become ways for us to show emotions.

Similes are comparisons that use "like" or "as," little words that announce a comparison. Metaphors omit the announcement. We write, "Her face bloomed with affection," and the word "bloomed" compares the girl to a flower; the face-flower is pretty, it is coming into its maturity, and it is associated with spring or summer. The writer may wish to go on talking about the girl in similes that use garden images. Perhaps her dress "rustles like leaves" and her skin is "as soft as petals." The difference between similes and metaphors is small — a signal is there or not there — but it is real; the simile, be-cause it announces itself, is more reasonable, more conscious of what it is doing.

For clarity, we must distinguish this brief comparison from the word "comparison" as it is used later in this book, when we discuss comparison and contrast as structures used in argument and exposi-tion; also, we must distinguish it from the grammatical sense — the "comparison of adjectives." A comparison between the gross national products of Greece and Turkey, or between "less" and "least," is not like comparing an old cheese to an untidy hog.

Creating a new, verbal comparison — simile, metaphor, and anal-ogy — is our most original act of speech; the originality comes from the dreaming part of the self. Although we cannot always manufacture metaphors at will, we can learn to be alert for comparisons, and we can stimulate their coming. The dead grandfather's funeral happened during a thunderstorm. When the girl tried to write about it, she encountered the trite associations of thunderstorms and death. She began simply.

> The funeral was 2 p.m. He was laid out in the front parlor, which was always closed except for weddings and funerals. Fifty people were there, some crowded into the parlor, others backed into the living room. The minister talked a little and read scripture. Then the sky turned dark.

The prose is simple and direct but it lacks energy. "The minister talked a little and read scripture" would probably be better if it included direct and indirect quotation. "Then the sky turned dark." *How* dark? How did she *feel* about the sky turning dark? We have the sense reading this prose that the feelings (formerly denied and lied about in journalistic clichés) are still restricted, held back, reserved.

Suppose the sky turned "as dark as" something. If it turned "as black as the ace of spades," we would be nowhere. What does the ace of spades have to do with her grandfather or her feelings? Even if she had told us that the old man was a poker-playing farmer, the simile is so hackneyed that no one will see the black of the playing card when she says it. The useful comparison will be new. But to say "the sky turned as dark as the soot from a factory chimney" would seem inappropriate; what would a factory have to do with a farm? The comparison must be more than new, it must relate to the context: to her memories of the man, to the funeral, to the idea of death. "The sky turned black as my grandmother's dress" would be a better direction; but maybe that's too black, or the texture is wrong. Or she might want to compare it to something she remembers and associates with the dead farmer: "The sky turned black, like inside the barn after milking." "The sky turned dark as a blueberry."

Sometimes one phrase will not be adequate. You want your comparison to go on longer than that. "The sky turned dark. I could see a black round storm cloud coming. I remembered leaning over the open well, staring down into the round black eye of the water." Here, we find a comparison within the comparison; the water is an "eye," and the reader alert to the insides of words will reconstruct the dead metaphor: "the eye of the storm" — and revive it — although (or because) the author has not stated it.

Originality and Memory

To find the right comparison, we must draw on memory and daydream; imagination newly combines old things remembered; it is always present, and often hard to discover. Memory is crucial to our writing, thinking, and feeling. By scrutiny of the retained past, we begin to understand and to express that understanding. In the floating world, we connect feelings in the present to feelings about the past. We express these connections mostly by making comparisons. In the uniqueness of each of us, we can find something that the sky grew as dark as.

Analogy

We use the word analogy for a comparison that makes or illustrates a point, and usually takes longer to say than a metaphor or a simile. An analogy can be extended into a whole essay; ministers' sermons are sometimes analogies — life is like the hundred-yard dash: birth is the starting gun, death is the tape, God is the judge. A whole book, or system of thought, can be based on analogy. Oswald Spengler, in *The Decline of the West*, at the beginning states an analogy, that a civilization is an organism, is born, grows old, and dies; then he writes a long book to make a factual case for his analogy.

Analogy often works best within a unit no longer than the paragraph. Frequently, it illustrates the sense in which an abstraction is intended. Analogies may make points; they don't prove them; they show how you feel, or they clarify your use of an ambiguous or all-inclusive word. Suppose we were tempted to support the stick-figure philosophical assertion, "Love is better than hate." We would not get far with such a proposition, because it is too vague for support, but we would at least put eyes and ears on our stick figures if we went on, "It is a meadow in the country compared to an alley of garbage and broken glass."

An analogy often runs through a paragraph like a thread in tweed, not separated into patches of assertion followed by comparison, but interwoven. James Thurber wrote this paragraph about working with the editor of *The New Yorker*, Harold Ross:

> Having a manuscript under Ross's scrutiny was like putting your
> car in the hands of a skilled mechanic, not an automotive engineer

with a bachelor of science degree, but a guy who knows what makes a motor go, and sputter, and wheeze, and sometimes come to a dead stop; a man with an ear for the faintest body squeak as well as the loudest engine rattle. When you first gazed, appalled, upon an uncorrected proof of one of your stories or articles, each margin had a thicket of queries and complaints — one writer got a hundred and forty-four on one profile. It was as though you beheld the works of your car spread all over the garage floor, and the job of getting the thing together again and making it work seemed impossible. Then you realized that Ross was trying to make your Model T or old Stutz Bearcat into a Cadillac or Rolls-Royce. He was at work with the tools of his unflagging perfectionism, and, after an exchange of growls or snarls, you set to work to join him in his enterprise.

James Thurber, *The Years with Ross*

Thurber begins by announcing his subject, "Having a manuscript under Ross's scrutiny," departs from it for the rest of a long sentence, returns to the manuscript for a sentence, then in the final three sentences develops his analogy, makes it funnier, and makes his point about Ross as an editor. He makes points by contrasts: "mechanic" not "engineer"; not "automotive engineer" but "guy." And he makes it by developing his analogy into impossibility (repairing a Model T into a Cadillac), and developing it out of all touch with reality; the customer joins with the mechanic to rebuild his torn-up machine. The analogy expresses feeling, it is witty, and it is a pleasure to read. Consider this alternative, omitting the garage and substituting abstraction and generality for analogy:

Having a manuscript under Ross's scrutiny was an edifying if terrifying experience. He was a skilled editor, not an academic, but a practical man. When you first gazed, appalled, upon an uncorrected proof of one of your stories or articles, each margin had a thicket of queries and complaints — one writer got a hundred and forty-four on one profile. You beheld all your work torn apart, and it seemed impossible to put it together. Then you realized that Ross was trying to make ordinary prose into prose of the highest order. He was using his editorial skills with unflagging perfectionism, and, after an exchange of growls or snarls, you set to work to join him in his enterprise.

This eviscerated version is slightly shorter, but the cutting loses rather than gains: the paragraph diminishes in energy and expression.

The Unintended Comparison

With analogy as with other forms of comparison, you must be wary of the dead, the mixed, and the inadvertently comic. Often a writer will trap himself in an unconscious analogy expressing an attitude that he really feels but denies to himself. The comic disparity is as slapstick as a top-hatted man with his trousers missing. Here is an English critic, writing about American music in the London *Times Literary Supplement.* He writes in attempted praise of American energy and vitality, but other messages come through his bad prose.

> The American composer is neither enriched nor shackled. He had nothing to start from but old rags and bones of European culture that, imported to a new environment, soon lost their savor. Then gradually, in the pulping machine of a polyglot society, the rags and bones began to acquire a taste of their own.

Look at the main analogy, rags and bones. When they were imported here, they "soon lost their savor." Did the gentleman actually expect rags and bones to taste good? His idea of the American stew expresses his distaste by an analogy to eating the product of something like a paper factory: "in the pulping machine . . . the rags and bones began to acquire a taste of their own." This writer expressed his feelings, but he expressed feelings he didn't know he had. He appears to believe that he likes American music, but something unacknowledged inside him is holding its nose.

For another example, we could look at a headnote in a textbook I recently published. Speaking of Virginia Woolf, I wrote, "Handicapped by her sex . . . she persevered against prejudice to refine and develop her abilities." Professor Sandra Donaldson, of the University of North Dakota, wrote me an inquiring letter about my "most puzzling remark." "Did she wear a brace on her arm to help her develop her ability to write, thus overcoming this handicap? Or are there pills women can take, to overcome this curse? Or did she follow a regimen of exercises?" Of course I *intended* to imply that the handicap was male chauvinism; but in my unintended comparison, I revealed my hidden bias. Perhaps my consciousness had been raised, but my unconsciousness nevertheless compared being female with being crippled. I never paused to examine closely what I really said.

To express a feeling without examining it is worthless. Originality combines opposites: we dream — with our eyes open; we are inspired — then we scrutinize and revise. Scrutiny provides the motive for revision. We need to look into words — to see the connection between "rags and bones," "savor," and "taste" — and we will sometimes discover feelings we had not wished to acknowledge. Then we can revise ourselves or our prose or both. We must again float on daydream and memory for new words, and then put the new words under scrutiny again. Only by developing all these mental abilities can we begin to be honest. The paradox is that to be sincere we must struggle; we must struggle to be spontaneous, and then struggle to revise, refine, and order our spontaneity. To speak our most intimate selves we must revise.

One way to cultivate our sensitivity to the insides of words is to develop an ear for the unintended comparison. (The unintended comparison is often an overt, and sometimes extended, version of the dead metaphor.) On a Monday-night football broadcast, Howard Cosell said of a new quarterback that he "walked in the wake" of a great predecessor. In this example, the unintended comparison approaches blasphemy.

Looking for Analogies

We can think out an analogy more easily than we can create the lone metaphor, which, to most writers, seems a gift from the god within us, an inspiration. Suppose you are discussing what makes a love affair succeed. Suppose you decide that it takes a lot of work. The word "work," itself a metaphor nearly dead, can lead you into analogy. What kind of work is it like? Is it like a nine-to-five job? You can make an analogy in the negative: "This work is no nine-to-five job." Is it like building a house? Rebuilding a destroyed city? Making the sets for a play? Being a skilled mechanic or an automotive engineer?

The liveliest prose moves from analogy to analogy without strain. It takes practice to learn how to invent, and practice to learn when to stop inventing. When analogy shifts abruptly, the effect is usually ridiculous, and comic writers can use these sudden shifts to their advantage; if in one sentence you compare tennis with big game hunting, do not compare it in the next sentence with knitting unless you want a laugh. Often a sentence or a paragraph of general summary or narrative separates passages of differing analogies, keeping them from clashing.

One more example of writing brings imaginative combinations of comparisons to Brooklyn, New York. The author is expressing complex feelings about its space.

> Manhattan is large, yet all its distances seem quick and available. Brooklyn is larger, seventy-one square miles as against twenty-two, but here you enter the paradoxes of the relative. You know, here: only a few miles from wherever I stand, Brooklyn ends; only a few miles away is Manhattan; Brooklyn is walled with world-travelled wetness on west and south and on north and east is the young beaver-board frontier of Queens; Brooklyn comes to an end: but actually, that is, in the conviction of the body, there seems almost no conceivable end to Brooklyn; it seems, on land as flat and huge as Kansas, horizon beyond horizon forever unfolded, as immeasurable proliferation of house on house and street by street; or seems as China does, infinite in time in patience and in population as in space.
>
> The collaborated creation of the insanely fungoid growth of fifteen or twenty villages, now sewn and quilted edge to edge, and lacking any center in remote proportion to its mass, it is perhaps the most amorphous of all modern cities; and at the same time, by virtue of its arterial streets, it has continuities so astronomically vast as Paris alone or the suburbs south of Chicago could match: on Flatbush Avenue, DeKalb, Atlantic, New Lots, Church, any number more, a vista of low buildings and side streets of glanded living sufficient to paralyze all conjecture; simply, far as the eye can strain, no end of Brooklyn, and looking back, far as the eye can urge itself, no end, nor imaginable shore; only, thrust upon the pride of heaven, the monolith of the Empire State, or different mode of life, and even this, seen here, has the smoky frailty of a half-remembered dream.
>
> James Agee, "Southeast of the Island: Travel Notes"

Though portions here may be overwritten — I have my doubts about "is walled with world-travelled wetness" as a way to say "borders the ocean" — there is imagination and order in the connected comparisons. Look at the order of sizes: Brooklyn, Kansas, China; then from an adverbial peak, downward: "astronomically vast as Paris alone or the suburbs south of Chicago." Look at the body metaphors, perhaps coming from the phrase "the conviction of the body": "arterial," "glanded," "paralyze." Look at the brief analogy with a quilt in the second paragraph. The energy and import of this prose derive from simile, metaphor, and analogy.

Revising for Comparison

First, check your sentences to make sure that you are controlling the comparisons you make. Make sure that you do not inadvertently turn a quarterback into a deity, or an art form into a bad smell. Second, see that you have not made cliché comparisons that no longer function, like "black as the ace of spades."

Then do the more difficult. *Add* simile, metaphor, and analogy. Most of us in our first drafts lack energy and feeling. Our prose resembles the pale version of Thurber, after the analogy was deleted. The prose is too plain to reach the reader with excitement and precision. Float on memory and daydream to invent; scrutinize with critical intelligence to cut and to improve. Ask yourself if your invention is new, if it is appropriate, if it does not clash with anything else. In a paragraph of exposition, think if you can clarify by analogy. What was it like, to have your prose edited by Ross? What was it like, the day your grandfather died?

___ EXERCISES ___

1. In the passage by James Agee, how useful are the phrases or words, "beaver-board," "fungoid," "glanded," and "smoky?" How do they work or how do they fail?

2. Using different colors of pen, underline words in the Agee passage — verbs in red, nouns in blue, and modifiers in green. Notice how the parts of speech work together. Notice how the metaphors and other comparisons contain all parts of speech.

3. These clichés began life as new metaphors. Can you figure out how each of them might have started? Invent a new metaphor that communicates what the cliché fails to communicate.

toe the line	a shred of compassion
an axe to grind	school of thought
chip on his shoulder	it dawned on me
pick a bone with you	bathed in sunlight

4. Here are six common comparatives. Taking any three, write sentences in which you make a new simile.

as long as	as green (or any color) as
as bright as	as sour as
as wet as	as heavy as

5. In these passages, underline analogies, metaphors, and similes. Choose three examples that you particularly like, and explain your reasons for preferring them.

a. But his position was weak. Like a cougar, the army was constantly perched above him, ready to pounce.

John Gerassi, *The Great Fear in Latin America*

b. After thousands of years we're still strangers to darkness, fearful aliens in an enemy camp with our arms crossed over our chests.

Annie Dillard, "Strangers to Darkness"

c. Many of us grow to hate documentaries in school, because the use of movies to teach us something seems a cheat — a pill disguised as candy — and documentaries always seem to be about something we're not interested in.

Pauline Kael, "High School and Other Forms of Madness"
(in *Deeper into Movies*)

d. The average American judge, as everyone knows, is a mere rabbinical automaton, with no more give and take in his mind than you will find in the mind of a terrier watching a rathole. He converts the law into a series of rubber-stamps, and brings them down upon the scalped skulls of the just and unjust alike. The alternative to him, as commonly conceived, is quite as bad — an uplifter in a black robe, eagerly gulping every new brand of Peruna that comes out, and converting his pulpit into a sort of soap-box.

H. L. Mencken, "Mr. Justice Holmes"

e. I lay down on a solitary rock that was like an island in the bottom of the valley, and looked up. The grey sage-brush and the blue-grey rock around me were already in shadow, but high above me the canyon walls were dyed flame-colour with the sunset, and the Cliff City lay in a gold haze against its dark cavern. In a few minutes it, too, was grey, and only the rim rock at the top held the red light. When that was gone, I could still see the copper glow in the piñons along the edge of the top ledges. The arc of sky over the canyon was silvery blue, with its pale yellow moon, and presently stars shivered into it, like crystals dropped into perfectly clear water.

Willa Cather, *The Professor's House*

f. . . . Women have served all these centuries as looking glasses possessing the magic and delicious power of reflecting the figure of man at twice its natural size. Without that power probably the earth would still be swamp and jungle. The glories of all our wars would be unknown. We should still be scratching the outlines of deer on the remains of mutton bones and bartering flints for sheepskins or whatever simple ornament took our unsophisticated taste. Supermen and Fingers of Destiny would never have existed. The Czar and the Kaiser would never have worn their crowns or lost them. Whatever may be their use in civilised societies, mirrors are essential to all violent and heroic action. That is why Napoleon and Mussolini both insist so emphatically upon the inferiority of women, for if they were not inferior, they would cease to enlarge.

Virginia Woolf, "A Room of One's Own"

g. But the thing that really tormented them was the thought of those two old-age pensioners living in their house, usurping floorspace, devouring food, and paying only ten shillings a week. I doubt whether they were really losing money over the old-age pensioners, though certainly the profit on ten shillings a week must have been very small. But in their eyes the two old men were a kind of dreadful parasite who had fastened on them and were living on their charity. Old Jack they could just tolerate, because he kept out-of doors most of the day, but they really hated the bedridden one, Hooker by name. Mr. Brooker [the landlord] had a queer way of pronouncing his name, without the H and with a long U — "Uker." What tales I heard about old Hooker and his fractiousness, the nuisance of making his bed, the way he "wouldn't eat" this and "wouldn't eat" that, his endless ingratitude and, above all, the selfish obstinacy with which he refused to die! The Brookers were quite openly pining for him to die. When that happened they could at least draw the insurance money. They seemed to feel him there, eating their substance day after day, as though he had been a living worm in their bowels.

George Orwell, *The Road to Wigan Pier*

4

Sentences

STYLE AND THE SENTENCE

A sentence is a group of words with a period, exclamation point, or question mark at the end. But no definition of the sentence is likely to help us much in writing one. Sentences — the spoken kind — happened first; grammarians named them later. We learn sentence structure by speaking and listening, by reading and writing, more than by studying types of sentences. Still, after studying sentences we can listen more carefully, read more closely, speak more eloquently, and write more clearly. We can learn to *control* the style of our sentences to express feelings and ideas — to make contact with our reader and to hold our reader's interest. We can learn to make sentences that hang together, cohering part with part, achieving unity in the service of clarity. We can learn as well to *vary* our sentences.

PARTS OF SENTENCES

Before we go into the types of sentences, we need to know something about the parts of sentences and the names of those parts.

Sentences have two main parts, subjects and predicates. The *subject* is what we make a statement or ask a question about. Usually the subject is a noun, or a pronoun like "she" or "who"; but on occasion the subject can be something else that substitutes for a noun, like a clause or a phrase. (Even a verb can be a subject: *"Is* is a verb. *Is* is the subject of these sentences.") In the following sentences, the subjects are in italics:

> The *frogman* dove.
> The *theory* was valid.
> *Who* committed this brutal crime?
> *Whoever committed this crime* must be insane.

In this sentence the *simple subject* is "woman," and the *complete subject* is "the woman in the blue house by the river":

> The woman in the blue house by the river wrote bizarre sentences on the walls.

The *predicate* is the verb along with its modifiers and complements. The predicate is what the sentence says about the subject; most often, the predicate is the action that goes on in the sentence. In these sentences, the simple predicates are in italics:

> The frogman *dove.*
> The theory *was* valid.
> Who *committed* this brutal crime?

The *simple predicate* in the next sentence is "wrote"; the *complete predicate* is "wrote on the walls with invisible liquids."

> The woman in the blue house wrote on the walls with invisible liquids.

Objects come in four forms: direct objects, indirect objects, objects of prepositions, and complementary objects.

The *direct object* is the part of a sentence that the predicate acts upon. Here, the direct objects are in italics.

> She designed the *atomic reactor.*
> The president washed the *dishes.*
> *What* did the elephant say?
> Underline *the predicates.*

An *indirect object* usually comes before a direct object, and tells us to whom or for whom (or to what or for what) the predicate acts.

> She gave the *team* a case of beer.
> Sam wrote *her* a new song.

Most of the time, the indirect object replaces a prepositional phrase using "to" or "for."

> She gave a case of beer *to the team.*
> Sam wrote a new song *for her.*

In the last two sentences "team" and "her" are *objects of prepositions,* nouns or noun substitutes that a preposition relates to another word or word group. Here are more prepositions followed by objects.

> When you are defenestrated you are thrown *out a window.*
> Dick the Bruiser was barred *from the premises.*

Another construction has two objects, in which the second modifies or describes the first. The second, or *complementary object,* may be a noun or an adjective. In these examples the complementary object is in italics.

> They made her *bartender.*
> He called her a *humbug.*
> Margaret painted the tree *purple.*

Complements follow linking verbs like "is" and "become" and "appear." When they modify or describe the sentence's subject, we call these words *subjective complements.* These words can be adjectives or nouns.

> She's an *artist.*
> They appeared *pretty.*

A *phrase* is a group of words which work together as a unit, but which lack a subject and a predicate. There are several kinds of phrases, defined by the word introducing it:

Prepositional phrase	The bat *in the attic* is not a vampire.
Verbal phrase	More and more people *will be buying* subcompact cars as gasoline prices rise.
Infinitive phrase	Hockey fans tend *to enjoy violence.*
Gerund phrase	*Establishing a fascist state* requires ruthlessness and ambition.
Participle phrase	*Doubting the medical assumptions of his time,* Pasteur sought further knowledge about what causes disease.

A *clause* is a group of words that contains a subject and a predicate. A clause may be *main* (also called independent) or *subordinate* (also called dependent). A *main clause* can be a simple sentence in itself.

> *The thin dog barked.*

A *subordinate clause* is not a complete sentence and cannot stand by itself; rather, it works as a noun, as an adjective, or as an adverb within a sentence.

Noun clause	*Whether the new league will flourish* is a question that no one can answer with certainty.
Adjective clause	The cricket, *which appeared to be wearing a tiny tuxedo,* did not answer his naive questions.
Adverb clause	She ordered the troops to attack *when it became apparent that to delay any longer would be suicidal.*

Each of these last two clauses is a *modifier*. A *modifier* is any word, phrase, or clause that functions as an adjective or adverb.

> The bat *in the attic* is not a vampire.

Here the prepositional phrase "in the attic" does something to, *modifies*, "bat"; it tells us *which* bat. If we say, "the vampire bat is in the attic," then the word "vampire" is an adjective that modifies "bat."

> The vampire flew slowly around the room when he assumed the form of a bat.

Here we have three modifiers, all acting as adverbs. One modifier tells us about the way the vampire flew: the single word "slowly"; then a prepositional phrase tells us where: the vampire flew "around the room"; then a subordinate clause tells us when it happened: "when he assumed the form of a bat." Manner, place, and time.

Now that we have the names of parts, we can examine types of sentences.

TYPES OF SENTENCES

Simple Sentences

A sentence is "simple" as long as it remains one clause, containing one predicate. "John laughed" is a complete, two-word sentence, simple and common in its structure: subject / verb. We could add modifiers, "Big John laughed loudly," or a preposition, "John laughed at her," and the sentence would remain simple.

A sentence can be quite long and yet still be simple. This sentence is simple, but elaborates the predicate with prepositional phrases:

> Neal *runs | with his wife | at Waterman Gymnasium | before classes.*

We can add as many modifiers as we wish; the sentence will remain simple unless we add a subordinate clause.

A subject can be long, too.

> *The ape-man in the gray loincloth, a wooden spear in his hand, attacked.*

Either subject or predicate can be compounded, and the sentence remain simple.

> *John and his zebra cried.*
> John *laughed and cried.*

Or the verb can be elaborated.

> The ape-man *attacked swiftly, with a sharp cry, from behind the rocks.*

Or we can have a direct object, and the object can be elaborated.

> The ape-man attacked *the sluggish warriors, those intruders tired from their lengthy searching.*

Or the simple sentence can have all its parts elaborated and remain simple.

> *The ape-man in the gray loincloth, a wooden spear in his hand, attacked the sluggish warriors swiftly from behind the rocks, the boulders shining in the hot sun.*

The basic sentence is still "The ape-man attacked," though by this time we have more definition for each of the parts, more information, and too many adjectives.

Compound Sentences

A compound sentence has two or more main clauses, each containing a subject and a predicate, each describing an action complete in itself. The clauses in the compound sentence are joined by a connective — "and," "but," "or," "nor," "yet," "for," or "so" — or by a semi-colon or colon.

> The economy stagnates and prices rise.

> We can lower the price of admission or we can stage fewer plays.

> He never went to the snake house again; he had been revolted by the alligator.

The clauses in each of these sentences are independent. Each sentence could become two sentences, with a minimal change of meaning.

> The economy stagnates. Prices rise.

> We can lower the price of admission. We can stage fewer plays.

> He never went to the snake house again. He had been revolted by the alligator.

In the compound sentence, notice that the two complete clauses are nearly equal in importance, or *coordinate*. A compound sentence, of course, can have more than two parts.

> Seaver pitched a curve, the runner on first sprinted toward second, and Morgan ran to cover the base.

But a string of coordinate clauses is usually boring.

> There was more crime in the street, the criminals were running around free, the judges were letting people go, nobody was safe in the streets, criminals were out on bail, murderers were on parole, and nobody did anything.

Complex Sentences

If, however, one part of the sentence depends on the other — if the one is the cause of the other, for instance — we have a complex rather than a compound sentence. We call the clause that depends upon the other for explanation or completion, the *subordinate clause*. A complex sentence would be,

> *Because the economy stagnates,* high prices find few buyers.

The first clause in this sentence is subordinate.

We can vary sentences even when we use only simple clauses and compounds of equally complete clauses. But the complex sentence provides further variety, and allows us additional conciseness and precision. Clauses introduced by relative pronouns, "that," "which," or "who" — sometimes called *relative clauses* — are subordinate to a main clause; they depend on it.

> Do you remember the face of the man *who sold you this ticket?*

> The king executed the horse *that had thrown him.*

In other sentences, we attribute cause or sequence, and we do it by a conjunction like "because" or "after."

> *Because the Girl Scouts had proved to be unscrupulous,* the neighbors burned the cookies they had purchased.

> *After the movie ended,* everyone in the audience left.

Many other conjunctions — like "although," "after," "if," "since," and "when" — can introduce subordinate clauses, each with its own precise meaning to be used by the careful writer.

Compound-Complex Sentences

Frequently, we combine compound and complex sentences, using at least two main clauses and one subordinate clause.

> The young heiress jumped under the covers *when her uncle walked in wearing his gorilla suit,* and she refused to come out.

> *If you had only proofread the article more carefully,* Mr. Crumbly would not have been so insulted, and we wouldn't have this lawsuit on our hands!

In each sentence the clause in italics is subordinate; the main clauses are in roman type.

Incomplete Sentences

Another type of sentence commonly used is the incomplete sentence, or fragment. It is incomplete because it lacks a subject or a predicate. "John laughed" is a brief complete sentence. Neither "John" nor "laughed" would be complete by itself, but we could use either of them alone in the proper context.

> She thought about whom she might ask to the picnic. Harry? Harry was too grubby. John? John.

> When she saw him she covered her mouth and, though she tried to suppress it, laughed. Laughed. He could not believe it.

But the more common incomplete sentence is a phrase or a clause of several words.

> The essay by Ellsberg shows great control of sentence variation.
> Like the variety in the first paragraph.

The incomplete sentence is informal. In more formal prose, other ways could have been found to work "like the variety in the first paragraph" into a long sentence. We use the incomplete sentence also with many common phrases like "No comment," "Not at all," and "Of course."

Although the incomplete sentence occurs frequently in good informal prose, the beginning writer should avoid using sentence fragments entirely, until he has learned to control the varieties of sentences.

Student writers usually make sentence fragments accidentally, without noticing that their sentence lacks a main verb. Often it is the most ambitious sentence that wanders off into incoherence. Here is a vagrant sentence from a theme.

> As a result of American military incursion into Indo-China, which was begun in a gradual and secretive way just beyond the bounds of public awareness, and which was modeled on the French attempts that had failed consistently, with heads of state of any interested foreign countries bribed and enormous amounts of economic and military aid being given to the pseudo-leaders, and the American politicians continuing to conceal the true purposes and the true nature of our interests.

By the time this student came to the fifth clause of this huge sentence fragment, he had forgotten the place he started from. The sentence confuses us, and remains incomplete. What *did* happen "as a result of the American military incursion into Indo-China"? Proofreading and patient revision could have prevented this problem. A good solution here would be to rewrite the sentence fragment as two or three shorter, complete sentences. The first rule is clarity.

Another possible danger in incomplete sentences is that they tend to avoid committing themselves. If we take notes on a history lecture, using fragments rather than sentences, we may look at them a month later and read something like, "Too many wars. Bad economy." Unless we remember the context, these phrases may leave us puzzled. They could imply that the number of wars, at some time in history, destroyed a nation's economy. Or they could imply that bad economy created the wars. Or both. With neither a verb nor the expected order of subject and object to complete the action, the meaning is left vague. Of course it is ambiguity — not having to make up our mind — which appeals to the part of our mind that likes to absolve itself from responsibility.

> The recession put everybody out of work in Flint. All those rich people in Cadillacs driving past the homes of the unemployed.

Here the sentence fragment avoids responsibility for making connections, and leaves the meaning unclear; an incomplete sentence leaves the thought illogical. Are the rich people responsible for the unemployment? Should the rich people take detours to avoid the workers' parts of town?

We must remember, at the same time, that a writer *can* use the sentence fragment, *when he knows what he is doing.* If the prose is informal enough, the sentence fragment is yet another possible variation in rhythm and structure. It isolates a fragment in time, because the period creates a pause longer than the pause inserted by a comma or a semicolon.

> We were going to be consumed by fire once more, and once more the world would let it happen. As usual. What was true yesterday will be true tomorrow.
>
> Elie Wiesel, *A Beggar in Jerusalem*

Only be careful to use incomplete sentences in an informal context, and deliberately, like Elie Wiesel, to establish pause and emphasis. A careless writer may make clauses into sentences (with periods and capital letters) without purpose, and with choppy results.

> He was a writer. Which is a difficult profession. She looked tall. Although she was really only 5'3".

Avoid slack, incoherent sentences like these. These sentences need to become complex, with commas replacing periods.

EXERCISES

1. In these sentences, identify subjects, predicates, objects, indirect objects, and objects of prepositions:

   a. The Empire State Building is no longer the tallest building in New York.

b. When we sent Ambassador Buntwell to South Africa, we gave the guerillas tacit support.

c. Which of the fity states spends least on education?

2. In these sentences, identify phrases as prepositional, verbal, infinitive, gerund, or participial:

a. Remembering the tradition of the Old South, Rhett was unable to dishonor his name.

b. The Senator from Arkansas tried voting the way he felt.

c. In the morning, the sun will be drying the dew off the grass.

3. Identify the clauses in these sentences as main or subordinates. Are the subordinates used as nouns or as modifiers?

a. She rose when he walked through the door, and when he spoke she turned her back.

b. The jury, which was white and male, took twenty minutes to arrive at a decision.

c. Although brown rice is highly nutritious, people cannot live on brown rice alone.

4. Identify each sentence as simple, compound, complex, compound-complex, or incomplete.

a. Because Margaret had brought the elephant into the house, Sandy had to take her sculptures down to the basement.

b. Rose ordered an apricot sour although she had been drinking daiquiries, and winked at her companion as she did.

c. This sentence, for example.

d. Rocking back and forth on her heels, the professor lectured.

e. Although the rainfall is minimal, irrigation waters the valley and nourishes the corn.

f. Australopithecus reasoned, he cooperated, he hunted in large bands, and he used tools.

g. The man in the Foster Grants strolled down the crowded street, a beret on his head, a cane in his hand.

h. Always cheerful, Mr. Sputter the mailman smiled, although a German shepherd hung by its teeth from his sleeve.

i. Without hesitation, thinking only of the trapped ocelot, Branny dashed through the rising flames.

j. He grabbed the chicken feathers and threw them off the cliff, screaming and dancing all the while, although the rites were not yet due to begin and he, a crazed poet, was forbidden to take part.

5. Here are five contexts, each including an incomplete sentence. Which fragments succeed, and which fail? Revise the failures into successes.

a. Henry Moore was born in 1898, in a country not known for sculpture since the Middle Ages. Son of a coal miner, raised in Yorkshire, trained to be a teacher, when Moore learned that he could attend an art school on an ex-serviceman's grant.

b. Nevertheless, advocates of strip mining persist in their rhetoric. We hear of "vast untapped natural resources." It makes strip mining sound like pouring a glass of beer. Instead of like destroying the earth.

c. When I came back from Canada, my friends were all tanned. Everybody. I looked like a pale dime in a pile of rich, copper pennies. And I felt like ten cents.

d. They looked up and saw it. The second stage of the launch vehicle.

e. Whenever the Congress decides to tangle with the president, and the people need tax relief or something of that order of magnitude, although the country needs immediate help, and the newspapers are all complaining, except that nothing ever gets done.

6. Here are three passages taken from student themes. What is wrong with the writing? Revise each passage.

a. We used to eat when my father got up. Because he wanted it that way.

b. When inflation rises above 6 percent annually, and the consumer can no longer afford essential services, but the rich can still get whatever they want.

c. We looked at the mountain. Four inches of light snow were on it. It was a good day for skiing.

7. Looking into your daily writing, or old themes, find and copy examples of these: (a) A simple, complete sentence. (b) A compound sentence. (c) Three complex sentences of two clauses, in which you use different conjunctions. If you do not have three examples, revise until you do. (d) A compound-complex sentence. (e) An incomplete sentence.

CLARITY, COHERENCE, UNITY

To be understandable, our sentences must hang together. *Clarity* and *coherence* are needed in writing at all levels — from words, to sentences, to paragraphs, to themes, to whole books. We start pursuing clarity when we choose the right word; when we bring that word together with a second word, we begin to pursue coherence. Phrases and clauses must cohere in the unity of sentence and paragraph. In the larger unit — the paper or the ten-volume history of the world — we make meaning by the *shape* that we give the assembled whole.

We first discover clarity and coherence, most obviously, in the next-to-smallest unit, the sentence. We must make clear sentences before we can make clear paragraphs or clear themes. Unity, clarity, and coherence; we must define these goals before we enumerate ways to reach these goals.

One way of trying to define a quality — something as abstract as "unity," as "clarity," as "coherence" — is to look at its opposite. Here is an obscure and incoherent sentence.

> The attention brought to Campus Management's mismanagement of its rental property at 410 Observatory makes a convincing case for the need of a strong and active tenants' organization in Ann Arbor.
>
> From an editorial, *The Michigan Daily*

Nothing holds this sentence together; it lacks unity, and sprawls disconnected across the page. When we try to rewrite this sentence, we run into difficulty, because before we revise, we need to know what the writer wants to say. What does he mean when he asserts that "attention" itself "makes a convincing case . . ."? Perhaps he confuses two ideas. (In another chapter, we will look into logic, and speak about clarity as it relates to methods of thought. See pages 238–241.) Maybe the meaning is something like this: "When we see how this property is mismanaged, we realize that we need a strong and active tenants' organization in Ann Arbor."

Here is another incoherent sentence.

> It seems to be delivering a message right up to the end, but to decipher it, one has to dig deep within his subconscious and then he may not be sure of the nature of the manner in which it has affected him.
>
> From a theater review, *Ann Arbor News*

It is hard to rewrite phrases like "the nature of the manner." Maybe this sentence could become two sentences. If we put a period after "within his subconscious," we could make a sentence like, "Even then, one may not be sure of how the film-makers have done their digging."

Or take a sample from a student theme.

> All these shortages are eventually going to put people in a position which forces them either to take some type of action that will level

off the population somewhere, or people are slowly going to make
life difficult for the whole human race.

All these examples have faults in punctuation and grammar — but
they come to one common result: the sentences are unclear. The writers were unable to use language to make their thoughts clear to another person.

When we speak of unity, clarity, and coherence, and later when
we speak of variety, we use different words as angles of vision toward
the same purpose. It would be difficult to find a clear sentence that
was not also coherent and unified. Coherence makes unity, which is
necessary to clarity. Variety of sentences can be *added* to our writing,
in pursuit of the reader's attention; but we pursue the qualities of
unity, clarity, and coherence all at once, in the act of writing and
thinking. In this book, we discuss grammatical errors, and proper
grammar, in the service of these qualities only. When you read in this
book advice on not misplacing modifiers, or on avoiding the comma
fault, or the sentence fragment, remember that the goal is not mere
correctness but unity, clarity, and coherence — qualities we cultivate
in order to make contact with other people.

Unity: Coordination and Subordination

The poet W. B. Yeats said that a finished poem made a noise like
the click of the lid on a perfectly made box. Prose makes that noise
too, only less loudly and clearly than poetry. A good passage of prose
resolves rhythm, emotion, and idea into a pleasing whole — a unity.

Our tools for achieving this unity are the types of the English
sentence. A good simple sentence is direct and clear; but the simple
sentence will not always embody a complete thought. Writers have
the choice of simple sentences, compound sentences, and complex
sentences — and variations within each type, and a combination of the
latter two types. Beginning writers usually run to simple sentences,
and collections of simple sentences bound together, which become
compound sentences. Usually, the beginning writer needs to practice
the art of the complex sentence, the art of subordination.

Subordination, often using conjunctions, saves words and makes
connections between ideas. *Coordination* happens when phrases work
together like equals, like *co*-workers.

I climbed the mountain and worshipped the sun.

When we use *subordination,* one clause leads the other; the subordinate clause hangs from the main clause, depends on it, is underneath — *sub,* as in *sub*marine — the main clause.

> When I climbed the mountain, I worshipped the sun.

Here, "I worshipped the sun," is a main clause, and "When I climbed the mountain," is a subordinate clause. The main clause could stand by itself. "I worshipped the sun" could be a perfectly fine, coherent, simple sentence. "When I climbed the mountain," all by itself, is only a sentence fragment; it does not stand by itself; it hangs from, it depends upon, it is subordinate to a main clause.

We could write:

> Hamilton was tired of the game. He took out his doughnut cutter.

These sentences are correct, and they are understandable, but too many of them in a row would be boring, and they may not give us a full idea. We could write:

> Hamilton was tired of the game, and he took out his doughnut cutter.

This version is a compound sentence, two whole and simple clauses joined by "and." If this sentence differs from the earlier version, it differs by enforcing, with its grammar, the notion that the two statements are intimately connected. But with a conjunction and a complex sentence, we could make the connection more explicit.

> When he tired of the game, Hamilton took out his doughnut cutter.

> Because he tired of the game, Hamilton took out his doughnut cutter.

Syntax, like words, has insides. Each arrangement makes a gesture of meaning. The last two examples, with subordinate clauses beginning with "when" and "because," make alternatives to the simple sentences or to the compound sentence. They also make alternatives to a sentence using a participle:

> Tired of the game, Hamilton took out his donut cutter.

In all the examples but the complex sentences, the closeness of the two notions implies a connection between them, but does not state it. The explicit conjunction makes a statement. If we want to emphasize causation, we can use the conjunction "because." If we want to emphasize the temporal, we can use the conjunction "when."

We must always remember the insides, the implications or connotations, of our syntax. In some contexts, "because" might seem overinsistent or bullying. If we write that Bill's best friend has stolen his wife, ruined his business, turned his friends against him, and hired someone to kill him, it is enough to say, "Bill had grown to hate his former friend." If we write, "Because Sam had done these things, Bill had grown to hate his former friend," we have wasted the reader's time. He is likely to feel insulted, because we have slighted his intelligence so. We have no way of deciding, without knowing the context, what form of the sentence about Hamilton and his doughnut cutter would be best. In relaxed, informal writing, the participle might feel right. But the participle might leave questions for the reader, that conjunctions like "when" or "because" would answer. The writer has to decide, with each sentence, how much, and with what precision, to tell the reader.

Subordination: The Correct Conjunction

When we make complex sentences using words that imply sequence or cause, or other forms of subordination, our sentences will be whole and solid only if the context supports the idea implicit in the conjunction. We only achieve unity if we are sensitive to the insides of syntax. For this unity, we must use conjunctions responsibly; beginning writers frequently violate this duty. If a writer omits something important, the conjunction may appear illogical; with all the information, the conjunction would have made sense. If we read,

> The work was hard; however, John was an extraordinary worker.

the word "however" is illogical. The hardness of the work should not be a potential contradiction of John's ability. If we read,

> The work was hard; however, the pay was good.

"however" functions logically: pay is compensation for difficulty. The first sentence omits something like this.

> The work was so hard it was difficult to imagine anyone doing it; however, John was an extraordinary worker and therefore he could do it.

Here the protestations in the second half of the sentence ("however ... extraordinary") balance the extremity of the first half ("so hard it was difficult to imagine anyone doing it"). The two parts of the sentence go together, and the conjunction earns its place.

A beer commercial (the brand changed) has an interviewer ask,

"As a lawyer, what do you think of Fitz's?

The relationship between the two parts of the sentence is mysterious. The possible sentences in this pattern are without limit. We could say, "As a retired major league relief pitcher, would you tell me the median rainfall in the Canary Islands?" Really, the beer commercial hides the meaning; it only appears to be as pointless as the parody. Its illogic conceals a social statement. Other commercials for that beer include women who don't find beer drinking unfeminine, a black man who identifies himself as a professional artist, and several working-class males. The lawyer finds his way into the series to imply that beer drinking is acceptable among rich chaps too. He likes beer best after sailing all afternoon in his catamaran. Beer, then, is *not* just lower class, white, and male, and the interviewer means something by his weird sentence. But what he means, he is not allowed to say: "We want to show you that upper class, professional, chic sailing types drink Fitz's. You are a lawyer who sails. You like Fitz's?" Information is suppressed, and the result is "As a lawyer, what do you think of Fitz's?"

Probably the most important function of conjunctions is to establish relationships and notions of cause and of time. And they save words. However, always be careful not to use them falsely, as transitions, when they do not really move from one thing to another. An example is commonplace in the commentary supplied to football games. The announcer blends two sorts of information into one sentence, with brevity but without logic: "And of last year's graduating class two-thirds went on to graduate school while down on the field O'Leary makes three yards on an end-around."

Other forms of subordination — without using conjunctions — save words and strengthen sentences. Subordinate phrases and clauses, used as modifiers, give our prose density and variety.

In the *absolute construction*, we omit the connective and the verb, or sometimes a preposition, and modify directly and clearly. The absolute construction is in italics.

Day done, he raised his pitchfork to his shoulder.

Here we have cut from "When day was done," or a longer construction.

The desk ordered, pencils sharpened, paper blank, he was ready for a day of combat with the English language.

The fullback twisted and plunged, *his legs pistons, his head an iron wedge.*

A construction much like the absolute is the adjective with a prepositional or comparative phrase.

Spring air, *thick with odor of lilac,* moved through the gardens of Montgomery.

Similar in effect is the *appositive,* a construction that identifies the word preceding it.

Joe, *the mailman,* said hello.

The appositive is more direct than the adjective with prepositional phrase, and briefer than clausal versions: "Fred the horse thief walked in" is more concise than "Fred, who is the horse thief, walked in." In relative phrases not in apposition we can also omit words when the relationship is clear without them; when they can be omitted, they should be. Any unnecessary word, in writing, makes it more likely that the reader will become bored and inattentive. Say, "The flowers she picked were lying on the newspaper," not "The flowers that she picked. . . ." This device is often useful in expository prose. "He had taken a position that was both unworthy and untenable" becomes more forceful when we say, "He had taken a position both unworthy and untenable."

The participle is also helpful. Participles are verb forms used as adjectives, *usually* ending in -ing, -ed, or -en.

Breathing heavily, he plopped down on the bench.

"Breathing" modifies "he."

The *broken* umbrella was afraid of the rain.

"Broken" modifies "umbrella."

Impressed by her credentials, Mr. Jefferson stroked his *unshaven* chin, muttering, "Yes, yes, just what we have in mind."

"Impressed" modifies "Mr. Jefferson," and "unshaven" modifies "chin."

We can frequently use participles in modifying phrases in place of whole subordinate or independent clauses, saving words. Participles can be past or present:

> Tiring of the game, Hamilton took out his doughnut cutter.
>
> Tired of the game. . . .

Coordination: Punctuating Compounds

We have concentrated on forms of subordination only because subordination is more complicated than coordination, and needs more practice to become habitual. But compound or coordinate sentences form an important part of our prose style. And often when we use coordinate clauses, we find ourselves confused about punctuation.

We use a comma, generally, when the two independent clauses in a compound sentence are long.

> The man wore a green bandana around his neck, but his wife wore
> a Brooks Brothers suit and a black silk tie.

Short compound sentences, however, need no commas. "He was fat and she was thin." The contradiction inside "but" often suggests a comma's pause, but it is a matter of ear, of judgment, rather than of rule. "He was thin, but he was tall" draws more attention to the speaker's insistence on two opposed ideas than does the same sentence without a comma, "He was thin but he was tall," which seems more matter-of-fact, more conversational. Context determines choice.

Compound sentences are loosely held together; a semicolon can substitute for the connective "and." The semicolon implies the close relationship between two clauses, which "and" also implies, but the semicolon makes a different rhythm, by substituting a pause for a connective word. It is a useful variation, and it feels more formal. Avoid tacking together loose compounds, correlative clauses all in a row. Prose that repeats the same loose structure comes to feel too lax. We are all familiar with the speaker who cannot pause.

> I saw her and she was carrying a kitten and it had a crooked tail
> and I think it was part Siamese and . . .

Some of the same boredom afflicts us when the writer multiplies compounds.

> I saw her and she was carrying a kitten. It had a crooked tail and it
> was part Siamese. The cat was making tiny squeaks and struggling

in her arms. She smiled and then she let out a shriek. The cat had
clawed her and jumped out of her arms and run away.

It is easy enough, without radical change, to introduce variety;
we vary the type of sentence, using some subordination, and we vary
the punctuation in the compound sentences.

> When I saw her she was carrying a kitten with a crooked tail. It
> was part Siamese. The cat struggled in her arms, making tiny
> squeaks. She smiled. Then she shrieked. The cat had dug its claws
> into her, jumped out of her arms, and run away.

Without variety we will be bored. But the variety we choose can be
more or less expressive. In this small anecdote the action in the last
sentence may best be expressed by the three loose clauses, which were
there in the original version; however, the long compound has more
effect when it follows the two short sentences — two periods make
the rhythm choppy with pause — than it had when it followed other
compounds. It is like coming from a dark theater into daylight; the
light is brighter because we are used to darkness. In a small way, the
grammar and the rhythm add to the feeling, or the expression, which
is the meaning.

When we join two or more clauses in a compound, we use a
connective word or a semicolon, except on rare occasions when we
join brief clauses by commas. The classic example is Caesar's "I came,
I saw, I conquered," in which the commas make the pauses appropriately brief. Periods — "I came. I saw. I conquered." — make too much
space between these clauses. Remember that if the clauses are long, a
comma will not hold them together by itself. We need a comma *and* a
connective, or a semicolon. In

> The hair fell to the floor of the barbershop, the man with the broom
> was dozing in the corner.

the comma is misleading. The sentence could be two sentences, with
a period and a capital letter. Or a semicolon could take the place of the
comma. Or we could insert the word "and" or "but" after the comma.

The distinction between "long" and "short" in this advice is
vague, and must remain so. It is clear that with clauses as brief as,

> John blushed, Sara wept, Linda shrieked, the whole class erupted
> at once.

the commas work. In the bad barbershop example above, the comma would not work. When you come to clauses of middling size, you must decide. It could be,

> I climbed the hill, Susan climbed with me.

or

> I climbed the hill; Susan climbed with me.

We might well prefer a subordinate phrase:

> I climbed the hill, Susan with me.

No rule will decide among these arrangements. Context and tone should decide. The writer should first be aware of the alternatives, and should refine his sensitivity to the differences.

The insides of syntax and punctuation show themselves in slight differences in meaning. The first version of "I climbed the hill" is rapid and idiomatic and informal. The semicolon in the second example increases the pause slightly, and the formality considerably. A period would make the longest pause, and creates a choppiness, perhaps even a Dick-and-Jane tone — that boring monosyllabic simplicity we remember from learning to read in the first and second grades. (All comments on the implication of these forms are generalities, not rules; a context could make the choppiness rhythmically satisfying.) The final example is the loosest, the most lax; it is not so grammatically informal as the first, but it is closest to loose speech. The first example, by omitting the connection, is a tighter unit.

We have been talking as if "and," "but," or "or" either took a comma or didn't, depending on how long the clauses were, or on whether the sense would benefit from a pause. Sometimes when the clauses on each (or either) side are long, we may want to use the semicolon, even when we use a connective, so that we can take a longer breath, yet still indicate a close relationship by keeping the two clauses in the same sentence.

> The block was dilapidated, gray, the houses raw and the sidewalks sprouting grass; but he knew he was home.

This semicolon before the connective is more common with "yet" and "so." We can write,

> The lion was sleeping in the corner of the cage, yet his feeder approached him warily.

But we are more likely to use the greater pause.

> The lion was sleeping in the corner of the cage; yet his feeder approached him warily.

When we use adverbs as connectives — words like "however," "therefore," and "consequently" — we always use a semicolon.

> The lion stirred awake in the corner of the cage; consequently, his feeder threw down the pail of food and ran away.

Notice that the adverb connective takes a semicolon in front of it and a comma after it. Or we can make the two clauses into separate sentences.

_____ **EXERCISES** _____

1. Scrutinize these sentences, from student themes, for clarity, coherence, and unity. Rewrite each of them. If you have to, make assumptions about the writers' intended meanings.

a. It is hard for a graduate student to hold down both a teaching position and work for their degree.

b. He takes one student, Mike, who says he can trust anyone and also that he only has acquaintances and no friends since when is unclear

c. When a friend of mine, Robert Olds, who I had known for years converted to Christianity in high school and I began to resent him.

2. Make the following sentences more concise.

a. When he had finished eating the birthday cake, he stretched out on the sofa.

b. The magnetic pole, which is not the same as the North Pole, governs the compass.

c. United States Customs destroys tons of food every year. These fruits and meats are illegally imported.

d. A vacuum-cleaner salesman, who was nearly seven feet tall and who smiled continuously, fell down the cellar stairs.

3. Revise the following passage into one complex sentence. You will have to make your own assumptions about causal and tem-

poral relationships. Do more than one version if you can see different meanings.

> It was raining. It was about seven o'clock the next morning. The
> jeeps sloshed through the street outside the window. We couldn't
> sleep. We had breakfast. We all felt hungry. All there was was some
> beans and brown bread left over. We felt better. The sun came out
> about nine o'clock.

4. Try to write one long, silly sentence using as many devices as
possible; try to make it compound and complex, with an appositive, a participle, an adjective with a prepositional phrase, and
whatever else you can get into it. Then dismantle it and change it
into a short passage of more than one sentence, with varied, more
reasonable structures.

5. Analyze these passages, finding the structure in each sentence, and noticing the variety of sentences within the same paragraph. Praise or find fault, as you see fit.

> a. Down the hall in Apartment 2 the reporter found a very "strong
> case." There were holes in both the floor and the ceiling, big enough
> for the biggest rats. Cockroaches crawled up the kitchen wall. A cur-
> tain divided off a section of the room for a bedroom, and out from it
> peeked an old woman. She smiled at the visitors and watched them
> with interest. Isabel Sánchez, the head of the house, was pointing out
> some more ratholes. A teen-age girl sat staring at a television set
> whose screen was filled with a constantly wavering, almost undistin-
> guishable cowboy movie, spoken in Spanish. The reporter walked to
> the kitchen to watch the cockroaches, and observed that some dishes
> were sitting on the table that contained the remains of rice and beans.
>
> Dan Wakefield, *Island in the City*

> b. The greatest sea power in Europe and the greatest land power
> faced each other in war. The stake was the leadership of Europe. Each
> was fighting to strengthen her own position at the expense of the
> other: in the case of the sea power to hold her widely separated empire;
> in the case of the land power to challenge that empire and win one for
> herself. Both, as the war began, were uneasily conscious that an im-
> portant and even decisive factor might be an Asiatic nation, enormous
> in extent of territory, which had a foothold in Europe and was believed
> by many to be interested in watching the two chief Western powers
> weaken and perhaps destroy each other until in the end she herself
> could easily dominate Europe.
>
> Edith Hamilton, *The Greek Way*

> c. The young officer, to whom this seemed a matter of routine,
> continued to give his orders, in accordance with the general directions
> of his Group Commander, in a calm, low monotone, and the three

reinforcing squadrons were soon absorbed. I became conscious of the anxiety of the Commander, who now stood still behind his subordinate's chair. Hitherto I had watched in silence. I now asked: "What other reserves have we?" "There are none," said Air Vice-Marshal Park. In an account which he wrote about it afterwards he said that at this I "looked grave." Well I might. What losses should we not suffer if our refuelling planes were caught on the ground by further raids of "40 plus" or "50 plus"! The odds were great, our margins small; the stakes infinite.

Sir Winston Churchill, quoted in *The War in the Air*

d. The universe and everything in it constitutes God. The universe is a gigantic human organism and man is a tiny image of it, a toy replica of God. Because he is a miniature of the universe, by a process of spiritual expansion a man can mystically extend his own being to cover the entire world and subject it to his will. It is because all things are aspects of one thing that all things are grist to the magician's mill. The complete man, who has experienced and mastered all things, has vanquished Nature and mounted higher than the heavens. He has reached the centre where man becomes God. The achievement of this is the Great Work, the supreme magical operation, which may take a lifetime or many lifetimes to complete.

Richard Cavendish, *The Black Arts*

e. Many women have given their lives to political organizations, laboring anonymously in the background while men of far less ability managed and mismanaged the public trust. These women hung back because they knew the men would not give them a chance. They knew their place and stayed in it. The amount of talent that has been lost to our country that way is appalling.

Shirley Chisholm, *Unbought and Unbossed*

f. There under a spotlight, two Oriental gentlemen in natty blue suits were doing some amazing things with yo-yos. Tiny, neat men, no bigger than children, they stared abstractedly off into space while yo-yos flew from their hands, zooming in every direction as if under their own power, leaping out from small flicks in arcs, circles, and straight lines. I stared open-mouthed as a yo-yo was thrown down and *stayed down,* spinning at the end of its string a fraction of an inch above the floor.

Frank Conroy, *Stop-Time*

g. The American does not enjoy his possessions because sensory enjoyment was not his object, and he lives sparely and thinly among them, in the monastic discipline of Scarsdale or the barracks of Stuyvesant Town. Only among certain groups where franchise, socially speaking, has not been achieved, do pleasure and material splendor constitute a life-object and an occupation. Among the outcasts — Jews, Negroes, Catholics, and homosexuals — excluded from the com-

munion of ascetics, the love of fabrics, gaudy show, and rich possessions still anachronistically flaunts itself. Once a norm has been
reached, differing in the different classes, financial ambition itself
seems to fade away. The self-made man finds, to his anger, his son
uninterested in money; you have shirtsleeves to shirtsleeves in three
generations. The great financial empires are a thing of the past. Recent
immigrants — movie magnates and gangsters particularly — retain
their acquisitiveness, but how long is it since anyone in the general
public has murmured, wonderingly, "as rich as Rockefeller"?

Mary McCarthy, "America the Beautiful" in *On the Contrary*

Grammatical Unity

The good prose already quoted has exemplified unity in agreement,
consistency, and coherent conjunctions. I bring such grammatical matters together in this section because they can help to unify and clarify
our sentences.

Misplaced Modifiers. Placing modifiers properly is essential to
unity in content and construction. We must always be careful that a
clause does modify the word that its position makes it appear to modify. The dangling participle, with its often comic effect, destroys unity.

Being six years old and rusted through, I was able to buy the car for
a song.

Arranged in this way, the participle phrase "being six years old and
rusted through" modifies "I"; it implies that "I" was six years old and
rusted through. Here the best solution would be a subordinate stating
cause.

Because it was six years old and rusted through, I was able to buy
the car for a song.

A similar mistake is the dangling appositive.

A good teacher, his superiors saw to it that he was promoted.

But this would imply that "his superiors" were "a good teacher." Solutions:

He was a good teacher; his superiors saw to it that he was promoted.

> Because he was a good teacher, his superiors saw to it that he was promoted.

Yet another kind of misplaced modifier is the dangling participle introduced by a preposition.

> On achieving the age of twenty-seven, his parents threw him out of the house.

(The author may have intended the parents to be twenty-seven, and expelling a small child; but we would know that much from the context.)

Or the dangling phrase can be adjectives.

> Tall and strong, the job was easy for him.

There is a prevalent dangling adverb.

> Hopefully, this book will be done by late July.

Does the book really hope? The simplest rewriting would be,

> I hope this book will be done by late July.

In all such misreferences, ambiguity is a possible problem; the reader may not be able to tell what we really *did* mean. We lose clarity, we lose coherence. Even if our *intended* meaning is apparent, however, the laxity behind the misapplied language is a flaw, and cannot be excused as informality. The reader is appalled by the frayed edge left by incorrect order. The disunity itself is unpleasant.

For the unity of a sentence, nothing is more important than the precise placement of all modifiers. The dangling construction is a common error; everyone falls into it from time to time. We also make mistakes — sometimes amusing ones — merely by misplacing modifiers. For instance, this sentence appeared in the want ads of a newspaper:

> For sale: Piano by owner with large carved legs.

In an earlier edition of this book, the author perpetrated this sentence:

> Look at the examples elsewhere in this book of carelessly constructed sentences . . .

Errors in agreement. These errors are common when we use indefinite pronouns. "One" and "none," and distributives like "each," "every," "everybody," "nobody," and "everyone" — all take singular verbs. Here are typical errors.

> Everyone says they had a good weekend.
> Everybody had their tennis racket with them.

Common speech accepts most of these errors in agreement; but the most unified style rejects them. We should write:

> Everyone says he had a good weekend.
> Everybody had his tennis racket with him.

We should write *he* and *his,* to be correct in grammar. Grammar in this standard use of "he" and "his" may, however, conceal sexism. No one has yet found an alternative that fails to seem confusing or awkward, like "Everyone says they had a good weekend." For some of us, surely, an awkward style is preferable to the bias implicit in correctness. Perhaps we can only insist that everyone should *know* the traditional rule; then, if someone wishes to break the rule, he will know what he is doing and why he is doing it.

Frequently we fall into disunity, not by using a singular pronoun together with a plural one, but by using singular nouns with plural pronouns, or other mixtures of singular and plural.

> Although a person may not be hungry, a piece of pastry can stimulate their appetite.

Maybe his appetite, maybe her appetite, but not their appetite. We could say "their appetite," correctly, if we used a plural in the first part of the sentence,

> Although people may not be hungry, a piece of pastry can stimulate their appetite.

Vagueness of pronoun reference is more insidious than disagreement, because it is harder to detect in a draft. We misuse "this" and "that," by using them without having a clear connection to something earlier. Thus we destroy unity, clarity, and coherence. We say

> When I went home at Christmas, the tree wasn't up yet and my dog was sick, my mother had to have an operation, and my father was worried about money. This bothered me.

What bothered you? "This" properly refers to one thing, and the reader is forced to choose at random among the items listed. The author might have talked about "This group of circumstances," for instance. Or we say

> When the Panama Canal opened for shipping, the elapsed time for sending merchandise coast to coast in the United States diminished by 80 percent, and the cost accordingly. That pleased manufacturers especially.

Was "that" the time? The cost? Both? The last sentence lacks clarity, fades into vagueness and disconnection.

Often we misuse reference by confusing parts of speech, and ignoring antecedents.

> My father is a doctor and that is the profession I want to enter.
> Because we put wire fencing around the chicken yard they cannot escape.

Each of these sentences is understandable. Each is sloppy, improperly connected, and without grammatical unity. "That is the profession" fails to connect, because "a doctor" is a person not a profession. And the chickens are nowhere mentioned in the second example, so that "they" can refer to chickens only when we derive these animals from the phrase "chicken yard."

Consistency of Tenses. The tense, or time, is the form by which a verb signals past, present, or future. We should stick to one verb tense in describing one action. An account of something that happened to us usually sounds best in the past tense, but occasionally fits the present. Summarizing a book, we use either tense, often the present. But it is not choosing past or present that matters most (context decides, as ever); it matters most that we stick to the tense we start with. In careless writing, we drift back and forth without noticing it.

> The maple turned red in September, a bright range of reds from near-gold to near-Chinese. The sky is blue, and the maples show fiercely against it, making the colors more deep. On October the first frost came, and . . .

The second sentence should take the past tense, to agree with its neighbors. On rare occasions, and usually at a paragraph break, we can change tenses. A leisurely description moves into sudden action, and a break from past to present signals this change. Be careful if you try this device; and know that you are doing it.

Consistency of Point of View

Shifts in tense violate unity, and so do other sudden shifts. Pronoun disagreement, already discussed, makes a shift in number. We must not shift the person of the sentence, unless there is compelling reason to. We might carelessly write:

> First you put on your skis, one at a time for most people, and then we take a quick look at the slopes.

The "you" and the "we" are inconsistent. Either pronoun will do.

Equally, we do not move from active to passive in the same sentence, unless there is a compelling reason. We need not say:

> We looked forward to the party and it was greatly enjoyed.

Disunity makes unclarity. Instead, say:

> We looked forward to the party and enjoyed it.

Do not shift among imperatives and indicatives either. We do not say:

> Keep your eye on the teacher and you should take full notes.

The sentence gains unity if it is one or the other.

> Keep your eye on the teacher and take full notes.

or

> You should keep your eye on the teacher and you should take full notes.

When it is half each, it is a minor monster.

All of these directives ask the writer, for the reader's sake, to keep his voice coming from the same place, in the same tone, with the same number and gender and mood. It is disconcerting — finally impossible to follow — when a voice comes from high and from low in the landscape, from past and from present in time, from singular and from plural in number. Inconsistency and incoherence curse the work of most beginning writers. Here is a paragraph from a theme in which the author lost clarity and coherence through neglecting grammatical unity. He (or she) had no single point of view. The inconsistencies in this passage occur from sentence to sentence in the paragraph, as well as within individual sentences.

> The mountain from a distance is long and low, about eight miles in fact, and when you climb it you find that it is covered with tiny

bushes. The climbing itself went easily, and it was fun for everybody. I was there by 6 a.m., and all through our climb by three in the afternoon.

In revision, the writer found unity, clarity, and coherence:

From a distance the mountain shows itself long and low, eight miles long and only three thousand feet in elevation at its highest. As we drove close to it, and began our climb, we discovered that its sides were dense with small bushes. All of us enjoyed the easy climb, which took us from six in the morning until three in the afternoon, when we drove west again, into the setting sun, and back home.

_____ **EXERCISES** _____

1. Rewrite these phrases, to give them emphatic unity, or to remove errors or ambiguities:

a. Without knowing which one was best, the chocolate covered one appealed to me most.

b. Having arrived at the airport fifteen minutes ahead of schedule, my friends were nowhere to be seen.

c. A genius at seven, his parents were worried about his relationships with second-grade classmates.

d. Hopefully, some of these exercises are simple.

e. Everyone wore levi jackets with their names printed on them

f. While the sunset was beautiful, the aroma of the garden was more beautiful still.

g. In Zambia, Russia, Poland, and in Venezuela . . .

h. When the game was over, when the stands emptied, when the popcorn was swept up, and the lights were extinguished, a vast silence overtook the stadium.

i. Intelligent, pretty, sympathetic, a good friend, Jane was known to everyone in the dormitory.

j. She danced to prove she didn't care, and implying she did.

k. He answered that he didn't care what she did, that he was furious with her, and he would never speak to her again.

l. Either you come inside, or get a spanking.

2. Destroy the grammatical unity in these sentences by misplac-

ing modifiers, creating dangling participles, undoing agreement of
different kinds, and by any other devious means you can invent:

> a. When the *Titanic* set sail, the world waited for a new speed
> record for an Atlantic crossing.
> b. Too many cooks spoil the broth.
> c. Climbing Mt. Everest, breaking the four-minute mile, the En-
> glish of that Coronation year seemed to be true Elizabethans.
> d. Sheila sighed, and reached into Dan's pocket to find her hand-
> kerchief, which was not there.
> e. Nervous, pacing in their hallway, Roger and Marie looked over
> the narrow island of their universe, crammed with the minute details
> of their deadly life, suspended now in a moment of terror.

Structural Unity

Many attributes that give stylistic finish and polish come from
the organization of the sentence, rather than from the words the writer
uses. Ranging from the definable *parallelism* to the intangible *rhythm*,
these structural attributes are harder to define than the grammatical
unity that is obligatory in good prose.

Parallelism. Parallelism is essential in formal prose; sometimes
we use it in informal prose as well. Parallel constructions are phrases
or clauses within the same sentence that repeat the same word forms
(nouns, verbs, adjectives, and the like) in the same order to perform the
same function.

> He quit the job because the boss was cruel, the pay was meager,
> and the work was dangerous.

> the boss was cruel / the pay was meager / the work was dangerous

After the conjunction, each subordinate clause follows the pattern of
article / noun / past tense verb / predicate adjective. Parallelism is not
a grammatical necessity, like agreement. It helps us to manage sentences, and to *clarify* grammar. It is a matter of clarity and symmetry,
not of correctness.

We use parallelism most obviously when we introduce the parallels with pairs of words: "both / and," "either / or," "neither / nor,"
"not / but," "not only / but also," "first / second / third." The sentence
beginning with one member of these pairs should pivot on the other;

also, the parallel clauses should be syntactically parallel. Do not write,

> Not only did he run into the fire, but also carrying a can of gasoline.

This nonparallel construction is comprehensible, but it feels stylistically lax. These clauses are not parallel because the second uses a participle instead of an active verb, like the first clause. We could rewrite it.

> Not only did he run into the fire, but also he carried a can of gasoline.

In writing many clauses together, it is common but confusing to depart from parallelism and destroy unity.

> His reasons were: first, the overwhelming size of the debt; second, that the company was ill-managed; third, having so little leisure in such a job.

The sentence can be rewritten in numerous ways; for instance,

> His reasons were: first, that the debt had grown huge; second, that the firm was ill-managed; third, that the job afforded little leisure.

The parallelism would remain the same — and we would still want parallelism — if we dropped the enumerations.

> His reasons were that the debt had grown huge, that the firm was ill-managed, and that the job afforded little leisure.

The briefest way to write the sentence would be to make parallels in the predicate subordinate to one "that," by using the verb "to be" once and then understanding it elsewhere in its absence.

> His reasons were that the debt was big, the firm ill-managed, and the job onerous.

The more concise the sentence becomes, the more formal the prose.

With "either / or," "not only / but also," and similar correlative expressions, be sure that by position in the sentence you make the words correlate the same parts of speech in each clause. We frequently misplace our "eithers" and "onlys." We say,

> Either she committed the crime or someone else did.

and we are right. This "either" and this "or" correctly refer to "she" and "someone else." But too often we say,

> Either she ironed all morning, or she watched television.

Because the verbs are being related, the sentence should read,

> She either ironed all morning or watched television.

Here are other ambiguous uses followed by clear ones.

> Either the professor was asleep or drunk.
> The professor was either asleep or drunk.

> They not only ran to the grocer, but also to the florist.
> They ran not only to the grocer, but also to the florist.

In making a list, either use an article or a preposition once, at the beginning of the list, or use it throughout. Either

> The soup, spaghetti, lamb, and salad . . .

or

> The soup, the spaghetti, the lamb, and the salad . . .

but not a mixture.

> The soup, spaghetti, the lamb, and salad . . .

Not for formal prose, at any rate. For rhythm and emphasis, in informal prose, or in a poem, one might depart from parallelism and profit by the departure.

When one or more prepositional phrases contain several words, parallelism always repeats the preposition. Say,

> Through wind, through sleet that stung his cheeks, and through snow . . .

not

> Through wind, sleet that stung his cheeks, and snow . . .

When you use long clauses, introduced by parallel conjunctions, repeat the conjunction. With long clauses, we need the repetition for clarity. In short clauses, we need only the first.

> Although day was done, and night approaching, he kept on ploughing.

But

> Although the sun had gone down more than twenty minutes ago, and although shadows thickened in the field, he kept on ploughing.

Also, use parallel parts of speech. Verbs go with verbs in a parallel, nouns with nouns, and adjectives with adjectives. We often violate this rule in making lists:

> From a distance, he looked tall, gray, well-dressed, and a foreigner.

Instead of "a foreigner," which is a noun, the sentence should fulfill its unity with the adjective "foreign." A common departure from parallelism pairs a participle and an infinitive.

> He talked to prove he was intelligent and showing off his cultural background.

This writing is stylistically inconsistent, jarring the ear like an untuned piano. We should say,

> He talked to prove he was intelligent and to show off his cultural background.

Two participles would be stylistically acceptable, but the infinitives make a more vigorous sentence.

Another frequent lapse in parallelism is to omit a "to" when infinitives follow each other. In formal prose, we preserve the "to" for all infinitives in a series even when simple verbs follow each other. We do not say,

> To see, want, and buy is the essence of the American consumer.

We say,

> To see, to want, and to buy is the essence of the American consumer.

The longer the clause, the more upsetting it is when we omit a "to."

> His desires were few: to live on the ocean, to spend at least a portion of each day sketching the sea-birds, to sleep alone, and cook for himself only.

Unity departs when the "to" is omitted before "cook." Yet in informal prose, and speech, we occasionally do something that resembles our practice with articles and prepositions, the "to" remains with the first infinitive, and is understood with the rest.

> He wanted to move back, get a job, buy a convertible, and drive through town in style.

As with the rule on prepositions and articles, the word "to," once omitted after the first use, may not slip back in again.

Constructions on two sides of coordinates should agree. If we find ourselves writing,

Either he was rotten or a badly misunderstood young man.

we should improve it by keeping the parts of speech parallel.

He was either rotten or badly misunderstood.

The same rule applies even when pairs like "either / or" aren't used. Sometimes we make sentences like this one:

He hoped that she would come and she would wear the blue dress.

The first clause uses "that" and the second violates unity by omitting it. The sentence should read,

He hoped that she would come and that she would wear the blue dress.

The word "that" can safely be omitted entirely, when no parallel clause is used. "He hoped she would come" by itself is fine, but when "he hoped" more than one clause, we need parallel "thats." In the single clause, follow your ear.

Emphasis. Since emphasis works to construct a sentence firmly, emphasis promotes unity. When we use emphasis well, we make a unity between sentence structure and meaning and between sentence structure and appropriate emotional tone. Repetition, contrast, and order are three means of emphasis.

Parallelism is emphatic, and parallelism is a form of *repetition.* Where the politician's speech as a whole gathers speed by repeating a phrase, like "and what is your answer to *this,* Mr. President?", so the sentence gathers firmness by repeating parts and structures. The repetition creates dramatic heightening, like quickening drumbeats on a movie sound track.

We must agree that *the present administration is* bankrupt, *that it has* no cash reserves of the spirit, *that its morale is* a total liability.

Balance, our subject in the next section, also contributes to emphasis.

Careful development in the sentence can contribute emphasis. This is emphasis by *order.* For emphasis, we put the most important words in the sentence at the beginning or at the end — and it's best at the end. (See Concluding the Sentence, pages 160–161.) If a sentence has three parts, which we could score from one to three from least to most interesting, the emphatic sentence probably would be 2, 1, 3; it could be 3, 1, 2, and it could be 1, 2, 3; it could not end with 1 and remain emphatic.

When the sentence saves the most crucial or dramatic part for last, we call it a *periodic* sentence. We postpone the most important part of a sentence — often the simple predicate — by using clauses or phrases or parenthetical remarks, in order to build suspense and gain attention. Periodic sentences promise that something is coming, but hold it back, teasing us, so that the resolution comes with power.

> That the spring was late this year, that the dogwood never bloomed and that the flowers struggled wanly out of the garden, all of these failures must have contributed to the moment when Frederick, suddenly and without warning, shot his wife.

When we have several details or ideas to present in a sentence, the emphatic order is the *crescendo*. If one of the details is a surprise — something that may seem out of place, but really belongs there — it should come last. Otherwise the order is simply the order of intensity.

> After the flood, we saw great willows uprooted, houses ripped from their foundations and drifted against canyon walls, and the swollen bodies of the dead.

> The president has tricked the workers, ignored the military, soaked the rich, and plundered the poor.

Departures from an emphatic order destroy unity by appearing accidental. A periodic sentence feels constructed and planned, sturdier than a loose sentence, which trails off into "many other instances of this kind." An emphatic order makes us feel control, not randomness. It is one more device contributing to the click of the box.

Varying sentence types can also become emphatic (and thus variety can lend its power to unity) when we shift suddenly from one sort of sentence to another. This is *contrast*. Most commonly, we see a short sentence provide emphasis after several long sentences.

> We cannot agree that the Cabinet has been ineffective, because as far as we can tell the Cabinet does not exist. If it exists, will someone please tell us if it has met? For we have been unable to discover when it meets, or where, or with whom in attendance, or if the President knows his own Secretaries by name. We think he doesn't.

By contrasting sentence types we build emphasis into the developing of the paragraph.

Balance. **Balance** and parallelism are related; both have to do with repetition. Both create emphasis. But parallel construction is a matter of maintaining equal grammatical structure, and balance has to do with getting the sentence parts, each with its own weight, where they fit. Balance is style, it is not grammar, nor can it be described grammatically. Parallelism is style, too; but it can be described grammatically. A balanced sentence is one in which the main parts of the sentence have approximately the same rhythm and importance. A balanced sentence need not have two parts in balance; it may have three or four or more. Balance is similarity and *sense*; parallelism is similarity and *structure*. Balance is a less precise matter than parallel construction.

> In his day, Frank built model airplanes of balsa wood and went to the movies on Saturday; / now, at the same age, Jim cruises around in his own car and flies to New York for the weekend.

> Fred said it was dangerous, / but Bill insisted on going.

These sentences have balance but do not have precisely parallel construction. For accurate expression, and without ambiguity, they depart from exact parallelism. Of course balance and parallelism are not necessarily exclusive. Not only are they similar in the unity they create, but both can work in the same sentence.

> The Grogs wanted only to share and be reconciled; the Kogs wanted only to kill or be killed.

Balance and parallelism give emphasis to a sentence and help us to remember it. Many proverbs and epigrams employ them for these reasons.

Here is parallelism without balance.

> We are to have what we have as if it were loaned to us and not given; to be without proprietary rights to body or soul, mind or faculties, worldly goods or honors, friends, relations, houses, castles, or anything else.
>
> Meister Eckhart

Balance without parallelism:

> People possess four things
> that are no good at sea:
> anchor, rudder, oars, and
> the fear of going down.
> > Antonio Machado

Balance and parallelism:

> The foxes have their holes and the birds have their nests; but the
> Son of Man has no place to lay his head and to rest.

Extreme balance and parallelism, as in wise sayings:

> The old pine-tree speaks divine wisdom; the secret bird manifests
> eternal truth.
> > Zen proverb

Rhythm. Rhythm and resolution, which we name together because they seem related, are more difficult to define or exemplify than any other words used in this book. By rhythm we mean sounds pleasingly arranged, the sort of emphatic arrangement we might wave our arms to accompany, or want to tap our feet to. The Hemingway passage quoted on page 16 succeeds by its rhythm. Here is another example of superb rhythm, quite different from Hemingway's, more lush and energetic.

> Witches, werewolves, imps, demons and hobgoblins plummetted
> from the sky, some on brooms, others on hoops, still others on
> spiders. Osnath, the daughter of Machlath, her fiery hair loosened
> in the wind, her breasts bare and thighs exposed, leaped from chim-
> ney to chimney, and skated along the eaves. Namah, Hurmizah
> the daughter of Aff, and many other she-devils did all sorts of
> somersaults. Satan himself gave away the bride, while four evil
> spirits held the poles of the canopy, which had turned into writhing
> pythons. Four dogs escorted the groom.
> > Isaac Bashevis Singer, "The Gentleman from Cracow"

Rhythmic pleasure is essential to the resolutions that make good style, but rhythmic effects cannot be separated from the meanings in the words embodying the rhythm. Look at the examples of carelessly constructed sentences elsewhere in this book, for instance on pages 8, and 169–170. In these examples we can feel the difference between prose that is strong in rhythm and resolution, and prose that is weak in rhythm and resolution.

I suspect that a writer's ear is his most subtle, and possibly his most valuable, piece of equipment. We acquire a good ear by reading the great masters until their cadences become part of our minds. The stored memory of a hundred thousand sentences becomes the standard of the writer's own ear.

Resolution. Resolution is the art of ending a thing so that the reader feels satisfied. Resolution partakes of sound, sense, feeling, and emphasis. The periodic sentence, holding back its emphasis until the end, is an obvious method of achieving resolution. Here is another periodic sentence.

> Without schooling, without friends, without money, without the accent that is necessary for success in Britain, he arrived in London.

This device is so pointed that we cannot do it often, and must usually rely on more subtle resolutions. No rules can govern resolution or rhythm, only example and exhortation, because each click of the box is original. The more we know the materials that make style, the more extensive our ability to improvise. Look at the passage by F. Scott Fitzgerald (page 179) and see the slow, rising beginning, the calm plateau at the center, and the slow, peaceful descent at the end. Then contrast it with quicker-moving, informative prose by Garrett Mattingly (page 179). Each sentence is its own little dance, in which variety arrives at unity by way of improvisation; and each sentence relates to each other sentence as part relates to part, so that the paragraph is a round of dances that become one dance.

In talking about rhythm and resolution, we are not so much covering new material as looking at old material from another point of view. Asking you to practice rhythm and resolution is asking you to write well.

Concluding the Sentence. I have been speaking — in Emphasis, and in Resolution — about ending the sentence well. No sentence can have resolution if it trails off in flatness or emptiness. Let us look at some common failures. In conversation, and in unedited writing, we frequently start a sentence with high energy and then collapse when we try to conclude it: we have a subject, but we haven't the faintest notion for a predicate. We say,

> The increase in heroin consumption in the early seventies

because we are worried. But we don't know exactly what to say about it, so that we reach around for a predicate filler, to end our sentence.

> is a matter of the utmost importance,

or

> requires our immediate attention,

or

> is an aspect of contemporary life that must concern us all.

Sometimes a writer will string such sentences together — all strong subjects with weak predicates.

> The increase in heroin consumption in the seventies is of paramount concern to us all. Firm international controls are of the utmost necessity. The identity of heroin-producing nations is a matter of public knowledge. The destruction of crops at their source is one way of dealing with the problem.

Each sentence achieves the art of falling. These dancers trip on their skirts. The writer has a partial idea — like a sentence fragment — but makes it into a pseudocomplete sentence with trite predicates. The mind that writes such sentences seems to be disorganized, or lazy about organizing. The unresolved, trailing-off sentences communicate a vacuum. Yet, with a little attention, the writer could have talked plainly, with decent whole ideas, and an attendant fullness.

> The increase in heroin consumption in the seventies requires international controls to destroy the crops at their sources in the heroin-producing countries.

We used only a third of the words, in this version, and the sentence is unified.

Formulas for ending sentences are like other verbal formulas. All formulas are to be avoided, but some are more destructive than others. The filler predicate is certain to destroy any possibility of a satisfactory coda, an ending that satisfies us by its rhythm and resolution.

——— **EXERCISES** ———————————————

1. Write three balanced sentences without parallel construction, three with parallel construction but without balance, and three with balance and parallel construction.

2. Revise a page or two from your daily writing, keeping in mind unity, emphasis, parallelism, balance, rhythm, and resolution. Not only avoid disunity, but employ unity for the sake of expression.

3. Revise this passage so that it has a more satisfying rhythm:

> The old man lived in the gloomiest part of the forest. He had a house there. It was made of crude bricks. All kinds of trees grew around the house. There were oaks, fir trees, and kinds that had no name. They shut out the sun. Only scattered patches and changing shapes of sunlight showed on the ground. The old man didn't mind. He had lived in the city for many long years. He had grown to hate the neurotic scurrying about. And the hypocritic smiles and cement-block faces.
>
> He loved the peaceful and sensuous darkness. He felt at home in it. He loved the freedom that the darkness gave to his imagination. He spent hours sometimes filling the darkness with memories, with images, and with fantasies. He filled it with the bodies of beautiful women. He filled it with the faces of kindly young men. He filled it with seas that held treasures and monsters. His demons terrified him sometimes. But it was exciting at the same time. And after a while he couldn't tell if he was telling stories to the darkness; sometimes he thought the darkness was telling the stories to him.

4. Revise these sentences so that they are resolved more specifically.

a. The Boer War was a conflict which was a matter of the utmost importance.

b. *Moby-Dick,* a masterpiece of the nineteenth century, is a great piece of writing.

c. The dark-haired girl that he had only glimpsed before was very attractive.

d. If David and Susan don't manage to compromise somewhat they'll have trouble.

e. The dog was strangely reserved, almost sinister; Dan didn't like it much.

f. The two of them were excited and pleased with their new car; it performed well.

g. The murder of the senator was a senseless and tragic act.

h. In the face of the increasing violence in our city drastic measures must be taken.

i. We must try to write better.

j. Racial hatred in this country affects all of us.

5. Decide whether each of these sentences has balance, parallel construction, both, or neither:

a. Let him who seeks cease not in his seeking until he finds; and when he finds, he will be troubled, and if he is troubled, he will marvel, and will be a king over the All.

The Gospel According to Thomas

b. Only when you have no thing in your mind and no mind in things are you vacant and spiritual, empty and marvelous.

Zen Buddhist saying

c. He who knows does not say; he who says does not know.

Lao-Tzu

d. But logic does not always win popularity, and a man who points out the gloomy end of things can hardly expect to gain popular esteem.

Robert L. Heilbroner, *The Worldly Philosophers*

e. A common opinion prevails that the juice has ages ago been pressed out of the free-will controversy, and that no new champion can do more than warm up stale arguments which everyone has heard.

William James, "The Dilemma of Determinism"

f. Another odd feature of the human landscape in these climactic years is that both sides claim to be moved by the purest impulses of human brotherhood.

I. F. Stone, *The Haunted Fifties*

g. Let the actor for the time being keep to himself, store up his emotions, his spiritual materials, his reflections about his part, until his feelings and a definite, concrete, creative sense of the image of his part have become crystallized.

Constantin Stanislavski, *Creating a Role*

h. I think a nation such as ours, with its high moral traditions and commitments, has a further responsibility to know how we became drawn into this conflict, and to learn the lessons it has to teach us for the future.

Alfred Hassler, *Saigon, U.S.A.*

i. A self that consisted of conventional lies, shams, self-deceptions, memory images, a self just like that of other people, grew in me again but behind and above it stood a greater and more comprehensive self which impressed me with something of what is eternal, unchanging, immortal and inviolable and which ever since that time has been my protector and refuge.

Karl Jaspers, *General Psychopathology*

j. My father and mother were certainly of vital importance, not only in themselves but because they created a world for me to revolt against.

Ingmar Bergman, *Four Screenplays of Ingmar Bergman*

Unity of Tone

Earlier, we called some words "fancy," and we have alluded to formal and informal styles. Now, in a chapter on the sentence, it will be wise to consider the levels of diction, the tones of voice our prose can aim for. We think of them now, as we consider unity in sentences, because consistency of tone is another means of holding our writing together, another means to unity. Logically, tone could be part of other chapters, but this place seems most convenient, because unity of tone begins inside the sentence.

In the chapter on Words, we mentioned formality and informality, fanciness and colloquialism, which pertain to the tone of diction. Speaking of tone in this chapter, we mean the tone of syntax, and the tone of sentence structure.

Formality and Informality. Choosing a tone requires *tact.* You do not use the same vocabulary, sentence structure, or organization of thought on contrasting occasions. The doctor delivering a paper to his colleagues writes a formal and scientifically exact prose; the same person, writing an alumni newsletter, writes a relaxed and conversational prose. If one style wandered for a moment into the opposite, we would have disunity.

> The amino acids were observed to disappear from the patient's urine which was a helluva note.

or

> "Pa" Barker writes that he and his child bride have settled into suburbia where they are expecting obstetric surgery.

The alumni note could be an attempt at humor. Much humor depends on disunity. More examples will follow presently.

Of course "formal" and "informal" are relative, and many points fall between the extremes. We must think about three things: first, what distinguishes formal from informal; second, the occasions requiring or suggesting different tones; third, how much unity of tone is appropriate to an essay or a story, and how much variety it will tolerate, accept, or enjoy.

It will be good to start with formal and informal prose writings as touchstones, or concrete reference points for our abstractions. For formal prose, look at this passage from Ecclesiastes in the King James translation of the Bible. The King James Bible always combines vigor and formality.

> I returned and saw under the sun, that the race is not to the swift, nor the battle to the strong, neither yet bread to the wise, nor yet riches to men of understanding, nor yet favour to men of skill; but time and chance happeneth to them all.

Or look at this contemporary passage of literary criticism:

> But to make the modern world possible in art is not the same, as Lawrence would have insisted, as making life possible in the modern world. The myths that Mr. Eliot is at such pains to parallel are, almost without exception, not acceptable to Lawrence. They were, indeed, the very things that made living his life all but impossible. He chose, both as an artist and as a man, not to manipulate myths but life itself. It is this that stigmatizes him as a dangerous heretic. He was, in fact, anarchy compounded, which may explain, if not justify, the element of panic in Mr. Eliot's attack that leads him into such unwarranted abuse.
>
> Wright Morris, *The Territory Ahead*

For informal prose, here is a passage from James Thurber's *The Years with Ross.*

> Ross began as a dice shooter in the AEF, and ended up with a gambling compulsion. Nobody knows how many thousands of dollars he lost in his time at poker, backgammon and gin rummy, but it ran way up into five figures. He finally gave up sky's-the-limit poker, but would often play all night in Reno or Colorado, on his trips West, in games where the stakes were only a dollar or so. He must have won at poker sometimes, but I don't think he ever really got the hang of the game; certainly he didn't bring to it the intuitive sense he brought to proofs and manuscripts. He once told me about what he called the two goddamdest poker hands he had ever seen laid down on a table. "One guy held a royal flush, and the other had four aces," he said. When I asked, "Who got shot?" he looked puzzled for a moment and then said, "All right, all right, then, it was a straight flush, king high, but I've been telling it the other way for ten years." His greatest gambling loss occurred in New York, in 1926, when he plunged into a poker game with a tableful of wealthy men. He got off to a lucky start, and was two thousand dollars ahead and going to drop out when one of the players said, "Winners quitters, eh?" Ross, who was drinking in those days, stayed in the game, kept on drinking, and lost thirty thousand dollars.

The more formal the prose, as a rule, the more complicated the sentence structure, and the more pronounced the parallelism.

In diction, formal prose avoids the slangy, the colloquial, or the novel. A writer attempting a formal style sometimes falls into temporary informality because he cannot think of the appropriate word, because his vocabulary is inadequate, or because he is too lazy to look for the word. Writing a research paper on exports from a small nation, we want to imply that the minister of the treasury lacked financial integrity; but "lacked financial integrity" is a pompous formula. What do we say of him? If we call him "a crook," we will intrude an alien vocabulary upon this paper. The slang is like tactlessness. The best solution is to say something particular, and avoid the generality. Perhaps we can say that he was convicted of taking bribes.

In a more informal context, "crook" might be just the right word, bringing in a slangy touch of roughness, a little asperity. Tact is all. And it is like social tact, which is often called hypocrisy. When you see an old friend for the first time in six months, you may call him all sorts of names that you would not use in front of your priest. When you are introduced to the Rumanian ambassador between the acts of the ballet, you do not use the same epithets you would use with your old friend; you are more apt to say something original, like, "How do you do, Mr. Ceascu?" If you called him "you old son of a bitch" (which is no more original, of course), you would have a social problem.

Formality Gone Bad. We can help to define our terms by looking at what they are not. The virtue of informality can slide into the vice of obscurity, wasted words, or vague terms. The virtue of formality can wiggle in a hundred directions into the vices of pomposity, fanciness, pretense, jargon, and meaningless abstraction. George Orwell turned a good formality into a horrid one by rewriting the passage from Ecclesiastes that I quoted earlier. His modern version is the High Abstraction of academic sociology. Orwell takes,

> I returned and saw under the sun, that the race is not to the swift, nor the battle to the strong, neither yet bread to the wise, nor yet riches to men of understanding, nor yet favour to men of skill; but time and chance happeneth to them all.

and turns it into,

> Objective consideration of contemporary phenomena compels the conclusion that success or failure in competitive activities ex-

hibits no tendency to be commensurate with innate capacity, but
that a considerable element of the unpredictable must invariably
be taken into account.

Orwell's parody, which would pass for good prose with many people,
sounds untouched by human hands, like a monstrous frozen dinner
fabricated from sawdust and boiled crayons.

Some years earlier, Sir Arthur Quiller-Couch did a parody of part
of Hamlet's "To be or not to be" soliloquy. Quiller-Couch's parody is
not sociological jargon in particular. His parody is a little anthology of
typical modern faults in formal writing, formal attempts ending in
pomposity and verbosity. As in Orwell's parody, the result is the abstract and the general rather than the metaphorical and the particular.
Here is the Shakespeare, and then the Quiller-Couch.

> To be, or not to be: that is the question:
> Whether 'tis nobler in the mind to suffer
> The slings and arrows of outrageous fortune,
> Or to take arms against a sea of troubles,
> And by opposing end them? To die: to sleep;
> No more; and by a sleep to say we end
> The heart-ache and the thousand natural shocks
> That flesh is heir to, 'tis a consummation
> Devoutly to be wish'd.

> To be, or the contrary? Whether the former or the latter be pref-
> erable would seem to admit of some difference of opinion; the
> answer in the present case being of an affirmative or of a negative
> character according as to whether one elects on the one hand to
> mentally suffer the disfavour of fortune, albeit in an extreme de-
> gree, or on the other to boldly envisage adverse conditions in the
> prospect of eventually bringing them to a conclusion. The condi-
> tion of sleep is similar to, if not indistinguishable from, that of
> death; and with the addition of finality the former might be con-
> sidered identical with the latter: so that in this connection it might
> be argued with regard to sleep that, could the addition be effected,
> a termination would be put to the endurance of a multiplicity of
> inconveniences, not to mention a number of down-right evils in-
> cidental to our fallen humanity, and thus a consummation
> achieved of a most gratifying nature.

Neither the Orwell nor the Quiller-Couch parody can be called formal.
Because of their imprecision, they could be called sloppy, but not informal; imprecision is a quality in most bad prose, whether it is formal

or informal in its intent. These parodies are in a stiff prose style that *passes for* formality among many writers.

Pompous Language. We use pompous language to paint over a reality we wish to avoid seeing. Earlier, I mentioned euphemisms; sometimes, whole sentences are euphemistic. The airline has the flight attendant say, "Would you care to purchase a cocktail?" instead of, "Do you want to buy a drink?" because the second sentence sounds crass, plain, and barmaidish. For the same reasons, "beverage" is often substituted for "drink." These words are fancy substitutes for plain talk, and we use them (or they are used on us by commerce) for deceit. They are a vice which formality sometimes supports. But they are not genuinely "more formal." "Wealthy" is not more formal than "rich," it is just more fancy. "Rich" is not slang; it belongs in the most formal discourse. It is plain, and formality can include plainness without disunity, as it cannot include slang without upsetting its wholeness of tone. Think of the difference between "crook" and "rich." And think of the difference between "tool" and "implement." Like "rich," "tool" is plain, and perfectly suited to formal discourse; "implement" is polysyllabic and general, and often a pompous alternative to "tool."

Formal and Informal Sentence Structure. The question "Do you want to buy a drink?" is neither formal nor informal in itself. "Would you care to purchase a cocktail?" is pompous. "Want to get sloshed?" is slangy, which is not the same as informal. We could use "Do you want to buy a drink?" in a context that was either formal or informal, because its words are plain. Informally:

> The girl came down the aisle looking tidy and cheerful. In back of the makeup and the hair, which looked as if it would break off in chunks if you touched it, perhaps there was a living girl, somebody with a name like Eileen or Carol. She wanted to say, "Do you want to buy a drink?" But the airline had enamelled her talk along with her hair. "Would you care to purchase a cocktail?"

or, more formally:

> When you arrive at the age of fifty, your ability to choose has narrowed, and you find yourself at the narrow end of the funnel, blocked from expanding or wandering, focused instead on one bleak point at the bottom of the page. When you were young, you

questioned: Do you want to be an actor, or a poet? Will you live in London, New York, or Paris? Now you are no longer young: Will you eat lobster for dinner? Do you want to buy a drink?

The difference here is less a matter of vocabulary than it is of sentence (and paragraph) structure. The difference includes words also, but the difference in vocabulary is relative. "Tidy" and "cheerful" could go in either passage. The idiomatic gesture of "along with," in the first passage, is relatively informal; perhaps "as well as" would be the formal equivalent. "Chunks" has an informal sound. But the sentence structure in the second passage — complex, pointed, controlled — mainly accounts for its greater formality.

Informality Gone Bad. The fault typical of informal prose, when it goes bad, is incoherence. It does not hang together. (Pompous formal prose, or jargon, at least *seems* to hang together.) Here is a journalist's parody of what the Gettysburg Address would have sounded like if President Eisenhower, who was famous for his meandering style, had delivered it.

I haven't checked these figures but 87 years ago, I think it was, a number of individuals organized a governmental set up here in this country, I believe it covered certain Eastern areas, with this idea they were following up based on a sort of national independence arrangement and the program that every individual is just as good as every other individual. Well, now, of course, we are dealing with this big difference of opinion, civil disturbance you might say, although I don't like to appear to take sides or name any individuals, and the point is naturally to check up, by actual experience in the field, to see whether any governmental set-up with a basis like the one I was mentioning has any validity and find out whether that dedication by those early individuals will pay off in lasting values and things of that kind.

Well, here we are, at the scene where one of these disturbances between different sides got going. We want to pay our tribute to those loved ones, those departed individuals who made the supreme sacrifice here on the basis of their opinions about how this thing ought to be handled. And I would say this. It is absolutely in order to do this.

But if you look at the over-all picture of this, we can't pay any tribute — we can't sanctify this area, you might say — we can't hallow according to whatever individual creeds or faiths or sort of religious outlooks are involved like I said about this particular area. It was those individuals themselves, including the enlisted men, very brave individuals, who have given this religious character to the area. The way I see it, the rest of the world will not remember any statements issued here but it will never forget how these men put their shoulders to the wheel and carried this idea down the fairway.

Now frankly, our job, the living individuals' job here, is to pick up the burden and sink the putt they made these big efforts here for. It is our job to get on with the assignment — and from these deceased fine individuals to take extra inspiration, you could call it, for the same theories about the set-up for which they made such a big contribution. We have to make up our minds right here and now, as I see it, that they didn't put out all that blood, perspiration and — well — that they didn't just make a dry run here, and that all of us here, under God, that is, the God of our choice, shall beef up this idea about freedom and liberty and those kind of arrangements, and that government of all individuals, by all individuals and for all individuals, shall not pass out of the world-picture.

Oliver Jensen, "The Gettysburg Address in Eisenhowese"

And here, in case you do not remember it, is Lincoln's formal original.

Fourscore and seven years ago our fathers brought forth on this continent a new nation, conceived in liberty, and dedicated to the proposition that all men are created equal.

Now we are engaged in a great civil war, testing whether that nation, or any nation so conceived and so dedicated, can long endure. We are met on a great battlefield of that war. We have come to dedicate a portion of that field as a final resting-place for those who here gave their lives that that nation might live. It is altogether fitting and proper that we should do this.

But in a larger sense, we cannot dedicate — we cannot consecrate — we cannot hallow — this ground. The brave men, living and dead, who struggled here, have consecrated it far above our poor power to add or detract. The world will little note nor long remember what we say here, but it can never forget what they did here. It is for us, the living, rather, to be dedicated here to the unfinished work which they who fought here have thus far so nobly advanced. It is rather for us to be here dedicated to the great task remaining before us — that from these honored dead we take increased devotion to that cause for which they gave the last full measure of devotion; that we here highly resolve that these dead shall not have died in vain; that this nation, under God, shall have a new birth of freedom; and that government of the people, by the people, for the people, shall not perish from the earth.

The parody is twice the length of the original, yet doesn't convey any more information. In fact, it is much less specific — substituting nebulous phrases like "this big difference of opinion, civil disturbance you might say" for clear and simple ones like "a great civil war." The sentences wander and repeat themselves ("It was those individuals themselves, including the enlisted men, very brave individuals . . .").

It would be easy to continue listing the faults, because they were planted deliberately. But it is more important here to notice how they change the effect the statement makes. The writing is so diluted and drifting that we don't feel the speaker cares for the subject; we don't believe that he is genuinely moved. One fault that helps to create this impression — a fault common to many writers — is repeating pointless qualifications like "I think," "I believe," and "I would say." Many people mistakenly think that such qualifications make writing more informal and natural. But these personalisms are understood without being said, and they make one feel that if the speaker (or writer) is so tentative about speaking his mind then he is probably not certain of it.

Be wary of becoming careless in trying to be informal. Carelessness is partly a matter of vagueness of words: "individual," which is jargon for "person," is vaguer than "person" or "people." But carelessness is also lacking sentence and paragraph structure, trailing off at the ends of sentences, lacking resolution and emphasis. Series of simple and compound sentences that bore us are usually careless; parts do not mesh into a whole; there is no consistency. If you write with some respect for variety and unity — if you write with a sense of shape and finish — you will avoid such failings, and inhabit some point along the line that stretches from formality to informality.

Subject and Audience. We choose a level of diction to fit subject and audience. We know, before we think it over, that a recollection of family reunions will be more informal than an essay advocating that the post office be abolished. Content and circumstance determine permissible areas on the line from formal to informal, and will determine whether we choose "crook" or "criminal" before we come to it. If a student remembering junior high school writes,

> After a month of missing wallets and empty purses, we decided that somebody in the classroom was a crook.

we read along easily, and the slangy word is vigorous at the end of the sentence. If the student had written,

> After a month of missing wallets and empty purses, we came to the conclusion that someone in the classroom was a criminal.

we would find the style ponderous — "came to the conclusion that" — and serious to the point of comedy. "Criminal" is a heavy word for petty thievery in the junior high.

On the other hand, if the student, in an essay on the traffic in heroin, wrote,

> In 1975, an investigation organized by Interpol showed that high officials in three Mediterranean countries, in which opium grew, in which opium was refined into heroin, and from which illegal shipments started for the United States, were crooks making vast profits by virtue of their public positions.

the word "crooks" would be inappropriately informal, in a sentence so formal in diction and structure. "Criminals" would be the better word.

We must learn to look for errors in tact when we revise; we must look for the low word in the high place, and for the high word in the low place. When we have used the wrong word or construction, we can revise it out. If we had written "crook" because we could not think of "criminal," we can consult the dictionary. If we had fallen into repeated compound sentences in a formal context, we can complicate some of them. If in a modest piece of prose, we had slipped unwittingly into polysyllables and long, complex sentences, we can simplify. But in order to learn to revise we must learn what to look for.

Mixing Formal and Informal Diction. We would write more easily if prose were either informal or formal, if nothing lived between the poles. But most good prose lives in the temperate regions on either side of the equator. The informal essay enjoys an occasional periodic sentence, or unusual word. The formally deft argument uses a sudden colloquialism with charm and wit.

A sentence by E. B. White exemplifies the mixture a witty writer can make. White has been talking with appropriate disdain about a pamphlet on writing that, among other things, admonishes us, "Whenever possible, personalize your writing by directing it to the reader." "Personalize" is a slimy word. As White says, "a man who likes the word 'personalize' is entitled to his choice, but we wonder whether he should be in the business of giving advice to writers." The word is used commercially to mean an imprinted name, "personalized stationery" for instance, and does not mean "to make personal" or "to direct toward another person." White's comment, after he quotes the advice, is the sentence,

> As for us, we would as lief Simonize our grandmother as personalize our writing.

The mini-analogy expresses White's feeling: it would be monstrous to "personalize our writing." He compares the offensive diction to an unnatural act. At the same time, he uses a cunning and *personal* oddity of diction. The plain way to say the sentence is "we would as soon Simonize our grandmother," but White uses the old fashioned "as lief." And "lief" nudges against "Simonize," the old-fashioned word against the trademark. The bizarre mixture of dictions — the *disunity* — makes its point.

So the mixture of dictions can be expressive as well as comic. Often it is chiefly comic. W. C. Fields' polysyllables are comic because he uses high words in low matters — or for low purposes, like conning people.

Revising for Unity. Unity brings us much to consider in revision. Go over your prose, thinking of it as something that ought to be as whole and as shapely as a clay pot or an automobile fender. Maybe a little less shiny and symmetrical than an automobile fender.

Look for rhythm and resolution, paying special attention to the ends of your sentences. Look for parallelism, emphasis, and balance. Repair any grammatical disunity that may have crept in. Look for places in which your tone shifts for no good reason, and make repairs.

_____ **EXERCISES** _____

1. Rewrite these sentences as simply as possible. Cut out all the pretentiousness.

a. He couldn't comprehend how the thermostat mechanism was to be operated.

b. The general voiced the personal opinion the defoliation was a reasonable measure in a police action such as this.

c. Your utilization of the word "sensuality" is improper.

d. That wedge is merely a portion of the circle's entirety.

e. We subscribe to the belief that negligence on your part was responsible for the damage incurred by our apartment's furnishings.

f. My lower appendage does not have a great deal of mobility, confined as it is by the plaster cast.

g. She doesn't minister to my emotional requirements for affection with a great deal of conscientiousness.

h. His investment in the emotional complex of their relationship, which had been ongoing for somewhat over five years, was minuscule.

i. Due to private considerations the precise nature of which I cannot reveal I will not be adopting the course of action you proposed as a substitute for my own.

j. The culinary offerings of this establishment are not of a very high quality.

2. Looking into textbooks, magazines, newspapers, college catalogues, find five sentences in which the writer uses a pompous or fancy construction in place of a plainer one. Rewrite for plainness, and speculate on the reasons behind the pomposity.

3. Rewrite this passage as clear informal prose, without wasted words:

I was walking on down by the Forum and I saw this guy I know whose name is Gaius Marcellus. He looks all shaken up and I wondered why, so I asked him. He could hardly talk he was so upset. He said, "Caesar's been murdered!" I was so shocked I couldn't believe it. He told me how it happened, that Brutus, Cassius, and some other guys tricked him and got him when he wasn't looking. They stabbed him all over, shouting that he was a tyrant and that it was for the good of the people. As he was telling me this stuff, we saw a big crowd and we heard a lot of noise from the direction of the steps of the Senate. And we saw Marc Antony getting up on the steps and making motions like he wanted the people to be quiet.

4. Write ten sentences, five formal and five informal, in which one word stands out as being inappropriate to the diction in the sentence. For instance, "The senator, having risen to the platform with difficulty, stated that he believed the measures the Senate had taken in the recent crisis, despite their intentions, were crummy."

5. Take this passage from Ecclesiastes, or this Shakespearean speech, and make a parody like those done by George Orwell and Sir Arthur Quiller-Couch.

And I hated all my labour wherein I laboured under the sun, seeing that I must leave it unto the man that shall be after me. And who

knoweth whether he will be a wise man or a fool? Yet will he have
rule over all my labour wherein I have laboured, and wherein I have
shown myself wise under the sun. This also is vanity.

Now my co-mates and brothers in exile,
Hath not old custom made this life more sweet
Than that of painted pomp? Are not these woods
More free from peril than the envious court?
Here feel we not the penalty of Adam,
The season's indifference, as the icy fang
And churlish chiding of the winter's wind,
Which when it bites and blows upon my body
Even till I shrink with cold, I smile, and say
This is no flattery; these are counsellors
That feelingly persuade me what I am.
Sweet are the uses of adversity,
Which, like the toad ugly and venomous,
Wears yet a precious jewel in his head.
And this our life, exempt from public haunt,
Finds tongues in trees, books in the running brooks,
Sermons in stones, and good in everything.

As You Like It, II, 1

6. Use the clause or sentence, "he never wanted to write again,"
in two paragraphs, one formal and the other informal.

7. Make two paragraphs, one using the word "phoney," and one
the word "insincere." Keep unity of tone in each paragraph.

8. In these passages, analyze diction and structure for formality
and informality. Be prepared to find some mixture.

a. A dramatic necessity goes deep into the nature of the sentence.
Sentences are not different enough to hold the attention unless they
are dramatic. No ingenuity of varying structure will do. All that can
save them is the speaking tone of voice somehow entangled in the
words and fastened to the page for the ear of the imagination. That is
all that can save poetry from sing-song, all that can save poetry from
itself.

Robert Frost, *Selected Prose of Robert Frost*

b. "Omit needless words!" cries the author on page 17, and into
that imperative Will Strunk really put his heart and soul. In the days
when I was sitting in his class, he omitted so many needless words,
and omitted them so forcibly and with such eagerness and obvious
relish, that he often seemed in the position of having short-changed
himself, a man left with nothing more to say yet with time to fill, a
radio prophet who had outdistanced the clock. Will Strunk got out of
this predicament by a simple trick: he uttered every sentence three
times. When he delivered his oration on brevity to the class, he leaned

forward over his desk, grasped his coat lapels in his hands, and in a husky, conspiratorial voice said, "Rule Thirteen. Omit needless words! Omit needless words! Omit needless words!"

E. B. White, The Elements of Style

c. So Elvis Presley came, strumming a weird guitar and wagging his tail across the continent, ripping off fame and fortune as he scrunched his way, and, like a latter-day Johnny Appleseed, sowing seeds of a new rhythm and style in the white souls of the white youth of America, whose inner hunger and need was no longer satisfied with the antiseptic white shoes and whiter songs of a Pat Boone. "You can do anything," sang Elvis to Pat Boone's white shoes, "but don't you step on my Blue Suede Shoes!"

Eldridge Cleaver, Soul on Ice

d. Every adult, whether he is a follower or a leader, a member of a mass or of an elite, was once a child. He was once small. A sense of smallness forms a substratum in his mind, ineradicably. His triumphs will be measured against this smallness, his defeats will substantiate it. The questions as to who is bigger and who can do or not do this or that, and to whom — these questions fill the adult's inner life far beyond the necessities and the desirabilities which he understands and for which he plans.

Erik Erikson, Childhood and Society

e. This is a society which has little use for anything except gain. All is hacked down in its service, whether people, ideas, or ideals. The writer, say, who achieves some entrance into the mainstream of American letters is almost immediately in jeopardy of being stripped of his insight by the ruffians of "success." A man who writes plays and poems, for instance, is asked to be a civil rights reporter, or write a dopey musical — if he is talked about widely enough — if not, there is no mention of him, and perhaps he is left to rot in some pitiful mistake of a college out in Idaho. A man who writes or makes beautiful music will be asked to immortalize a soap, or make sounds behind the hero while that blond worthy seduces the virgins of our nation's guilt. Even a man who is a great center fielder will still be asked to kick up his heels at Las Vegas.

Leroi Jones, Home

VARIETY AND UNITY

Sentences find variety through the necessities of thought and expression. Subordinate clauses often make appropriate qualifications, for instance. The short, succint sentence embodies the rhythm of an idea. If our prose has unity, clarity, and coherence, it is usually varied in its sentence structure as well.

But not always. We get in a rut. We lack experience of the long, periodic sentence, or even of the complex sentence, and we tend to fall into a monotony of construction. It helps us, in revision, to look for variety of sentence structure, and if we lack this variety to see if we can appropriately impose it.

Unity and variety need each other. They are the two poles, and the world spins between them. Without variety, there is nothing to be unified. Identically constructed sentences strung together in a row have the unity of chicken wire. Dick-and-Jane stories have this unity, which is perhaps why we want to leave first grade for the second. Paragraphs of successive compound sentences are similarly boring. In this passage from a student theme, the writer, lacking confidence in his ability to use complex sentences, writes chicken wire prose.

> Student government at the high school level is pointless. Principals never allow students any power. School boards are the same. Every year people get elected and nothing happens.

We could revise this passage, for variety, into these words — which also supply greater unity and clarity:

> Student government in high school is pointless because no high school principal is prepared to grant real power to students, and no school board would support a principal who experimented with student power. Although elections take place every year, office without responsibility makes nothing happen.

By using different sentence types, we can vary the speed and style in our prose, and at the same time make it more precise. If for no other reason, we must vary our sentences to keep the reader interested and involved. Monotony destroys attentiveness; if the reader sleeps, our clarity is wasted. But more important than keeping the reader's attention, variation allows us subtle expression, it increases the range and conciseness of our expression. The means are not separate from the ends. *A change in style, however slight, is a change in meaning, however slight.* You will find meanings that you cannot express, cannot convey, unless you can find in your box of varied sentence structures the shape you require.

Long Sentences

Short sentences are easy. They are also useful, when they are mixed with longer sentences of different types. Longer sentences give student writers more trouble; the more parts a machine has, the more things can go wrong. But to become a skillful writer, we must be able to handle varieties of the long sentence.

In the most controlled prose, in the long sentences made by writers being formal, clause follows clause, the sentence is compound as well as complex, and absolutes, participles, and appositives combine with prepositional phrases — a combination of combinations that includes, balances, and ultimately unifies.

If we took the sentence above and reduced it to one complete clause for each idea, we might end with something like this:

> Some prose is highly controlled and each sentence is long. This happens when the writer is being formal. There are many clauses. The sentence can be compound and it can also be complex. The sentence can also include absolutes, participles, appositives, and prepositional phrases. This combination makes the sentence inclusive. It gives it balance, and it gives it unity.

Seven sentences, in this version, and fifty-nine words. The earlier version was one sentence, and forty-four words. The gain in brevity is trivial, but the shorter version is more accurate. It is more accurate by its use of subordination, not only in bringing form and content into agreement, but by making direct syntactic connections instead of continually stopping the flow of sense and picking it up again with a pronoun.

But we don't need to make such sentences up; we can find them in the work of many writers. W. H. Auden uses long, formal sentences to define the sea as a symbol in religion and in literature.

> The sea, in fact, is that state of barbaric vagueness and disorder out of which civilization has emerged and into which, unless saved by the effort of gods and men, it is always liable to relapse.
> W. H. Auden, *The Enchafed Flood*

This sentence starts slowly, with "in fact" and "state of," but ends with a flourish. Auden carries us up the hill, as far as the phrase "and into which," and then holds us at the summit for a while with "unless saved by the effort of gods and men" before he takes us downhill to resolve the main thought. The parallelism between the prepositions and relatives "out of which" and "into which" finds its action in the exact verbs "emerged" and "relapse," interrupted, with precise syntactic sense, by the "unless" clause that separates the relative and the verb in the final clause. We might try once more to supply a version of the sentence as someone else might have written it.

The sea literally depicts a state of being that is barbaric. Also, it is vague, and it does not have any order in it. Civilization is what has come out of the sea. Civilization is always liable to go back into the sea. But civilization is saved by the efforts of gods and men. Or it has been so far, anyway.

Let us find more long sentences, graceful and agile.

In the early morning the distant image of Cannes, the pink and cream of old fortifications, the purple Alps that bounded Italy, were cast across the water and lay quavering in the ripples and rings sent up by sea-plants through the clear shadows.
F. Scott Fitzgerald, *Tender Is the Night*

The passage begins and ends with prepositional phrases ("In the early morning . . . through the clear shadows") and in between are more of them, and adjectives, and a varied use of verbs: "bounded, cast, lay quavering." The verbs, which follow each other in time, have as subject the three phrases and clauses before — an elaborated subject, which includes the verb "bounded" as well as nouns and adjectives. Then we move into more prepositions and nouns, another verb, preposition and noun, preposition, adjective, and noun. At the center stand the verbs that carry the sentence

Fitzgerald's prose is ornate and well-ordered, but not so formal as the prose of some historians and essayists. Here is a whole paragraph, beginning with a simple sentence.

Perhaps Philip had not made up his mind either. The English had given him provocation enough; Drake's impudent raid down the Spanish coast and across to the West Indies, Leicester's army in the Netherlands, the worsening fate of the English Catholics for whom, ever since his marriage in England, Philip had felt a special responsibility. The Pope exhorted him to act, the English exile begged him to hurry, and among his counsellors the war party was in the ascendant. It may be that Philip was only making haste slowly because, as he had once written, in so great a matter it was better to walk with leaden feet.
Garrett Mattingly, *The Defeat of the Spanish Armada*

Here is classic prose that is vigorous and formal at the same time. Try to recast the second sentence into simple sentences. Notice the colon used to imply that something follows which had been announced by the phrase before the colon. Notice how Mattingly starts listing provocations with a long compound subject, varies into a short subject, and then concludes with a long subject ending with a subordinate clause.

After this long, complex sentence, the historian varies the pattern by writing a three-part compound and ends with a longer complex sentence.

The long, complex sentence lends itself to organizing things that are related to each other, like events in history, plots of stories, or arguments with several parts.

Mixing the Types

We can manipulate the types of sentence we use for variety, and to create an expressive effect, to establish a mood, or to emphasize a point. Here are some examples. Keep in mind that the passages get their effect not by the sentence structure alone, but by the whole apparatus built into them — words and ideas. Sometimes, for the sake of sense or mood, we manipulate phrases to achieve more regularity than variety.

> In a little house on the mountain slopes above Delphi lived an old woman with her witless son. The house consisted of a single room; one wall was the mountainside itself, and always dripped with moisture. It was really not a house at all, but a ramshackle hut which herdsmen had built for themselves. It stood quite alone away up in the wild mountain, high above the buildings of the city and above the sacred precincts of the temple.
>
> Pär Lagerkvist, *The Sybil*

The sentence structure here is simple and stable. The construction is uncomplicated and regular. All the sentences except the first are regular in word order, beginning subject / verb and continuing evenly, without parenthetical expressions, or phrases set off by commas, or any other complications in the syntax. The syntax is as undisturbed as the scene. The sentences are medium in length, and similar in length, establishing a rhythm that reinforces the stability and simplicity in the scene described. We participate in the rhythm of untroubled isolation. That rhythm is established, even more, by the uniform length of the main phrases within the sentences. If we listen to ourselves reading the passage we will find that natural pauses divide the phrases in this way:

> In a little house on the mountain slopes above Delphi /
> lived an old woman with her witless son. /
> The house consisted of a single room; /
> one wall was the mountainside itself, /
> and always dripped with moisture. /

It was really not a house at all, /
but a ramshackle hut which herdsmen had built for themselves. /
It stood quite alone away up in the wild mountain, /
high above the buildings of the city /
and above the sacred precincts of the temple.

It has enough variation to avoid monotony. The even length contributes not only stillness to the scene, but our sense of the narrator's calm, unemotional objectivity.

The following passage taken from Annie Dillard's *Pilgrim at Tinker Creek* exhibits different sentence constructions, with different effects:

> When I slide under a barbed-wire fence, cross a field, and run over a sycamore trunk felled across the water, I'm on a little island shaped like a tear in the middle of Tinker Creek. On one side of the creek is a steep forested bank; the water is swift and deep on that side of the island. On the other side is the level field I walked through next to the steers' pasture; the water between the field and the island is shallow and sluggish. In summer's low water, flags and bulrushes grow along a series of shallow pools cooled by the lazy current. Water striders patrol the surface film, crayfish hump along the silt bottom eating filth, frogs shout and glare, and shiners and small bream hide among roots from the sulky green heron's eye. I come to this island every month of the year. I walk around it, stopping and staring, or I straddle the sycamore log over the creek, curling my legs out of the water in winter, trying to read. Today I sit on dry grass at the end of the island by the slower side of the creek. I'm drawn to this spot. I come to it as to an oracle; I return to it as a man years later will seek out the battlefield where he lost a leg or an arm.

Ms. Dillard starts with a long complex sentence of description, with three strong verbs in a subordinate clause, and then an elaborated predicate in the main clause. She follows this sophisticated sentence with two simple clauses, a compound joined by a semicolon. The next sentence elaborates the pattern of the second one. The fifth sentence is long and rich, its mass of description tending to obscure the fact that its construction is simple, direct — and compound. Following it is the shortest sentence, and the simplest one so far, in the paragraph. Two sentences later, we find a sentence even shorter and simpler, followed by a compound-complex sentence of great sophistication, and a final image that is startling, almost shattering. Dillard plays the octaves of syntax like a skilled musician improvising at the piano.

Revising for Variety and Conciseness

Look over your writing for the construction of sentences. Ask yourself if you vary enough to avoid monotony, if your variations are as expressive as they might be, and if your informal sentences are appropriate and sufficiently precise.

Also, see if you can be more concise. To revise for conciseness often requires conjunction and complex sentences. Conciseness and precision go together. We ramble on, in our first drafts or in our daily writing, assuming connections and causes but not stating them. If we try to make our prose more concise, by writing complex sentences with precise conjunctions, we often discover that what we wanted to imply does not really derive from what we said. So this device of revision — by adding the conjunction — becomes another way of testing, and achieving, the identity of expression and meaning. Precision of time and cause is a responsibility that the loose or compound sentence may evade. In an earlier example, a tiny revision illustrated a small gain in brevity and responsibility.

> I saw her and she was carrying a kitten. It had a crooked tail . . .

became

> When I saw her she was carrying a kitten with a crooked tail.

Maybe the greatest change here is in the tone; the writer seems to be controlling something, not merely rattling on.

Here is a passage from a student theme in which the writer dumps things together without showing relationships. He wastes words by repetition, and he wastes the power in those words by poor organization.

> The building was still burning and firemen couldn't put it out. An hour or so went by. The National Guard looked nervous and young. They drove around in their jeeps with their guns. They tried to look tough. We didn't know if their guns were loaded or not. They were scary just because they had guns but they looked scared themselves. They were about the same age as the students. Yet they were guarding them.

Because the relationship between remarks is often vague in this passage, we could not rewrite it with certainty unless we knew more facts, or the feelings the author tried to express. Reading the passage, we may doubt that the student had arranged the facts in his mind with clarity, or had understood his feelings. Later, he revised the passage, and his sentence structure accounted for much of the improvement — though as with writing always, the *whole* assembles everything we label; the whole is better, partly because of sentence structure.

As we watched the building burn for hours, the firemen standing by helpless, we became aware of the patrolling jeeps of the National Guard, young men the same age as the students they were guarding, young men who tried to act tough but looked as frightened of their guns as we were.

The gain in economy and vividness is great, and so is the gain in clarity of thought and feeling.

—— EXERCISES ——

1. Revise the following passage to introduce varied sentence structure. Use variation not just for its own sake, but to make the writing more precise. Remember that commas, semicolons, colons, and periods are aids to rhythm, and therefore to meaning, to expressiveness, and to clarity.

Every man who worked on the docks had to wear a hard hat. He also had to wear heavy canvas gloves. The hats protected the men from falling objects. Sometimes crates fell into the hole. Sometimes steel beams were swung down to the dock on cables. There was danger of metal splinters and serious abrasions. These dangers were increased because the longshoremen might work for 12 hours straight. They might work from 6 P.M. to 6 A.M. Some of the men also had jobs during the day. And many of the men drank heavily. This was because they got depressed. Sometimes there would be a shipment of whiskey. The men might pretend to have an accident. They would let a crate fall. It would break open. They would stash the unbroken bottles. And they would hide them. They would drink some when the officials were not around. The officials were paid by the shipping companies. They didn't want to be blamed for missing goods.

2. Find and identify, in the passage you made from exercise 1, a subordinate clause, a main clause, an appositive, a participle, and an adjective with a preposition. If you cannot find one of each, revise the passage to include them.

3. Examine these passages to discover the way sentence structure and variation express the content.

a. Shortly, everybody in Coach House Road was aware that Eli Peck, the nervous young attorney with the pretty wife, was having a breakdown. Everybody except Eli Peck. He knew what he did was not insane, though he felt every inch of its strangeness. He felt those black clothes as if they were the skin of his skin — the give and pull as they got used to where he bulged and buckled. And he felt eyes, every eye on Coach House Road. He saw headlights screech to within an inch of him, and stop. He saw mouths: first the bottom jaw slides forward, then the tongue hits the teeth, the lips explode, a little thunder in the throat, and they've said it: Eli Peck Eli Peck Eli Peck Eli Peck. He began to walk slowly, shifting his weight down and forward with each syllable: E-li-Peck-E-li-Peck. Heavily he trod, and as his neighbors uttered each syllable of his name, he felt each syllable shaking all his bones. He knew who he was down to his marrow — they were telling him. Eli Peck. He wanted them to say it a thousand times, a million times, he would walk forever in that black suit, as adults whispered of his strangeness and children made, "Shame . . . shame" with their fingers.

Philip Roth, "Eli, the Fanatic"

b. And then the Arab drew his knife and held it up toward me, athwart the sunlight.

A shaft of light shot upward from the steel, and I felt as if a long, thin blade transfixed my forehead. At the same moment all the sweat that had accumulated in my eyebrows splashed down on my eyelids, covering them with a warm film of moisture. Beneath a veil of brine and tears my eyes were blinded; I was conscious only of the cymbals of the sun clashing on my skull, and, less distinctly, of the keen blade of light flashing up from the knife, scarring my eyelashes, and gouging into my eyeballs.

Albert Camus, *The Stranger*

c. Familiarity has perhaps bred contempt in us Americans: until you have had a washing machine, you cannot imagine how little difference it will make to you. Europeans still believe that money brings happiness, witness the bought journalist, the bought politician, the bought general, the whole venality of European literary life, inconceivable in this country of the dollar. It is true that America produces and consumes more cars, soap, and bathtubs than any other nation, but we live among these objects rather than by them. Americans build skyscrapers; Le Corbusier worships them. Ehrenburg, our Soviet critic, fell in love with the Check-O-Mat in American railway stations, writing home paragraphs of song to this gadget — while deploring American materialism. When an American heiress wants to buy a man, she at once crosses the Atlantic. The only really materialistic people I have ever met have been Europeans.

Mary McCarthy, "America the Beautiful" in *On the Contrary*

5

Paragraphs

USES OF PARAGRAPHS

The paragraph is a small box of sentences, making a whole shape that is at the same time part of another whole. It is a miniature essay itself, with its own variable structure.

In that bible for stylists, *Modern English Usage*, H. W. Fowler writes, "The purpose of the paragraph is to give the reader a rest." I called the paragraph a mini-essay; it is also a maxi-sentence: the blank space at the end of the paragraph, before we indent and begin a new one, is like the period ending the sentence, only longer. Paragraphs punctuate, not by a mark but by arrangement on the page. Paragraphs, like sentences, tell us that something completes itself. The paragraph tells us that we have come to the end of a group of statements composing a larger statement; now the reader must pause a moment, and see what the paragraph was doing.

Look at the preceding paragraph. Its organization is only one of many possible, but it is a common one. It begins with a quotation from Fowler, which announces the purpose of the paragraph. Then it compares paragraph and sentence. Fowler does not make such a comparison; my paragraph develops the comparison from Fowler's word "rest." The last sentence suggests the function that rest fills. A paragraph elaborates and supports the first sentence, and the pause at the end should grant us a sense of wholeness.

Paragraphs rest the eye as well as the brain. Unbroken print leaves no landmarks for the eye that wanders and returns; we sometimes find ourselves using a finger to keep to the correct line. Though context gives us other reasons for longer or shorter paragraphs, paragraphs are useful as visual aids to comfort in reading. Those little identations are hand- and footholds in the cliff-face of the essay.

FOCUSING WITH PARAGRAPHS

Paragraphs become units of thought and feeling. The content makes the paragraph, and paragraphs become ways of organizing our complexity (for ourselves and for others) into units we can comprehend. One breakthrough in writing an essay comes when we see which part belongs with which part. We take tiny pieces, and assemble them into larger units, and assemble the larger units into the focused paper. The middle unit is the paragraph. It associates detail into order; it concentrates; it begins to narrow our focus. We may start with notes like these (from an autobiographical essay):

> summer I was eight
> going hunting with my uncle
> gun laws and the NRA
> the bounty on coyotes
> my .22
> killing the coyote pup
> how I felt afterward
> my uncle and the VFW
> fourth of July parade

Before we can order the whole essay, we must associate these small units with each other. If these notes are on file cards, we can simply make piles of them. Each pile would be a potential paragraph. If the notes are listed on a piece of paper or in a notebook, we can associate one with the other by lettering and numbering each item, linking like to like with the same number. The most obvious order might start with the old summer, and hunting with an uncle and a new .22, then switch moods to tell an anecdote of killing a coyote pup, then consider gun laws and the National Rifle Association; then it might mention a parade of VFW members, including the uncle, carrying rifles. A different order might begin with the recent parade, and return to the memory. Any order is arbitrary, but some orders are better than others. I wish to show here not so much a *best* ordering of the whole, as a useful, preliminary sorting of material into units, small collections of notes, which may turn out to be paragraphs. For instance:

B_1	summer I was eight
B_3	going hunting with my uncle
D	gun laws and the NRA
C_1	the bounty on coyotes
B_2	my .22
C_2	killing the coyote pup
C_3	how I felt afterward
A_2	my uncle and the VFW
A_1	fourth of July parade

This way is only one of many. It is the second ordering suggested, from parade to memory. The units represented by the capital letters are not necessarily single paragraphs. Maybe A would be two paragraphs — first a description of the VFW parading, the uncle puffing along in step, and then a close up on the uncle, leading to a memory. The items grouped under C — the anecdote about killing a coyote pup and the consequent feelings — might take several paragraphs. But regardless of how many paragraphs each subject takes, the *order* would be:

fourth of July parade
my uncle and the VFW

summer I was eight
my .22
going hunting with my uncle

the bounty on coyotes
killing the coyote pup
how I felt afterwards

gun laws and the NRA

Many a beginning writer, or a writer who has not learned to paragraph, might write the essay following the order in which the notes originally appeared. The result would be chaos, moving back and forth in time by random association. That is the way we talk, thinking of points afterward and crying, "Oh, I forgot to say . . . !" But writing is harder, and requires organization. The paragraph is our middle unit of organization between sentences that incorporate raw data and the finished, shapely essay. In developing explanation or narration, the rest or the handhold lets the reader know that a limited subject has been dealt with, finished or put on hold, and that we now move to another topic — perhaps arising from the last one, perhaps in contrast to it, certainly different. The paragraph becomes a semantic unit. It carries meaning. The look of it on the page makes a statement; it tells us that a topic, or a detachable unit of an argument, or that an event, or a detachable unit of an event, is complete here. Like commas and sentence structure, paragraphs create meaning in our prose.

In order to make statements with paragraphs, we must be able to construct good ones. The paragraph must have *unity,* and for unity we often require a *topic sentence.* The paragraph must have coherence within itself, and a series of paragraphs must cohere to form the essay; *coherence* requires *transitions.* Finally, we must learn to *develop* the paragraph until it is adequate in its fullness and in its *length,* and until it presents its material in the best possible *order.*

UNITY IN THE PARAGRAPH

In pursuing unity of thought and of feeling, the paragraph must contain nothing extraneous. The writer must omit the odd fact which happens to be true, but which is irrelevant to the topic. The odd fact violates unity, and distracts the reader.

> We never had enough time to eat lunch in high school: half of the time I'd get a stomachache from hurriedly wolfing down the food. The food was lousy, anyway. We complained to the administration, but it didn't do any good. We were often held up in getting into the cafeteria because the lunchroom helpers were slow in getting the tables and the food ready. Then, if you were one of the people who got in toward the end, you would have to wait a long time in line. Sometimes the jocks, who acted as lunchroom police, would hold you up, too, trying to bully you into buying a football schedule.

The sentence about the food being lousy doesn't fit here; it is a digression from the topic, "We never had enough time to eat lunch in high school."

We must remain alert, to maintain a unity of subject matter in our paragraphs, because the associations in our thought constantly lead us into irrelevance. When we begin to write about a subject, our mind drifts from one thought to another, by personal association. We ramble, we appear disorganized, because our impressions are unified *only* by personal association. Because the reader does not share our private memories and feelings, he cannot see the connections we make — and we fail to make contact with the reader. Here is an example from a student theme.

> All of the recent concern over the slaughter of whales whose species are nearly extinct has reminded me of my childhood interest in whales and other wild animals, especially animals who prey. I was particularly fascinated by the killer whales, which travel in packs like wolves, often attacking larger whales. They will tear off the lips and tongue first, their favorite parts. But man has been almost solely responsible for the dangerous depletion of some of the whale populations, such as the blue whale. Still, I can remember the fear that animals like puff adders, tarantulas, and sharks could inspire in me as a child. So I wonder if, in certain cases, we aren't being hypocritical for blaming the people who actually live in lands inhabited by animals like tigers and wolves for killing them. We might be just as frightened and irrational as they are. But that still doesn't make it right.

The thoughts in this paragraph make connections for the writer, but not for the reader. The writer jumps from the threat to whale populations to his childhood interests, then to the habits of killer whales, then to questions of man's rational and irrational fears of predatory animals. To write a unified paragraph, he would have to decide what the topic of his paragraph ought to be, and then stick to that topic. We cannot expect readers to be patient with a rambling, disorganized paragraph, nor can we expect them to read our minds, and recognize an order that is personal to us.

Exposition and argument need especially careful paragraphing, because the writer must carry the reader's mind along a path that leads to understanding or agreement. Paragraphs in argument or exposition are mini-essays. They deal with one topic, or with closely related data, or with an integral segment of a topic. The paragraph is homogeneous. It is orderly — and we must remember that there are many varieties of order. (See Some Ways to Develop Paragraphs, pages 202–207.)

Unity and Topic Sentences

Probably the most common paragraph construction begins with a topic sentence, which brings to the paragraph not only order but also unity. The topic sentence announces the topic and an attitude toward it. Several sentences follow to explain, elaborate, or enumerate examples or analogies supporting the topic sentence. Then a final sentence draws the elaboration to a conclusion, in a way that leads to the next paragraph. Here is a paragraph that begins with a topic sentence.

> To live in America today is to be constantly impressed by the ability of the superfluous to displace the useful, and by the ease with which the gratuitous can triumph over the imperative. Witness the growth of the so-called leisure-time industries, most of which exist to fill the emptiness left by a diminishing sense of purpose. Our media afford some familiar examples: our TV news is presented to us as a sideshow of irrelevancies, and what news there is comes presoftened; the richness of the real world eludes our major novelists, so circumscribed are they by an illusory circle of their own making. Our public demonstrations were once aimed at such self-evident evils as hunger, racism, and war. Now we object to the "potential" harm (and presumably to the potential benefit) that may be caused by the nuclear-power industry. We call for an end to the potential dangers of recombinant DNA research, which recently gave us unlimited supplies of insulin. At the same time we accept without fuss the auto industry's abolition of that lifesaving device, the serviceable car bumper.
>
> Peter McCabe, "Vanity Fair" in *Harper's*

The author supports an elegant topic sentence with a quick series of examples.

Many variations upon this order are possible. Variations are also desirable, because a long essay composed of paragraphs equal in length and identical in construction would be boring. Sometimes a topic sentence is not present, or is understood or implied, in much the same way as a transition can sometimes be understood. A writer may mention that he spent a day in the town of Omaha, then follow with this paragraph.

> The visitor can enjoy the aroma of the stockyards. He can watch the rich sit at their clubs, drinking gin next to pools of chlorine, beside flat golf courses. The visitor can walk up the sides of ugly buildings on dry Sundays. He can watch grass grow, at least in early spring and early fall. He can listen to the medley of transistor radios in several parks. He can try sleeping for a week or so, until he is able to leave.

He needs no topic sentence; we already know what the topic is. The topic is the place, and the paragraph has unity because we can see that every sentence describes an activity possible in this place.

Sometimes we find a topic sentence ending the paragraph, as a summary. We can create drama or tension by starting with the arguments and details, and building to a conclusion. Here is a paragraph about government funding for the arts; in which the author gathers information and opinions toward a conclusion; her final sentence locates the topic of the paragraph.

> The virtue of the American program has been in stimulating competition, initiative, and originality in the arts across the nation. On the negative side, because of the project-only philosophy of the Endowment, many ill-suited institutions have been forced into annual paroxysms of justification to get money earmarked for this or that passing "great idea," while, bit by bit, the economic foundations of their operations have been caving in. The resulting competition for short funds now threatens to destroy that carefully achieved harmony of opposites among the constituencies in the arts.
>
> Eleanor Munro, "Money for Art's Sake"

Notice how this structure involves us. We are pulled into its movement by the suspense, not knowing exactly where the argument will lead us. The author seems to carry us with her, and our ideas seem to arise from the material, just as hers do.

For the opposite effect, look back at the paragraph quoted from Peter McCabe. Paragraphs that begin with topic sentences differ greatly, in rhythm and in tone, from paragraphs that end with them. McCabe tells us our destination as we start; he begins with his primary idea, and then fleshes it out.

The McCabe and Munro paragraphs have different purposes, which make their different structures appropriate. McCabe wants to inform and explain; it makes sense for him to let us know where we stand as soon as possible, to give us a sure basis from which to proceed. But Munro wants to persuade us to share not only her ideas but her sympathies. It makes sense for her to keep us off balance at first, and to involve us in the accumulating fabric of her thought and feeling.

Sometimes the topic sentence can come in the middle of a paragraph, where it provides summary or generalization tying together the particulars that come before and after.

> We hesitated before we stepped into the garden, so heavy was the odor of flowering quince. The garden was orderly, comfortable, and gorgeous, with little benches artfully placed for the weary guest. *Our host, as generous as he was clever, introduced us to his hobby.* We toured among hardy perennials, and walked past an

nual borders. We strolled among fig trees, past palms, to a density of shrubs. We floated in joy on the tropical air.

Hermann von Kreicke, *The Migrant Swan*

Sometimes we even find the topic sentence at the end of the previous paragraph. The paragraph break serves almost as a colon.

In general, chronology is the most satisfactory organization. *However, we must not rely on it alone.*

We would reduce our psychological world to the order of the clock. We would become slaves of "then" and "afterwards." . . .

The first two sentences in the second paragraph elaborate the negative topic sentence which ends the first paragraph, but which could have introduced the second paragraph just as well.

We have been talking mostly about exposition and argument. In narrative and descriptive writing, topic sentences often change the scene, introduce signposts in complicated country. Here are some sentences that could be lead-ins to new paragraphs.

Finally, he thought it was time to return.

The weather turned fine.

When they turned the corner, the street changed abruptly.

Election night began with a bad omen.

When he heard footsteps outside in the darkness, he turned off the oil lamps and reached for his gun.

The final chapters seem pointless.

In argument or exposition, the topic sentences have the flavor of philosophical propositions. For instance:

When a man needs help, he must know where to turn.

The nineteenth-century politician's Biblical oratory is no longer effective.

The paragraph is a unit of sense, a discrete idea or topic.

When we revise our prose, it is useful to look into our paragraphs for topic sentences. We do not demand that every paragraph have one — but the *idea* of a topic sentence is an idea of focus and unity, and therefore essential to clear and forceful prose. We look for the topic sentence of a paragraph — overt or implicit, at beginning, middle, or end — to see if the paragraph is sufficiently unified.

COHERENCE IN THE PARAGRAPH

Frequently, in unfinished writing, a sentence seems extraneous or irrelevant; the writer has a use for the information, but he has been unable to build the sentence smoothly into his thought. If a fact does not belong in a paragraph, it causes disunity. If it only *seems* not to belong, it causes incoherence.

The writer must learn how to blend his information so that it coheres in a meaningful whole: the relationship between the sentences must be clear, and the paragraph must seem a whole, not just a collection of individual sentences. Here is a paragraph, from some daily writing, which has little coherence.

> I had been having severe headaches and frequent dizzy spells. I was terrified of doctors. I went to the health clinic. I waited three days. It was the time of finals and I was very busy. I saw a doctor. He prescribed some pills. The problems continued.

It is impossible to tell what the relationships are between the bits of information related here. Did the speaker wait three days before or after going to the health clinic? Did he wait because of his fear of doctors or because he was busy? Was he busy studying for finals, or doing something else? Not only is the sense confused, but the rhythm is irritatingly choppy. Here is a revised and more coherent version of the passage.

> I had been having severe headaches and frequent dizzy spells, but I hesitated to go to the health clinic because I was terrified of doctors. It was the time of finals and I was busy studying for them, so I made the excuse to myself that I didn't have time and that there was nothing the matter with me, just fatigue. Finally, I went, although I waited three days before making an appointment. I saw a doctor, and after he examined me he prescribed some pills. But despite the medication, the problems continued, even after I'd been taking the pills for two weeks.

Notice that much of the coherence comes from using conjunctions and subordinate clauses. Although most facts remain the same, the author has given the reader much more information, because he has connected the facts in a coherent paragraph, using complex sentences and transitions. The revision illustrates how a writer can take a mere list of facts, and by keeping his audience in mind, build them into a **statement** that leaves no question unanswered. In revising, the writer found it necessary to add a few facts — that he was busy studying for exams, that he took the pills for two weeks — which he had omitted from the original paragraph, before he had realized that his audience would need to know them.

We achieve coherence, in our writing, when our paragraphs answer the questions that they raise in the reader's mind. If we merely write,

> I was terrified of doctors. I went to the health clinic.

the reader is going to ask, "If you're so afraid of doctors, what compelled you to go?" If we don't answer the invisible question, the paragraph will lack coherence, and the reader will be frustrated or confused.

Similarly, when we make a general assertion, we create the expectation that we will defend it. The reader expects us to justify or explain a statement like, "The public was responsible for the war's continuation," or "Statistics show us that cassettes will eventually drive out the eight-track." The reader does not, presumably, know as much as we know about our chosen subject; we must give the detail, background, statistics, reasons, or explanations that our audience requires and expects of us. We write exposition to deliver information or ideas to other people.

We establish another type of expectation when we use an extended metaphor to enliven and organize a paragraph. Here is a passage from a student theme.

> The beast of civil war lay outside the sheepfold, and its roaring could be heard within the gates. At first its voice, as it had begun to slink out of the foothills, had been low and faint. Then, as it drew nearer to the town, the explosions of large artillery shells had been its approaching steps, and the different pitches of the voice — the snarling of machine guns, the howls of mortar shells — had grown distinct. Now the beast clawed at the walls and breathed heavily on the gates with its mouth aflame. The sheep within huddled together, knowing their throats would soon feel the enemy's teeth, knowing the shepherd had fallen asleep.

The extended metaphor compares the enemy to a predatory beast, the city to a sheepfold, and its citizens to helpless sheep. The metaphor makes another kind of coherence, which we would violate if we shifted metaphors in the middle of the paragraph.

. . . At first its voice, as it had begun to slink out of the foothills, had been low and faint. Then, as it drew nearer, the internal machine could be heard stomping out death on the plain with the press of bombs, and the different sounds — the grinding of machine gun fire, the chunking of mortars — had grown distinct. Now the beast clawed. . . .

Coherence and Consistency

We should know a few more mechanical ways in which coherence can be maintained in the paragraph. Just as we need agreement within a sentence, we need agreement within a paragraph. We should stick to the same verb tense. It is easy, if we let our minds wander, to begin writing a passage or paragraph in one tense and then switch to another. We may begin in the present tense to be dramatic, and then slip into the past tense because the events described actually occurred in the past.

> He sits on the dock, his feet bare on the warm wood, his eyes half-closed in the hot sun, daydreaming about women in black silk dresses. Suddenly he felt a violent tugging on the pole, and a long shape thrashed in the water ten feet away.

Or we may begin in the past tense and abruptly shift to the present tense, without realizing it, because we want greater immediacy.

> He sat on the dock, his feet bare on the warm wood, his eyes half-closed in the hot sun, and daydreamed about women in black silk dresses. Suddenly he feels a violent tugging on the pole, and sees a long shape thrash in the water only ten feet away

In rare instances, when skillfully done, a shift in verb tense can serve a purpose — but almost always such shifts are only mistakes that proofreading should correct.

Another common violation of coherence is to shift pronouns within a paragraph. If we start with "we," we should not switch to "you." We must be careful, if we have chosen to use the formal "one," that we do not fall back into "I" or "you."

> But if *one* has experienced the mystical conversion described by adepts in almost every culture in the world, *one* may still fall back into the old dualities and pettinesses. But once we have felt that stronger intensity of being, *you* can never again remain satisfied

with less. The ghost of that experience haunts *us* like a dead loved one.

Coherence and the Paragraph: Transitions

Transitions in our writing are devices for moving from one place to another. They range from single words like "but" to phrases like "on the other hand," and to more subtle devices like repetition or parallelism. Transitions are essential to the coherence of paragraph and paper. You might expect to find this topic with the last chapter, on sentences, or with the next chapter, on whole essays, but I put it here because transitions happen *within* the paragraph as a way to move from one sentence to another, or *between* paragraphs, as a way of moving from topic to topic while keeping the essay whole. *And transitions are essential to coherence in paragraph and paper.* A prose insufficient in transitions is nervous and obscure. It leaps from subject to subject, without stated or implied connection. The connection remains in the writer's mind.

Overt Transitions. Often a transition needs to be obvious, to carry the reader along our passage of thought, to make sure we don't lose him. Perhaps we are making an overt contrast. To draw attention to the contrast, we say, "on the one hand / on the other" — which is trite but hard to avoid. Or we use the context of our discussion: "Although most transitions are best left implicit, some are properly overt."

Often we need overt transitions when ideas or actions conflict, when the essay's meaning depends upon fully exploiting the reality in that conflict. Or if we are piling detail upon detail, we might want to use a transition that calls attention to our multiplicity: "not only . . . but also." Prose that explains, reasons, or argues frequently uses overt transitions. In this example, the transitional phrases are in italics:

> This attitude makes him a kind of "Pop automatist," *and he is heir to other aspects of Surrealism as well.*
> *Unlike most of the Surrealists, however,* and unlike their successors in the "messy" vein, for instance, Oldenburg is not dependent on juxtaposition for effect. *Like all the Pop artists* he takes his objects whole and unadorned. *But unlike most of them,* he has never made the complete transition from rough to pristine handling. . . .
>
> Lucy R. Lippard, *Pop Art*

Repeated Words or Phrases. One way to achieve continuity within a paragraph (or between paragraphs), to make transitions between sentences and between statements, is to repeat words or phrases. One of the simplest of these devices, so simple that we might not think of it as one, is repeating pronouns. We use it for both economy and continuity.

> But towards Aumeister the paths were solitary and still, and *Aschenbach* strolled thither, stopping awhile to watch the lively crowds in the restaurant garden with its fringe of carriages and cabs. Thence *he* took *his* homeward way outside the park and across the sunset fields. By the time *he* reached the North Cemetery, however, *he* felt tired, and a storm was brewing above Föhring, so *he* waited at the stopping-place for a tram to carry *him* back to the city.
>
> Thomas Mann, "Death in Venice" (italics added)

But you should be careful when using a repeated pronoun, because if it is repeated too often it can become monotonous. You can get variety by occasionally using the name the pronoun refers to; Mann, in the story from which I've just quoted, uses "Aschenbach" every now and then instead of "he" or "him." You can also use constructions like "His nose itched" rather than "He felt his nose itching" to avoid using "he" too much. A writer also has to make sure that the reader knows what each pronoun refers to. If we say "Mr. Cortazar saw that the man was following him closely; he stared at him," it is not clear who is doing the staring. Here we may need to be more explicit: "Mr. Cortazar saw that the man was following him closely; Mr. Cortazar stared at him."

Any word or phrase, not just pronouns, can be repeated to make effective transitions — if it is important to the meaning or the emotional tenor in the passage.

> If we once accept the premise that we can build a better world by using the different gifts of each *sex*, we shall have two kinds of freedom, freedom to use untapped gifts of each *sex*, and freedom to admit freely and cultivate in each *sex* their special superiorities. We may well find that there are certain fields, such as the physical sciences, mathematics and instrumental music, in which *men* by virtue of their *sex*, as well as by virtue of their qualities as specially gifted human beings, will always have that razor-edge of extra gift which makes all the difference.

. . .

This has meant that *men* had to be willing to choose, win, and keep women as *lovers,* protect and provide for them as *husbands,* and protect and provide for their children as *fathers.* It has meant that women have had to be willing to accept *men* as lovers, live with them as wives, and conceive, bear, feed, and cherish their children. Any society disappears which fails to make these demands on its members and to receive this much from them.

But from *men,* society has also asked and received something more than this. For thousands of generations *men* have been asked to do something more than be good *lovers* and *husbands* and *fathers,* even with all that that involved of husbandry and organization and protection against attack. . . .

Margaret Mead, *Male and Female* (italics added)

If we want to avoid monotonous exact repetition, we can use variations (near-synonyms) for the key words in some places.

His *sculptures* seem like men and women stripped naked. They are *works of art* that seem to lack all artifice, *plastic creations* which, in their emotional if not in their physical presence, have the feeling of natural, organic creations.

These methods are commonly used for transition *between* paragraphs as well.

. . . and the importance of spatial form in *modern* literature.
Modern thought, as well, has used the metaphor of dimensionality. . . .

Parallel Constructions. We can repeat structures as well as words. Parallel constructions (see Parallelism, pages 152–158) can fulfill a need for transition that is not only structural and logical, but emotional; passages with parallel sentences can work like sentences with parallel phrases, to produce a dramatic effect, or to maintain emotional tension.

Today, now that he is no longer among us, *who can replace* my old friend at the gates of this kingdom? *Who will look after* the garden until we can get back to it? . . .

Albert Camus, "Encounters with André Gide"
(italics added)

We describe how the poor are plundered *by the rich. We live among the rich.* Live on the plunder and pander ideas *to the rich. We have described* the *torture* and we have put our names under appeals against *torture,* but we did not stop it. (And we ourselves became *torturers* when the higher interests demanded torture and we became the ideologists of torture.) Now *we once more can analyze* the world situation and and *describe* the wars and explain why the many are poor and hungry. But we do no more.

We are not the bearers of consciousness. We are the whores of reason.

Jan Myrdal, *Confessions of a Disloyal European*
(italics added)

Parallel contructions that repeat part of a phrase are common and useful transitions, especially in exposition and in argument.

. . . and they never decided whether they were *Bulgarians or Americans, rich or poor, artists or dilettantes.*

And we, on our part, could not decide whether they were *heroes or frauds. . . .*

On our part, in the last sentence, is an overt transition.

Transitional Words and Phrases. We use many transitional phrases to establish the relationship between sentences and between paragraphs, and to prepare the reader for shifts in subject or meaning. The most common are words like "and," "but," "or," and "for." Some are words of sequence and time — "meanwhile," "afterward," "before"; of qualification — "again," "also," "nonetheless"; and of reasoning — "for example," "because," "therefore." Although we often try to avoid phrases like these in fiction or narrative, they are useful and often essential to exposition or argument. Their very commonness and simplicity make them valuable to clarify a sequence of thought. These paragraph openings use common phrases to accomplish transitions; they are taken from *The Naked Ape* by Desmond Morris:

Up to this point I have been concentrating on the social aspects of comfort behaviour in our species . . .

In addition to problems of keeping clean, the general category of comfort behaviour also includes . . .

Because of his exploratory and opportunist nature, the naked ape's list of prey species is immense . . .

For the next major category, that of parasites . . .

In order to find the answer to this question we must first assemble some facts . .

We commonly use comparison and contrast for transitions, especially in criticism and analysis. The means of transition are relatively simple. We describe one of the objects for examination in one paragraph and then, in a following paragraph, compare and contrast traits of the other. When we turn to the second object, we often begin with one of the transitional phrases that make for comparison or contrast, like "similarly," "in the same vein," or "however," "on the other hand," "in contrast," or "contrary to."

> Freud gave a picture of the unconscious mind as containing primarily memories and the remnants of suppressed desires. He saw the sexual drives as being the foundation of the unconscious.
>
> Jung, *on the other hand,* claimed that Freud's depth psychology wasn't deep enough, that there was another aspect of the unconscious which contained spiritual drives as important as the sexual drives. . . .

Remember that even in expository prose it is better to leave out well-worn phrases *if the sense is just as clear without them.* Many times, we can cut out the obvious direction signals, and rely on implicit transition.

Some of the most obvious clues to transition — within the paragraph or between paragraphs — are words of sequence, like "therefore," "later," "so," "then," and "next." They are so obvious that it is pleasant to do without them, if we can.

Implicit Transitions. The order within the paragraph can itself be a means of transition. It gives the paragraph motion; it gives a reason for one sentence following another: left to right, down to up, smaller to larger: or other sorts of order: color to shape, spring to summer to fall to winter; or orders of ideas: from more obvious to less obvious; from less complex to more complex. These motions are clear enough in themselves to allow the movement from subject to subject without explicit directions. We need not say "after spring came summer" within a paragraph, unless we are writing for people we can presume unaware of the order the seasons follow. We would be more likely to move from rain and early flowers to the longest day of the year, to hot sun and to swimming and to no school.

Sometimes the rest between paragraphs acts as transition. We take a breath, and we pivot on the pause. It shows that we are moving from one grouping to another. We don't always have to be reminded that we are moving. Sometimes we do, and sometimes we do not. Develop *tact* for transitions. Develop a sense also for the multiple means of transition. A good writer uses implicit, overt, parallel, repetitive — and many other forms of transition, and uses them in rapid sequence as he moves through his paragraphs, and from paragraph to paragraph. Transitions in complex expository writing are constant and multiple, overt and implicit. Much that is implied depends on the best order of thinking, and a clear sense of what the reader needs to know.

Suppose we catalogue everything in a boy's pockets. The next paragraph could begin, "Therefore, his pockets bulged as he walked, and he bumped into tables when he passed them. In fact, he bumped into almost everything. . . ." The paragraph could go on about his clumsiness. But the "therefore" at the beginning is unnecessary. It is obvious, if I have catalogued twenty items, that these items bulge out his pockets. Transition can be found in image. No reader need be led by the hand so carefully. The paragraph break could read like this:

> He had on his person two rubber bands, a golf tee, two notes from a teacher, a bottle cap, and a gray-brown handkerchief.
> His pockets bulged as he walked, and he bumped into tables when he passed them. In fact, he bumped into almost everything.

The word "his," referring to an antecedent in the previous paragraph, holds the two paragraphs together.

Transitions are a glue that holds parts together. You need enough, or the parts will fall apart. But if you have too much, you will see the glue instead of the parts. The space between the catalogue and the bulging pockets is a sort of invisible glue — but it holds, because we have sense enough to know that the objects listed cause the bulging. The next transition, from pockets to clumsiness, is less obvious and more necessary. It takes more doing. The only thing that bulging pockets share with clumsiness is that the little boy possesses both of them. Of course we could use a generality for a transition.

> . . . a bottle camp, and a gray-brown handkerchief.
> In fact, he was generally rather gross and clumsy. He bumped into everything. . . .

This transition would work, but it is not elegant. It is obvious and general. Suppose in the next paragraph we want to talk about his table manners, do we say again that he was "gross and clumsy"? No, we have used these words up. The stylish transition happens without drawing attention to itself. We move from pockets to bumping into things by picturing the boy bumping into tables with his fat pockets, and then we do a turn on the word "bumping" and we are off into a new subject before the reader knows it. He has been led from one subject to another by the elbow, as a kindly person helps a blind man across the street. But if we have done the job well, the reader does not feel the guiding fingers touch his arm.

DEVELOPMENT IN THE PARAGRAPH

Once we pass beyond the single sentence, we become involved in development and its problems. We discussed development in earlier sections of this chapter, when we mentioned using topic sentences to achieve unity and explaining general statements to achieve coherence. The requirements of unity and coherence overlap with the requirements of development. As we must develop paragraphs to substantiate generalizations, so we must develop paragraphs to make our associations clear to the reader. Frequently, we lack fullness of development because we do not take the reader into account. We put forward a generalization, perhaps, and a conclusion that we have arrived at, but we do not lead the reader through the process of thinking that leads from introduction to conclusion. Perhaps in our own thinking we have leapt from generalization to conclusion by intuition — but the reader will not necessarily leap along with us.

Eventually, as we go over development, we will need to investigate length and order. But first, we must list methods for developing paragraphs.

Some Ways to Develop Paragraphs

We can develop a paragraph in countless ways. No list can be comprehensive. But looking at some methods of paragraph development can help us to see the range of possibilities. The type of development we choose — the *how* in the paragraph — depends on the material we are using — the *what* in the paragraph, and the purpose we have in mind — the *why* of the paragraph. If we are listing Paraguay's annual imports, we develop by listing, and not by comparison and contrast. *The container takes its shape from what it contains.* One of our tasks in organizing a paper is to find the means of development that is *most appropriate to our material.*

We need to list some useful ways to develop paragraphs. We have mentioned chronology, and we have mentioned spatial contiguity. On occasion the reader must learn *what* something is; the writer must develop a paragraph by means of definition. Sometimes a reader needs to know what something is *like;* the writer must develop a paragraph of comparison, or comparison and contrast. Sometimes the reader needs to know the *parts* of a thing, what makes it up; the writer must supply analysis. Or the writer must use *classification,* he must tell us the species of something perhaps; is it animal or vegetable? Sometimes we must develop our notion of a thing by discussing its *cause* and its *effect*. Here are examples of paragraph development by these rhetorical forms and others.

We may organize a paragraph to *make an assertion and give reasons:*

> The country is vastly indebted to him [Louis Brandeis] for his creative work in the field of labor relations, in dispelling misunderstanding between management and labor, and in making collective bargaining an effective instrument for industrial peace. He successfully arbitrated or conciliated many labor disputes. In 1910 he was arbiter of a serious strike in the New York City garment trade. Not content with settling the immediate dispute, he devised the famous "protocol" for the permanent government of labor relations in the industry, with provision for the preferential union shop, for a Joint Board of Sanitary Control, and for a continuing Board of Arbitration composed of representatives of the public as well as of the employers and the union. The procedures thus developed and successfully tested served as a model in other industries. For several years he served as impartial chairman of this board of arbitration.
>
> Irwin H. Pollock, *The Brandeis Reader*

The writer begins with a contention, and then substantiates it by reciting information upon which he bases it.

Or to *make a statement and then give relevant facts:*

> Gandhi recognized that the whites in South Africa thought they needed protection against a majority consisting of Negroes and Indians. The province of Natal, in 1896, had 400,000 Negro inhabitants, 51,000 Indians, and 50,000 whites. The Cape of Good Hope Colony had 900,000 Negroes, 10,000 Indians, and 400,000 Europeans; the Transvaal Republic 650,000 Negroes, 5,000 Indians, and 120,000 whites. In 1944, the five million Negroes hopelessly outnumbered the million and a quarter whites.
>
> Louis Fischer, *Gandhi: His Life and Message for the World*

This last category resembles the one before it, except that "facts" (or statistics) take the place of "reasons," which are arguments based on a value put on events.

Or to *list:*

> Now the leadership elements of the Democratic Party began to filter through the suite of the nominee in a parade that was to last the rest of the day, to assist him in making up their mind. First of the big-city leaders to arrive was David Lawrence of Pennsylvania.

> Following him came the New York crowd — Wagner, Harriman,
> DeSapio and Prendergast; then William Green of Philadelphia;
> then DiSalle of Ohio; then Bailey and Ribicoff of Connecticut;
> then all the others.
>
>> Theodore H. White, *The Making of the President 1960*

First, White tells us what sort of men they are whose names will
follow, and then the occasion that brought the men together, and then
the names.

Even in the examples chosen, these methods are not exclusive.
One paragraph may use more than one method, or one method may
involve another. "Relevant facts" usually come in "lists." In this next
paragraph, the author develops the paragraph primarily by an assertion
followed by reasons, and his final sentence is a list.

> If conventions epitomize the mythology and legendry of Ameri-
> can national politics, then Chicago epitomizes the convention city.
> For one hundred years, ever since the nomination of Abraham Lin-
> coln at the Wigwam, it has been the favorite city of political con-
> vention-goers. Counting notches for fourteen Republican and nine
> Democratic national conventions in the last twenty-five quadren-
> nials, Chicago can boast that here were first named all the follow-
> ing Presidents of the United States: Lincoln, Grant, Garfield,
> Cleveland, Harrison, Theodore Roosevelt, Harding, Coolidge,
> Franklin D. Roosevelt, Truman and Eisenhower.
>
>> Theodore H. White, *The Making of the President 1960*

We can also develop paragraphs to *classify:*

> We can thus say that while the average human being is a mix-
> ture, some people are mainly "digestion-minded," some "muscle-
> minded," and some "brain-minded," and correspondingly diges-
> tion-bodied, muscle-bodied, or brain-bodied. The digestion-bodied
> people look thick; the muscle-bodied people look wide; and the
> brain-bodied people look long. This does not mean the taller a man
> is the brainier he will be. It means that if a man, even a short man,
> looks long rather than wide or thick, he will often be more con-
> cerned about what goes on in his mind than about what he does or
> what he eats; but the key factor is slenderness and not height. On
> the other hand, a man who gives the impression of being thick
> rather than long or wide will usually be more interested in a good
> steak than in a good idea or a good long walk.
>
>> Eric Berne, "Can People Be Judged by Their Appearance?"
>> in *A Layman's Guide to Psychiatry and Psychoanalysis*

Berne separates people into groups according to their bodily appearance, relating psychological classifications to physical ones.

This paragraph, from an essay about television advertising, is developed to *show cause and effect:*

> There is good reason to suspect that this manic obsession with cleanliness, fostered, quite naturally, by the giant soap and detergent interests, may bear some responsibility for the cultivated sloppiness of so many of the young in their clothing as well as in their chosen hideouts. The compulsive housewife who spends more time washing and vacuuming and polishing her possessions than communicating to, or stimulating her children creates a kind of sterility that the young would instinctively reject. The impeccably tidy home, the impeccably tidy lawn are — in a very real sense — unnatural and confining. Yet the commercials confront us with broods of happy children, some of whom — believe it or not — notice the new fresh smell their clean, white sweatshirts exhale thanks to Mom's new "softener."
>
> Marya Mannes, "Television Advertising: The Splitting Image"

In the course of her argument, the writer observes negative results of advertising, where an image of cleanliness leads to a slovenly reality. Or we can develop paragraphs to *compare and contrast:*

> In other respects, the film follows Hearst's career with mixed fidelity. The plot adjustments are significant. Both Hearst and Kane were only children, born in 1863, and both were expelled from Harvard. Hearst's father and mother were not, like Kane's, poverty-stricken boardinghouse keepers. George Hearst was a well-to-do farmer's son, whose silver strike at the Comstock lode made him a millionaire, and whose later interest in the Homestake Mine still further increased his massive fortune; he became a senator and earned a respected place in the American Dictionary of Biography. In the film these parents are left a deed to the Colorado Lode by a defaulting boarder, Fred Grange, and the Kane fortune is thus founded not by the acumen and push of a paternal figure but by blind chance.
>
> Charles Higham, *The Films of Orson Welles*

Comparison and contrast works when we talk about relationship or conflict, and are not merely separating facts about two or more subjects. Here, the first sentence states the mixture that is the paragraph's topic, and the rest of the paragraph gives examples of each ingredient in the mixture. Notice that the paragraph, when it compares and contrasts Hearst's life with Kane's, carefully maintains the order in which it first mentions them: Hearst-Kane. This order helps to avoid confusion, and makes for coherence.

Or to *analyze:*

> The nature of the inequality needs, however, to be understood precisely. The smaller firm will invest more adequately and thus produce more economically if it has the security of a contract on which it can reliably survive. The larger firm derives no advantage from negotiating a price lower than that at which the smaller firm can continue to supply the product. A contract that is so unfavorable or so inflexible that it destroys the small firm is self-defeating. The effect of power emerges in the way price is graded to need. The larger firm can calculate the income that the smaller firm requires for survival and minimal satisfaction of its affirmative purposes, and it does so as a matter of course. The small firm can make and enforce no similar calculation on the larger firm. The consequence is that a smaller firm doing business with a larger one will almost always have its returns more nearly at the necessary minimum than the larger firm doing business with the smaller one.
>
> John Kenneth Galbraith, *Economics and the Public Purpose*

We analyze when we need to explain or to demonstrate the mechanism inside a process or an act. We tell how it works rather than what it is. Here the author announces the need for better understanding, and then reasons step by step to show that larger firms have a bargaining advantage over smaller firms.

Or to *define or elucidate:*

> For eros is the power which *attracts* us. The essence of eros is that it draws us from ahead, whereas sex pushes us from behind. This is revealed in our day-to-day language when I say a person "allures" me or "entices" me, or the possibilities of a new job "invite" me. Something in me responds to the other person, or the job, and pulls me toward him or it. I participate in forms, possibilities, higher levels of meaning, on neurophysiological dimensions but also on aesthetic and ethical dimensions as well. As the Greeks believe, knowledge and even ethical goodness exercise such a pull. Eros is the drive toward union with what we belong to — union with our own possibilities, union with significant other persons in our world in relation to whom we discover our own self-fulfillment. Eros is the yearning in man which leads him to dedicate himself to seeking *arête,* the noble and good life.
>
> Rollo May, *Love and Will*

We are presented with a partial definition of *eros* at the start, but the idea is so large that it calls for further explanation. The paragraph expands and builds upon that original definition, until the author brings to his audience an adequate understanding of the word defined.

Or to make clear by *elaboration or rephrasing:*

> The "duende," then, is a power and not a construct, is a struggle and not a concept. I have heard an old guitarist, a true virtuoso, remark, "The 'duende' is not in the throat, the 'duende' comes from inside, up from the very soles of the feet." That is to say, it is not a question of aptitude, but of a true and viable style — of blood, in other words; of what is oldest in culture; of creation made act.
>
> Federico García Lorca,
> "The Duende: Theory and Divertissement"

Here, since the word names something more spiritual than intellectual — something harder to define than a concept — the author does not try so much to define and to elucidate as to name and rename, to offer description and metaphor, until we begin to comprehend the intangible.

Notice that in these quoted paragraphs the progress within the paragraph is the motion of thought. The exact detail, the example that locates the general in the particular, the comparison, the logical steps — these motions develop the thought and unify the paragraph at the same time. Paragraph development makes coherence.

Development: Length and Completeness

We need here to talk about paragraph length. Our paragraphs will vary in length, rarely following a set rule. The length must be *adequate*, first; we must take the time and space to flesh out our arguments, to justify our contentions, to explain our theories, or to describe our characters. We discussed this need for completeness in Coherence in the Paragraph, but we must repeat it here. We must never forget that the reader is another person, who must be given reasons if he is to be persuaded of our opinions, and must be given details if he is going to see what we see. We must not simply assert, "President Smith is the worst, most dishonest president we've had," and then propose to circumscribe his power. We must tell *why* he is so bad. We must supply reasons, facts, arguments, details — *adequate* to the assertion. We must develop the paragraph, to make our assertion coherent.

Undeveloped paragraphs bedevil beginning writers. Many times paragraphs remain undeveloped because the writer does not adequately imagine the reader. Here is a paragraph from a student theme.

> When you study dance, you learn either modern or classical ballet. Some people prefer one kind of dance and some another. I learned modern dance and I prefer it.

The writer continued the theme by describing the pleasures of modern dance. But her opening paragraph is undeveloped, and lacks a sense of audience, because it begs either for definition or for comparison and contrast. One or two sentences of development, giving the reader an insight into the difference between forms of dance, would establish the necessary background for the discussion of modern dance.

Less frequently, writers are afflicted with too much detail, so that the writing loses force. We must keep in mind what is important and what is not. We must give reasons, but not every one we can think of. We must give only so many as we need to make our point. With too many reasons the reader will be bored, or feel bullied.

To decide whether our detail is adequate — neither too little nor too much — we must develop judgment and tact; we must look at what we've written not only as a writer, but as a reader.

Since adequacy always depends on context, it's useless to lay down rules for paragraph length. Different kinds of writing, however, usually need paragraphs of different lengths. The more formal the writing, usually the more lengthy the paragraphing. In narrative and fiction, we use paragraphs with more varied lengths, and in informal writing our paragraphs shorten. Newspaper writing breaks up the solid column of print by making a paragraph out of every sentence or two.

In exposition, or in writing up research, we may move from topic to topic by long paragraphs that introduce a subject, elaborate it, enumerate it, explain it, or conclude it. We may frequently write paragraphs as long as a typewritten page. If the paragraphs get much longer, we should cut them down. We can always find a place where we can make a break that is not wholly arbitrary, and give the reader a rest. One argument could make a six-page paragraph, but it would be tiring to read. If we look back at it, we can find the steps in the argument. We can break between one step and another, even though the pause in reasoning is small. In a long description, we can break between one part of the subject and another. Talking of a barn, we can break between remarks about the colors things have, about the shapes they take, and about the uses they are put to. Talking about a block we grew up on, suppose we want to write equally about ten houses. Ten tiny paragraphs would be too choppy; one paragraph would be two pages of solid print. Here, we can subdivide our houses by talking about one side of the block and then the other, or by making a division for three architectural styles, or different shades of paint, or lengths of time houses were occupied by the same tenants.

Some paragraphs must be short. When we write dialogue, we show a change of speaker by indenting a new paragraph.

> "Did you go downtown after lunch?" He was tapping the arm of his chair with his index finger. Behind his glasses his eyes wandered.
> "Yes," she said. "I suppose I did."
> "Why?"

But that paragraphing is mechanical. In descriptive or expository or narrative writing — usual ingredients in essay or autobiography, and frequently in story — short paragraphs are choppy, a rash of blurts, like someone who talks in the manner of a machine gun. When we move from dialogue to description or narration, we should provide a change of pace by keeping the paragraphs relatively long. The long paragraph is a rest, a relief after several short ones: here is a bed big enough to lie down on. We do not want:

> The room was large, the chairs comfortable. He sat down on the overstuffed sofa.
> All around him the ticking of clocks wove a mesh of sound.
> There was dust on the windowpane, and the rugs were shabby.
> Dark pictures hung on the walls, and the woodwork was dark

It is too much like standing up and sitting down all the time. We want to relax and read the description straight.

> The room was large, the chairs comfortable. He sat down on the overstuffed sofa. All around him the ticking of clocks wove a mesh of sound. There was dust on the windowpane, and the rugs were shabby. Dark pictures hung on the walls, and the woodwork was dark.

And the paragraph should continue for another five or six lines.

Sometimes when we chop our prose into too short paragraphs we may be deceiving ourselves with handwriting, which can make a few words into full-sized paragraphs, and think that we are writing a long paper when we are not. Or perhaps we find it difficult to move from one thing to another within the paragraph, and so we break the paragraph to indicate a switch to another topic. And at times, short paragraphs reveal our laziness. We fail to collect and to develop our thoughts, and so write paragraphs that are little more than a sentence announcing a topic, paragraphs lacking detail, elaboration, and support. We need to think of further ideas to support arguments; details to make description carry feeling.

In narrative, the paragraph break is rather arbitrary. We could justify one after every sentence, we could justify none at all; but neither of these solutions would be tolerable. So we break for a rest when it is most nearly logical, as when the character turns a corner, or sees something new, or understands what is happening.

It is tempting to be dogmatic, and to say, "Outside of dialogue, keep your paragraphs between 200 and 250 words." Life would be more comfortable, and writing easier, if simple prescriptions solved our problems. Although a highly formal essay might follow some such rule, most good modern writing has much more variety to it. As it is hard to type the best contemporary stylists as formal or informal, so it is hard to put limits on paragraph size. Although formal writing leads toward a more uniform length of paragraph, it can use something as short as a one-line paragraph. A skillful writer may make a long statement in periodic sentences, a 350-word paragraph that concludes with a flourish, and follow it by a paragraph that reads, in its entirety,

> On the other hand, maybe this reasoning is haphazard.

Then he may write another long paragraph. The one-liner has been a change of pace — at the same time restful, offhand, and revivifying: it keeps us on our toes. We don't know what might come next, we are perpetually a little off balance. Look at this example from a student theme:

> When you approach the city from the East, you enter a downtrodden world with shabby filling stations, electric signs with letters missing, potholes, boarded-over houses, and bars which never close — dark holes of degradation and hopelessness. Next to them often you see old men asleep in gutters. No one looks young or happy or as if there is any future. The only thing you see which is bright and shiny and new is a police car.
>
> But that is only a part of the city.
>
> To the west and to the north, the lakes attract fine houses. To the south, past the new buildings of prosperous businesses, the farmlands spread in abundance. . . .

Here, the one-line paragraph — which makes a transition between the two longer paragraphs — could easily become a first sentence for the second paragraph, but the student has chosen this rhythmically shocking brevity to underline, to make even more emphatic, the totally changed scene that his prose begins to describe.

On the other hand, look at these paragraphs of definition, more nearly equal in length:

A classical understanding sees the world primarily as underlying form itself. A romantic understanding sees it primarily in terms of immediate appearance. If you were to show an engine or a mechanical drawing or electronic schematic to a romantic it is unlikely he would see much of interest in it. It has no appeal because the reality he sees is its surface. Dull, complex lists of names, lines and numbers. Nothing interesting. But if you were to show the same blueprint or schematic or give the same description to a classical person he might look at it and then become fascinated by it because he sees that within the lines and shapes and symbols is a tremendous richness of underlying form.

The romantic mode is primarily inspirational, imaginative, creative, intuitive. Feelings rather than facts predominate. "Art" when it is opposed to "Science" is often romantic. It does not proceed by reason or by laws. It proceeds by feeling, intuition and esthetic conscience. In the northern European cultures the romantic mode is usually associated with femininity, but this is certainly not a necessary association.

The classic mode, by contrast, proceeds by reason and by laws — which are themselves underlying forms of thought and behavior. In the European cultures it is primarily a masculine mode and the fields of science, law and medicine are unattractive to women largely for this reason. Although motorcycle riding is romantic, motorcycle maintenance is purely classic. The dirt, the grease, the mastery of underlying form required all give it such a negative romantic appeal that women never go near it.

Although surface ugliness is often found in the classic mode of understanding it is not inherent in it. There is a classic esthetic which romantics often miss because of its subtlety. The classic style is straightforward, unadorned, unemotional, economical and carefully proportioned. Its purpose is not to inspire emotionally, but to bring order out of chaos and make the unknown known. It is not an esthetically free and natural style. It is esthetically restrained. Everything is under control. Its value is measured in terms of the skill with which this control in maintained.

To a romantic this classic mode often appears dull, awkward and ugly, like mechanical maintenance itself. Everything is in terms of pieces and parts and components and relationships. Nothing is figured out until it's run through the computer a dozen times. Everything's got to be measured and proved. Oppressive. Heavy. Endlessly grey. The death force.

Within the classic mode, however, the romantic has some appearances of his own. Frivolous, irrational, erratic, untrustworthy, interested primarily in pleasure-seeking. Shallow. Of no substance. Often a parasite who cannot or will not carry his own weight. A real drag on society. By now these battle lines should sound a little familiar.

Robert M. Pirsig, *Zen and the Art of Motorcycle Maintenance*

These even, full, adequate paragraphs march in rank and in good order, helping to convince us — even by their shape itself — that they are calm, logical steps in a progressive statement of thought or opinion.

The variety and unity of the paragraph resemble the variety and unity of the sentence. The effective contrast, when the one-line paragraph follows the complex one, resembles the pleasure we take in a short, simple sentence after a long, complex sentence. One can mix a stew of variety without violating a unity that holds the essay together.

Development: Order and Clarity

If we do not want to irritate or confuse the reader, our information or argument must be orderly. Things must follow each other with a sense of purpose. Purpose makes clarity. We cannot say, "Oh, I forgot to say . . ." or leave out steps in our progress. We must move in an orderly way, from earlier to later, or from less to more important, or from periphery to center, or from smaller to larger, or from larger to smaller. Sometimes we will want to move from center to periphery, from present to past. But we must not scatter our sequence — from larger to smaller to larger to larger to smaller to largest to larger to smallest to large. We may want A B C D E F. On occasion we may want Z Y X W V, but never A Q I X L D.

The order in this paragraph is fine; we move from generality in the topic sentence to particulars that describe and substantiate it:

Winter is a catastrophe. Life on skid row is lived out of doors, and the cold and the snow bring with them intense suffering. The men often get drunk enough to lie in the streets in the midst of a storm. The first time one sees a body covered with a light blanket of snow, stretched out on the sidewalk, the sight comes as a shock

and a dilemma. Is the man dead or just drunk? Or worse, the habi-
tués are so obsessed and driven that stealing goes on in the dead of
winter, and a man who needs a drink will take the shoes of a fellow
alcoholic in the middle of January.

Michael Harrington,
The Other America: Poverty in the United States

The following paragraph, organized in a different way, moving from
pieces of information to a general conclusion, is also well constructed:

Last January as he was about to leave office, Lyndon Johnson
sent his last report on the economic prospect to the Congress. It
was assumed that, in one way or another, the Vietnam War, by
which he and his Administration had been destroyed, would come
gradually to an end. The question considered by his economists
was whether this would bring an increase or a decrease in military
spending. The military budget for fiscal 1969 was 78.4 billions; for
the year following, including pay increases, it was scheduled to be
about three billions higher. Thereafter, assuming peace and a general withdrawal from Asia, there would be a reduction of some six
or seven billions. But this was only on the assumption that the
Pentagon did not get any major new weapons — that it was content
with what had already been authorized. No one really thought this
possible. The President's economists noted that plans already existed for "a package" consisting of new aircraft, modern naval vessels, defense installations, and "advanced strategic and general purpose weapons systems" which would cost many billions. This
would wipe out any savings from getting out of Vietnam. Peace
would now be far more expensive than war.

John Kenneth Galbraith, *How to Control the Military*

The organization in this paragraph, however, is not satisfactory:

The birds often flock in huge numbers on trees, sometimes
breaking limbs off. They may bury a car parked below them in
white dung. Starlings can be a terrible nuisance. The dark pur-
plish-black pests may tear up a whole lawn in the process of
searching for worms and insects, particularly as winter approaches
and live food gets scarce. Their antics can drive a homeowner out
of his tree. In large enough numbers, they can create a din of voices
that blocks out all other sounds in the area. Their cries are strident
and irritating.

The order is unclear. In this paragraph we move from specific to specific to general to specific to general to specific to specific, without

meaningful progression. It would make much better organizational sense to begin "Starlings can be a terrible nuisance" and to end "Their antics can drive a homeowner out of *his* tree."

In writing a paragraph we usually have to settle on some controlling principle of order or sequence and then keep to it. Earlier we showed some methods of developing paragraphs for exposition. Two of the simplest and clearest means of ordering — appropriate for all sorts of writing — are simple chronology and spatial proximity, discussed briefly when we looked into transitions. Here we see chronological order in exposition.

> Then the Phillips staff compiled descriptions of about a hundred pieces of legislation that the Department had proposed or intended to propose to Congress, along with a list of the likeliest clashes over issues when the Ninety-first Congress convened a few days later. Memoranda were also prepared on the Department's involvement in certain pressing urban problems and its responsibilities vis-à-vis the District of Columbia. Since most of the Department's business with Congress is conducted through the Senate and House Judiciary Committees, Phillips and his staff drew up biographies of their members, which included information about where each man stood on important issues and the relative influence of the chairmen and the ranking members of both parties, along with an assessment of the strength of the coalition between Southern Democrats and Northern Republicans, which was expected to be more influential than ever. Finally, Phillips prepared a paper describing the procedure to be followed in the confirmation hearing that Mitchell would have to attend before the Senate Judiciary Committee in a couple of weeks.
>
> Richard Harris, *Justice*

Chronology is probably the easiest method for ordering the material in a paragraph, and perhaps the most common. At times, in narration and exposition, we want to leap ahead and then catch up. We must use this violation of chronological sequence, however, only when we are fully aware of what we are doing.

> In December, 1941, Congress declared war on Japan, Germany, and Italy. The declaration was an immediate result of the Japanese attack on Pearl Harbor, but earlier events had made such a move inevitable. Perhaps the Treaty of Versailles. . . .

Here, the opening sentence states the ultimate topic, an event to be reached by way of causation, and the paragraph develops by reverse chronology. Presumably, the writer will turn around and advance through the twenties and thirties in a conventional forward direction. If this essay began by referring to the earliest event mentioned — that is, if it had followed regular chronology — the reader might have expected, for a moment, that the Treaty of Versailles was the subject.

Development: Order and Forcefulness

Clarity is not our only consideration when we organize paragraphs; we must also organize for appropriateness and forceful effect. Look again at the paragraphs by McCabe (page 190) and Munro (page 191), keeping in mind the discussion of topic sentences. Look at the order in the paragraphs compared with the effects achieved. By their positions the topic sentences give *force* to these paragraphs.

Or take the method that lets us order according to spatial proximity. It can be more than a means to clarity; it can direct the reader's attention significantly, and achieve dramatic effect. Here is a passage from *Gandhi* by Louis Fischer.

> At Rajghat, a few hundred feet from the river, a fresh pyre had been built of stone, brick, and earth. It was eight feet square and about two feet high. Long, thin sandalwood logs sprinkled with incense were stacked on it. Mahatma Gandhi's body lay on the pyre with his head to the north. In that position Buddha met his end.

Notice how the paragraph moves gradually closer to its subject, like a camera that dollies in for a close-up in a film. We start from far back, and move gradually closer. If the author had described the body of Gandhi first, and then its surroundings, the passage would be less forceful.

When we consider how we organize our paragraphs, we must always consider our *purpose* in writing. In expository writing, we may want to be sure that the reader knows what we are doing at all times. We may want to avoid listing statistics before telling what they demonstrate. Imagine the other paragraph I quoted about Gandhi with the first sentence placed at the end.

> The province of Natal, in 1896, had 400,000 Negro inhabitants, 51,000 Indians, and 50,000 whites. The Cape of Good Hope Colony had 900,000 Negroes, 10,000 Indians, and 400,000 Europeans; the Transvaal Republic 650,000 Negroes, 5,000 Indians, and 120,000

whites. In 1914, the five million Negroes hopelessly outnumbered the million and a quarter whites. Gandhi recognized that the whites in South Africa thought they needed protection against a majority consisting of Negroes and Indians.

Revised as above, the paragraph's order makes the paragraph confusing and pointless. The reader does not know what is going on until he finishes reading the paragraph. He will be confused, bored, and inattentive.

And yet if our purpose in writing is to create an ominous or tense atmosphere — in narrative, perhaps, either fictional or autobiographical — we might want to list unexplained details first, waiting for the end of the paragraph to offer an interpretation. This suspenseful order would give our paragraph *force.*

> The forest, all at once, had grown silent. The monkeys had stopped their chattering, and the birds darted their heads apprehensively. The wind in the trees became audible, and then, faintly, the sound of drumming rose from the village enclosure. It could only mean that Godzilla had awakened once more.

Imagine how anticlimactic it would be in a film to show the monster suddenly appearing, and then to pan around the trees. It wouldn't make emotional or dramatic sense.

Revising Paragraphs

Make sure that your paragraphing is useful, to the mind that understands and to the eye that reads. Consider your paragraphs for their unity and variety, their coherence and adequacy of development, and their clarity and effective ordering. Consider their internal organization, and their transitions both internal and between paragraphs, both overt and implicit.

——— EXERCISES ————————————————————————————

1. These phrases might be notes for an essay. Arrange them into four or five groups, each group capable of development into a paragraph. Consider the essay's shape, over its whole length. Consider

the shape of each paragraph, and how the paragraph might move from one item to another.

> the 747 and airborne mass transit
> the modern airport
> ground transportation to and from airports
> the handling of baggage
> the outlook for aviation's future
> the SST
> the aerospace industry and the airlines
> competitive routes
> faster airlines
> midair collisions
> VTOL
> the declining railroads
> the trouble with buses
> youth fares
> charter flights

2. Here is a short essay on baseball. I have mixed up the paragraph order, and numbered the paragraphs in the mixed-up order. See if you can restore them to their original sequence.

1. At any one point, there's anticipation, deliberation, preparation: "Now" is a building-up. "Now" is never only for itself. It's cumulative "progressing," in strife, to form the game's unfolding. Nor are any two games alike, any more than two art works that push themselves into being through the resistance of time, incident by incident, in head-on conflict by two complicated machines designed to win through accidents and opportunity. "What's happening" is contingent. There's a whole game to be gotten through.

2. This is to see baseball as an art-work-in-the-making affair, totally unrehearsed, improvised by more than eighteen men, who thrust in their various skills while the moving parts pass through innings, highlighted by crucial plays, to the conclusion being thereby created.

3. The game in progress is a structure in the becoming, if you see it, through time, as a whole, all the separate episodes can come flashing together, and interlock, to shower aesthetic illumination on a drama of its own devising.

4. Like literature, music, opera, theater, and the dance, baseball takes place in time. (Architecture, sculpture, and painting don't — they're purely spatial.) The performer and the observer, while a game is in progress, look back and look ahead: the present action is laid out in a shifting, dramatic time field. A rhythm, of sorts, weaves its way through the "accidents" on the playing field. A current play, involving positioning and decisions, is affected by what was previous in the game, and is having its effect on what's to come later; the game may

be seen as an organic unit. Every pitch has its place in there, somewhere.

Marvin Cohen, Baseball the Beautiful

3. Analyze these paragraphs for their unity. (a) Do any of these
paragraphs have extraneous material? (b) Does each paragraph contain a topic sentence? Underline topic sentences, and discuss in
class. (c) What does the position of each topic sentence accomplish,
if anything?

a. The sea, autumn mildness, islands bathed in light, fine rain
spreading a diaphanous veil over the immortal nakedness of Greece.
Happy is the man, I thought, who, before dying, has the good fortune
to sail the Aegean Sea.

Many are the joys of this world — women, fruit, ideas. But to cleave
that sea in the gentle, autumnal season, murmuring the name of each
islet, is to my mind the joy most apt to transport the heart of man into
paradise. Nowhere else can one pass so easily and serenely from reality
to dream. The frontiers dwindle, and from the masts of the most ancient ships spring branches and fruits. It is as if here in Greece necessity is the mother of miracles.

Towards noon the rain stopped. The sun parted the clouds and appeared gentle, tender, washed and fresh, and it caressed with its rays
the beloved waters and lands. I stood at the prow and let myself be
intoxicated with the miracle which was revealed as far as the eye
could see.

Nikos Kazantzakis, Zorba the Greek

b. A philosopher — is a human being who constantly experiences,
sees, hears, suspects, hopes, and dreams extraordinary things; who is
struck by his own thoughts as from outside, as from above and below,
as by *his* type of experiences and lightning bolts; who is perhaps himself a storm pregnant with new lightnings; a fatal human being around
whom there are constant rumblings and growlings, crevices, and uncanny doings. A philosopher — alas, a being that often runs away from
itself, often is afraid of itself — but too inquisitive not to "come too"
again — always back to himself.

Friedrich Nietzsche, Beyond Good and Evil

c. Franco's reestablishment of the Catholic Church as a dominant
force in Spanish life, through the restoration of religious education, of
state financial support for the Church, and by the repeal of Republican
anti-clerical laws, led in 1941 to a working arrangement with the
Vatican that was finally formalized by a treaty in 1953.

These measures, however, did not serve to protect the Franco regime
from the severe censure of the Allies after the Second World War. In
July 1945, Spain found herself branded by the Potsdam Declaration as
unfit to associate with the United Nations. In December 1946 the
United Nations formally ostracized the Spanish government and recommended that all its member nations withdraw their ambassadors

from Madrid. Thus Spain found itself practically friendless in the post-war world, with only the dictatorships of Portugal and Argentina still lending the Nationalist regime their support.

Robert Goldston, The Civil War in Spain

4. Here are some incoherent paragraphs. (a) Consider the different sorts of incoherence in each paragraph. Which paragraphs can profit by reorganization? In class, reorganize them. (b) Which paragraphs need further development, in order to achieve coherence? In class, speculate on the directions development might take.

a. The heavy wooden door was painted red, but the wood showed through in many places where the paint was flaking off. Dandelions covered the lawn, but there were few weeds in the dark grass. A white and black cat lay curled by the door. Three huge oaks threw their shadows across the wide lawn. Far off, a deer was watching from the edge of the woods. There was no knob on the door.

b. The days were unusually hot and humid, even for that part of the state. Joe didn't want to go to the beach. His girlfriend, Linda, did. She wasn't a good swimmer. She loved to swim. Joe was working on his car. He was a fanatical sports enthusiast.

c. He had found that the wolves subsisted mainly on a diet of mice. Farley had been dropped in the middle of the Canadian tundra. He discovered that the hunters were lying, and that they themselves were the insane murderers. Hunters had been complaining that the wolves were slaughtering thousands of caribou for the sheer pleasure of killing. He had made an astonishing discovery. He had been assigned to investigate the killing of caribou by timber wolves.

d. *Delivery* by Paul Jamesy is a story of the adventures of a group of department store delivery boys sent on a mission into the suburbs of a large metropolis. The journey is a revelation of the inner world of modern man — the wanton violence of five-year-old footballers, the vast boredom of the swinging teens, the horrors of afternoon romance in respectable families. The author himself is a former cheerleader and national frog-jumping champion. All but one of the young men become trapped in a labyrinthine and nightmarish Kresge's store. Only one, who wins the voluptuous blonde named Shirley, succeeds in making his big — *Delivery*.

e. Robert and Daniel crouched in the cave, listening for the sound of approaching footsteps. He thought the troops must have left the area by now. For the moment he was reassured by the silence, but he worried about the sharp pain in his knee, and he wondered if he would be able to walk on it if he had to. He was glad to have his old friend with him. He looked at him. Their gazes meeting, he felt tears come to his eyes from straining to see in the half-darkness, and from thinking where he and his friend had been just yesterday.

f. When the gate opens at last, four thousand music lovers push, crush, and shove each other forward in an immense mass. The sun glares down, the musicians struggle to tune their sweaty instruments, and the ice cream salesman exhausts his stores in twenty minutes. Finally the music started at 1:30.

5. Here are two coherent paragraphs, from the essay by E. B. White in which he speaks of Simonizing his grandmother. Look at these paragraphs for their unity and their coherence. (a) Which words help White move his paragraphs along? (b) How does he accomplish transitions?

Communication by the written word is a subtler (and more beautiful) thing than Dr. Flesch or General Motors imagines. They contend that the "average reader" is capable of reading only what tests Easy, and that the writer should write at or below this level. This is a presumptuous and degrading idea. There is no average reader, and to reach down toward this mythical character is to deny that each of us is on the way up, is ascending. ("Ascending," by the way, is a word Dr. Flesch advises writers to stay away from. Too unusual.)

It is our belief that no writer can improve his work until he discards the dulcet notion that the reader is feeble-minded, for writing is an act of faith, not a trick of grammar. Ascent is at the heart of the matter. A country whose writers are following a calculating machine downstairs in not ascending — if you will pardon the expression — and a writer who questions the capacity of the person at the other end of the line is not a writer at all, merely a schemer. The movies long ago decided that a wider communication could be achieved by a deliberate descent to a lower level, and they walked proudly down until they reached the cellar. Now they are groping for the light switch, hoping to find the way out.

E. B. White, *The Second Tree from the Corner*

6. A student writing a theme about a teachers' strike wanted to make these points in one paragraph:

1. Teachers have no legal right to strike.
2. The teachers' union claims the strike is their constitutional right.
3. Some school boards try to fire striking teachers and hire new ones.
4. Striking teachers sometimes find judges who will issue injunctions against this firing and hiring.
5. Picketing disrupts the classes with new teachers.

Here is a first draft of the paragraph.

Of course it's against the law for teachers to strike anyway. Some teachers say that the law against striking is unconstitutional. So the school board fires the teachers who are striking and hires new teachers who are looking for work. The striking teachers get a judge to make an injunction against the school board. The picketing disrupts classes with the new teachers.

This first attempt was incoherent. Does the paragraph have a topic sentence? Does it have *a topic?* Does one sentence follow from another? Does the last sentence appear to belong in the paragraph?

Here is the paragraph as it appeared in the final draft of the theme.

> Although a state law forbids strikes by teachers, teachers still strike, claiming that the state law violates the U.S. Constitution. When a school board tries to break the strike, firing the old teachers and hiring new ones, some judge usually agrees with the strikers, and puts an injunction against the school board. Meantime, if one set of teachers is picketing another, whatever the argument between legislators and judges, the children in the classroom suffer.

(a) How does this paragraph improve over the previous one? (b) By what means does this student connect sentences to each other? (c) In the last sentence, why does the student write, "whatever the argument between legislators and judges "?

7. Analyze these paragraphs for their transitions, both within paragraphs and between them.

When Saint-Exupéry begins his second paragraph, which word especially links it to the end of the first paragraph? What binds the third paragraph to the second? When the fourth paragraph follows the third, an idea rather than a word makes the transition: underline the words that are intellectually related to each other.

> Once again I had found myself in the presence of a truth and had failed to recognize it. Consider what had happened to me: I had thought myself lost, had touched the very bottom of despair; and then, when the spirit of renunciation had filled me, I had known peace. I know now what I was not conscious of at the time — that in such an hour a man feels that he has finally found himself and has become his own friend. An essential inner need has been satisfied, and against that satisfaction, that self-fulfillment, no external power can prevail. Bonnafous, I imagine, he who spent his life racing before the wind, was acquainted with this serenity of spirit. Guillaumet, too, in his snows. Never shall I forget that, lying buried to the chin in sand, strangled slowly to death by thirst, my heart was infinitely warm beneath the desert stars.
>
> What can men do to make known to themselves this sense of deliverance? Everything about mankind is paradox. He who strives and conquers grows soft. The magnanimous man grown rich becomes mean. The creative artist for whom everything is made easy nods. Every doctrine swears that it can breed men, but none can tell us in

advance what sort of men it will breed. Men are not cattle to be fattened for market. On the scales of life an indigent Newton weighs more than a parcel of prosperous nonentities. All of us have had the experience of a sudden joy that came when nothing in the world had forewarned us of its coming — a joy so thrilling that if it was born of misery we remembered even the misery with tenderness. All of us, on seeing old friends again, have remembered with happiness the trials we lived through with those friends. Of what can we be certain except this — that we are fertilized by mysterious circumstances? Where is man's truth to be found?

Truth is not that which can be demonstrated by the aid of logic. If orange-trees are hardy and rich in fruit in this bit of soil and not that, then this bit of soil is what is truth for orange-trees. If a particular religion, or culture, or scale of values, if one form of activity rather than another, brings self-fulfillment to a man, releases the prince asleep within him unknown to himself, then that scale of values, that culture, that form of activity, constitute his truth. Logic, you say? Let logic wangle its own explanation of life.

Because it is man and not flying that concerns me most, I shall close this book with the story of man's gropings towards self-fulfillment as I witnessed them in the early months of the civil war in Spain. One year after crashing in the desert I made a tour of the Catalan front in order to learn what happens to man when the scaffolding of his traditions suddenly collapses. To Madrid I went for an answer to another question: How does it happen that men are sometimes willing to die?

Antoine de Saint-Exupéry, *Wind, Sand and Stars*

8. In this passage from Thoreau, underline the topic sentence of the first paragraph. (a) How does the paragraph grow from this sentence? (b) Is every other sentence in this paragraph related to the topic sentence? (c) How do the sentences proceed? Underline transitions. (d) Do you find implicit transitions in this paragraph, and later between paragraphs? Find the basis for each implicit transition.

The mass of men serve the State thus, not as men mainly, but as machines, with their bodies. They are the standing army, and the militia, jailers, constables, "posse comitatus," &c. In most cases there is no free exercise whatever of the judgment or of the moral sense; but they put themselves on a level with wood and earth and stones; and wooden men can perhaps be manufactured that will serve the purpose as well. Such command no more respect than men of straw; or a lump of dirt. They have the same sort of worth only as horses and dogs. Yet such as these even are commonly esteemed good citizens. Others, as most legislators, politicians, lawyers, ministers, and office-holders, serve the State chiefly with their heads; and, as they rarely make any moral distinctions, they are as likely to serve the devil, without intending it, as God. A very few, as heroes, patriots, martyrs, reformers in the great sense, and *men*, serve the State with their consciences also, and so necessarily resist it for the most part; and they are commonly treated by it as enemies. A wise man will only be useful as a man, and will not submit to be "clay," and "stop a hole to keep the wind away," but leave that office to his dust at least: —

"I am too high-born to be propertied,
To be a secondary at control,
Or useful serving-man and instrument
To any sovereign state throughout the world."

He who gives himself entirely to his fellow-men appears to them useless and selfish; but he who gives himself partially to them is pronounced a benefactor and philanthropist.

How does it become a man to behave toward this American government to-day? I answer that he cannot without disgrace be associated with it. I cannot for an instant recognize the political organization as my government which is the *slave's* government also.

All men recognize the right of revolution; that is, the right to refuse allegiance to and to resist the government, when its tyranny or its inefficiency are great and unendurable. But almost all say that such is not the case now. But such was the case, they think, in the Revolution of '75. If one were to tell me that this was a bad government because it taxed certain foreign commodities brought to its ports, it is most probable that I should not make an ado about it, for I can do without them: all machines have their friction; and possibly this does enough good to counterbalance the evil. At any rate, it is a great evil to make a stir about it. But when the friction comes to have its machine, and oppression and robbery are organized, I say, let us not have such a machine any longer. In other words, when a sixth of the population of a nation which has undertaken to be the refuge of liberty are slaves, and a whole country is unjustly overrun and conquered by a foreign army, and subjected to military law, I think that it is not too soon for honest men to rebel and revolutionize. What makes this duty the more urgent is the fact, that the country so overrun is not our own, but ours is the invading army.

> Henry David Thoreau, "On the Duty of Civil Disobedience"

9. Read these paragraphs and classify them according to their methods of development. (See pages 202–207.)

a. It's sometimes argued that there's no real progress, that a civilization that kills multitudes in mass warfare, that pollutes the land and oceans with ever larger quantities of debris, that destroys the dignity of individuals by subjecting them to a forced mechanized existence can hardly be called an advance over the simpler hunting and gathering and agricultural existence of prehistoric times. But this argument, though romantically appealing, doesn't hold up. The primitive tribes permitted far less individual freedom than does modern society. Ancient wars were committed with far less moral justification than modern ones. A technology that produces debris can find, and is finding, ways of disposing of it without ecological upset. And the schoolbook pictures of primitive man sometimes omit some of the detractions of his primitive life — the pain, the disease, famine, the hard labor needed just to stay alive. From that agony of bare existence to modern life can be soberly described only as upward progress, and the sole agent for this progress is quite clearly reason itself.

Robert M. Pirsig, *Zen and the Art of Motorcycle Maintenance*

b. But there is an aspect of the crystal of our nature that eschews the harness, scorns sublimation, and demands to be seen in its raw nakedness, crying out to us for the sight and smell of blood. The vehemence with which we deny this obvious fact of our nature is matched only by our Victorian hysteria on the subject of sex. Yet, we deny it in vain. Whether we quench our thirst from the sight of a bleeding Jesus on the Cross, from the ritualized sacrifice in the elevation of the Host and the consecration of the Blood of the Son, or from bullfighting, cockfighting, dogfighting, wrestling, or boxing, spiced with our Occidental memory and heritage of the gladiators of Rome and the mass spectator sport of the time of feeding Christians and other enemies of society to the lions in the Coliseum — whatever the mask assumed by the impulse, the persistent beat of the drum over the years intones the chant: Though Dracula and Vampira must flee the scene with the rising of the sun and the coming of the light, night has its fixed hour and darkness must fall.

Eldridge Cleaver, *Soul on Ice*

c. For twins they are very dissimilar. Colin is tall and active and Johnny is short and middle-aged. Johnny doesn't kick off his shoes, he doesn't swallow beer caps or tear pages out of the telephone book. I don't think he ever draws pictures with my best lipstick. In fact, he has none of the charming, lighthearted "boy" qualities that precipitate so many scenes of violence in the home. On the other hand, he has a feeling for order and a passion for system that would be trying in a head nurse. If his pajamas are hung on the third hook in the closet instead of on the second hook, it causes him real pain. If one slat in a Venetian blind is tipped in the wrong direction he can't have a moment's peace until somebody fixes it. Indeed, if one of the beans on his plate is slightly longer than the others he can scarcely bear to eat it.

Jean Kerr, *Please Don't Eat the Daisies*

10. Take this excerpt from the *Detroit Free Press*, tiny newspaper paragraphs, and copy it out into longer paragraphs, as you would organize paragraphs in a theme. Break the paragraphs logically and usefully.

Here's what the historic arms limitation agreements signed here Friday night in the Kremlin mean.

What they do, essentially, is to freeze a "balance of terror" between the world's two nuclear superpowers.

Each side, in these agreements, retains the ability to kill millions of defenseless civilians on the other side.

Washington and Moscow will be defended from nuclear attack with anti-ballistic missile systems (ABMs).

But Detroit and every other major city in the U.S. will remain undefended. So will Leningrad and Kiev, and other major cities in the Soviet Union.

Thus each side, in a sense, will hold the civilian population of the other side hostage — as a means of discouraging the other side from launching nuclear war.

The fact is, as Henry Kissinger, White House national security adviser, has put it: "Both sides are now vulnerable to each other . . . this has been a fact now for five or six years."

The new SALT agreements seek to freeze the 25-year-old nuclear arms race at that point — on the theory that a "balance of terror" is the best guarantee either side has, in this terrifying age, of preventing war.

But what of other major questions?

How important are the agreements? Can they work? Can they be monitored? Don't the agreements give the Soviets a numerical advantage? What will they mean to the average citizen?

                                                                James McCartney

11. Look at the length of paragraphs in this example. Does the author provide variety in length and type of paragraph? Do any paragraphs seem choppy? Are transitions adequate? Make notes in the margin for class discussion.

What, in our human world, is this power to live? It is the ancient, lost reverence and passion for human personality, joined with the ancient, lost reverence and passion for the earth and its web of life.

This indivisible reverence and passion is what the American Indians almost universally had; and representative groups of them have it still.

They had and have this power for living which our modern world has lost — as world-view and self-view, as tradition and institution, as practical philosophy dominating their societies and as an art supreme among all the arts.

By virtue of this power, the densely populated Inca state, by universal agreement among its people, made the conservation and increase of the earth's resources its foundational national policy. Never before, never since has a nation done what the Inca state did.

By virtue of this same power, the little pueblo of Tesuque, in New Mexico, when threatened by the implacable destroying action of government some twenty-five years ago, starved and let no white friend know it was starving. It asked no help, determined only to defend its spiritual values and institutions and its remnant of land which was holy land.

If our modern world should be able to recapture this power, the earth's natural resources and web of life would not be irrevocably wasted within the twentieth century, which is the prospect now. True democracy, founded in neighborhoods and reaching over the world, would become the realized heaven on earth. And living peace — not just an interlude between wars — would be born and would last through ages.

John Collier, *Indians of the Americas*

6

Exposition, Argument, Description, Narrative

In the opening chapters of this book, we looked briefly into whole essays. The first chapter used examples of autobiographical narrative to discuss the honesty and freshness necessary to all writing. The second chapter investigated the process of writing — gathering ideas, collecting details, shaping and revising — in making an expository paper. Then for three chapters we concentrated on *parts* of writing: word, sentence, paragraph. Now we must return to the whole essay, and take a longer look. We must investigate the different kinds of writing appropriate to different purposes; within each kind, we must discuss the variety of patterns possible for construction or development. Essays differ in intention and in construction: purpose makes pattern.

Our purpose may require us to explain something, or to argue or persuade, or to describe something, or to tell a story. If we explain how to pick apples, we write *exposition*. If we argue for hiring local apple pickers in place of migrant workers, we undertake *argument* or *persuasion*. If our purpose is to evoke for the reader an orchard of Northern Spies in full bloom, we undertake *description*. If we tell the story of Johnny Appleseed, or recount the spread of apple farming in the Pacific Northwest, we use *narration*.

Of course many essays make mixed demands, and mixed purposes make mixed patterns. In order to explain how to pick apples, it may well be necessary to describe the way apples distribute themselves on apple trees, and to narrate a small story including ladders and pails. When we argue or persuade, we need exposition of facts; for instance, we may need to explain the economics of migrant labor. When we narrate the story of northwestern apple farming, most likely we will need passages of description or explanation; we will need perhaps the look of hills in Oregon, or the reasons why the soil in the Northwest is best for apples.

EXPOSITION

Most writing assigned in college is exposition. So is almost all writing required in professional life — in business, in teaching, in science, in law, in medicine. When social workers deliver papers, when geologists make reports, when hospital directors release information on new diagnostic equipment — they write exposition. Expository writing explains. It does not argue — though exposition can form part of an argument. It does not tell a story — though it might explain something essential to telling a story.

Exposition is usually the essay's foundation. It can also take pure form, in whole essays of exposition. But generally the essayist will narrate and describe, and by contrasting passages of exposition he may argue. Argument lacking in exposition moves toward bombast or harangue. If you did an exchange year in England, you might feel called upon to write an essay explaining baseball or percolator coffee to your teacher and classmates. If you tried to demonstrate the superiority of baseball or coffee, you would be adding argument to exposition. If you wrote a biography of Albert Einstein, you would certainly write a narrative of his life, you would probably use dialogue, and you would probably use description. But you would need exposition also.

But there was another consequence which Einstein now brought forward for the first time. If light is produced in a star or in the sun, an area of strong gravity, and then streams down on the earth, an area of weak gravity, its energy will not be dissipated by a reduction of speed, since this is impossible, light always having the same constant speed. What would happen, Einstein postulated, was something very different: the wavelength of the light would be shortened. This "Einstein shift," the assumption that "the spectral lines of sunlight, as compared with the corresponding spectral lines of terrestrial sources of light, must be somewhat displaced toward the red," was spelled out in some detail. However, he was careful to add the qualification that "as other influences (pressure, temperature) affect the position of the centers of the spectral lines, it is difficult to discover whether the enforced influence of the gravitational potential really exists." In fact the Döppler shift, produced by the motion of the stars relative to the solar system, was to provide an additional and even more important complication.

Ronald W. Clark, Einstein

Clark, pausing in his biography to explain a scientific discovery, analyzes a natural process. *Process analysis* is a rhetorical pattern common to expository writing, which answers the question: "How does it happen or work?" Now we must look into the many patterns — process analysis among others — that recur in exposition, and consider the advantages and disadvantages of each. We will call them *rhetorical patterns*. Rhetoric is an old word for the art of discourse, the way we use spoken or written language in order to make ourselves clear to listeners or readers; rhetoric is this book's subject.

RHETORICAL PATTERNS

Each of the most common patterns answers a question. *Example* answers, "For instance?" *Classification* answers, "What kind is it?" *Division* answers, "What are its parts?" *Cause and effect* answers, "Why did it happen?" *Comparison and contrast* answers, "What is it like? What is it unlike?" *Definition* answers, "What is it?"

These rhetorical patterns represent ways of thinking, of understanding — and of explaining. Suppose our subject is community colleges. We could give one or more *examples* of community colleges, with concrete detail. We could *classify* different sorts of community colleges, according to size, location, sources of funding, or curriculum. We could *divide* one community college into its component parts — faculty, administration, staff, and student body. We could talk about social *causes and effects* — events that led to the formation of such colleges, and their social results. We could *compare and contrast* community colleges with four-year colleges, with residential colleges, or with technical institutes. We could *analyze the process* by which a community college is founded. We could *define* the community college, listing the attributes that make an institution correctly carry the name.

Most likely, a paper on community colleges would use more than one of these rhetorical patterns. A mixture is possible because these patterns persist on all levels of writing; when speaking of ways to develop paragraphs, we mentioned these patterns also. As we may develop a whole essay using one or more of these rhetorical patterns, so we may develop a part of an essay — a paragraph — using one or more of these patterns. Each of these devices can structure an entire paper, or support one segment of the paper — even as short a segment as a sentence. Good essays combine rhetorical patterns in a sequence demanded by the essay's purpose.

Example

Examples are fundamental to expository prose. In the previous chapter, when we looked into paragraph development, the first three methods used example: assertion followed by reasons, statement followed by relevant facts, and listing. Example is the concrete instance that gives substance to generalizations and abstractions. We support statements by giving examples. If we argue, "Philosophers show us how to live," we need to continue by giving an example: "For instance, Plato. . . ." Whenever we might say, "For instance," or "For example," we are explaining by example. "Meats are fattening; a hamburger patty two-and-a-half inches around contains about 250 calories." Examples often lead to more examples, as we avoid the error of generalizing from a particular. If we speak of paintings we may need to exemplify by speaking of Turner or Picasso. If we speak of Turner or Picasso, we may wish to exemplify these painters by naming periods in their work, or canvases within a period. Example is indispensable to expository prose, and supplies the factual detail necessary to other rhetorical patterns.

Composition teachers commonly demand *detail* from their students; details are examples. Writing that lacks example is abstract and unsupported. A paper satisfied to speak of "outdoor sports" lacks detail, lacks example. We need to hear of skiing or horseback riding. Reading about "skiing areas," the reader longs for the concrete detail of an example: "King Ridge, in New London, New Hampshire, offers thirty-seven trails for novice, intermediate, and advanced skiers."

The shape of our thought determines our best use of example. In a paper on representative government, perhaps one or two extended examples of real governments in practice — Canada, Italy — may provide the needed particularity. On the other hand, a paper on fast-food franchises meant to emphasize the multiplicity of possible offerings might exemplify endlessly — Arbie's, Arthur Treacher's, Cap'n Salt,

McDonalds, Burger King, Burger Chef, Gino's — to the point of useful nausea.

In revising expository prose, we do well to interrogate our examples. First, do we have enough detail to support our statements or generalizations? We must be careful not to generalize from a particular. Second, is the detail or example relevant to the generalization? It is easy to make a mistake, in a first draft — to confuse an example of one thing with an example of another; we must learn to check over our thinking, as well as our punctuation and our spelling. Third, does our prose make each example as clear and as vivid as it can?

Classification and Division

Classification is characteristic of human thought. We classify among many things: apples, towns, automobiles, left-handed people, musical instruments. When we consider friends we have known, towns we have lived in, apples we have eaten, or cars we have driven, our minds tend to classify these things. We group according to similarities, and then we discriminate differences. If we classify voters, we separate people into Republicans, Democrats, Socialists, Prohibitionists — but this discrimination depends on their shared identity as voters. Thinking of cars we have driven, we classify according to mileage, price, country of origin, size, or any other discernible quality; they are all automobiles. Of course classification leads to comparison, often to contrast, because the large class depends on similarities — what all seashells or automobiles have in common — and the subdivisions depend on contrasts of striping, handling, size, and horsepower.

Outline form uses classification. Classification keeps our thinking orderly. Essential to good order in classification is parallelism. If we classify forms of literature, we may speak of fiction, drama, and poetry, and the classification remains parallel. If we were tempted to classify literature into novel, drama, short story, poem, and sonnet, our thinking would become muddled: drama is a general category while novel and short story are subcategories of the general notion of fiction; poetry is a general category, and sonnet a particular form within the category of poetry. Keep classifications parallel.

Division is also characteristic of human thought. While classification sets many things in order — apples classified as McIntosh, Baldwin, Northern Spy — division analyzes single things into their parts. An apple, for instance, is composed of skin, stem, flesh, and seeds. To analyze the Federal government, we divide it into three parts. To analyze our Buick, we divide it into chassis, engine, and body. When we analyze by division, we analyze a static thing: the finished automobile, the ripe apple. It is important to distinguish between the analysis of a single, static object — for which we use the rhetorical pattern of division — and the narrative analysis of action or process, a pattern we will take up later.

In writing, when we follow the rhetorical pattern of classification, or of division, we should not confuse the two. Sometimes a good writer will begin an essay by classification, and end it with division — with careful logic and excellent results. We could classify plays as tragic, comic, historical, and pastoral — and then analyze the anatomy of the tragedy, dividing the one dramatic form into components; Aristotle in his *Poetics*, for instance, distinguished plot, character, diction, thought, spectacle, and song.

But the two patterns are different. Be careful. Often in careless writing we may start using one pattern and end using the other, not knowing what we do, with monstrous results — as if the Creator's attention had wandered, and He set a robin's head on a daffodil's stem. Do not wander, like a careless talker, from one to the other without noticing it. The result makes disunity, much as mixed constructions do in individual sentences. If we began a paper with an analytic division of the federal government into its components, we would wander into incoherence if we took off from the legislative third of the division and started classifying the different legislatures of the world.

Cause and Effect

We commonly think and explain in terms of cause and effect as we try to answer the question: "Why did (or does) something happen (or not happen)?" Scientific writing frequently examines phenomena in terms of causes and effects. Historical speculation, less objective than science, marshalls evidence to suggest what caused certain events, and editorial writers announce the likely effects of legislation. In literary criticism, we may name the causes for the decline of a writer's work, or speculate upon them. In an essay on skiing, comparing downhill with cross-country, we may use cause and effect for a sentence or two: "Goggles are necessary to downhill skiing *because.* . . ." In an autobiographical essay on a favorite vacation place, we may explain that old buildings, bright sunsets, and long beaches affect us pleasurably.

Using cause and effect as a rhetorical pattern, we must be wary of possible misuses. We must be wary of assigning single causes, or of assuming that because B follows A, B was caused by A. (The logical fallacy of the latter assumption, *post hoc ergo propter hoc,* is discussed on pages 248–249.) Most effects we can observe have more than one cause, and it is immodest to assume that observation can discern all the causes of any event. If we see that our roommate acts the way one of his parents acts, we may safely assume that the parent's behavior has affected the child. But we would be foolish and presumptuous to declare that we had discovered the entire cause of our roommate's actions.

Comparison and Contrast

Like all rhetorical patterns, comparison and contrast is basic to thought, and to the exposition of thought. We use it to shape whole papers — as we saw Sharon Rustig do in Chapter II — or we use it as part of a paper. In an earlier paragraph, I used the caloric count of a hamburger as an example of an example. Perhaps that detail by itself would mean little to most readers; in order to let that detail speak to an audience, I could supply meaning for "250 calories" by comparison and contrast.

> Meats are fattening; a hamburger patty two-and-a-half inches across contains about 250 calories. On the other hand, a medium-sized potato, a member of the starch family often accused of fattening us, contains only 100 calories. On a scale the potato outweighs the hamburger patty two-to-one; in my metabolism, the hamburger alone — without bun, without ketchup, without fried onions — is two-and-a-half times more fattening than the potato.

Comparison and contrast can be a tool for judgment and decision. We compare sweaters or used cars before we buy one; we compare colleges before we choose where to apply. But we also compare and contrast simply to define or to explain. When we say that a hamburger is fattening, what does the statement mean? Is it fattening compared to a mushroom? Is it fattening compared to a gallon of ice cream? To make the word "fattening" mean anything, we require comparisons; comparison and contrast define a single word.

In a paper for a government course, we might compare another country's representative government with America's, to illuminate the differences, or to understand our own system better, by seeing its familiar shape against the unfamiliar background of a different system. It is not necessary, in comparison and contrast, to take sides. Although comparison and contrast often contribute to argument, we can use them for exposition alone.

We compare and contrast things which have something in common, and which have some differences as well. Bicycles and cars get us places — and also differ. *War and Peace* and *Anna Karenina* are both novels, both by Tolstoy — and differ considerably. Things compared must have enough in common, and enough in contrast. To compare *War and Peace* and *Love's Latest Gothic,* it may not be enough that both are novels. To contrast Senator Buffalo's campaigns in 1972 and 1978 may be difficult, if he said exactly the same things both times.

Whenever we compare and contrast, we face a structural problem. How long do we go on, talking about A's qualities, before we move to the contrasting qualities of B? If we balance each sentence with a look at both A and B, the alternation will be too swift; our heads snap back and forth as if we were watching Ping-Pong, and our necks get stiff. On the other hand, if we talk about A for ten pages before we get to B, we create another problem. When the reader starts seeing, on page eleven, the qualities of B that correspond to the earlier qualities of A, he has forgotten the details ten pages back. Always keep the audience in mind, and beware the confusion of too swift alternation, and the other confusion of too distant comparison.

In comparison and contrast the order of the points is essential; we must keep them parallel. If we are comparing and contrasting educational institutions according to admission policy, class size, and tuition, be sure that the points proceed in the same order in speaking of each institution. If we use one order for one institution, and a different order for the other, we lose the reader in a jumble of incoherence.

Finally, we should mention comparison and contrast through analogy. (Analogy is discussed on pages 114–115.) Maybe in an autobiographical essay we will say that human growth is like the progress of the seasons, and that we are in our spring, looking ahead to the long summer of maturity, before the autumn of old age, and the winter of death. A historian tells us that civilizations are born, grow old, and die—just like organisms. But beware—when you use analogy—of stating something as an analogy, and then taking it as literal truth. Beware of saying that because civilizations are organisms, our society must die. (See page 249.)

Process Analysis

When exposition uses the pattern of process analysis, it answers the question *how. How* is a car manufactured? *How* does the internal combustion engine work? *How* do you change a tire? The answers to these questions differ from each other in tone: the answer to the first would make a scientific article in an encyclopedia; the answer to the second would be a feature story in a newspaper; the answer to the third would be practical directions. But the three are alike in *pattern:* in each answer, exposition analyzes a process, an ongoing sequence of events. Process analysis describes sequence or chronology. This pattern demands that we follow chronological order, advancing from a beginning by steps to an end.

When our analysis of process explains how something is made — automobile, perfume, skyscraper — we have something like an encyclopedia article. The writer's task is narrative, and often descriptive; the writer must struggle to clarify scenes and actions for the reader. Where process analysis gives directions — how to change a tire, how to make waffles, how to find an apartment in Manhattan — the writer must take special care to consider the audience's level of knowledge. It is easy through carelessness to speak of lugs to people who may not know what a lug is, or to ask the reader to add "a little" salt without indicating how much "a little" is.

We must be wary of confusing process analysis with cause and effect. If we write an essay on *why* yeast makes flour and water rise in a bread pan, we write a scientific explanation, in which necessary effect follows particular cause. If we write an essay on *how* to bake bread, with a recipe and steps of action, we analyze a process. If we intrude the chemistry lab upon the kitchen, mixing up how and why, the essay may become incoherent through internal disorder, and the bread smell like a Bunsen burner. Keep *why* distinct from *how,* cause and effect from process analysis. Or if the shape of your essay requires that you use both patterns, the one after the other, be certain that you retain control, and for the sake of clarity indicate the difference between the two rhetorical patterns.

Encyclopedia articles often exemplify exposition as analysis —

both of process's *how,* and of cause and effect's *why.* The encyclopedia explains how crude oil becomes gasoline, and how gasoline makes the internal combustion engine work. At the same time, the scientific entries in the encyclopedia tell us why gasoline is flammable, and why certain parts of the world are richer in petroleum deposits than others. Cause and effect analysis is analogous to the science of the laboratory; process analysis is analogous to engineering and applied science.

Process analysis, like the other rhetorical patterns, can make a whole essay, or a small part of one. Suppose you had a general interest in forms of energy. You might begin a paper by classifying energy into its sources; oil, fusion, wind, coal, water, sun. You might compare and contrast the different sources. Focusing on petroleum, you might narrate the journey of crude oil from discovery to extraction to refining to transportation to retail sales to vehicle. This narration would be a sequential, chronological analysis of process. This analysis could occupy most of an essay, with much detail; or, cut down with skill, it could become a paragraph or two in a larger structure.

Definition

Definition uses a variety of rhetorical patterns — which is why we discuss it last. A dictionary often defines a word by offering near synonyms. If we need to know what a "portal" is, words like "entrance" and "door" and "entryway" can help us. Sometimes a dictionary begins defining something by telling us what class it belongs to. A car is a vehicle. A sparrowhawk is a bird. Then the definition distinguishes the particular species from other members of its genus by means of contrast: a car is mechanical, unlike a horse; it is self-propelled, unlike a bicycle. If we look up "sparrowhawk," we find first that it is a bird, and then, by a series of narrowing details, what sort of a bird it is: its characteristics, its markings, its habits. We go from the broadest classification — "bird" — to the narrowest description of bands of color.

Definition must often move deeply into description. Some portions of definition — like naming the bands that distinguish one bird from another — require exact observation, adjectives of color, details of width in inches or millimeters. An icthyologist, telling us about a newly discovered Antarctic fish, needs description as much as he needs classification.

Frequently we need definition in exposition in order to clarify matters for an audience. In analyzing the process of changing a tire, we may realize that the reader needs to know what a lug is. In writing about downhill skiing perhaps we mention moguls. If we think of our audience, we know that we must define a mogul, because readers who have not skied may find "mogul" an obscure word.

Always define a word that comes from a particular sport or pastime, discipline or profession. Such definition is invaluable, in the service of clarity. We use simple definition in our writing when we recognize: this is the kind of word that would drive me to the dictionary, if I wasn't familiar with its use in this context.

When we organize a whole essay in the pattern of definition, usually we define another kind of word. The meaning of "sparrowhawk," like the meaning of "broadax" or "Abraham Lincoln," is agreed upon. But suppose we define a subjective or philosophical word: "conservatism" or "imagination" or "passivism" or "romanticism" or "democracy." We can write an entire essay to define such an idea; we can write a book — we can write a library of books. Definition is the rhetorical form most common to philosophical writers. Wanting to understand wisdom, or good, or literature, or social class, we pursue philosophical definition. These definitions require other patterns of rhetoric, in the course of their accomplishment. In order to define democracy, we must compare and contrast it to other forms of government. In order to define "Maturity" we need to classify stages of growth. Our thinking's purpose determines our essay's pattern.

ARGUMENT AND PERSUASION

In writing expository prose, we assemble details — facts, anecdotes, descriptions — to understand and to explain, not to take a position and defend it. On occasion, we might seem to argue that something is superior to something else — say, the Cubist painters to the Impressionists — when we are really only giving reasons for personal preference. If we are explaining our own likes and dislikes, we are writing exposition; we are not arguing that anyone else should feel as we do. Exposing our preference is valid exposition. When I read someone's praise of crocheting, I can enjoy and understand it, without feeling any pressure to make an afghan.

On the other hand, sometimes we do write arguments, in which we try to persuade the reader of a thesis, to convince him. In an argument, we will use exposition, but we will also have a thesis to defend, so we will need to use the techniques of argument and persuasion: clear thinking, reasonableness, and taking account of the opposition.

Therefore, we will speak of argument mindful of the treatment of rhetorical patterns in exposition. We must remember what we have learned about ways of explaining, because exposition is the core of argument.

Most of the time, in writing an argument, we are dealing with debatable material. We cannot *prove* our thesis as a mathematician or a philosophical logician can, by manipulating his own terms. We cannot measure our results in a cyclotron like a physicist. We are dealing with probabilities and persuasions, not certainties or proofs. Or say that we are dealing with an old-fashioned sense of the word "proof," an inexactness that we might call "the agreement of reasonable people." We have an opinion; we may feel it is true; we may believe it strongly. But we must recognize that other people have other opinions, and respect those opinions, if we are going to try to persuade them.

The honest writer avoids some forms of persuasion, or attempted persuasion. "The rhetorician would deceive his neighbors. / The sentimentalist himself"— as I quoted before from W. B. Yeats—and in much dishonest writing the writer is both sentimentalist and, in Yeats's sense, rhetorician. The loaded word— when the dictator's police shoot "unarmed civilians" or "a traitorous rabble"— or loaded syntax— when the beer company asks, "As a lawyer, what do you think of Fitz's?"— can combine to make a whole essay into loaded argument, or propaganda. Arguments, ideas, or phrases seem to say one thing, and really say another. In good writing, we must avoid such subterfuge.

Clarity in Argument

To avoid fooling ourselves, and trying to fool others, we must apply to our arguments all the standards for clarity and forcefulness that we have discussed. Misusing the passive verb can help us avoid responsibility, and confuse an argument. Abstract nouns are misused often by the writer reluctant to *see* what he is talking about; this reluctance makes a vagueness, which fuzzes over a reality that might do damage to an argument. To argue well, we must be wary of misusing conjunctions, and implying cause or sequence or another relationship that the evidence cannot support. Most first drafts leave us with problems in verb forms, abstract nouns, and askew syntax; but in arguments, these errors often defend us against understanding what we are saying and cover holes in our argument. These errors are not merely mechanical; they are *learned* errors by which we fool ourselves. Here is some hasty thinking from an impromptu.

> Last night Kiss played at the gym. I started thinking about Mr. Williams back in Harbor Springs (my counselor). Because he was forty or fifty, he hated the new music, and once a terrific trick was played on him. He was acting principle and some guys got the key to the p.a. and hooked up a two hour tape of rock and turned the p.a. up loud and jammed the lock and split. (Kiss was part of the tape.) People like him should never be in high schools. They hate kids. They never remember that they were kids and they've got no sense of humor at all. In fact, middle aged people should never be allowed to teach teen-aged kids. They don't understand. This fact was true in my whole school except for Miss Casey since she never grew up anyway.

Mr. Williams may well have been annoying, and the practical joke amusing, but we cannot take an argument seriously when it is so one-sided.

Reasonableness in Argument

Most of the time, we persuade by being reasonable — and also by seeming so. The *being* is clear thinking; the *seeming* is tone. We will *be* reasonable by writing with clarity, and by avoiding typical errors of thinking that I will mention later. We will *seem* reasonable by refusing to be dogmatic, by allowing time to opposing points of view, and by writing with the modesty that distinguishes between fact and opinion. It is not that we should continually qualify our remarks by tagging them with phrases like "in my opinion"; it is more the attitude we take. If it is in fact raining, it will not be dogmatic to assert that the grass is wet. But if we look at a girl and call her pretty, obviously we are uttering a feeling of our own, nothing *necessarily* follows except within ourselves.

Of course fact and opinion are mixed; the mixture is humane and necessary. We are only obligated, for the sake of honest writing, to know which we are writing. A fact is information that can be documented from historical and scientific sources. ("Truth" is elusive; the scientific "facts" of one century may be illusion to another; a "fact" is what we can reasonably accept as true.) It is also a statement of personal experience that can be accepted as reasonable. "It rained all day, July 5, 1971" can be fact; "Hester looked pretty" is opinion, or surmise,

and not fact. When we refer to someone else's documented opinion —
"her minister thought that Hester looked pretty" — we are on the
border between fact and opinion. It is a pity that human life is so full
of twilights; day and night are so easily distinguishable; but everything
human seems to flourish in twilight.

When we quote the minister, we have quoted an outside source,
which makes us appear objective, yet we have quoted only an opinion.
With this sort of reference, we can write as if the reference were fact if
we do not lean on it too heavily. On the other hand, if we make the
minister's opinion the fulcrum in our essay ("But contrary to her doctor's statement, we know from her minister that Hester looked pretty.
Therefore . . ."), the opinion will crumble and the essay collapse. We
have let ourselves seem to be unreasonable.

For persuasive argument, we must discover a tone that uses fact
when it is relevant, inserts opinion modestly and reasonably, allows
time and space to doubts, and builds a sequent argument by paragraph
steps that the reader can follow. In the current debate about federal
funding for the arts, it is common for dogmatists to pretend that their
antagonists either hate *all* the arts, or love the arts at the expense of
all other social amenities. The useful argument listens to both extremes. A student wrote in a theme:

> Although it may seem a waste of money to provide symphony
> orchestras with millions while people starve, if we don't provide
> food for people's minds as well as their stomachs, we will find that
> there are many kinds of starvation.

Here, the attempt to classify kinds of deprivation — nutritional and
artistic — indicates a mind that refuses to close itself off. The student
went on to favor artistic subsidies, but with economic limitations on
them, because the student was open to more than one idea.

For a purer example of argument, we might go to the editorial
page.

> Studded tires are definitely out of season in July and they may be
> out of season permanently if legislation banning tire studs gets to
> the governor's desk, as now seems likely.
> The News supports this legislation, not because it doubts the
> margin of safety that studded tire users claim is increased but
> because the case against their continued usage in Michigan is
> stronger and more economically defensible.
> Even the safety factor of studded tires may be overrated. In ap-
> plying the studs ban, enough senators accepted the contention that

studs cut grooves in highways which, when filled with water during rainstorms, set up conditions for hydroplaning.

Hydroplaning may occur when a cushion of water builds up between the pavement and the tires, causing the driver to lose control.

Studding tears up highways, there doesn't seem to be any question about that. Road repair programs are accelerated under the pounding of stud wear. Instead of getting a 20-year life expectancy out of concrete highways, Michigan motorists may get only half that, when studded tires are permitted.

. . .

All this means is that state taxpayers will be paying more and more to keep their highways in decent shape. Snow tires already provide some safety without the disadvantage of chewing up roads. And of course, winter-time driving requires special care and restraint on the part of drivers anyway.

Studded tires are best on glare ice, a condition that occurs only a few times during winter. With or without studded tires, glare ice conditions or sleet requires the utmost in driver caution. In fact, drivers are urged not to take to the roads in these conditions.

Continued use of studded tires is not warranted for the few occasions in which they work best. Do they save lives? Their supporters say they do. But caution and restraint save lives without the disadvantages studded tires have. Highways are for the pleasure and utilization of all motorists, not just those who believe in studded tires.

"Highways Are for Everyone, Not Just Studded Tire Users,"
The Ann Arbor News

This editorial is pure argument in the sense that it contains little exposition, little explaining, and much advocacy. Still, to advocate its points, it must stop to explain what "hydroplaning" is, and it must refer to facts like the life expectancy for highways.

Also, it must try, at least, to account for the opposition's arguments.

Time for the Opposition

When we hope to persuade, we should pay court to the opposition. We should seek to imagine all possible rebuttals to our position, and figure out how to answer them. We should be both sides of the debating team, like any good debater. Then in our written argument we should deal with the most important objections. Sometimes we can take on the objections directly. Suppose we are arguing that football is superior to baseball, presenting not merely a personal preference, which would be exposition, but an argument or a persuasion of general superiority. Recognizing a common objection to football, we might say, "People have argued that football glorifies violence, and baseball skill, but. . . ." Then we could contradict by means of anecdote, by appeal to a hypothesis, or whatever. And we could do the same for other objections.

Thinking of opposing arguments is a natural system for multiplying ideas. Put yourself on the other side. Gather evidence and argument against your thesis. Counter every notion of your own, and by this means gather material. But when you write, don't arrange your essay like a dialogue between disputants. A pro-con structure jerks the head from right to left to right. You don't need to give equal time. You need not say:

> It has been argued that middle-aged people have more experience than the young, because they have lived longer.
> But mere time does not give understanding. In fact, age seems to diminish understanding. . . .

Brainstorming the opposition's argument, you can accept it and counter it in the flow of one sentence.

> Although middle-aged people obviously have more experience than the young, they don't seem to profit from it.

Similarly, you find positive ideas because you have thought up answers to negative ones. Suppose you are attacking the SST. Trying to gather arguments, you think of a proponent saying, "Time to cross the Pacific will be cut by a third." You turn this to your own purposes by saying, "Surely we do not need to spend billions of dollars in order to give businessmen three fewer hours to drink Scotch in the lounge of a 747." Of course on some occasions, the opposition's voice, droning in the Senate of your head, may come to sound more and more reasonable. If it happens, you might as well take a deep breath, cross out your old title, and begin again: "The Necessity for Studded Tires."

Our most persuasive argument, in the long run, is positive praise, and not attack on the opposition. We persuade by praising football more than we do by attacking baseball. If we record straightforwardly too many opposing arguments, we lose focus; we are spending most of our time dealing with the contrary to our thesis, even suggesting ways in which the reader might disagree with us, and our statement becomes fuzzy. We lose not only unity but argument as well. Often, it is wise to deal with opposing arguments obliquely, raising them in dependent clauses, while the main clauses carry the argument, as in the argument above about the middle-aged and the young. This device raises the issues that the opposition would raise, but keeps clear direction. We might say, "Although football is violent, there is a skill to its violence that is greater and more subtle than the skill of baseball."

Time for the opposition is part of tone, and is part of the honesty in openmindedness. We do not win many arguments by asserting that no other point of view is possible, and that anybody who disagrees with us is stupid. *Admit* that football is violent, that studded tires may stop a skid on glare ice, or that middle-aged people sometimes understand the young. If you don't admit these facts, you are telling lies and leaving your valid argument unsupported. Also, you are losing your reader, especially the one you want to reach — the idiot who disagrees with you.

The Order of Argument

Once you have gathered valid arguments, you must organize them. In your catalogue of argumentative points and details of evidence, some entries will make a stronger case than others, and some will be more interesting. The general rule is to save the best for last. Argument or persuasion is ordered by increasing intensity. We start with the arguments in which we have to concede most to our opponents, or the arguments to which we hear our mental adversary objecting, "But . . . but. . . ." Then while he is still spluttering, we pin him to the ground with our best points. The persuasive effect derives from the crescendo. Suppose we are arguing that a national educational television network should be set up, equal in budget to NBC, CBS, and ABC. We might list:

> success of PBS, despite low budget
> annoyance of advertisements
> higher cultural level
> pressure of advertisers
> guards against government control
> expense small compared to other expenses of govt.
> public service broadcasts
> service for minorities.

Of course the relative weight carried by each item, in this limited list, would depend on the evidence and argument the writer could adduce in support. We will show one way of ordering the list, but another writer might find a different order more persuasive.

Let us speculate on what we have here. Two arguments are rebuttals of the imagined adversary, who tells us, "Government television will be the mouthpiece of the state," and, "All this money should go to more worthwhile uses." Perhaps the essay could begin by generally stating the thesis, and then proceed by acknowledging that, of course, laws should provide a certainty that government could not interfere with programming. In answering the objection about cost of the enterprise, we might turn it in the opposite direction, and use it to further the thesis. Money spent on a national network, we could say, could be used for minority representation, and for educational programs; the network would *serve* social welfare, not *starve* it. For many an essay, this point might be strong enough for a conclusion.

We might give examples of the annoyance that advertising causes; personal anecdote could supply detail. Anecdote from library research might also indicate pressure from advertisers on the networks, and this topic might lead to the content in commercial television, contrasted to the content possible on public television. The final point might be the PBS example. "You say it will never work? Here it is, and it works."

There is no one way of organizing this material. Each of us has a way to order our argument *best,* according to our best material. In general, the crescendo is the right kind of noise. In the essay imagined above, an alternative conclusion might talk about the network's high cost — as if we were giving away a point — and then turn it around and say that, despite the cost, the social effects would be so great that the network is cheap at any price. We would certainly *not* end it, after the PBS example or the argument about social effects, by remarking that, of course, it would be essential to avoid government interference.

We should organize the arguments in ascending form. But one kind of exception might come up. Our opening — our zinger — ought to be *interesting,* and not merely our least effective argument. We might open with an anecdote about a PBS program, and not mention that institution again until the end, when we reap the crop that grew from the seed we planted. Or we might start with an anecdote about a tasteless commercial, one that annoys everybody, and will not only catch the reader's attention but engage his sympathy. In the beginning, we are most interested in holding readers so that we can persuade them later. At the end, we are interested in convincing them once and for all.

A relay team in track has four runners. Usually the fastest one runs last. The second fastest runs first, slowest is second, and third is third: 2, 4, 3, 1. It is a good arrangement for arguments, also.

Logic and Emotionalism

If we wish to persuade, we must avoid illogic. Logic is not the only mode of persuasion, goodness knows; poems and stories convince us, but although they are sometimes logical in form, they usually convince by embodying feeling in character and image. Arguments embody feeling also, usually in anecdote and detail. But when we think publicly, and preferably when we think privately, we must understand logic in order not to think badly. We all know some logic without perhaps calling it that; it is common sense. Suppose I told you an anecdote about a bald man who hijacked a schoolbus. Suppose I told it well, embodying feelings of fright and outrage. But suppose then I added, "Therefore, bald people are dangerous criminals." You would laugh at my thinking; and you would be right. I would have committed an error in logic, generalizing from insufficient evidence. If I had been more modest in my declaration, I could at least have shown you my opinion without raising laughter; if I had said, for instance, "I know it is dangerous to generalize from a particular, but this sort of news item seems to me to characterize what is wrong with the United States today. At least to my prejudiced eyes, bald people are always making the trouble." Here, the anecdote is used not for pseudoargument, but as a device to introduce an opinion. There is no false logic, because there is no claim to logic.

When we decry "emotionalism" we are blaming not feelings but misuse of them, or misunderstanding of how to use them. Emotionalism uses an appeal to feelings to disguise a defect in thought. If we say:

> I love this country, its history and its landscape, and I would die to defend it against an invader. I don't believe that anyone who refuses to defend his country should enjoy the rights of citizenship.

we are taking a rather extreme position, based on emotion, but we are not covering bad thinking with camouflage made of feeling. We are openly displaying our patriotism and our prejudice. We do not say that the second sentence follows *logically* from the first. It certainly depends upon it *emotionally*. But if we write,

> Cowards who ran away to Canada to keep from getting a scratch in defense of their great country ought to be jailed for life because of all the brave men who have died for freedom

we write loaded words, we beg questions, and we state an illogical cause. The errors in writing and thinking are manifold, but we may lump them under a general label, "emotionalism pretending to argue." We find this kind of bad writing on any heavily charged issue: busing, abortion, legalizing marijuana.

Common Fallacies in Thinking

If we wish to study logic seriously, we should go to the philosophy department. The philosophical study of logic resembles composition-course logic as a 747 resembles a balsawood glider. Yet knowing a little about common errors in thinking is essential, if we are to make arguments for our essays that are likely to persuade a reasonable reader.

Many common fallacies in thinking are misuses of induction or deduction.

To begin with, here are two quick definitions. *Inductive reasoning,* or *induction,* draws general conclusions from particular examples or evidence.

> As a result of these experiments we conclude that if the temperature of water falls below 32 degrees it will freeze.

Deductive reasoning, or *deduction,* applies a general truth to a specific instance.

> All men are mortal. My editor is a man. My editor is mortal.

Here are some fallacies that most of us fall into, from time to time.

Generalizing from a Particular. Arriving at a general statement from a single supporting fact, or from too narrow a range of particulars, is a common error of induction. We do not collect enough evidence, and we assume that because X happens twice, X will always happen. Because the one Eskimo in our circle of friends likes to read Trollope, we generalize that Eskimos enjoy Trollope. Clearly, such an assumption is illogical. We need a greater sample, we need to spread the net wider for evidence; if we cannot support a generalization, we must abandon it, or admit its worthlessness as proof. When we use the rhetorical pattern of example, we must take care to avoid this error.

This advice is not to be construed as advice to avoid the particular. Often an argument takes on persuasive power because a specific bit of evidence is taken as *typical* of the generalization. The argument's effectiveness, however, still depends upon the validity of the assertion, not on the one particular. In the essay on public television, if one began by describing a nauseating commercial, and then said, "Therefore, we must have at least one national network without advertising," one would be illogical. If, after the particular, one listed other offensive commercials, and perhaps gave statistics on the time devoted to commercials, one would be ready for a generalization without having relied on only one particular.

The Overinclusive Premise. In the furnace of argument, many logical errors are forged from flawed metal like the overinclusive premise. All of us are guilty. "Everybody who goes to medical school is out for money." "All people who act like that are Communists." These statements are generalizations (possibly from a limited sample) that common sense will not tolerate. If we say "some" instead of "all," we are more sensible — and we have admitted that our charge is not inclusive.

Guilt by Association. Guilt by association (or holiness by association, for that matter) is another common form of faulty thinking. The Mafia, we believe, is an Italian organization. Whenever we identify someone as Italian, the Mafia may cross our minds. Everyone *knows* this sort of thing is absurd; yet if we do not keep constant scrutiny over ourselves, we fall into it again and again. Politicians thrive on guilt by association. Because socialists believe in free medicine, anyone who believes in free medicine is a socialist. If we attach an emotional negative to the word "socialist," we can think that we have just argued free medicine down. We have only associated emotively; we have not *argued* at all.

Begging the Question. In this error the arguer assumes the truth of a premise that readers may question. The arguer could try to prove the assumption, but does not. Someone might say, "The rising incidence of mongolism proves that early advocates of a test-ban treaty were correct." The writer neither demonstrates that mongolism *is* rising, nor shows that nuclear testing causes mongolism. Causation asserted but unsupported is common in sloppy thinking. In an earlier example, we quoted, "Cowards who ran away to Canada. . . ." Here the reader hears the assumption that anyone who went to Canada to avoid the draft is a coward. The question is not raised and explained or argued. A questionable idea is asserted. Sometimes misused conjunctions beg the question: "Although middle-aged, he wore levis."

Evading the Issue. Cleverly avoiding facing an issue is another favorite tactic of politicians, usually introduced by an assertion that they will *not* evade this issue: "I'm glad you asked that question." Sometimes a politician will say something like, "I believe in freedom of assembly, and the freedom of all Americans regardless of race, creed, or color to assemble with people of their own choice." If we look at the context, we may see that the speaker is not defending freedom but segregation, the rights of associations to exclude members on account of race. "Right to work" laws are laws against forms of union organizing. "Freedom of the press" is sometimes an umbrella for pornographers. Ignoring the question is frequently a deliberate illogic, an attempt to deceive the public by diverting attention from a real goal, which might seem disreputable, to a substitute goal, of which anyone might approve. Evading the issue is euphemism in paragraph form. The gap between expression and meaning is large enough to power the buses of Cincinnati for twelve years and six months.

Non sequitur. "Non sequitur" is Latin for "it does not follow." We use the term for a statement or idea which *appears* to grow out of an earlier one (by causation, by chronology, by logic, or whatever), but which upon examination fails to make the trip.

> He was a doctor, and therefore an all-around man.
> She left an hour ago, although her car wouldn't move.

Non sequiturs sometimes afflict us when we are trying to make complex sentences for conciseness. When we use the rhetorical pattern of cause and effect, we sometimes wander carelessly into non sequitur, or into the next fallacy.

Sequence as Cause. Post hoc ergo propter hoc, literally "after this, therefore because of this," is a form of non sequitur. The assumption is that if B follows A, A causes B. This assumption is not logical

Because we saw one billiard ball hit another, and the second ball move, we *assume* cause and effect, but we cannot know it.

Again, the politics of paranoia adopts sequence as cause for its argument. "Rudolph Blast was in Newark the day before a bomb went off; therefore. . . ." Such evidence is not even circumstantial, and it does not hold up in court. If a hurricane comes after a bomb test, we cannot safely assume that the bomb test caused it. Sequence is not causation, and is inadequate evidence for it.

The Argument ad Hominem. The argument ad hominem — the Latin means "at the man" — rises in us frequently when we lose our tempers. The ad hominem argument diverts attention from issue to personality, and thus it is a refinement of evading the issue, and of the non sequitur. We ignore the issue and attack the person defending the issue or symbolizing it. When someone defends destroying trees to make a parking lot, we attack him for wearing white socks. A friend says, "I believe in a socialist form of government, because the profit motive, which is basic to a capitalist system, robs us of our humanity and corrupts our intelligence to serve materialism." We rebut him, "Your cousin sells lipstick."

Analogy as Fact. Analogies in argument are most useful. They illustrate the sense in which we mean a statement that might otherwise be too tenuous to be understood. They embody attitude and feeling, and they persuade by being exact carriers of feeling. But we can fall into another common form of illogic by arguing from analogy as if it were fact. Suppose we want to write about different civilizations, which seem to have features in common — like beginning, developing, fulfillment, and decay. To carry this idea to a reader, we invent an analogy, each civilization is like an organism: it is born, it grows up, it matures, it becomes old, and it dies. So far so good. We follow the abstract thought by associating it with concrete things. But many writers become so accustomed to a dominant analogy that they begin to take it literally. Arguing later that our own civilization must end, we say, "Like all organisms, our society must come to death." The argument is invalid because a civilization is not literally an organism and therefore we have not proved that what is true of an organism will be true of civilization. The analogy is not the thing itself.

The General Fallacy: Imprecision. These common fallacies are not exclusive. An issue is often evaded by a non sequitur, or by an argument ad hominem. Our terms overlap, as our errors do. Common to all these errors is the general fallacy, imprecision.

Ambiguity is a general term that can apply to various imprecisions, to misplaced modifiers, to pronouns with uncertain antecedents, and to words used carelessly for position and for meaning. Clarity is essential to argument. One of the commonest flaws in argument is using one word in several senses. We can fool ourselves into thinking that we have said something profound when we are really just playing with words. Abstractions lend themselves to ambiguity more readily than specific words. Watch out for prose like this, from a theme about campus politics:

> Jerry was liberal, but not so liberal as Mary Huncher. Some of the
> professors, even the most liberal, were conservative when it came
> to Mary Huncher, who claimed that they weren't liberal at all.

With ambiguity, or question begging, or whatever, we fall into fallacies unless we examine ourselves. By self-serving, or laziness, or in anger, we commit sloppy thinking, and when we think carelessly we lose the argument, if our reader is thinking well. We must discipline ourselves to honest clarity in thought, or we lose not only arguments but much more. The careless thinker is a liar, and will never learn to be clear.

Argumentation organizes exposition to make a point, to advocate and to persuade. Without an expository base — when we approach the pure opinion of the editorial or the political speech — we are more prone to emotionalism and imprecision. Writing well, we provide an expository basis to our argumentative thrust. By concentrating first on exposition, in its many rhetorical forms, and then on argument with the help of clear exposition, the beginning writer can learn to discover, and to tell, the truths that he perceives.

DESCRIPTION

In talking about patterns of rhetoric, we have shown how description becomes necessary to clear exposition — in classification, in definition, in comparison and contrast, and in other patterns as well. Description by itself is another kind of writing.

Description by itself *evokes* place, scene, or time of day; we feel that we are there. Evocative description, of course, forms a frequent part of fiction and autobiography.

The order we give to details, in description, is usually *spatial.* But words follow each other — they are not simultaneous in the way a picture seems to be — and we necessarily move in words from point to point in a sequence that has to be chronological. So in description we talk about space in a temporal way. In describing a scene, we can begin from the periphery and move to the center, or move from the center to the periphery. The order is not crucial: it is crucial that there *be* an order; that we do not move from center to periphery to center to periphery to periphery.

Some writers seem to think of description as filler, or padding. Not only beginning writers, but professional ones who write the less skillful stories in adventure or confession magazines — and are paid by the word. In these places, we will see description used to delay information, to tantalize.

> Rhonda turned from the window, her eyes wet. "Belinda," she said to me, "I could forgive you for Ron. I could forgive you for Bruce. I could even forgive you for Althea. But there is one thing I can never forgive you for!"
>
> She turned back to the window, her eyes flooded with tears. My cheeks suffused with shame. Over her shoulders, I could see the sweet meadows of home, adeck with lilacs and daisies, their sleepy heads waving in the soft breezes of June, while above, storm clouds gathered to chase away the white puff-ball clouds of early morning.
>
> "They Had a Name for Me," *Real Romance*

Description's main function here seems to be suspense, as a daytime television serial uses an advertisement. To be sure, it also shows a heavy-handed attempt to use description as a good writer does, *for the meaning and the feeling that images carry.* This anonymous writer has the protagonist look at the fields in an attempt to symbolize her past innocence, contrasted to the torment (storm clouds) of the sinful present.

When you write well, your description cannot seem to approach pure symbolism because then it will not seem to be real description. But there is room for invention, especially when we use comparisons (simile, metaphor, analogy) that carry feeling. Remember the girl writing about her grandfather's funeral. "The sky turned dark" was boring. "Storm clouds gathered" would have been a pathetic and trite attempt to appeal to our emotions. But the new comparisons would have worked.

In *Ulysses*, James Joyce has Stephen Dedalus look at the sea when he is feeling depressed. "The ring of bog and skyline held a dull green mass of liquid." Though the description is literal enough, it expresses

Stephen's emotions. Here is a passage from a book by a doctor who spent a year in Vietnam. He describes finding some bodies washed up on a riverbank.

> Four nude, markedly swollen, water-logged bodies lay side by side on their backs. Each had a massively swollen face. Eyes seemed to try to bulge out of sockets whose contents were as big as apples. Their lips were three times normal size and each mouth was open and round like that of a fish, with a massive splitting tongue protruding skyward. A thin, bloody fluid trickled from their nostrils.
>
> Massive edema and rigor mortis held their arms up and out in front of them with fat fingers reaching toward the clouds. Their scrota were the size of softballs, and their swollen penises stood as if erect. Their knees were bent in identical frog-leg positions. The smell was overwhelming and hundreds of flies circled around those which were already busy inspecting the mouths and nostrils. There was not a mark on the front of their bodies.
>
> John A. Parrish, M.D., *12, 20 & 5*

The accurate description has modifiers that come from observation, not from the worn tracks: *fat* fingers, *frog-leg* positions, *massively swollen*; it has statements of fact and measurement, like "massive edema" and "three times normal size"; it has comparisons that embody feeling, like "mouth . . . open and round like that of a fish," " . . . as big as apples," and "scrota . . . the size of softballs."

Statistical accuracy in description must never be confused with emotional accuracy. Again, sometimes we must lie, to tell the truth. A contemporary poem ends with a sudden vision: a hundred cows in a field. Reviewing this poem, a hostile critic (carried away by his anger into absurdity) asked *how* the poet could tell that exactly one hundred cows were in the field. He received a postcard from the poet: "I counted the teats and divided by four." The pseudoparticular has a long tradition. It does not lie, because we know it is not intended to be statistically accurate. When Wordsworth says of daffodils. "Ten thousand saw I at a glance," we do not suspect him of counting. If we write, "The sandwich was as thick as the toe of Italy," we are saying that it was very thick — so thick that it astounded and delighted us. If we say, "The sandwich was two-and-five-eighths inches thick," we are being pedestrian, and expressing little astonishment. Mere accuracy is all right, but the exaggeration is a lie that is truer to the feeling than accuracy is. Sometimes in writing, you can be accurate in both ways at once; maybe a list of ingredients could be literally true, and also carry an astonished reaction to abundance: "salami, bologna, ham, roast beef, corned beef, Swiss cheese, provolone, onions, lettuce, red peppers, olive oil, vinegar, and, I believe, oregano."

NARRATIVE

In talking about patterns of rhetoric, we saw how narrative was necessary on occasion to exposition — in process analysis, in the story that gives us an example, and in other patterns. It is time to look briefly at narrative by itself, as another kind of writing.

Narrative must find its way between two extremes. It must have enough detail so that the reader knows what is happening. It must not have so much detail that the reader gets bogged down. The detail must be appropriate; it must have the right quality, as well as the right quantity. Here is a fragment from a theme.

> When I heard the doorbell, I stood immediately, my heart pounding. I knew it was her. I didn't answer it quickly, and heard the door opening toward me. I must have forgotten to lock it! I looked around for a second. Then I picked up my suitcase and climbed through the open window.

The first version had been:

> When I heard the doorbell, I placed my hands against the arms of the chair and pushed myself upright immediately. My heart pounded in my chest. I knew it was her. For some reason, I didn't move toward the door right away. I just stood there and stared, my heart pounding, my legs shaking. Then I heard a sound like the doorknob turning, and a creaky noise as she must have started to push the door open. I realized that I had forgotten to lock it when I came in from the drug store. I looked all around to see if there was any way to escape. I saw the window open beside me. Without thinking of what I was doing, I picked up my suitcase, checked the fasteners on it, set it on the windowsill and lowered it to the ground, which was only about 2½ feet down. Then I sat down on the sill myself, swinging my legs through, and pulled the rest of my body after me.

This student was commendably rich in detail; but total recall is boring. We need the essential narrative, and nothing more. The revision does it. If the writer had gone further in cutting, and written,

> When I heard the doorbell, I climbed out the window.

we would have missed some crucial information.

Here is a passage from the book about Vietnam from which I quoted earlier. It begins with exposition and ends with narrative.

> The western perimeter of the camp bordered on a "free-fire zone." Anyone or anything that moves in that area is free game and can be shot, mortared, or bombed. All of the military maps had it marked as such and supposedly all civilians in the area had been informed.
>
> The camp dump was in this "free-fire zone." Each morning at the same time a truck drove out to the dump and all of the tin cans, cardboard containers, wrappers, and garbage from the camp was dumped about fifty meters inside the zone. Within minutes, the dump was filled with Vietnamese from nearby villes [hamlets] gathering cans and garbage. The marines in the watchtower would fire close to them to frighten them away. A few days earlier, an eight-year-old Vietnamese boy had been wounded by these warning shots and was brought to the aid station where he was kept until his wounds were healed. One day he stole an orange soda from a marine who shot and killed him as he tried to run away.
>
> John A. Parrish, M.D., *12, 20 & 5*

This is a good example of narrative used in exposition, and ultimately, as you can see, in an argument that does not need stating.

————— **EXERCISES** ———————————————————————

1. Here are ten topics. For each topic, think of three alternate treatments, each employing *one* rhetorical pattern. For instance, if the topic were thunderstorms, we could *classify* them, discerning different sorts of storms; we could tell how they occur, by *process analysis;* or we could *define* a thunderstorm.

pollution	snowmobiles
baseball	zoos
cousins	freshmen
state parks	graveyards
supermarkets	shoes

2. Here are five passages from essays. Discern the rhetorical pattern — or patterns — employed in each.

a. To test properly the mechanic removes the plug and lays it against the engine so that the base around the plug is electrically grounded, kicks the starter lever and watches the spark-plug gap for a blue spark. If there isn't any he can conclude one of two things: (a) there is an electrical failure or (b) his experiment is sloppy. If he is experienced he will try it a few more times, checking connections, trying every way he can think of to get that plug to fire. Then, if he can't get it to fire, he finally concludes that *a* is correct, there's an electrical failure, and the experiment is over. He has proved that his hypothesis is correct.

Robert M. Pirsig, *Zen and the Art of Motorcycle Maintenance*

b. Jim Murray, the great West Coast sports columnist, addressed one of his books to readers who did not need "larger-than-life heroics all the time. They can take their sport with a squirt of humor and a twist of irreverence."

In the spirit of this attitude I remember some years back, in the heat of a hectic football game at Harvard Stadium, a pigeon (Marianne Moore would have exclaimed in delight!) landed on the four-yard line — turning as soon as he put down and setting out toward the goal line with great determination, his neck bobbing in his haste. But then indecision, or perhaps something startling in the grass, diverted his attention, and he stopped a foot or two short. He revolved, peering here and there . . . and suddenly that immense crowd focussed on him, neighbors nudging each other and remarking on the pigeon's vacilla-tion just at the brink of the goal line: megaphones went up, cries of "Go, bird, go!" erupted from one side of the stadium and, "Hold that pigeon!" from the Harvard side.

George Plimpton, "The American Tradition of Winning"

c. So Grant and Lee were in complete contrast, representing two diametrically opposed elements in American life. Grant was the mod-ern man emerging; beyond him, ready to come on the stage, was the great age of steel and machinery, of crowded cities and a restless bur-geoning vitality. Lee might have ridden down from the old age of chivalry, lance in hand, silken banner fluttering over his head. Each man was the perfect champion of his cause, drawing both his strengths and his weaknesses from the people he led.

Bruce Catton, "Grant and Lee: A Study in Contrasts,"
in *The American Story*

d. The first baseline in defining Presidential types is *activity-pas-sivity*. How much energy does the man invest in his Presidency? Lyn-don Johnson went at his day like a human cyclone, coming to rest long after the sun went down. Calvin Coolidge often slept eleven hours a night and still needed a nap in the middle of the day. In between the Presidents array themselves on the high or low side of the activity line.

The second baseline is *positive-negative affect* toward one's activ-ity — that is, how he feels about what he does. Relatively speaking, does he seem to experience his political life as happy or sad, enjoyable or discouraging, positive or negative in its main effect. The feeling I am after here is not grim satisfaction in a job well done, not some philosophical conclusion. The idea is this: is he someone who, on the surfaces we can see, gives forth the feeling that he has *fun* in political life? Franklin Roosevelt's Secretary of War, Henry L. Stimson wrote that the Roosevelts "not only understood the *use* of power, they knew the *enjoyment* of power, too. . . . Whether a man is burdened by power or enjoys power; whether he is trapped by responsibility or made free by it; whether he is moved by other people and outer forces or moves them — that is the essence of leadership."

James David Barber, The Presidential Character

e. What is pornography to one man is the laughter of genius to another.

The word itself, we are told, means "pertaining to harlots" — the graph of the harlot. But nowadays, what is a harlot? If she was a woman who took money from a man in return for going to bed with him — really, most wives sold themselves, in the past, and plenty of harlots gave themselves, when they felt like it, for nothing. If a woman hasn't got a tiny streak of harlot in her, she's a dry stick as a rule. And probably most harlots had somewhere a streak of womanly generosity. Why be so cut and dried? The law is a dreary thing, and its judgments have nothing to do with life. . . .

One essay on pornography, I remember, comes to the conclusion that pornography in art is that which is calculated to arouse sexual desire, or sexual excitement. And stress is laid on the fact, whether the author or artist *intended to* arouse sexual feelings. It is the old vexed question of intention, become so dull today, when we know how strong and influential our unconscious intentions are. And why a man should be held guilty of his conscious intentions, and innocent of his unconscious intentions, I don't know, since every man is more made up of unconscious intentions than of conscious ones. I am what I am, not merely what I think I am.

D. H. Lawrence, "Pornography,"
in Pornography and Obscenity

3. If you have used an anthology of essays in your composition course, discuss in class the types of writing you have recently read. Which expository essays — and which parts of essays — use the rhetorical patterns discussed at the beginning of this chapter? Discover examples of the following patterns — and be prepared to defend your discoveries: example, classification, division, cause and effect, comparison and contrast, process analysis, definition.

4. Here are some argumentative passages. Analyze them for their logic, order, reasonableness, and fallacies, if they have any. Remember that these passages are excerpts.

a. A realistic discussion of the place of athletics in our educational program is long overdue. There is in both our schools and colleges today a vicious overemphasis on competitive athletics. Such overemphasis is seriously destructive of our entire educational system.

A short while ago, many Americans were disturbed because unofficial team scores showed that the Soviet Union had clearly taken first place, the United States second, in the Olympic games in Rome. These Americans were ready to argue that we must step up our concern with athletics in school and college as part of our struggle against communism. This line of reasoning needs to be examined. To understand my point, imagine that our independence as a free nation turned solely on the outcome of the next Olympic games — analogous to the ancient trial by combat between selected champions of opposing forces. Under such conditions, we would be forced to modify all our educational practices with the single aim of producing the greatest number of prize athletes.

This is pure fantasy, of course. One hardly needs to argue that we are engaged in a cold war — and in all probability, a long one. What we must have to win this real struggle are more and better scientists, engineers, doctors, lawyers, teachers, technicians. In short, we must improve the academic output of our educational system. Such being the case, overconcern with the development of prize athletes might well jeopardize our future.

That we need to have concern with the physical development of our youth goes without saying. Our society is heavily industrialized and urbanized. Our children and young people need to devote more time to effective body building and physical exercise. This problem was recognized nationally when, in 1956, President Eisenhower by executive order established the Council on Youth Fitness at the Cabinet level and the Citizens Advisory Committee. I have come to believe that all public-school pupils should devote a period every school day to developing their muscles and body coordination. This means that each school needs a gymnasium of ample size. It also means, in many schools, drastic changes in the content of the physical-education courses. However, in many junior and senior high schools, there is not room enough in the gymnasium to allow my recommendations to be adopted. Too often, physical-education programs are scheduled for all pupils only two or three days a week.

Yet, in some of these same schools, the facilities and instruction are excellent for the relatively few on the basketball or football team that competes in interscholastic contests. Why? Because the community demands public entertainment in the form of winning teams. Fuzzy thinking attempts to relate athletic spectacles to the physical well-being of all our citizens. But there is little real concern for what is of prime importance, namely, the physical fitness of all youth, both boys and girls. . . .

James B. Conant, "Athletics: The Poison Ivy in Our Schools,"
in *Look*

b. It should be obvious that even with schools of equal quality a poor child can seldom catch up with a rich one. Even if they attend equal schools and begin at the same age, poor children lack most of the educational opportunities which are casually available to the middle-class child. These advantages range from conversation and books in the home to vacation travel and a different sense of oneself, and apply, for the child who enjoys them, both in and out of school. So the poorer student will generally fall behind so long as he depends on school for advancement or learning. The poor need funds to enable them to learn, not to get certified for the treatment of their alleged disproportionate deficiencies.

All this is true in poor nations as well as in rich ones, but there it appears under a different guise. Modernized poverty in poor nations affects more people more visibly but also — for the moment — more superficially. Two-thirds of all children in Latin America leave school before finishing the fifth grade, but these "desertores" are not therefore as badly off as they would be in the United States.

Few countries today remain victims of classical poverty, which was stable and less disabling. Most countries in Latin America have reached the "take-off" point toward economic development and competitive consumption, and thereby toward modernized poverty: their citizens have learned to think rich and live poor. Their laws make six to ten years of school obligatory. Not only in Argentina but also in Mexico or Brazil the average citizen defines an adequate education by North American standards, even though the chance of getting such prolonged schooling is limited to a tiny minority. In these countries the majority is already hooked on school, that is, they are schooled in a sense of inferiority toward the better-schooled. Their fanaticism in favor of school makes it possible to exploit them doubly: it permits increasing allocation of public funds for the education of a few and increasing acceptance of social control by the many.

Ivan Illich, Deschooling Society

c. Women's roles have always been more tightly bound than men's to parenthood, more limited by conceptions of reproduction as mysterious, ritually impure, restricting the development of either mind or soul. As a result, women's rebellion against the simple maintenance role that has been their lot is more vivid than men's. Since the beginning of social life, the performance of men's activities, however tedious, dangerous, or humdrum, has been associated with ideas of achievement that both men and women have often mistaken for innate superiority. If men are conscripted and sent to war without ever being consulted by the distant old men who control the corridors of power, they, too, have no more choice over their lives than women without contraceptives have for preventing an unwanted pregnancy.

In this moment of vision, people caught in one kind of life that they have never questioned are getting a glimpse of the way other peoples live; the current questioning of the status of women is part of the whole process of questioning a social order that no longer meets the newly aroused hopes of the people who live within it. The voices of women are combining with voices all over the world against a new worldwide system of political and economic exploitation of the land, the sea, and the air, and the endangered populations that depend upon them.

But there is a difference between women's voices and the voices of all the others who live meaningless lives within a world where they have no part in decisions made too far away. The revolts of the oppressed — slaves, serfs, peons, peasants, manual workers, white-collar workers —:are part of the periodic attempts to correct social systems that are seen as exploitative and unfair. But this is the first time in history when the progress made in the control of disease and reproduction has offered to the female half of the population escape from a lifelong role that was defined for every one of them simply by gender. Having one or two children and rearing them together as parents who have chosen parenthood means for men and women — but most of all for women — permission to participate at every level in our highly complex society.

And it is not only women who gain — society gains. Where once half of the best minds were consumed in the performance of small domestic tasks, society can now draw on them. Where women's experiences — inevitably different from men's because women all had mothers with whom they could identify — have been fenced off from contributing to the high-level planning of the world, they can now be used in the attack on such problems as chaotic abuse of food, resources, human settlements, and the total environment. When women are once more able to participate in decisions and are free to be persons as well as parents, they should be able to contribute basic understandings that are presently lacking in the world. These basic new understandings include the fact that food is meant to be used to feed human beings, not to serve as a weapon or commodity; that towns were meant for generations to live in together, not only as barracks or bedrooms; that education can be used to make life meaningful; that we do live in a world community that is here but is unrecognized, in all its interdependence and need for shared responsibility.

Margaret Mead, "Needed: Full Partnership for Women,"
Saturday Review

d. In all previous consideration of class warfare there had been at least the assumption that the design of human beings was adequate, unbiased, functional, and not particularly in need of alteration. It was assumed that if the working class took over the functions of the ruling class, they would still be able to act with the conventional organs of men. But the ultimate logic of the sexual revolution required women to stand equal to the male body in every aspect — how could this equality prevail if women in competition with the other sex for the role of artist, executive, bureaucrat, surgeon, auto mechanic, politician, or masterful lover should have to cry quits every now and again for months of pregnancy plus years of uneasy accommodation between their career and their child, or else choose to have no children and so be obsessed with the possibility of biological harm, worse, the possibility of some unnameable harm to that inner space of creation their bodies would enclose?

One could speak of men and women as the poles of the universe, the universal Yang and Yin, offer views of the Creation in such abstract lands as seed and womb, vision and firmament, fire up a skyworks of sermon and poem to the incontestable mystery that women are flesh of the Mystery more than men — it would not diminish by a coulomb those electrics of wrath in the eyes of those women whose revolutionary principles are Jacobin. It was as if the High Grand *Geist* of the Jacobins had returned to state, "It was never enough to sever the heads of the aristocrats. The time is now come to get the first Aristocrat of them all. Since He designed women at a disadvantage, such Work must be overthrown!"

What a job! Men were by comparison to women as simple meat; men were merely human beings equipped to travel through space at a variety of speeds, but women were human beings traveling through the same variety of space in full possession of a mysterious space within. In the purse of flesh were psychic tendrils, waves of communication to some conceivable source of life, some manifest of life come into human beings from a beyond which persisted in remaining most stubbornly beyond. Women, like men, were human beings, but they were a step, or a stage, or a move or a leap nearer the creation of existence, they were — given man's powerful sense of the present — his indispensable and only connection to the future; how could a woman compete if she contained the future as well as the present and so lived a physical life on the edge of the divide? What punishment traveled into the future with the pile driver's clang? Whose unborn ear heard the loss of a note in the squawk of the static? The womb was a damnable disadvantage in the struggle with the men, a cranky fouled-up bag of horrors for any woman who would stand equal to man on modern jobs, for technology was the domain of number, of machines and electronic circuits, of plastic surfaces, static, vibrations, and contemporary noise. Yet through all such disturbance, technology was still built on conformity of practice. If it could adjust to rhythm, tide, the ebb of mood, and the phasing in and phasing out of energy in the men and women who worked its machines, nonetheless such adjustments were dear to technology, for each departure from a uniform beat demanded a new expensive control. The best operator was the uniform operator, and women had that unmentionable womb, that spongy pool, that time machine with a curse, dam for an ongoing river of blood whose rhythm seemed to obey some private compact with the moon. How this womb, unaccountable liaison with the beyond, disrupted every attempt at uniform behavior!

Did women get into automobile accidents? Count on it, more than half their accidents came on a particular week of the month — just before and during menstruation was the time of that week. So, too, were almost half of the female admissions to mental hospitals in that week, and more than half of their attempted suicides, half the crimes committed by women prisoners. . . .

Norman Mailer, *The Prisoner of Sex*

5. Describe the flaws in these arguments.

a. You're stupid! That's why I'm right.

b. In 1979, Rupert Hudmill announced that he was no longer associated with the Virgin Vampires. When he decided to destroy the punk rock group, Hudmill gave no reasons.

c. When Luke hit the first pitch of the game into the left-field stands, it was obvious that Mitchell could no longer pitch.

d. When we consider the question of aid to underdeveloped nations, we should always consider first that we, too, are an underdeveloped nation.

e. Since democracy died in Rome with the elevation of Augustus, one can no longer go to the Romans for lessons in the democratic process.

f. No one who dresses like that could possibly know Mozart from Mantovani.

g. Warmongers who masquerade as friends of Egypt or Israel attempt to deceive the gullible.

h. Everybody who votes for Cynthia is a racist.

6. Take a subject in which you have some interest. Meteorology, for instance. Set up an argumentative thesis for a paper, like "Long-range weather forecasts are futile." Collect notes for arguments. Then take the opposite tack, and try to establish arguments against your original position.

7. Make up examples for each of the common fallacies of thinking listed in this chapter. Read aloud in class.

7

Autobiography, Fiction, Criticism, Research

When we write autobiography or fiction, we write narrative, we describe and we use dialogue. Literary criticism is a common form of exposition. A research paper may use many rhetorical patterns as it shapes and organizes material assembled from library work. It is time to investigate these special kinds of writing.

AUTOBIOGRAPHY

In the Vietnam book quoted in the last chapter, Dr. Parrish was writing autobiography; not a book about his whole life, but about a bad year of it. We are all authors of a continual autobiography. In letters we tell what we have been doing and thinking; we confide to a diary or a journal; in conversation we tell anecdotes about experiences lived through or observed. We may even tell an old friend what we did last summer, that traditional theme is only as far away as paper and ball-point pen.

Your own life is your greatest source for writing. Even when you are explaining, arguing, doing research, or writing fiction, your own experiences — eating, reading, loving, being tired, playing checkers — are what you think with and what you argue by. Analogy and metaphor derive from experience. The problem is reaching the source, and bringing the experiences back for use, so that a reader can understand them.

In writing out of your own life, you confront that mass of experience directly. The exercise we furnish the imagination, in recovering the past for autobiography, aids other writing. The same spirit that floats to recall the old summers, in autobiography, will float to discover the precise analogy, in argument.

Memories of childhood make good subjects. Many writers seem to need the distance years give — the long mellowing in the mind — before they can write fully and with feeling. Everyone alive has the material to fill a thousand books. Our minds are huge storehouses of material — the look and smell of a room on an afternoon in May, five years ago, the sun making stripes on the wood floor, the sounds of mother in the kitchen, and the newspaper hitting the door. Nothing fully understood is trivial. Any difficulty lies in a heaviness in our spirits that will not float. We must recover in order to make new. Sometimes it helps to close the outward eyes to let the light reach the inward eyes of memory; to feel, see, hear, and taste the vivid past. Then if we hold the mental image close, we can describe it in original words, and the words will release other memories, and by soft explosions we remake an old world in new words. From description we can move to action, and bring narrative into our autobiographical writing. Remembering the people we know, we hear them talk the way they talked. We write dialogue, in autobiographical prose, not as a word-for-word transcript of ancient conversations, but as imitated style joined to remembered content. We write dialogue by ventriloquism.

In the first chapter of this book, I talked about "getting ideas." I have just been talking about it again. Of course our own experience should be our happiest source in writing. *It is all there.* But many young people are curiously alien to their pasts. They write more easily about Egypt than they do about Shaker Heights. I suspect that this happens when writing is entirely mental, and is even subsumed by the intellect. By daily writing, and by deliberate brainstorming — *by cultivating daydream* — we can learn to recover the past, and to reconstitute it by means of style. Here is a passage of reminiscence, which the author has organized by place.

> The first I heard of Runkel's Saw Mill was when the oldest Johnson boy, Dave, who was working there at one dollar a day, came home from the doctor with his arm in a sling. When the doctor looked at the arm hanging like a rope with every bone crushed into fine splinters, he told Dave he would have to cut it off up close to his shoulder and Dave said, "You cut off my arm and some day I'll kill you. You put those bones back in place." Dave had noticed

that a wide leather belt was running a bit to one side of its pulley and tried to push it back in place with his hand while it was running, and his whole arm had been pulled around the pulley. The doctor had done his best to put the bone splinters together, but he told the boy that he had no hope that he would ever have any more use of that arm. There were days and weeks when everybody thought the doctor was right, but Dave's healthy body and fine spirit fooled them all. His elbow was always stiff and bent so he appeared to be wanting to shake hands with you, but within a year he was able to do a man's work again.

My next contact with Runkel's Mill was when I dropped my new jackknife into the mill race. One of my brothers and I were fishing above the race, and I caught a small bass that had swallowed the hook so far down that I had to use my knife to cut it out. Just as I did that I dropped both the fish and my knife into water moving rapidly towards the mill wheel. When my brother saw how quickly both fish and knife disappeared he said, "Let's get away from here. If we ever fell in we'd be ground to pieces by that wheel."

It wasn't the water wheel but one of the circular saw blades that killed the mill owner. And it wasn't the big seven-foot blade used to rip lengthwise through the logs, turning them into boards and planks, but a small eighteen-inch blade used to cut boards into various lengths. Mr. Runkel had left the saw running and had gone some distance from it when the lock nut turned off and then the blade went spinning through the air, striking him across his back as he was bending down. It cut his body nearly in half and went on to embed itself in a beam on the side of the mill. It was said that his death must have been instantaneous. After that the family operated the mill a few years with hired help, but its usefulness was about at an end.

When the creek left the mill and pond it flowed on through a wide valley. About once a year, in the spring rains, it overflowed its banks and the whole valley became a shallow river. . . .

Tracy Redding, Hoosier Farm Boy

And the author goes on about the creek, *remembering*.

FICTION

Writing fiction is writing out of your life with imagination added. It is autobiography to write about what happened last summer. It is fiction to write about what happened next summer. We are most apt to write fiction by using last summer, but revising it in our imaginations. Sometimes we write what we *wish* had happened last summer. Sometimes we write what we *fear* might have happened last summer. Suppose we went swimming, were frightened by undertow, but made it safely to shore. We could write it autobiographically. Or we could "make up" a story: a character ("he") drowns trying to make it to shore; or he saves a pig from drowning / discovers a cache of perfume bottles / meets a grandmother who flies balloons. Starting from real experience, the daydream can take us anywhere. And wherever we go, we must ultimately take care that our story is structured, economical, and makes its point — just as we do in other forms of writing.

Daydream can take off from next to nothing. You are in a store, and you have an impulse to shoplift. You resist the impulse, but walking home you dramatize in a daydream what might have happened. Perhaps you get away with it and feel guilty. Then what do you do? You return the stolen goods surreptitiously. And are accused of shoplifting! Or you mail them back. Or you give them to someone who needs them, and relieve your guilt, but then wonder further about your action. On the other hand, perhaps you daydream that you are caught: police, trials, disgrace. The daydream can lead to a story in the third person. "She" does some shoplifting. You describe her, her feelings, her actions, her responses to actions by others, and the end of her story. It all started from your own impulse and your subsequent daydream. Or the daydream can be a happy one, a wish fulfillment. You do the impossible feat, and everyone loves you. But in writing make it "he" or "she." When the daydream is glorious, the word "I" is self-glorifying. For that matter, sometimes "he" or "she" sounds narcissistic, when the character shares obvious background with the author. Beware of writing about a noble freshman. Scrutinize your daydreams for dealing with the wholeness of an experience. In fiction as in autobiography, we often omit a discreditable feeling because we don't want to admit it to ourselves.

Fiction by definition is a lie. But more profoundly, good fiction is telling the truth, because fiction embodies an emotional truth. The wishes and the fears in daydream are as real as tables or days of the week. Fiction *can* lie badly, and often does, when it distorts human nature to flatter the author's or reader's ego, or when it gives the reader or the author an easy way out of a real dilemma, or when it substitutes comfort for anxiety by turning birth and death into something like cotton candy. Situation, comedies on television — those endless hours of cute children, cranky husbands, and kooky wives: the television family — distort our lives wholly, to manufacture a light narcotic that induces the passive consumer to buy products. We have all been nurtured on these lies; they are big as mountains inside us, and we must be wary, or we will spend our lives reciting lies under the impression that we are speaking the gospel of observation. Truth to feeling requires vigilant scrutiny.

A good deal of fiction, in fact, is more autobiography than invention. Only the names are changed to protect the guilty. Good fiction is seldom written out of daydream widely detached from the author's experience. In good historical fiction, and in good science fiction, the authors are able to daydream feelings from their own experience into situations they imagine. But historical novelists know history, and science fiction writers know science. Writers do well to stick close to their own background. Northern liberals write bad fiction about southern racists or the black world of northern cities. Farm girls write badly about the jet set, and boys from expensive prep schools write badly about camps of migrant laborers.

We make up stories, and we use our experience as the starting point and as the continuing reference point. Making up stories is an acquired ability. If we write much fiction, we develop a story-making facility. If we see a stop sign punctuated with bullet holes, we begin to imagine the hunters who used it for target practice. We see them, we hear their dialogue, we imagine or create their motives. Imagination depends on experience, on understanding ourselves and the people we have known. The story-maker creates a world of strangers based upon a lifetime of friends and acquaintances.

Description, narrative, and dialogue are ingredients of fiction, but the most important ingredient is the imagination which makes form. The same instincts for shape that lead you to cut irrelevances in autobiography, and to distort the real for the sake of the whole and the probable, work in fiction. Many writers find it necessary, in fiction as in autobiography, to write big and to cut small. In the first draft they cannot be sure which details are going to be expressive, and which not. They float to gather. It is important for many writers not to adhere too closely to a plan. If you start to write a story about shoplifting, and then find yourself getting more and more interested in the storekeeper's character, let it happen. You may find that you have written a story about the day of a storekeeper, and in rewriting you can shift your attention to accord with what you find you have written. Let the characters have a life of their own. Let your imagination take over from your planning intellect. Let it ride. Then revise to make a whole.

One of the most useful ways to keep a story whole is to stay with one viewpoint: either your own, viewing all your characters' minds as if you were God; or one of your characters, a "he" or an "I," whose mind you read. Point of view helps unity and focus, which are as important to fiction as they are to essays.

As there are clichés of adjective / noun, and of dead metaphor and of analogy, so there are clichés of plot. Though we write from experience, we must be sure that it is our experience of people we have observed in real life, and not our experience of that television family. Formula plots fill television, movies, confession magazines, and best-sellers. Boy meets girl, boy loses girl, boy gets girl. Good man appears evil, usually by his own nobility; good man is vindicated and keeps his ranch. Be wary of pat resolutions, problems solved along commonplace lines. As with all writing — from single words to trilogies — originality is honesty / is knowing yourself / is hard-headed scrutiny *as well as* the loose invocation of dream. We arrive again at the paradox of the miserly spendthrift.

Dialogue and Quotation

Dialogue belongs with narrative, in fiction and autobiography. In exposition or argument we may use *quotation,* repeating conversations to explain or to persuade; and in writing up research it sometimes lends authority to quote directly from an interview, or from a source of speeches like the *Congressional Record.*

Dialogue moves best with fewest direction markers. Here are two passages for contrast

> The door opened. Nancy stood there, wearing a white coat.
> "What do you want?" inquired Jim quizzically.
> "I want my ring and my record player," she spat. Her eyes flashed.
> "Get out!" he exclaimed.
> "Don't you care at all, any more?" she beseeched him tearfully.
> "Shut up!" he shouted, slamming the door.

Let us revise this passage.

> The door opened. Nancy stood, wearing a white coat.
> "What do you want?" said Jim.
> "I want my ring and my record player."

"Get out."
"Don't you care at all, any more?"
"Shut up!" He slammed the door.

Maybe the second example is too sparse, but it is better than the first. Beginning writers often explain things too much, telling us twice what we know the first time. (It is like speaking of "white snow.") And in dialogue, it is usually better to use varieties of "say," or to use nothing, than it is to use verbs like "growled" and "whimpered." (See H. W. Fowler, in *Modern English Usage*, on "Elegant Variation"; he says fine things about substitutes for "say.") In other contexts, we prefer the particular because it is more expressive, but these dialogue verbs have been overused, and if the dialogue is adequate, the verb usually over-explains what we know from the speech itself. Sometimes, we might want to know that "he whispered," because we need the information that he was trying not to be overheard. When you can, omit this information. The writer of dialogue should try to convey the speaker's tone *within* his speech, and avoid the stage directions.

⭐ CRITICISM: WRITING ABOUT WRITING

Often we are asked to write about something we have read. Sometimes we write to investigate something about writing; we may analyze the argument of an essay, or its paragraph structure, or its use of narrative and description. But here, I want to deal briefly with the kind of writing we usually call "criticism," essays that talk about the content, the form, and the value in other essays, in stories, and in poems.

When we write on an essay, we judge its clarity, its persuasiveness, its unity, its interest — and we apply appropriate standards. If the essay is wholly expository — say, a disquisition on constructing golf courses — we are silly if we blame it for its lack of persuasiveness. If we read a polemic between a feminist and a male chauvinist, we miss the point if we don't deal with the argument. It is sensible to draw a line between explaining and evaluating. Though the two activities are not wholly separable, we should try for clarity to know which we are doing. It is perfectly possible to explain without evaluating. It is not possible to make an understandable evaluation without giving some concrete reasons for your position — without quoting or paraphrasing, examining, and explaining.

In looking at an essay — or even, sometimes, at a story or a poem — it is sensible to ask three questions. It helps you to avoid mistakes in reading. First, consider the purpose, moment, or occasion behind the writing. Is this a reminiscence or an editorial? A recipe or a denunciation? You must ask: *What is it for?* Second, you must ask: *Who is it talking to?* Is it addressed to friends or strangers, to initiates or adversaries, to Kiwanis or the Hell's Angels? Third, *What is its tone*, or assumed vantage point? Is it written by the humble investigator or the omniscient intelligence? Is it sharing a discovery, piece by piece, or is it handing us results from a discovery already consummated?

For more guidance in criticism, look at a book like Sylvan Barnet's *A Short Guide to Writing about Literature*. Here, we must be content to name two general ways of dealing with literature, to look at two common fallacies in dealing with literature, and to present a few examples of criticism from the classroom and from printed sources.

One way to deal with poems and stories is to analyze them, to separate the qualities in the work of art — requiring the mental act of taking stock by stepping back inside your mind and looking — and report on them separately. In dealing with a story or a novel, for instance, you can analyze the author's characterization, use of setting, and development of plot. Also, you can analyze *within* these categories. The writer will show character by dialogue, by description, by action, and by other characters' reactions. In analyzing poetry, we may deal with character, setting, and plot (and speaker and occasion) also. Or with sound, or imagery, or metaphor.

In analysis we dig into the methods a writer uses, to explain what he has done. Never worry, as so many beginning critics do, that analysis will destroy a work of art. Ten million words have been written about *Hamlet. Hamlet* still sits on the top shelf, looking down at all the books written about it, smiling a little.

Remember as in all essays to narrow your topic. You cannot write a six-hundred-word essay about *Hamlet* and approach your topic. If you are going to write about *Hamlet,* or *Huckleberry Finn,* or "The Love Song of J. Alfred Prufrock," find a tiny topic and be adequate about it. Write about "Mark Twain's Use of the River in *Huckleberry Finn,*" or "Hamlet's Puns," or "Eliot on Prufrock's Character."

Another kind of critical paper is explication, analyzing line-by-line a short poem or a passage from a longer poem or a work of fiction. We use explication more with poems, like character and metaphor. Analysis means attempting to deal with larger units, and must be more summary. Explication is more narrow and more thorough, dealing with the words as they come — somewhat as Chapter III of this book deals with words — and therefore lacking the overview. In a paper of explication on *Hamlet,* you might take the Queen's lines about Ophelia's death.

> There, on the pendent boughs her coronet weeds
> Clambering to hang, an envious sliver broke;
> When down her weedy trophies and herself
> Fell in the weeping brook. Her clothes spread wide;
> And, mermaid-like, awhile they bore her up:
> Which time she chanted snatches of old tunes;
> As one incapable of her own distress,
> Or like a creature native and indued
> Unto that element: but long it could not be
> Till that her garments, heavy with their drink,
> Pull'd the poor wretch from her melodious lay
> To muddy death.

and go through them line by line; you find the *use* of flowers, as a parallel to Ophelia and as a value put upon her; you also find the vivid imagery that carries the action — those floating clothes! — and the metaphor of drunkenness. And more.

Of course a million pitfalls await anyone writing criticism. One of the greatest is the reader's sense of the author. Too often in reading we ask ourselves silly questions: "Did T. S. Eliot really mean all these hidden meanings?" The whole notion of "hidden" meanings begs the question: who is hiding what from whom? And to suggest intention is naïve. With anything complicated in our own lives, are we ever really certain of our own intentions? Then how are we able to know Eliot's intention in 1909, or Shakespeare's in 1601? We must keep our eyes on the text, not on the imagined "idea of the author." If something is *there* in the text (if we can show that it is *there*) then it's there — no matter if the author rises before us in ectoplasm and denies it. The only qualification we need make is historical, and governs the meanings words had at the time they were used. "King" meant something to Shakespeare it cannot mean to us. The OED is especially helpful in reading old books.

Avoid the biographical fallacy. First, avoid arguing from intentions, which are always unknowable. Second, avoid using the work of literature to illuminate the author's life. Of course if you are writing a biography, write a biography — and use the literature as you will. But do not write biography that pretends to be criticism, as so many critics have done. People writing about a novelist try to explain his novels by referring to his first marriage, his depressions, and his isolation. But novels are novels and we learn nothing about them by learning what experience *may* have informed them. Critics writing about W. B. Yeats's poems seem to run from the poems to the life as fast as they can. When a poem is about a woman, they cry "Maud Gonne!" — the name of a woman whom Yeats loved, unrequitedly — and lift their eyes from the page. They have said nothing about the poem. Keep your eyes on the words in front of you, when you write criticism. If you love an author's work, it is fascinating to know something about his life, and nothing is wrong with this knowledge. But when you are writing about the work, write about the work.

The beginning critic should avoid the biographical fallacy, even if it seems artificial to avoid using what he knows. Probably it is more difficult to avoid *the autobiographical fallacy.* This kind of criticism is not really about the poem; it is about the reader's response to it. At the extreme, it can read like this passage from an examination:

> I like this poem. When I first read it I felt scary, and then when I read it over again I felt good. I like the images and the sounds and the ideas. The poem is *right on!*

There is no need to quote the poem that the student is writing about — it could be any poem. All he talks about is himself.

This kind of paper often comes from enthusiasm, and is an understandable excess. We *respond* to something! We want to tell people. We want to copy our response in our prose, making it equivalent to a printout of our heartbeat, body temperature, and brain waves. We try to name our feelings. But in our enthusiasm, we have forgotten the object about which we are enthusiastic. Our subject, instead, is I, I, I. Unwittingly, we have fallen into egotism, and we praise the poem because it was able to create such a response in us. Remember two things especially, when you write criticism: *the poem is important, not the poet.* And equally, *the poem is important, not the reader.*

Robert Frost has a poem called "Acquainted with the Night."

> I have been one acquainted with the night
> I have walked out in rain — and back in rain
> I have outwalked the furthest city light.
>
> I have looked down the saddest city lane.
> I have passed by the watchman on his beat
> And dropped my eyes, unwilling to explain.

I have stood still and stopped the sound of feet
When far away an interrupted cry
Came over houses from another street,

But not to call me back or say good-bye;
And further still at an unearthly height
One luminary clock against the sky

Proclaimed the time was neither wrong nor right.
I have been one acquainted with the night.

One student on a final examination wrote this "analysis" of this poem:

> I really love this poem. I chose to write about it because I know
> just the feeling that Frost is writing about. It reminds me especially
> of one night at home last summer. All afternoon I had been feeling
> depressed, listless. I turned on the television and turned it off. After
> supper I helped my mother with the dishes but then I didn't want
> to hang around with my brothers the way I usually did but I felt
> like taking a walk. It was really funny, because I never take walks,
> but that night I really wanted to.
> I didn't walk outside town, so that part isn't the same. But it
> rained! When I read the poem it all came back to me, so clearly! . . .
>   . . .
> The poem is excellent because it is so realistic and so moving.
> Reading it, my whole body felt just what was happening. It made
> me remember the strangest feeling of my life, when I too was one
> acquainted with the night.

This reader, partly because of coincidence, will not let herself see the
poem itself. Another student wrote about the same poem.

> Robert Frost's "Acquainted with the Night" recounts an experi-
> ence of loneliness and of restlessness. Frost — or the man who says
> "I" in the poem — is all alone. He listens as if somebody might be
> calling for him but it is never him. It seems as if it couldn't be him,
> or even as if he wanted to be alone. Why does he walk back and
> forth in the night if he doesn't want to be alone? He is *sad* (a lane
> isn't sad unless you are) and he is guilty or shameful about some-
> thing ("dropped my eyes, unwilling to explain") — maybe about
> wanting to be alone? When you come to the clock at the end of the
> poem, at first it seems to be some sort of symbol of what he is
> looking for. It is "luminary," which can just mean that it was
> lighted up, but which sounds mysterious and grand. And it was "at
> an unearthly height." What does this mean? Well, it could just
> mean that it was really separated from the earth a lot — as Frost

(the walker) isn't, concerned with street and lanes and feet. But it is *sort* of a hint of God or some mystery too. But just when he thinks he's going to get an answer, it turns out that the time of day isn't what matters. It's "neither wrong nor right" so the walker must be worried about right and wrong, or about not being able to tell them apart. Maybe that's why he wants to be alone?

The poem has fourteen lines. It is some sort of a sonnet. It doesn't have much colorful language in it. It's mostly just what happens, but there are words (like the ones at the end I mentioned) which are really well used. "Acquainted" is a funny word, like an "acquaintanceship" not a "friendship." It sounds as if Frost knew the night *very well* but didn't like it very much. And the part I like best is when he says

> stopped the sound of feet
> When far away an interrupted cry
> Came over houses from another street.

It's so *cold*, that way of referring to your own walking by hearing it.

The poem is a good one. It's more complicated than it looks. It gives a feeling — of desolateness — and a reason for it.

This sensitive examination answer, pondered over and revised into an essay, would make a good piece of criticism.

Here is an example of polished criticism. The paragraph is from a book about Thomas Hardy, and introduces a discussion of *Tess of the d'Urbervilles.*

> With *Tess of the d'Urbervilles* we come to one of the most contentious novels in the language. Once again the theme is preposterous human suffering, an ill-starred individual, fighting the good but lonely fight against invincible odds. But this time the sufferer is an attractive peasant girl, "a pure woman" who, although she had "passed the Sixth Standard in a National School," was still a child, still a country innocent, when she was sordidly raped. Yet in *Tess,* a Transcendental purity of spirit, embracing all that is charitably humble and devotedly unselfish, survived long enough to enthrone humanity in a brief splendour. The book, too, is a commentary not only on Victorian morality but on the complexity of sexual morality as a whole. Despite the martyrdom and literary canonisation of Tess, there is no vindication of unchastity, and this is a factor not necessarily forced by the magazine-readers. All Hardy's heroines are chaste.
>
> George Wing, *Hardy*

Because this is a paragraph from a book, I do not print it as a model for a theme, but as an example of a writer beginning to cope with fiction and fictional character. It is easier to find explications and analyses of short poems or parts of poems. Here is R. P. Blackmur going to work on a few lines by a poet named Hart Crane.

> To illustrate the uniformity of approach, a few examples are presented, some that succeed and some that fail. In "Lachrymae Christi" consider the line
>
> Thy Nazarene and tinder eyes.
>
> (Note, from the title, that we are here again concerned with tears as the vehicle-image of insight, and that, in the end, Christ is identified with Dionysus.) Nazarene, the epithet for Christ, is here used as an adjective of quality in conjunction with the noun tinder also used as an adjective; an arrangement which will seem baffling only to those who underestimate the seriousness with which Crane remodelled words. The first three lines of the poem read:
>
> Whitely, while benzine
> Rinsings from the moon
> Dissolve all but the windows of the mills.
>
> Benzine is a fluid, cleansing and solvent, has a characteristic tang and smart to it, and is here associated with the light of the moon, which, through the word "rinsings," is itself modified by it. It is, I think, the carried-over influence of benzine which gives startling aptness to Nazarene. It is, if I am correct for any reader but myself, an example of suspended association, or telekinesis; and it is, too, an example of syllabic interpenetration or internal punning as habitually practiced in the later prose of Joyce. The influence of one word on the other reminds us that Christ the Saviour cleanses and solves and has, too, the quality of light. "Tinder" is a simpler instance of how Crane could at once isolate a word and bind it in, impregnating it with new meaning. Tinder is used to kindle fire, powder, and light; a word incipient and bristling with the action proper to its being. The association is completed when it is remembered that tinder is very nearly a homonym for tender and, *in this setting,* puns upon it.
>
> R. P. Blackmur, "New Thresholds, New Anatomies"

You don't have to know all the references Blackmur makes to see his method. And you don't have to write with such references to write criticism.

By and large, I suspect that it is good policy, when you are about to write a critical essay, to avoid reading critics — especially critics of the work you are writing about. (Sometimes it is useful to write a research paper on the criticism of a work of art, to sample the range of opinion. But this is another matter.) If we are going to write on Huck Finn, we can easily drown ourselves in the contradictory criticism of Huck Finn, and end by being too frightened to have an opinion of our own. I think we do better, once we have found out what we need to know about the vocabulary in a work, if it is old, to deal intensively with the work itself, and avoid the secondary material that comes from biographers and critics.

For writing criticism is a matter, not of knowing about criticism, but of knowing about the work criticized. Committing ourselves, in our own words, to interpret and evaluate a literary work, we may find that we have read more deeply than we have read before, and think more deeply about what we have read. Criticism helps us learn to read, while we are learning to write.

WRITING RESEARCH

Although research can support an argument, the research paper differs from an argumentative paper by paying most of its attention to assembling information. Sometimes a research paper has no thesis at all. It sets out to answer a question — by what means did the United States acquire Alaska? — and not to prove a point. Research is a way of learning, important in formal study, which we can use the rest of our lives: we can research voting records of members of Congress, recipes, genealogy, precedents in zoning for the neighborhood, or types of schooling for information to give the PTA. Research is a method. The research paper is a particular embodiment of the general method. It applies findings from library research, or other investigation, to the aims and forms that make the essay.

First you must choose a subject. Choosing a subject often resembles discovering Chinese boxes, starting with a large box, moving to the smaller one inside it, then to a smaller one inside *that*, until finally we arrive at something of suitable size. We must, as always, *limit the topic*. Often — maybe *usually* — the hardest part of a research paper is finding a suitable topic, and then limiting it. (On pages 35–37, I talked about focus, and about narrowing a topic.)

Broadness, however, is not the only problem that can afflict a topic. In fact, broadness need not be a grievous problem; one can almost always whittle a broad topic down. "Vegetable Gardening" can become "Raising Organic Tomatoes," and "Voting in a Democracy" can become "Absentee Balloting: Its Effects on the Two Parties." When a subject is too scientific or too technical, on the other hand, only years of specialized study will prepare a student to write about it, and "Genetics," for all its breadth, is no more difficult than "The Effects of Gamma Rays on Drosophila." Here, we must abandon our desired topic and look for something less technical. Other subjects prove impossible because research material is unavailable, or insufficiently available. "Vampires in Brazil" sounds fascinating enough, but the library is unlikely to provide the reading necessary. Still another kind of problem is the subject about which there is little to say — a subject adequately covered by an encyclopedia entry, like the history of basketball.

In writing a research paper, the most important decision is choosing a manageable topic — a topic neither too large nor too small to be handled in the assigned number of pages, and a topic neither too technical for a lay audience, nor too specialized for the facilities of a university library.

Since the library is essential to the research paper, let us look at ways to use it.

Using the Library

Libraries hold the past of the species. Large university libraries, with microfilm vaults that collect old books and manuscripts, as well as current periodicals, can satisfy the most specialized inquiries. But even the smallest library contains more than we are likely to learn and to retain in a lifetime. When we walk into a reference room, or among the stacks of coded volumes, we walk in a universe of possibilities. Everything thought and done in human history surrounds us. The first sight of a big library can be a terrifying vision. All these books! How do I find my way? Many a student, entering the largest library he has yet seen, has wanted to flee in terror, and perhaps to settle down in front of the television set, with a bag of potato chips.

But the road maps are there, and people to help. In the next few pages I will talk about card catalogues and reference collections, but first, I want to mention the most obvious things — things sometimes overlooked. Many colleges offer library orientation, and you should never ignore such help. Many also provide a small guide to their facilities, printed or mimeographed, which you can keep and consult when you need to. Finally, there are the librarians — at a desk labeled Information, or at the reference desk, or wherever, who sit there in order to help you out, to advise you, and to acquaint you with the resources stockpiled around you. *Never be afraid to ask a librarian a question.* Whatever you ask, the librarian has probably heard it before: Where do I find out about vampires? What do you have on blue whales? How do you spell "drosophila"?

The librarian will not find the answer for you, but will tell you where to start looking.

The Card Catalogue

The card catalogue records everything that is in the library. Thousands of 3-by-5-inch cards, in long trays, are alphabetized by author, title, and subject. Every book is represented by at least three cards. One card is alphabetized under the author's last name; to find Georges Blond, you look under B and not under G. Another card is alphabetized under the first major word of the title; *The Great Story of Whales* will be found under G, not under T. A third card is alphabetized under the subject, like Whales. Naturally enough, most books are listed under more than one subject; three cards is only the minimum that will represent each book.

Each card gathers all sorts of information, including a *call number* that, in conjunction with the library's own map of its collection, tells us where to find the volume. The cards list publisher, edition (if other than the first), publication date, the number of pages and illustrations, and usually the dates of the author's birth and death and the subjects covered in the book.

Subject, title, and author cards for a single book are on page 279. When we do research, we find the subject cards especially helpful. Under Whales, and Whaling, are more than a hundred and fifty cards in one large university library. But the other listings, of author and of title, are essential also. Sometimes in our background reading we will find a title but no author; then we require the title index. Sometimes we will find a person quoted, but not know whether he has collected his thoughts into a book. Perhaps he has published a book recently.

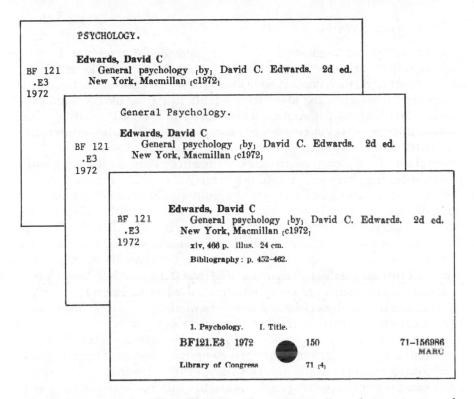

Such speculations will lead us back to the card catalogue, to see if there are books under his name that we should consult.

Here are some things to remember about the organization of a card catalogue.

Subjects are not always listed under the names we choose for them. Therefore the library cross-references for us. If we look up Farming, we will be told to See Agriculture. If there is no entry under the word you have chosen for your subject, try to think of near-synonyms. Or ask a librarian.

Abbreviated words are alphabetized as if they were spelled out. "St." — for "Saint" — is alphabetically ahead of "seraglio." Names beginning with "Mc," "M'," and "Mac" are alphabetized as if they were spelled "Mac." When names with prefixes like "de" and "von" are alphabetized, the prefixes are ignored; "de Kruif" comes under K.

A writer is an author before he is a subject. Books *by* W. H. Auden will appear before books *about* W. H. Auden.

Reference Works

First let me mention a reference book about reference books, appropriately titled *Reference Books,* by Saul Galin and Peter Spielberg. Most libraries have this book, and it is worth looking at; the table of contents indicates the material available in a good library reference room. The authors list encyclopedias first and then dictionaries. The *Encyclopaedia Britannica* remains the best general encyclopedia. Its newest edition divides itself into two multivolumed works. The Micropaedia of ten volumes provides short entries for most topics, and gives bibliographies and also cross references to the detailed, nineteen-volume Macropaedia which has immense articles — as long as a book — on the history of China, for instance. The bibliographies of course lead you straight to the card catalogue in your library.

The various dictionaries include the massive *Oxford English Dictionary* (see pages 68–69). (When you consult British dictionaries, beware of British spelling.) There are also, as Galin and Spielberg show, numerous dictionaries that come to our aid when research leads us in special linguistic directions: dictionaries of slang, of scientific terms, and even *A Dictionary of Clichés.*

Biographical dictionaries run from the common *Who's Who* through the *Dictionary of American Biography,* and into biographical dictionaries that cover all countries and all times. Invaluable to anyone researching contemporary problems are the indexes to periodicals and newspapers, from the *Readers' Guide to Periodical Literature* to the equally useful *New York Times Index.* Then there are bibliographies, catalogues of printed books on certain subjects by which we can discover books our library lacks — and can perhaps acquire by interlibrary loan. The *United States Catalogue* and *Cumulative Book Index* are important, as is the *Publishers' Trade List Annual,* of which most libraries keep back copies.

Then, still dealing with general material, there are all the almanacs and yearbooks, like the *World Almanac* and *Facts on File.* Here we find statistics. Even the *Guinness Book of Records* may be useful in a research paper, at least to provide a lighter moment. Of course there are atlases and gazetteers with much social and historical information, coded according to geography.

When we leave general categories and become specific, we find that there are reference books *within* all disciplines. There are *Who's Who's* that are scientific and medical. There are encyclopedias of music and of architecture, of archaeology and of anthropology. There are indexes to works of art. Many of these special reference books can be found in the card catalogue under the subject name of the discipline itself. And do not forget to consult the kindly librarian.

Under the subject literature are innumerable reference works, from histories of the literatures of various languages, to dictionaries — like the *Oxford* companions to English and American literature, and the *Oxford Classical Dictionary*. *Twentieth Century Authors* has been useful to at least a million students. Some of these books, like the last mentioned, quote criticism of the authors discussed, and most of them include bibliographies of works by the authors, and of works written about them.

In almost all fields of study are works of reference that can help us with research. I cannot list everything that might come in handy. (Galin and Spielberg, attempting to list only the *most* useful books, filled more than three hundred pages.) A few titles may hint at the range that you can expect. There is Grove's *Dictionary of Music and Musicians;* the *Congressional Record;* the *New Catholic Encyclopedia;* the *McGraw-Hill Encyclopedia of Russia and the Soviet Union;* the *Bibliography of Comparative Literature; Anthropology Today: An Encyclopedic Inventory;* the *Mental Health Book Review Index;* the *International Bibliography of Political Science; Nuclear Science Abstracts;* Chambers's *Technical Dictionary; Chemical Abstracts; Mathematical Reviews;* the *Encyclopaedic Dictionary of Physics* — and on and on and on.

Whether you find usable material or not, you will need to take a note for every book consulted, for your own bibliography. And when you find a fact or a notion that you might want for your paper, you need to record it. A 3-by-5-inch card is most useful. Any time you make a note, be sure to write down the information that you will need to include in a footnote. But to deal with this subject, we need another section.

Bibliography

A bibliography is a list of books or other printed sources that the writer has consulted in order to write a paper. Research papers depend especially on outside resources, but even an argument or a book review frequently takes the writer to the library. See the bibliography on page 300, at the end of "The Protector Unprotected." At the end of any paper for which you have done reading, list your sources alphabetically by author.

For a thorough summary of the manners to use in bibliography, consult the *MLA Style Sheet,* second edition. Here is a brief outline.

Underline the titles of books, and enclose the titles of essays and of articles from newspapers and magazines in quotation marks. (In a printed text, words that were underlined in the typescript are set in italics.) Include page numbers when you refer to periodicals, but omit them when you list a book. List publishers of books, cities of publication, number of edition when there is one, and date of publication. When you refer to a magazine, include the date and volume number, and underline the name of the magazine. When an article or book is anonymous, list it alphabetically by title, using the first word that is not "a," "an," or "the." Here are some of the possible varieties of bibliographical entry; notice punctuation.

A periodical article with an author:

> Mumford, Lewis. "The Cult of Anti-Life." *The Virginia Quarterly Review,* 46, No. 2 (Spring 1970), 198–206.

An anonymous article from a periodical:

> "Freud on Death." *Time,* 100, No. 3, 17 July, 1972, p. 33.

A book with one author:

> Graves, Robert. *Wife to Mr. Milton.* New York: Creative Age Press, 1944.

A book with more than one author:

> Cordell, Richard A., and Lowell Matson. *The Off-Broadway Theatre.* New York: Random House, 1959.

An edited book:

> *Page 2.* Edited by Francis Brown. New York: Holt, Rinehart & Winston, 1967.

An article from an edited book:

> Vonnegut, Kurt, Jr. "Science Fiction." *Page 2.* Edited by Francis Brown. New York: Holt, Rinehart & Winston, 1967.

A translated book:

> Chuang T'zu, *Basic Writings,* tr. Burton Watson. New York and London: Columbia University Press, 1964.

A book in several volumes:

> Johnson, Edgar. *Charles Dickens: His Tragedy and Triumph.* 2 vols. New York: Simon & Schuster, 1952.

A new edition:

> Kennedy, X. J. *An Introduction to Poetry.* 4th ed. Boston: Little, Brown, 1978.

[handwritten: pick closest city if more than 1]

Footnotes

Footnotes name the source of a quotation you use in the text, or the source of information used, or on occasion qualify or elaborate a portion of the text. The last use is the least common; it can detract from the flow of a text; we use it only when some information is half-pertinent.

If you quote or paraphrase anything without naming your source, you are plagiarizing. Footnotes are your acknowledgment of indebtedness, your statement of research done, and your contract for honesty. Footnote what you must, but omit footnotes if you feel that the material you are using is obvious. Telling us that whales are mammals, you need not footnote the *Encyclopaedia Britannica*; the information is readily available.

Type the footnote at the bottom of each page, rather than in a clump at the end, for the reader's convenience. To save the proper space for the appropriate footnotes takes planning ahead when you are typing. When you start a new page, in typing up your draft, estimate how many lines of manuscript you will cover, and how much space the footnotes to those lines will occupy. Single-space your footnotes at the bottom of each page. If a page has more than one footnote, double-space between them.

For meticulous advice on footnoting, covering various contingencies, consult the *MLA Style Sheet.*

Number footnotes consecutively throughout the paper; do not start each page with 1.

The number for the footnote is placed at the end of the material footnoted, and slightly above the line of the text, thus.[5]

If the name of the book or the author is given in the text, do not repeat the information in the footnote.

You can abbreviate long titles of periodicals and supply the full name in the bibliography. *The Review of Analytic Psychology* can be *RAP* in a footnote.

Here are some sample footnotes, followed by a list of short cuts and abbreviations frequently used in footnoting.

An article from a periodical:

> [1] Leslie Raddatz, "Actress-Equestrienne with a Problem," *TV Guide,* 20, No. 30 (1972), 16.
> [2] Audrey F. Borenstein, "Reflections on Woman's Identity," *The Georgia Review,* XXVI, No. 2 (1972), 156–58.

When a periodical has no volume number or issue number, give the exact date and indicate the page number as "p.," or "pp." if you refer to more than one page.

A book with one author:

> [3] Germaine Greer, *The Female Eunuch* (New York: McGraw-Hill, 1971), p. 57.

It is possible to omit the publisher's name and give just the city of publication. If no author is named, begin the footnote with the title and proceed as above. If no date is given, write "n.d." where you would have put the date. With no publisher listed, write "n.p."

A book with two or three authors:

> [4] Frederick J. Hoffman, Charles Allen, and Carolyn F. Ulrich, *The Little Magazine* (Princeton: Princeton University Press, 1946), pp. 64–66.

When a book has more than three authors, use the name of the first and "et al.," which means "and others" in Latin. Or use "and others."

A book with an editor:

> [5] *Poets on Street Corners,* ed. Olga Carlisle (New York: Random House, 1968).

A book with a translator:

> [6] Chuang T'zu, *Basic Writings,* tr. Burton Watson (New York and London: Columbia University Press, 1964), p. 33.

An encyclopedia article:

> [7] "Nicaraguan Relations," *Encyclopedia of American History,* Updated and Revised Edition, 1965, p. 323.

An essay in a collection:

> [8] Ned Rorem, "The Music of the Beatles," in Jonathan Eisen, ed., *The Age of Rock* (New York: Random House, 1969), p. 150.

An interview:

> [9] Russell Fraser, personal interview, Nantucket, Mass., July 30, 1972.

A newspaper item:

> [10] *The Ann Arbor News*, May 12, 1959, Section B, p. 1.

A quotation cited in a secondary source:

> [11] Stanislaus Joyce, *My Brother's Keeper*, as quoted in Richard Ellmann, *James Joyce* (New York: Oxford University Press, 1959), p. 12.

A review:

> [12] A. Alvarez, rev. of *Delusions, Etc.*, by John Berryman, *The New York Times Book Review*, June 25, 1972, p. 1.

In the last example we might have called the periodical *NYTBR* and referred the reader to the bibliography. Use initials, however, only if you footnote the periodical more than once.

Here are some short cuts and abbreviations used in footnoting. When you quote a book often in your paper, you need not repeat the whole citation of book and author after the first time you give it. In your footnote, refer to the book by the author's last name, and list the pages referred to. Repeating the author's name replaces the old citation, *ibid*, which you will find in older books, meaning "the same" book. If you mention more than one book by the same author, include the title along with the name in each footnote.

> Kenner, *The Pound Era*, p. 21.
> Kenner, *The Poetry of Ezra Pound*, p. 215.

Abbreviations that are frequently used and not previously explained include:

> cf. (compare)
> ch., chs. (chapters)
> e.g. (for example)
> ff (the following pages or lines)
> i.e. (that is)
> il. (illustrated)

ll. (lines)
ms., mss. (manuscript)
n. (note)
pass. (see mentions further in text)
q.v. (see for confirmation)
rev. (revised)
v. (see)
viz. (namely)

A Research Project

A student named Jennifer Case decided she wanted to write her research paper about ecology.

> "Fine. Come back in twenty years with thirty volumes. What *about* ecology?"
> "I think I would like to write about animals that become extinct because of what men do."
> "Fine. What animals?"
> "I don't know. There are birds and wild animals I could do. Some are extinct and some are going to be. But I like whales best."
> "Fine. *What* whales?"
> "I don't know."
> "Go to the library and find out."

This dialogue, between the student and her instructor (which can happen inside the student's head, too, between student-student and instructor-student) did the preliminary narrowing of the topic. To move from "ecology" to one species of whale is to move from thirty volumes to a possible research paper. But more preliminary work remained. Jennifer Case needed to read loosely among the whale books, looking for two things. One was a thesis or an argument; but the general tone of her argument was clear before she chose whales as a species to investigate. It was the specifics that remained to be found, to flesh out the thesis using a special whale. The first necessity was to find the whale to write about.

The *Encyclopaedia Britannica* seemed a good place to start, because it gave a brief and factual overview of this large subject, like a map of a whole country. Jennifer read the Britannica article, which talked about different types of whales, and was most attracted to two — the blue whale, because it is the largest mammal of all time, and the humpbacked whale. Thinking about it later, she said that the humpback reached her because of the record, "Songs of the Humpback Whale," which she had first heard Judy Collins mention on the old "Dick Cavett Show," and which she had later listened to; and also because, when she saw a picture of the humpback, she was drawn to it because of its ludicrous shape; it was an ugly duckling among the graceful whales. These last details — Dick Cavett, and maternal feeling toward an underdog — are examples of the reasons we choose to write about specific subjects, reasons that are eventually irrelevant to our argument and therefore extraneous to our paper, but human feelings that are originally pertinent to the choices we make.

Jennifer went to the card catalogue in the library and looked up Whales, and Whaling. She found a hundred and fifty library cards. Libraries cross-index by subject, and usually store the books in the stacks by subject. If your library has open stacks, you can find from the card catalogue which shelves in the library contain most of the books on any subject, and then browse in this section. In the University of Michigan library, SH 381 turned out to have the most cards on whales and whaling. A 11 was also helpful, and QL.

Jennifer checked out seven books, and began reading in order to investigate whales, before narrowing her choice of topic. She took few notes at this stage, writing something down only when she couldn't resist it. But for every book that she consulted, she made a bibliography card: call number, author, title, publisher, city, year. Then if she took a note from a book — either paraphrases or quotations — she wrote down the author's name in order to clue her to the bibliography card, and she wrote down the page number for her quote or reference. By this means, she saved herself time; when she needed later to check a fact or a quotation, she could refer herself back to the bibliography card and find the address of the book in the library. When she came to make her bibliography, she needed only to alphabetize her bibliography cards and type them up without the call numbers.

Jennifer read for eight or ten hours, gradually acquiring familiarity with the humpback. She also read much of *The Year of the Whale*, a good book about the blue whale, but could not use it because her choice was the humpback. She followed her humpback through various sources, taking notes frequently now, on 3-by-5-inch cards. *Whales*, by a Dutch author named E. J. Slijper, was particularly useful. In the bibliographies of books, and in footnotes, she found references to other sources of information, periodicals and government pamphlets and books. She consulted periodicals in the library, and discovered with a librarian's help how to use microfilm. She consulted the *Readers' Guide to Periodical Literature* for the latest publications. She built a collection of cards. Here are a few of them.

Bibliography cards for two books:

Sci. Lib.
SH
381
A57

Andrews, R.C. Whale Hunting.
New York: Appleton, 1916.

Sci. Lib.
QL
737
.C4
1622
1963

Norris, K.S. Whales, Dolphins &
Porpoises. Berkeley: U. of Cal.
Press, 1966.
        (proceedings of a symposium in
Wash. D.C. held in 1963, ed. by Norris)

A bibliography card for a periodical:

Hickel, W. J. "When a Race Breathes
No More; Extinction of 47 Species
of U.S. Wild Life"

Sports Illustrated, December 14, 1970

Three cards with information on them:

Matthews

p 59
highly dev. sense of hearing
in whales

Sanderson

    p. 311

        modern industry based first on fin whales, then hump backs, then blues

Slijper

    p. 378

        maternal ties and "aunts"

After another ten hours of disciplined reading and note-taking, Jennifer Case was ready to organize and begin writing.

In the meantime, she had developed respect for libraries. The card catalogue, the subject index, the microfilm machine, and the reference room were added to her experience. She had learned the beginnings of research in high school, but the high school library had limited resources. In the college library's reference room were the encyclopedias, the *Who's Who's*, the dictionaries of biography, indexes to the *Congressional Record* and to *The New York Times*, yearbooks on all sorts of subjects — and a reference librarian who helped her. At first, the walls of books in the stacks were threatening; how could she ever cope with such multiplicity? But gradually the library grew familiar, and she accepted the fact that she was not writing a Ph.D. thesis, and that her knowledge would remain limited.

In organizing the paper, she had only to try different orders for the 3-by-5-inch cards that held her notes. A stack of 3-by-5's is an instantly changeable outline. You can place them in piles according to topic, order them in each pile according to the best arrangement of facts, and then order the piles in the best sequence for the essay. Because each piece of information is a unit that might go anywhere in the paper — we cannot organize our information until we have collected all of it; when we start, we don't know where our facts will best fit our argument — it is wise to keep the notes short, to write on one side of the card only, and to make a series of 3-by-5's even when we are finding several things on one page in a book, rather than lumping different facts on one card. Later, organization will be easier.

Jennifer tried different orders. She found that she worked best by starting with general information, apparently objective but gathered around ideas about maternity and protection, and then moving onward to opinion, argument, and exhortation at the end. She worried about her beginning. She had read that a prehistoric mammal, ancestor to prehistoric whales, had a long horn protruding from its head, and might be the source of our myth about the unicorn. She played with the idea of suggesting that the humpback whale might one day be as extinct as the unicorn. But it seemed elaborate and strained.

She tried beginning with an analogy.

> The great whales graze on plankton floating in the sea as the bison once grazed in oceans of prairie grass. [That certainly takes itself seriously.] As the American bison was hunted to near extinction during the last few centuries, so is the number of whales now seriously and permanently reduced.

The bracketed aside (her own, in a draft) dismissed this attempt. Then she decided to begin abruptly, without a conventional introductory paragraph, and let the title do the introducing. The cards were in order and she was ready to begin. The first draft felt nearly right, because she had prepared and organized well. A few facts that interested her did not fit; she put the cards aside, to see if later she could find a place for them. She set the manuscript aside for a day, corrected it for style, inserted one new paragraph, drafted her footnotes, consulted *Writing Well* for the mechanics of footnoting and bibliography, and typed her paper.

                    The Protector Unprotected

                          Jennifer Case

      Humpbacks are mammals, as all whales are; they

breathe into huge lungs, bear live young, which they nurse

for the better part of a year, and have vestiges of hair

which scientists believe once covered the bodies of

terrestrial ancestors. The shape of the humpback's body,

when compared to the other great whales, is comical --

rotund, with long knobby flippers, and bumps, like

freckles, all over the head and snout. The dorsal fin is

small, sticking out slightly from its back. Behind this

fin are several more small, irregular bumps -- probably

the source of the humpback's name. The upper part of the

body is black while the underside is usually whitish.

The average length of a mature humpback is forty-five

feet.

      Unlike a toothed whale, like the sperm whale, which

uses its teeth to catch and devour its food, the humpback

is a filter-feeder, subsisting mainly on plankton, but

also on any small fish unfortunate enough to be in the

way. Even birds sometimes fly into the huge mouth. The

humpback is a baleen whale; as it swims through the water, mouth open, tiny organisms catch in a mesh of hairy bristles called baleen, which run the length of the whale's palate.

The migration of humpbacks relates directly to their feeding habits. They feed mostly in Arctic or Antarctic waters, areas particularly rich in plankton. But when winter comes to the poles, the whales are driven toward tropical waters which are, oddly, nearly barren of the humpback's food. So while ". . . 90 per cent of captured humpback whales had their stomachs filled to capacity . . ."[1] when taken in the Antarctic (in a study done in 1942), ". . . only one out of 2,000 humpbacks (taken in waters off Australia) was found to have food in its stomach."[2] The tagging of humpbacks has shown that they migrate along the coasts of the continents and that there are several rather distinct populations, one of these feeding in the Arctic, the other feeding in the Antarctic. There seems to be little intermixture between the two groups.

Although humpbacks are slow swimmers, they are famous for their playful behavior. They often jump completely out of the water, unlike most of the larger

---

[1] E. J. Slijper, Whales (New York: Basic Books, 1962), p. 257.

[2] Slijper, p. 316.

whales. Christopher Ash has suggested that humpbacks

jump and splash to shake off the barnacles that inevitably

attach themselves to the flippers and tail of the whales.[3]

According to E. J. Slijper, the humpback also:

> likes to roll on the surface, slapping the water
> with its flukes and wing-shaped pectoral fins as
> he does so. The slaps can often be heard many
> miles away. Moreover, humpbacks like to swim on
> their backs for a while and to display their white
> bellies. They often turn whole series of somer-
> saults both above and under the water.[4]

Sometime during their fourth year the humpbacks mate

in the warm waters of the tropics. After a long period

of love-play, they swim at each other, picking up speed.

At the last instant they turn toward the surface and,

belly to belly, jump out of the water. Probably they

copulate at this moment, although some scientists main-

tain that this jumping behavior does not include copula-

tion, but is rather an elaborate part of the whale's love-

play. Humpbacks also copulate while lying on the surface

of the water on their sides. In this case, they glide

past each other before mating, stroking and slapping with

their long, wing-like flippers. While the love-play is

rather long in duration, it seems that copulation lasts

only a short period of time -- from ten to thirty seconds.

---

[3]Christopher Ash, Whaler's Eye (New York: Macmillan, 1962), p. 61.

[4]Slijper, p. 97.

How many times the same pair of whales mates is unknown.

Eleven to twelve months later the baby whales are born, usually one calf to a mother, although there are records of multiple births among humpbacks. Humpback babies are born, like most whale babies, tail first, and large in proportion to the size of the mother. The average mature female is forty-five feet long while the average calf is fourteen feet long at birth -- nearly one-third the size of its parent. Almost immediately after the birth of the calf, the mother and perhaps one other mature female from the herd (called the "aunt") nose the baby gently toward the surface of the water where it will take its first breath.

Maternal ties are strong in whales; the mother stays very close to her calf for months after it is born, often allowing no other whale but the aunt to swim between her and her offspring. In its earlier stages, the American whaling industry capitalized upon this instinct. Whalers harpooned suckling calves knowing that the mothers would stay by their young and be easy prey. There is now an international agreement which protects calves and nursing or pregnant females.

The humpback's protectiveness is called "epimeletic" behavior. When this protectiveness is maternal, or the act of any older whale on the part of any younger whale,

it is specifically called "nurturant." An article called
"Epimeletic Behavior in Cetacea" includes descriptions of
strong maternal affection in humpbacks. There is a
report by a whaling captain of female humpbacks buoying
up dead young for hours.[5] In the same article, "succorant" behavior is described. This is care-giving behavior between mature whales: remaining in the area of
an injured companion, or supporting it so it can breathe,
or even attacking the source of the injury. Male humpbacks display succorant behavior more often than females,
but there are reports of "standing-by" in both sexes.

The most highly developed of the whale's senses is
its hearing. There is no particular reason for a whale's
sight to be highly developed since it often feeds at
depths which are dark. The humpback's sense of hearing
is used to locate food and to locate other whales.

Dr. Roger Payne has done considerable research on
the sounds made by humpback whales. He believes whale
songs like bird songs make contact with other members of
the species. Newsweek (June 8, 1970) quoted Dr. Payne as
saying that, ". . . in certain layers of the ocean, known
as sound channels, humpback songs can travel thousands of
miles without losing much power." Dr. Payne's recording,

---

[5]Kenneth Norris, Whales, Dolphins, and Porpoises
(Berkeley: University of California Press, 1966), p. 77.

"Songs or the Humpback Whale," is available commercially. In the notes on the record jacket he explains that:

> Humpback whale songs are far longer than bird songs. The shortest humpback song recorded lasts 6 minutes and the longest is more than 30 minutes.

It is difficult to describe the sounds humpbacks make. Sometimes their noises are like incredible belches. Sometimes the humpbacks sound like cows bellowing or jungle birds screeching far away. The pitch and the duration vary enormously. When my cats heard the record for the first time, they paced nervously back and forth in front of the speakers and then ran out of the room to hide under a bed.

For many years the humpback was of basic importance to the American whaling industry, partly because of the whale's habit of migrating close to shore, making him easy to catch, and partly because humpbacks yield a good amount of oil for their size. In a Congressional Hearing on the Conservation of Whales (1931), Dr. A. B. Howell had this to say: "For all practical purposes it may be said that the existing whaling industry is dependent upon the Blue Whale, Finback, and Humpback. . . . But at present all three species have been almost exterminated commercially in all but the most inaccessible portions of their ranges." (p. 3) The latest figure I could find on the number of remaining humpbacks is "a few thousand"

(<u>Newsweek</u>, Jan. 25, 1971), down from hundreds of thousands.

Until 1963, humpbacks were only partially protected
by the International Whaling Commission. In that year,
The Commission forbade even the limited four-day take of
humpbacks due to the near extinction of the species. As
reassuring as this sounds, the humpback is still the victim of whalers not belonging to the member nations of the
Commission and even, occasionally, of whalers from member
nations -- sometimes out of simple error and sometimes because of inadequate enforcement of the regulations. (Victor Scheffer, author of <u>The Year of the Whale</u>, would like
to see enforcement of whaling regulations by the United
Nations.) Another discouraging fact is that the whaling
industries of various nations have turned to other endangered species, especially the fin whale, to take their
quotas.

Given modern processing techniques, many products
can be made from the body of a whale. Not only oil and
meat come from the carcass, but cattle-feed, fertilizer,
glue, glycerin, and insulin. In 1955, Georges Blond
estimated the commercial value of an Antarctic blue at
four to six thousand dollars.[6] I should mention that the
blue whale is the largest of the great whales, in fact,

----

[6]Georges Blond, <u>The Great Story of Whales</u> (Garden
City, N. Y.: Hanover House, 1955), p. 16.

the largest mammal known to inhabit the earth, now or
ever.

The problem is this: either we continue whaling
policies as they now exist in order to acquire what the
whale affords, until we have killed off all whales, or,
we develop alternative sources for the products now supplied by the whaling industry. Since we would have to
find alternatives eventually, it seems sensible to look
for them now, and preserve the declining population of
whales in our oceans. In previous centuries, it was
fashionable for women to cinch their waists with corsets
stayed by whale-bone. That practice is no longer "essential." It never was. Science could make whale oil as
obsolete a source of lubricants as whale-bone is obsolete
in women's corsets. The same goes for cattle-feed and
glue and all the rest. With proper application of the
brain-power in this world we can find other means to
satisfy our wants. We need not exterminate one species
of animal after another.

If we should find ourselves unable to make alternatives in the laboratory, perhaps we should question how
badly we need the products in the first place. Perhaps,
to preserve a species, we could learn to do without
things like ambergris (which comes from the sperm whale
and is used in making perfume) and whale meat for cattle-

feed. A T-Bone steak is an incredible waste of matter
and energy if it comes from a steer that ate a whale that
ate a herring that ate some plankton that ate. . . . In
the portion of a poem that follows, Gary Snyder embodies
the interconnectedness of all living things. He is
talking about eating shark meat but it could as well be
whale steak:

> Sweet miso sauce on a big boiled cube
>   as I lift a flake
>   to my lips,
> Miles of water, Black current,
> Thousands of days
>   re-crossing his own paths
>   to tangle our net
>   to be part of
>   this loom.[7]

So far it seems that every generation thinks the next
generation is the one that will have to stop the destruction of the ecosystem. That kind of thinking can't go on.
We must protect our brother the humpback, as the humpback
protects his brother. The movement toward protection of
humpbacks by international agreement is a small move in
the right direction.

---

[7] Gary Snyder, <u>Regarding Wave</u> (New York: New Directions, 1970), p. 29.

Bibliography

Ash, Christopher. <u>Whaler's Eye</u>. New York: Macmillan,
    1962.

"Battle of the Whales." <u>Newsweek</u>, January 25, 1971,
     pp. 89-90.

Blond, Georges. <u>The Great Story of Whales</u>. Garden City,
     N. Y.: Hanover House, 1955.

Norris, Kenneth. <u>Whales, Dolphins, and Porpoises</u>.
     Berkeley: University of California Press, 1966.

Slijper, E. J. <u>Whales</u>. New York: Basic Books, 1962.

Snyder, Gary. <u>Regarding Wave</u>. New York: New Directions,
     1970.

U.S. Congress. Special Committee on Conservation of
     Wildlife Resources. <u>Whales</u>. Washington:
     Government Printing Office, 1931.

"Whale of a Singer." <u>Newsweek</u>, June 8, 1970, p. 106.

Jennifer Case wisely limited her paper, and it works well within its limits. She has a fine eye for detail, and embodies her ideas and feelings in the facts that fascinate her. As a result, she is able to interest the reader.

Perhaps this account of Jennifer's paper is misleading, because she found her topic rather easily, and no major problems got in her way when she proceeded to work. She narrowed her topic without a struggle, and she found her way through a large library without getting lost. A librarian helped her. Also, she gave enough time to the paper to write it well.

Many students fall into bear traps, and find themselves in trouble. But each trouble is particular; there is no *general* bear trap, once an adequate subject is found. Student X is intimidated by the library, and does research that is inadequately documented; Y gets involved in a technical side issue, fascinating to him but destructive to the paper's shape and purpose; Z becomes tied up in a Gilbert and Sullivan production, and does not take the time to do his research or write his paper, and tries to complete his paper in twelve hours, midnight to noon, on the day it is due. Maybe Jennifer Case's good luck has partly to do with being *sensible*.

Competent writing is the final ingredient in her paper. But we should not allow our pleasure in her writing to obscure the *basic* ingredients of research and organization. Reading and note-taking, hours and hours of them, supply us with the details we find ourselves using. We must be willing to put in the time and the thought to *accumulate* detail. Then we must use our shaping intelligence to set the right details in the right order, and *eliminate* the useless, even when it is amusing or intriguing. Then we must work over our words, sentences, and paragraphs for style. It is worth it.

——— EXERCISES ———————————————————

1. Bring to class a set of notes for a possible autobiographical essay. After students have read their notes aloud, discuss methods for organizing these notes into autobiographical essays, thinking of place, year, season, and character as potential organizing devices. See if you can't invent other possibilities for organization.

2. Consider the possibility of fictionalizing the autobiographical materials brought to class for the first exercise. The class can take one scene or situation from real life, reduce it to a set of notes, and each student can write a short story starting from the same materials.

3. Criticize these samples of autobiographical narrative and dialogue.

 a. When darkness came, we sat around the campfire telling stories about when we were kids. Warren my best friend told about going to Martha's Vineyard every year. Somebody I didn't know told about Nantucket. Then we started talking about Christmas and other holidays. Then we sang some songs. Suddenly we heard a scream.

 b. When my father drove to Salt Lake City he lost our dog.

 c. "Never mind what the doctor said," said Rupert without expression.
 "What?" exclaimed she.
 "You heard what I said," he barked softly.

4. Take notes on a poem or a story and arrange them as you would if you were going to write a paper. Use these notes as a start for class discussion.

5. Here is a list of general subjects that you might wish to investigate, pursuing a topic for a research paper. In class, discuss what sorts of reference books you might consult. Under what subjects would you look in the card catalogue?

coal mining
modern dance
the American labor movement
coinage in the ancient world
the history of hats
raising sheep
the geography of sport

6. In class discussion, consider the possible ways of limiting the topics listed above.

7. Looking at Jennifer Case's essay, "The Protector Unprotected," answer these questions: (a) Does she beg the question anywhere in the paper? (b) Might you have organized the material differently? Make alternative suggestions. (c) Does she use clichés? Are the sentences varied enough? Are the paragraphs well constructed? (d) Do you find any ambiguity of language in this paper? Does information seem to be lacking in some places? (e) Are there errors in logic in this paper? (f) Is the footnoting consistent? Is everything footnoted that ought to be? (g) Is the bibliography consistent? Is everything listed that ought to be? (h) Can you see when the author has omitted connectives and transitions? Are the omissions stylish? Are they obscure? (i) Are some details not sufficiently integrated into the whole? (j) What fundamental attitude toward the humpback whale supplies the structure of this paper? (k) Is this paper constructed more upon intellectual or emotional premises?

8

A Brief Review of Grammar, Punctuation, and Mechanics

This book is mostly about style and structure, about making writing lively, honest, energetic, and clear. As you move through the text, you find grammar when you need it. Here, I want to make a concentrated review of the most common errors of grammar, punctuation, and mechanics, so that the beginning writer who feels confused — what *is* a whole sentence? when *do* I use a colon? — will have a place to come for answers to questions. It may also serve the writer who, after a summer's vacation or a year away from the classroom, needs a quick review of grammar and mechanics that concentrates on errors frequently made.

If your grammar is loose and shabby, your punctuation random, and your mechanics haphazard, you will lose your audience. We must put sentences together by rules, because rules describe the readers' expectations. If your language ignores these rules — if you substitute commas for periods, or neglect to match parts of sentences to each other — readers will be confused and bored, they will not follow where you want to lead them, even if your ideas are profound and your information fascinating.

When things go wrong in mechanics and grammar, for an inexperienced writer, they go wrong usually because of a few mistakes. If you can follow six general rules, you will avoid most of the errors beginners fall into.

1. Make whole, clear sentences.
2. Match the parts of sentences that need matching.
3. Connect modifiers with what they modify.
4. Keep the sentence consistent.
5. Keep punctuation clear.
6. Keep mechanics conventional.

These rules will only become useful if I do some explaining and give examples. Almost everything mentioned here is repeated from earlier chapters; this chapter is repetitious, but it ought to be useful. It differs from the text in how it approaches writing. In the text I talk mostly about the choices a writer can make, to express meaning with vigor and clarity. Here, you can read about the swamps that you as a writer can sink into, which keep you from reaching your goal.

Many inexperienced writers have trouble with only one or two of the problems I list, and not with the rest. People sitting next to each other in class may have opposite troubles in writing. *A* writes sentence fragments, *B* uses commas for periods, *C* mixes up pronouns, and *D* dangles modifiers. None of them has the problem the other has, and each is thoroughly confused by his own problem. With this chapter, each student can go directly to his particular problem; I hope it can help the whole alphabet of writers.

MAKE WHOLE, CLEAR SENTENCES

Sentence Fragments

Beginning writers commonly make sentences — groups of words beginning with a capital letter and ending with a period — which don't complete an action. In a theme a student wrote

> The effects of World War II.

as if the phrase told us something. But the sentence is incomplete, a sentence fragment. What *about* World War II? Did he want to say,

> Hungary suffered the effects of World War II.

or

> The effects of World War II brought prosperity.

or what? In this theme, the writer had said:

> The economy began picking up finally in 1939. The effects of World War II.

He needed to connect the sentence fragment to the sentence, making something like this:

The economy began picking up in 1939 because of World War II.

The best writers sometimes put sentence fragments to good use (see page 131), but when you are inexperienced, you should avoid them entirely. Wait until you have developed a firm and exact feel for the whole sentence's shape. Do not write:

He was a good teacher. Being sympathetic with students and fascinated by his subject.

Instead, write something like,

He was a good teacher, sympathetic with students and fascinated by his subject.

Do not write:

The pumpkins froze. When the blizzard arrived unexpectedly in October.

Instead, write something like,

When the blizzard arrived unexpectedly in October, the pumpkins froze.

Here are some inadvertent sentence fragments, indicated by italics.

After the sun finally sank behind the hills. It was dark and we were ready.

The principal of my high school was a nice person. *Believing that every kid was potentially all right.*

Seeing the Buick with all its tires flat and rusted out in the grass, with no license plates on it.

The people at the fair stared at the twins and began to talk about them. *Because they looked different, I guess.*

Graduate students in my opinion do not have the right to strike and miss their classes. *When students have already paid their tuition.*

Inadvertent sentence fragments are mainly of two kinds.

Many fragments are subordinate clauses treated as if they were whole sentences. In the last three examples, the sentence fragments begin with *because, after,* and *when.* These words — like *although, since,* and *while* — mean that the clauses they introduce depend on, or hang from, a main clause; they are dependent or subordinate clauses. In the examples above, the main clauses (not in italics) make whole sentences by themselves. The sentence fragments could make subordinate clauses in complex sentences.

> Graduate students in my opinion do not have the right to strike and miss their classes, *when students have already paid their tuition.*

The other category, shown in the first two examples, is the fragment that modifies the main clause, and ought to be separated from it by a comma — not by a period and a capital letter.

> The principal of my high school is a nice person, *believing that every kid is potentially all right.*

Watch out for sentence fragments that begin with an *-ing* word, just as you watch for fragments beginning with *when* or *because.*

You can correct sentence fragments in several ways. But first, let me mention one way *not* to correct them. *Do not* substitute a semicolon for a period.

> The people at the fair stared at the twins and began to talk about them; *because they looked different, I guess.*

> Graduate students in my opinion do not have the right to strike and miss their classes; *when students have already paid their tuition.*

The semicolon fragment is just as confusing as the sentence fragment. A semicolon is closer to a period than it is to a comma; when we fall into the semicolon fragment, we still separate a dependent clause from the main clause it depends on. In both of these examples, a comma would make a whole, clear sentence.

You can correct *many* sentence fragments simply by using a comma instead of a period. Or you can add a verb to the fragment and make it a whole sentence, equal to the other. Or you can sometimes use the dash — things seem to move faster. (Use the dash with caution. See pages 334–335.)

Here are some alternate repairs for sentence fragments used earlier.

> He was a good teacher. He was sympathetic with students, and fascinated by his subject.

He was a good teacher because he was sympathetic with his students and fascinated by his subject.

The blizzard arrived unexpectedly in October, freezing the pumpkins.

The blizzard arrived unexpectedly in October, and the pumpkins froze.

Because the blizzard arrived unexpectedly in October, the pumpkins froze.

We saw the Buick with all its tires flat, rusted out in the grass, no license plates on it.

The principal of my high school was a nice person. He believed that every kid was potentially all right.

The people at the fair stared at the twins and began to talk about them; they looked different, I guess.

After the sun finally sank behind the hills, it was dark and we were ready.

The sun finally sank behind the hills. It was dark and we were ready.

Notice that frequently a sentence fragment can become a whole clear sentence when we remove the subordinating word, like *because*, or change the modifying participle into a verb — like *we saw* for *seeing*.

_____ **EXERCISES** _____

These five passages each contain one or more sentence fragments. Identify each fragment, and revise it into a whole sentence.

a. When the sun rose high in the sky, All of us gathered twigs and fallen branches to make a fire. Then making breakfast for the whole group.

b. No-fault insurance helps all motorists. The good and the bad. Every state should pass no-fault automobile insurance.

c. When the Ford Motor Company named a new car the Pinto, they did a lot of research into the power of names. Names on the final list were largely the names of animals. Based on the discoveries of a market research firm.

    d. The morning of our trip to school, the car all packed and ready, the rain falling in sheets outside.

    e. Never too late to learn! That is what my high school civics teacher always told us. Which we heard so often that we didn't hear it any more.

Comma Splices

Comma splices (or comma faults, and run-on sentences) are the opposite of sentence fragments. In the comma splice, a comma is forced into the work a period is meant for; in the sentence fragment, a period is pressed into the service a comma is designed for. Here is a typical comma splice, two whole sentences incorrectly joined by a comma.

> The Union stands back from the street about a hundred feet, it was built when land was still cheap.

Substitute a period for the comma, capitalize the next word, and you have two real, whole sentences.

Often the same writer makes sentence fragments and comma splices, because both errors depend on an insecure grasp of what makes a sentence. By reading our prose aloud, pausing according to the punctuation, we can sometimes discover these errors in time to revise them.

The comma splice is confusing to the reader, because two whole ideas are connected (spliced) as if they were not each whole and separate. The writer gives a signal by the comma but the sentence denies the message that the comma carries. The comma gives us the information that we are reading one continuous idea, which conflicts with the wholeness of each of the two spliced sentences. The best writers sometimes use the comma splice to good effect (see pages 141–142), but the beginning writer should avoid the device entirely, until he has developed a firm sense of the sentence. Here are comma splices taken from student themes.

> The port of New York has minimum safety requirements, some vessels have to dock in Hoboken.

> The inevitability of war became obvious to even the most casual observer, maneuvers were constantly being held.

My father grew up on a potato farm in Idaho, he never saw a movie until he was twenty-two years old.

She walked through the door into the dining room, she wore nothing but a bikini.

When they were little, they liked to play in the empty warehouse down the block, it was a spooky and exciting place.

I didn't know where the arboretum was, somebody had to show me.

Never eat vegetables from a can which looks puffed up like a balloon, that's something I learned at camp.

Whoever saw the man running away saw the burglar, that's the only possible explanation.

Making a sweater from acrylic gets you into other problems, wool is better when you are beginning.

The canoe started tipping as I approached the falls, I was terrified that I would lose all my gear.

When you correct a comma splice, you have four alternatives. Two of them require only a change in punctuation; two of them require another word.

1. Substituting a semicolon for a comma repairs most comma splices. Making a comma splice often means you want to show a close connection between two whole sentences. You try to move quickly from the one to the other, without the long pause implied by a period and a capital letter. The semicolon was invented for just this purpose: to show that two whole sentences follow quickly upon each other, and are closely related.

Here are comma splices repaired by semicolons.

The port of New York has minimum safety requirements; some vessels have to dock in Hoboken.

The inevitability of war became obvious to even the most casual observer; maneuvers were constantly being held.

When they were little, they liked to play in the empty warehouse down the block; it was a spooky and exciting place.

2. Or you can use the period and a capital letter; it will always be correct.

My father grew up on a potato farm in Idaho. He never saw a movie until he was twenty-two years old.

Never eat vegetables from a can which looks puffed up like a balloon. That's something I learned at camp.

3. On the other hand, you can make a complex sentence, if you find that one sentence can depend on the other, by using a subordinating conjunction.

When the canoe started tipping as I approached the falls, I was terrified that I would lose all my gear.

4. Or you can connect the two sentences into one compound sentence with *and, but, or, nor, yet* or *so;* the two clauses will be equally strong, or coordinate.

I didn't know where the arboretum was, so somebody had to show me.

The port of New York has minimum safety requirements, and some vessels have to dock in Hoboken.

She walked through the door into the dining room, but she wore nothing but a bikini.

Each of these four solutions makes a slight difference in tone or meaning. In your context, one of the four will be best.

_____ **EXERCISES** _____

Here are five passages from student themes. Identify the comma splices, and revise the passages into whole, single sentences, using any of the four methods listed above.

a. Carbon monoxide filled the foggy air, we could breathe only with difficulty.

b. Sunset fell rapidly, we had to hurry to set up our tent.

c. When the waitress removed an empty platter, she was back with a full platter a moment later, I never ate so much in my life, I was so full I thought I would burst.

d. Riding a bike you must never expect someone driving a car to notice you, you must always watch out for yourself.

e. The carrots pulled easily from the wet ground, it had rained for a week.

MATCH THE PARTS OF SENTENCES
THAT NEED MATCHING

Matching Subjects with Verbs

When the subject of a sentence is one thing (singular), the verb must be singular also. When the subject is more than one thing (plural), the verb must be plural also. In standard English, we say, "the newspaper covers the waterfront murders," not "the newspaper cover the waterfront murders"; or we say: "the newspapers, which share a reporter, cover the waterfront murders," not "the newspapers covers the waterfront murders."

Here are some frequent pitfalls, and how to avoid them.

Sometimes we get into trouble because a phrase comes between the subject and the verb, and confuses us. If we have a single subject followed by a prepositional phrase that ends with a plural, we may make the verb plural, because the plural phrase rings in our ears. "The newspaper of the six northern suburbs" is a singular subject. We should say,

The newspaper of the six northern suburbs covers the waterfront murders.

not

The newspaper of the six northern suburbs cover the waterfront murders.

We should say,

The newspaper with four ace reporters covers the waterfront murders.

not

The newspaper with four ace reporters cover the waterfront murders.

With words like *anyone, each,* and *everybody* (called indefinite pronouns) we should use a singular verb. It's confusing: *everybody* refers to many people, but it's a single thing, a single "body" — as single as the *one* in *anyone* or *everyone*. We must say, "everybody hurts this morning"; not "everybody hurt. . . ."

None can be either singular or plural, agreeing with a singular or plural noun elsewhere in the sentence. Context decides.

None is so happy as a cow in spring.
None are so happy as Venusians at a fly-by.

Do not say:

Everybody in town run down to the circus.

Each of the forty-seven students howl like wolves.

Many a humanoid, accompanied by slime and mist, step from the craft.

When you write a sentence that uses *either . . . or, neither . . . nor,* or *not . . . but,* use a singular verb if both subjects are singular.

Either the red-haired witch or her broomstick was on fire.

If one subject is plural, and the other singular, the rule says that the verb should agree with the subject closest to it. Thus the rule would allow,

Either her two broomsticks or the red-headed witch was on fire.

But such a sentence, technically correct, is stylistically ugly. For style's sake, when one subject is plural and the other is singular, put the plural subject nearer the verb, and use a plural verb. Say

Either the red-haired witch or her two broomsticks were on fire.

Do not say,

Either her two broomsticks or the red-haired witch were on fire.

or

Either the red-haired witch or her two broomsticks was on fire.

Do not say,

Neither the father nor the son want to follow the witch's track.

It should be *wants,* a singular verb. Do not say,

Not the Prime Minister but the Members of his Cabinet believes in amnesty.

It should be *believe,* a plural verb matching the plural *Members.* These sentences are incorrect:

Neither Hitler nor Ghengis Khan were conspicuous for humanitarianism.

Not the first potato but the second and the fourth contains the microfilm.

Either the roof or the shingling over the sheds were giving off a putrescent odor.

When your sentence uses a verb like *is* or *are* (a linking verb, a form of *to be*), make sure that the verb matches with the subject of the sentence, and not with a noun that comes afterward. Say

The best part of the team was its outfielders.

not

The best part of the team were its outfielders.

Say

The outfielders were the best part of the team.

not

The outfielders was the best part of the team.

These sentences are incorrect:

The middle chapters was the section of the book I liked best.

The best section of the book were the middle chapters.

___ **EXERCISES** ___

Identify and correct the errors in these sentences.

   a. Each of the colored pencils have a different shade.

   b. The store with its aisles of groceries, hardware, soft goods, and paperbacks, rest back from the road.

   c. The green part of Northern Spy apples always taste best.

   d. Neither the horse nor the cows in the barn hears the siren.

   e. Either Bozo or Emmett Kelly get the prize.

Matching Pronouns with the Words They Refer To

Pronouns (*he, she, it, this, that, you, we*) take their identity from a noun which comes before them, and which they refer to, called their antecedent. The noun can come before them in the same sentence, or it can appear in a sentence close enough to have the reference clear. Pronouns must match their nouns both in number (singular or plural) and in gender (male or female).

Mostly, we match pronouns to their antecedents without trouble. Here are a few troublesome exceptions.

In formal writing, we use a singular pronoun with an indefinite pronoun like *anybody, everybody, each, none* and so forth. We say,

> Everybody carried his tennis racket.

not

> Everybody carried their tennis racket.

This is a rule of formal writing. To avoid *his* as sexist, or to avoid *his or her* as awkward, we sometimes use the incorrect or informal *their*. If you do it, know that you are doing it. Perhaps it is best, if possible, to avoid gender entirely.

> Everyone carried a tennis racket.

Words like *team, committee, jury, class,* and *orchestra* are collective nouns. They are singular words that refer to plural collections of people. Use a singular pronoun when you describe the whole group; use a plural pronoun when you describe the many members. Say

> The team climbed on its bus.
> The team dispersed to their lockers.

Don't say:

> The jury went to its separate rooms.

> The committee voted to disband themselves.

> The team voted to distribute their winnings among twenty-four ballplayers.

> The group destroyed their petition to remove the governor.

When a pronoun matches two or more nouns joined by *and*, it is always plural.

> When the boy and his dog wanted supper, they went to the tavern.

When a pronoun matches nouns joined by *or, nor, either . . . or,* or *neither . . . nor,* and one of the nouns is plural, the pronoun matches the nearer of the two. When you use such a pair of nouns, the sentence sounds better if the second of the two nouns is the plural. Say

> Although neither Margaret nor the Hamiltons are elderly, they run to the chopping block.

Don't say,

> Although neither Margaret nor the Hamiltons are elderly, she runs. . . .

or

> Although neither the Hamiltons nor Margaret are elderly, they run. . . .

Never use a pronoun when it could refer to either of two words before it. We must use pronouns so that the reader will always be *certain* which previous noun they refer to. Uncertainty is intolerable. Don't say:

> When Wilhelmina declared herself to Bertha, she was aghast.

> Leaving his father's house and the dry valley, he was happy to see the last of it.

Both of these sentences lack a clear antecedent to the pronoun. Which of the ladies was aghast? Was he happy to see the last of the house, or of the valley, or of both?

Don't use the pronouns *this* or *that* or *it* to refer to general ideas in a previous sentence, or to an antecedent that is not there. Watch out for *this* or *that* when you use them as pronouns. Don't say:

> I couldn't find my way home because of the darkness and the strangeness of the streets. That's why I was late

That lacks a clear antecedent, and the sentence drowns in imprecision. Here are more examples of pronoun error from themes. Troublesome pronouns are in italics.

> The state legislature never got around to getting the bill out of committee until October, and *it* was the reason the scholarships were never funded.

> Susan's brother is in his third year at Harvard Medical School, and *this* is the profession she wants to enter.

> The next thing that happened was that the screen door got stuck

open and the mosquitoes could get in and the dog would get out whenever he wanted. My mother started crying about *this.*

Preferential voting is fair because it gives the voter a chance to give a graded opinion of the different candidates, and therefore opens the way to third parties. *That* is the real justification for preferential voting.

Down the block from me there was a family that had three cats. One of them was a big red tom named Mio, the biggest cat I ever saw — thirty-four inches long not counting his tail, and twenty-eight pounds. The kids in the neighborhood couldn't get over *this.*

We make another common error when we use a pronoun far removed from its antecedent. The result is more ambiguity, vagueness, and imprecision. Here are two examples.

The partnership of Hudnut and Greenall was breaking up; business had declined, Hudnut's wife was ill, and Greenall's son had run off to Tibet. One Tuesday, *they* suddenly stopped speaking to each other.

When Sharon looked across the classroom, Bill winked and Larry looked away. Outside the window the clouds gathered for rain, and students were beginning to drive off for lunch, many of them carrying no books at all. Suddenly two girls ran toward a car that had stopped to pick them up. She saw that *it* was Matt.

_____ EXERCISES _____

Underline the faulty pronouns in these sentences.

a. When the Senate and the House convene, on rare occasions, they do not know how to behave toward each other.

b. Panthers feed on zebras when they can, and zebras feed on grass. As a result of this, panthers live near the grasslands.

c. I was late for registration because my father had the flu and then our car broke down outside Tucson. That made me more nervous than ever.

d. Uncle Bruce is a career man in the Navy, stationed in San Diego now, and it makes me think about enlisting myself.

e. The department decided to hold their annual picnic on Riverside Drive.

f. The Boosters Club adjourned its meeting and went to its respective houses.

g. Either Rita or Carole were tardy last Tuesday.

h. Everybody had their ticket to the rock concert.

i. When Rosalyn and Alice finished dinner, she decided to provide dessert.

j. Penelope and Roger had been married seven years. Then Roger met Goneril, and fell in love. They did not know what to do.

CONNECT MODIFIERS WITH WHAT THEY MODIFY

In most sentences, we write phrases that describe (modify) other things in the sentence. We use prepositional phrases as modifiers (to define, to limit).

> the barn *with the lavender paint*
> the girl *in the human corner*
> the chapter *about grammar*

For similar purposes, we use clauses beginning with words like *that, who, since,* and *because.*

> the worst storm *since the winter of 1978*
> Herbert *who tipped his homburg*

And we use phrases beginning with *ing* words (participles), which also modify

> the chapter *containing the examples*
> *hanging from the skylight,* the plumber

Most of the time we have no trouble controlling these phrases or clauses. We will find no trouble at all if we avoid two common errors.

Make sure that modifiers beginning a sentence really modify what the sentence claims they modify. If we start a sentence, "Hanging from the skylight," we tell the reader something; we guarantee that the noun that will begin the main clause is what is hanging.

> Hanging from the skylight, the plumber screamed that he had climbed up there to escape the terrorists.

Too often, we are careless, and make a sentence like this next one —

which starts to seem like the sentence above, and then changes its mind.

> Hanging from the skylight, the plumber looked at the huge spider's web.

Common sense can untangle the mess. The reader will eventually understand that the spider's web is hanging, and not the plumber. In the meantime, the reader has been first confused and then annoyed, by the misdirection a careless sentence gave.

Here are more examples of dangling modifiers, which are shown by italics.

> *Being a wreck with no gears at all,* she got the bicycle free.

> *Riding in a new car,* the beagle chased me half a mile.

> *Driven by his desire to succeed,* the test was easy.

> *Before making a reservation,* my roommate recommended a travel agent to me.

> *Humbled by circumstances,* the town looked better to him now than it had looked before.

Make sure that your word order says what you want it to say, when you place modifiers in a sentence. This advice applies to adverbs and adjectives, as well as to phrases or clauses that modify. The wrong word order can alter your meaning.

> I tell myself frequently to practice.

means one thing.

> I frequently tell myself to practice.

means something else.

> She heard only the words that hurt.

means one thing.

> She only heard the words that hurt.

means something else.

> He said only that he loved her.

means one thing.

He only said that he loved her.

means something else. It is the writer's job to know the meaning and to say it. Here are some examples from student themes in which mistakes in word order made sentences that are ambiguous, misleading, or silly.

Hattie is the cousin who gave me the present in a housecoat.

Joseph borrowed an egg from a neighbor that was rotten.

The autobiography tells the exciting life of the man who lived it quickly and modestly.

The lecturer told us about the problem of alcoholism in room A–14.

—— EXERCISES ——————————————

Discover and correct the errors in these sentences.

a. Desperate, clinging to life, our teacher told us about the surrounded tribe.

b. Igor attempted one last time to climb the hill lacking food and ammunition.

c. Never certain of which side of the road to drive on, American roads drove the Englishman crazy.

d. Full of conceit, the application form looked like a cinch to him.

e. I walked the last five miles to the city tired and full of martinis.

f. She said that animals only hurt the way he did.

g. Without his fortune, or his youth, or his good health, the old house looked warm and solid to him.

h. I used the reference section without getting lost because of a librarian's help.

i. We walked on a neighborhood street without coats.

j. Without potholes we walked on a neighborhood street.

KEEP THE SENTENCE CONSISTENT

Once we start a sentence, we commit ourselves to continue it as we started it. In the second and third sections of this Review, we discussed the commitments to match number and gender, and to connect a modifier with what it modifies. We also commit ourselves to other consistencies.

When we write parallelisms, or parallel constructions, as in a series of clauses, we must keep the words grammatically parallel, for the sake of consistency. Otherwise, we find our sentences beginning to come apart, to veer off the road and into incoherence. We list adjectives or we list nouns, but we do not list three adjectives followed by one noun. Don't say,

> He was tall, rich, funny, and a bank robber.

Say something like,

> He was tall, rich, funny, and fond of robbing banks.

When one phrase is constructed by one grammatical formula, its parallel phrase must be constructed in the same way. Don't say,

> The dog had a long nose, a black tail, and barked loudly.

Instead, talk about the dog's *loud bark.* Don't say,

> The cities are deserted, the countryside parched, the government paralyzed, and the economy not healthy.

Instead, say something like,

> The cities are deserted, the countryside parched, the government paralyzed, and the economy diseased.

Here, the sentence must continue using phrases ending in *-ed* words (past participles), or it will be inconsistent.

Consistency is the rule. If you start a sentence — or a linked group of sentences — with one subject or person, be consistent. Don't say,

> When you get a good grade, one should be proud.

Say either *you* or *one,* and stick to it.

Don't use the active voice in one part of a sentence, and shift to the passive in another, when you could perfectly well keep the active and use the same subject.

> We could hear raucous sounds from the party as the house was approached.

Be consistent in using the past or present of verbs. Don't say,

> He went into the room, closed the door, opened the window, and goes to bed.

Remember that we need consistency within related sentences, as well as within the sentence. Here is an inconsistent paragraph.

> The median tax on houses in Centerville is $852 a year. You could appeal to the city assessor if you wanted to. But one is well advised not to; he can always hit you for more tax, and you are punished for asking.

_____ **EXERCISES** _____

Locate, name, and correct the inconsistencies of these sentences.

a. She walked like a princess, ate like an ape, and her hair was at least five feet long.

b. If you write a page a day in your notebook, you will discover that one learns from practice.

c. Harriet opened the window, to get some fresh air, and we all breathe deeply.

d. Geology is boring, chemistry fatiguing, history overwhelming, but English was a useful class.

e. We lifted the rock, peered into the mud, and a thousand grubs were seen.

KEEP PUNCTUATION CLEAR

Learning to punctuate correctly, we learn the conventions that an experienced reader expects of us. No one can argue that the conventions of English punctuation are ideal. But they are clear, and for the most part they are sensible.

End Punctuation

At the end of a sentence, we use a period, an exclamation point, or a question mark.

Period. Periods end sentences.

Periods also indicate abbreviations (Mr., no., st., St., etc., i.e., Mass., U.S.A.). (See pages 338–339.)

And periods indicate omissions in quoted material. (See pages 335–336.)

Exclamation Point. Use exclamation points only for a proper exclamation,

> Oh! Zap!

or for a remark almost shouted,

> It's Godzilla!

Avoid using them frequently, or they diminish in effect, like a vague intensifier.

> I could not make out the face! Then I saw. It was Algernon!

Question Mark. At the end of a sentence asking a direct question, we use a question mark.

> Did you ask Fernando?
> Have you bought the paper, the pins, and the manila envelopes?

Do not use a question mark to end a sentence that includes a question but does not ask it (an indirect question). These sentences are incorrectly punctuated:

> He asked what time it was?
> I waited to find out where the carnival was?

They should end with periods.

Commas

The most common mark of punctuation — and the most commonly misused — is the comma. I will not talk here about the comma splice, because I discussed it on pages 310–312. Here are some of the main uses of the comma.

We use commas to separate whole clauses.

In the compound sentence, where two or more whole clauses are connected by *and, or, nor, for,* or *but,* we use a comma just before the connective.

> The faculty senate debated for three hours, but no one could re-solve the issue of the blind pig.

When the main clauses are short, the comma is optional. The pause is shorter, and therefore the rhythm different. We might prefer,

> The wine was old, and we drank it slowly.

or

> The wine was old and we drank it slowly.

On the other hand, we can also opt to use the semicolon instead of the comma. It creates a longer pause. Sometimes we want this extra pause when the main clauses are especially long, when they themselves contain commas, or when we make strong contrast between the two parts of the sentence.

> The cliff was red, solid, and perpendicular; and the car disappeared into the face of it.

We use commas to separate items in a series.

> The dress was black, green, and purple.

to separate phrases in a series,

> She wore it to parties, in the bathtub, and at work.

and to separate subordinate clauses in a series,

> She explained that it was warm, that it needed washing, that it was comfortable, and that it was in good taste.

or whole clauses in a series,

> She shook her head, she stood up, and she left the room.

When we use "and" with each item of a series, we do not use the comma.

> He touched first and second and third.

It is possible to omit the comma before the "and," in a series of words or short phrases,

> He touched first, second and third.

but it can sometimes seem ambiguous, as if the baserunner were able to straddle, and touch second and third at the same time.

We use commas to set off introductory words and groups of words.

Adverb clauses, transitional phrases, and phrases introduced by verbals or prepositions, when they come at the beginning of the sentence, usually require a comma to set them off from the main clause. These adverb clauses need a comma:

> *If a dunce applies himself thoroughly,* he can dream of becoming president.

> *When I turned to the left at the end of the lane,* I found the old house intact.

Omitting these commas would leave the sentence hopelessly awkward and confusing. If the order of clauses is reversed, a comma, though possible, is no longer necessary.

> A dunce can dream of becoming president if he applies himself thoroughly.

> I found the old house intact when I turned to the left at the end of the lane.

An introductory adverbial clause, if it is short, need not always carry a comma. A comma is optional in,

> *If I lead* he will follow.

Introductory phrases of transition, like *on the other hand,* usually need a comma.

> On the other hand, sometimes they don't.
> In fact they are optional.
> In fact, they are optional.

Retaining the comma is appropriate in formal writing and is acceptable in all writing. Omitting the comma is rhythmically more colloquial. Interjections like *Oh,* or *shucks,* however, almost always take the comma.

> Gosh, that's not what you said the last time.

We use a comma when the sentence begins with a long phrase governed by a preposition.

In the century after the Civil War, progress in civil rights was minuscule.

When the introductory prepositional or verbal phrase is short, the comma is optional, and may be omitted when omission does not cause ambiguity.

At twelve she was full-grown.
Having won they adjourned to a saloon.

We use commas to avoid ambiguity.

Sometimes we need a comma to indicate a pause which the voice would make, in speech, for clarity, but which is not otherwise necessary.

Outside the fields spread to the river

is clearer with a pause:

Outside, the fields spread to the river.

To find such potential ambiguities in your prose, sometimes it is helpful to read it aloud, pronouncing it as it is written — which means pausing when there is a comma, and *not* pausing when there is *not* a comma.

We use commas to set off nonrestrictive, or parenthetical, clauses.

It is useful to know the difference between a restrictive and a nonrestrictive clause. A restrictive clause describes or limits its subject, providing essential information.

The knight who was dressed in black won all the events in the tourney.

Here, "who was dressed in black" defines the knight, as if we were pointing a finger.

The building that overlooked the river was the most popular of all.

In such restrictive clauses as these, no comma separates the clause from the rest of the sentence.

Nonrestrictive clauses, on the other hand, do not define; they could become separate sentences or coordinate clauses, and unless they are very short, they take commas at both ends. We could also write sentences in which clauses above become nonrestrictive.

> Sir Galahad, who was dressed in black, won all the events in the tourney.

This sentence, as opposed to the restrictive example above, could be broken into two sentences, with no violence done to the meaning.

> Sir Galahad was dressed in black. He won all the events in the tourney.

Or, using the clause from the other example, we could have the sentence,

> The library building, which overlooked the river, was built in 1975.

We use commas to enclose words, phrases, or clauses that are like a parenthesis.

Quotations are common parenthetical elements. So are phrases and words like *of course, naturally,* and *heavens to Betsy.* When asides or parenthetical expressions appear at the beginning of sentences, place a comma after them. When they appear at the end of sentences, put a comma just before them.

> God knows, the situation is desperate.
> The situation is desperate, God knows.
> Fellow Americans, I speak to you as a concerned citizen.
> I am a representative of the people, of course.

Omitting commas in these examples would make the sentence ambiguous or hard to read.

> God knows the situation is desperate.

Does He?

At times the commas can be omitted with no awkwardness or confusion, and the omission becomes optional. Short sentences in which word order precludes ambiguity give us this option.

> The situation was of course desperate.

On occasion one can take stylistic advantage of the rhythmic speed offered by this option.

Use a comma before and after parenthetical expressions within a sentence.

> I think you're tired, Fred, and hungry.

> The student worked, in a manner of speaking, for three whole days.

> I heard him calling, "There's my bubble gum," to the audience.

We use commas around appositives.

Appositives are nouns or noun substitutes placed next to another noun to explain or define that noun.

Peter, *the flying dwarf,* escorted Tarquina, *his good fairy.*

In many of our first drafts, we use too many commas, or put them where they do not belong. Beginning writers often feel that something is going wrong if they haven't used a comma lately, and so they shake commas over their prose like salt. Here are some sentences, taken from student themes, which have some commas they should not have.

But, it was not too late.
Clarke came by, later.
When I left she, followed me.
The dimensions were, approximately three by five.
I quickly saw Ed, and Sara.
He thought she was sickly, and studious.
The old barn was painted, red.
A runner, who likes to win, has to train, every day.
The agency sold, life, fire, and theft, insurance.

EXERCISES

The following sentences omit commas necessary to clarity. Add commas where they belong.

a. The indiscreet Martian insensitive to the feelings of Earthlings disintegrated the beagle.

b. Horrors I said to the surrounding observers

c. Of course the narrative begins to become incoherent when Hermione reaches this part of the journey.

d. If there is war in the Mid-East within the next decade the winners will be losers.

e. Beyond the river widened.

f. Deciding that cinnamon toast was preferable to fried sardines we looked in the bread box.

g. In a million or two million years the human toenail may disappear.

h. In truth the final dispensation of the profits available to the institution will not be accomplished until the end of the decade.

> i. When we take the S-curve at a speed of forty or more miles an
> hour we hold our lives in our hands as well as the steering wheel.
>
> j. He looked through his pockets and found a comb two matchbooks
> four paper clips six pennies and a piece of bubble gum.

Semicolons

Semicolons between Whole Clauses. Semicolons separate whole
clauses, making a pause longer or more emphatic than a comma, but
shorter and less definite than a period. The semicolon shows a close
connection between the clauses.

It may be used between two (or more) balanced and equal clauses.

> The sun rose; the sky lightened; day had come.

Or it can be used between clauses of unequal length and different
construction.

> The sun rose; instantly, the air was alive with birds singing so
> happily that anyone who heard them could not help but smile.

These sentences are compound, the semicolon replacing the conjunction.

Semicolons with Series. Sometimes, in a long sentence, semicolons separate series or divisions, making the divisions clearer than
commas would, particularly if commas are already within the divisions.

> There were three sorts of students waiting on table at the Inn:
> fraternity boys who were dating expensive girls; girls from Detroit
> whose Daddies cut off their allowances because they had moved in
> with their boy friends; and street people, boys and girls, working
> for a week or two until they got tired of it.

Semicolons with Conjunctions. A semicolon used with a conjunction shows more separation or pause between clauses than the
comma would show.

> He flew to Denver that night; and we were glad he did.

Adverbs acting as conjunctions in compound sentences (*besides,
nevertheless, also, however, indeed, furthermore, still, then*) take a
semicolon. Transitional phrases in the middle of compound sentences

(*on the other hand, in fact, in other words, on the contrary*) do the same.

Let us take the matter in hand; however, we must not be foolhardy.
The sun rose in a clear sky; in fact, the sky was painfully bright.

Semicolons with Incomplete Clauses. Semicolons also separate incomplete clauses when a verb in one of the clauses is omitted but understood.

Poetry is one thing; verse another.

Apostrophes

Possessives. We use the apostrophe to show the possessive, with singular words. (Notice that an apostrophe does not form part of the possessive of a pronoun.)

The bag was Sara's.
It was the weather's fault.

and with plural words:

the hens' feed
Mr. and Mrs. Jones's automobile
the women's club

Contractions. We also use the apostrophe to show contractions. Use an apostrophe to show that you have omitted one or more letters in a phrase, commonly a combination of a pronoun and a verb. *I'm, she's, he's, who's, we've, you've, they're,* etc; *we'd, you'd, he'd, she'd; he'll, she'll, who'll.*

Three contractions become problems. *They're* sounds like *their* and *there*, and we may spell one when we mean another. "*Their* out working" is as incorrect as "*there* work" and "working *their*." (Correct: "*They're* out working"; "*their* work"; "working *there*.")

It's always means *it is*. It is not possessive, like "*its* shadow." Whenever you write or see the apostrophe with these letters — *it's* — remember that the *'s must* stand for *is.* Or memorize the phrase,

It's afraid of *its* shadow.

Who's is another common contraction and once again there is a confusion. *Whose* gets mixed up with *who's*. Again, the *'s* means *is*, and *who's* always stands for *who is*, whereas *whose* is a possessive pronoun.

> *Who's* drinking *whose* soup?

Other common contractions involve a verb and the negative: *isn't, aren't, doesn't, don't, can't, haven't, won't.*

Plural of Numbers. We use the apostrophe to form the plurals of typographic symbols, words referred to as words, letters, and figures.

> The 7's on the new office typewriter are black as e's, 8's are un-readable, and half the time simple the's are obscure.

> *Her* book.
> The book was *hers*.

____ EXERCISES ____

Cross out the incorrect apostrophes in these sentences. Add the missing ones.

a. Poor dog! Its too late for it's supper.

b. That Morocco-bound volume of Tolkien was supposed to be her's.

c. Whose for tennis?

d. Is'nt English spelling irrational?

e. It's true he didn't know who's tax he had paid, his wifes or his own.

Quotation Marks, and Punctuating Quotations

The exact words of a speaker or writer, included in a paragraph, are set off by quotation marks. Put a comma at the end of the quotation before the quotation mark, or a period if the quotation ends the sentence. If the quotation ends with a question mark or an exclamation point, these marks of punctuation take the place of the comma and occur inside the quotation marks.

> Al asked Wayne, "Didn't you?"

On the other hand, sometimes we quote in order to exclaim about the quotation, or inquire about the quotation. In such a sentence, the exclamation point or question mark occurs after the quotation mark.

> What did he mean when he said, "Good morning"?
> She had the nerve to say "Hello"!

When we quote a passage longer than fifty words, in a research paper for instance, we can use a colon to introduce the quotation and detach the quotation from the text by indenting it. The quotation is not enclosed by quotation marks. Ellipses can help you avoid long, detached quotations.

We use quotation marks to indicate the exact repetition of words from speech or writing: As Macbeth would say, "Tomorrow and tomorrow and tomorrow. . . ." We also use them to indicate the titles of short literary works, like essays and short stories and poems and chapters or other sections of a longer work. We speak of Tennyson's short poem "Tithonos"; when we refer to a book-length poem by the same author, we use italics instead: *In Memoriam*. We speak of Hemingway's story "A Clean Well-Lighted Place" and his novel *A Farewell to Arms*. "The Dead" is part of James Joyce's *Dubliners*. We use italics for the names of newspapers and magazines: *The New Haven Register*, *Blair and Ketcham's Country Journal*.

Other Marks of Punctuation

Brackets. Brackets are useful in prose especially in three places, all within or close to quotations. We use them when we add to a quotation material which was not in the original but which is needed for clarity. Sometimes a bracketed word supplies information lacking in the quotation but available in the context. The brackets can contain the antecedent to a pronoun:

> "He [O'Toole] smashed his fist through the window of the bar."

or some important fact:

> "It was in mid-June [1976] that the storm began."

Sometimes, in quoting the spoken word, we use brackets to enclose an indication of action, like a stage direction.

> ". . . and, finally, I want to ask you willingly and cheerfully to share the huge burden of responsibility which the age has thrust upon us all." [Boos.].

Sometimes we use brackets to correct a quotation.

> "It all happened in the early hours of September 20th [actually September 21] when the sun began [to] rise over the boardwalk."

Colons. Colons direct our attention to what comes after them. Usually they follow an introductory statement that leads us to expect a follow-up, though sometimes the introduction is implicit, or the colon itself reveals that the clause preceding it was introductory. Here are some explicit introductions.

To a long quotation, either included in the text in quotation marks, or indented without quotation marks,

> E. B. White wrote of his old professor: "In the days when I was sitting in his class he omitted so many needless words, and omitted them so forcibly and with such eagerness and obvious relish, that...."

To a list,

> He narrowed his choices to three: Mary, Elizabeth, or Karen.

Less elegantly, to an appositive at the end of a sentence,

> He narrowed the field until he arrived at one name: Zona.

A comma, here, would be just as correct, and perhaps less prone to melodrama.

Sometimes we put a colon between two main clauses instead of a semicolon; it implies that the second clause is a result of the first.

> The hands of the clock seemed never to move: she had never been late before.

Here the colon adds a meaning that the semicolon would lack. The semicolon would present the two statements as closely connected, but without the implication that the second clause derived from the first.

Dashes. Use dashes with caution — but use them. Make them on your typed paper by putting two hyphens next to each other.

In the sentence above, the dash shows a hesitation in the voice, followed with a rush by something that seems almost an afterthought. Dashes are informal. For some careless writers, dashes become substitutes for all other forms of punctuation; they not only lose any special meaning dashes may contribute, they also rob other punctuation of its meaning. For instance:

Yet many people use them too often — they become substitutes for all other forms of punctuation — and thus lose their special meaning — at the same time they rob other punctuation of its meaning —

Two legitimate uses for the dash are the implied afterthought, as in the first sentence above, and the informal parenthesis. Marks of parenthesis ( ) look more formal; dashes give a sense of speech. These two sentences illustrate a slight, characteristic difference:

> The myth of connotative and denotative meanings was destroyed by Carnap (the logician who taught at the University of Chicago) some twenty-five years ago.

> The myth of connotative and denotative meanings was destroyed by a logician and philosopher — I think it was Carnap — about twenty-five years ago.

Ellipses. Three dots in a row . . . indicate that you have omitted something from a quotation. Use four dots if the words left out were at the end of a sentence: three to indicate the omission, a fourth for the period.

Ellipses are useful in research papers or arguments using references. Much of a paragraph we want to quote may be irrelevant to our point. To include the whole paragraph in our text would slow the pace and violate the unity in our argument. Therefore we piece-cut the quotation, and make it blend smoothly with our essay. Here is the long way to use the quotation:

> Marlowe was more direct than Shakespeare, and more vigorous. As Professor William Wanger puts it:
>
> > If the *Jew of Malta* is Marlowe's *Merchant of Venice*, it is at the same time better and worse than Shakespeare's famous comedy. The lesser-known play has fewer quotable passages, perhaps, and certainly fewer that are quoted, but we must acknowledge that Marlowe's play has more energy than Shakespeare's. What it lacks in finesse it makes up in vigor, and the character of the Jew is surely more complex, and more thoughtfully observed, than the character of the Merchant.
>
> What Professor Wanger says of two plays, we can say of all. . . .

Instead, we can use ellipses and build the necessary quotations into our text:

> Marlowe was more direct than Shakespeare and more vigorous. Comparing comedies by the two men, Professor William Wanger

found Marlowe "better and worse than Shakespeare . . . ," lacking "in finesse" but superior in "vigor" and "energy." He found Marlowe's characterization, in one comparison, "more complex, and more thoughtfully observed" than Shakespeare's.

When we are obviously making excerpts, as with single words like *energy* and detached phrases like the last quotation, we do not need ellipses, because ellipses provide information: if we already know that quotations are excerpted, we do not need rows of dots to tell us so. But after *Shakespeare,* earlier in the paragraph, when we cut between a noun and an apostrophe indicating possession, we need the ellipses.

Hyphens. We use hyphens to break a word at the right-hand margin. Dictionaries usually indicate the syllables that make up a word by placing a dot between them (com • pound • ed.). Hyphenate only at the syllable break. Write com / pounded, never comp / ounded. When the syllable to be isolated is only one or two letters long, avoid division (a-long; man-y, compound-ed).

We use the hyphen on occasion to join two adjectives, or words serving as adjectives, modifying a noun. They make a temporary compound word.

blood-red hair
mile-long avenue

Avoid the temptation to multiply hyphenated phrases, which can become a virulent form of adjectivitis.

The *purple-green cloud-forms sweep-crawl.* . . .

We use hyphens with some temporary compounds. Before *wheel* and *barrow* became the compound word *wheelbarrow,* there may have been a stage at which men wrote *wheel-barrow.* Consult your dictionary when you are in doubt. Hyphens in compounds are a matter of spelling.

We use hyphens in compound numbers from twenty-one through ninety-nine.

We hyphenate fractions used as adjectives and placed before the noun modified,

a *two-thirds* majority

but not otherwise:

three quarters of the population

We use the hyphen to avoid ambiguity. We must spell the word *re-creation* to avoid confusing it with *recreation*

We use the hyphen with some prefixes and suffixes.

governor-*elect*
ex-wife
self-determined

We use the hyphen as a typographic device to indicate a manner of speaking, when we indicate that someone is spelling a word by writing it *w-o-r-d*, or when we indicate a stammer, *w-w-word*.

Italics. When we type, or write by hand, we show italics by underlining the word: italics. It comes out in type, *italics*.

Use italics for the names of ships. the *Niña*, for the titles of books, films, and plays: *War and Peace*; for the titles of magazines: *Sports Illustrated*; and for foreign expressions: *faute de mieux, in medias res.*

Also, we use them to indicate a special use of a word.

We might call the directory an *encyclopedia* of has-beens.

We use them, from time to time, to indicate emphasis.

Do you really *mean* that?

Using italics for emphasis is tricky, however. Italics are a vague gesture, an attempt to register a tone of voice that often fails because it cannot indicate a *specific* tone of voice. A writer who relies on emphatic italics often is being lazy; a more careful choice of words, a more precise context, and the emphasis will be clear without italics.

Parentheses. Use parentheses to enclose material which digresses or interrupts the main idea of the writing, or which explains something but remains a detachable unit.

The minister continued to pace up and down (though he normally slept through the night) and to stare out the window into the darkness.

De Marque points out (not only in the Treatise, but in the Harmonics as well) that Jolnay was ignorant of Graf.

Fred Papsdorf (Charles Laughton bought his paintings) lives on Jane Street, near East Detroit, in a small bungalow.

She complained that she weighed ten stone (140 lbs.; a stone, an English measure of avoirdupois, is fourteen pounds) and had been seven stone a year ago.

Also, use parentheses for numbers or letters that divide parts of a list.

There are three reasons, (1) . . . , (2) . . . , and (3). . . .

—— **EXERCISES** ————————————————————————

In the following sentences, marks of punctuation are used incorrectly, or loosely. Discover errors, or places where exact punctuation would improve precision or clarity.

a. Two thirds of the population is semi-literate, and has read nothing more complex than "Readers Digest."

b. The triumvirate, a ruling group of three, resembling a contemporary troika, took over from the dying emperor.

c. The pumpkin stuffing October sun, as the poet (Rarity) called it in his sonnet, *Goose,* pumped calories into the uncoiling sausage of the valley.

d. "Whatever you do", the potato farmer told me; "remember one thing; eat starch four times a day."

e. The monk, with the Gucci shoes wearing the new tonsure, spoke, at last with a sigh, "Yes I am Ludwig Babo."

KEEP MECHANICS CONVENTIONAL

Like punctuation marks, the mechanics of English prose are conventions that make life easier. We can argue that the rules of spelling or manuscript form are irrational, and we can make a good case. But if we all agree to abide by the same mechanical conventions — irrational or not — we can more easily understand each other. Here are some remarks about abbreviations, capital letters, manuscript form, numerals, and spelling.

Abbreviation

For the use of abbreviations in footnotes and bibliography, see pages 281–286.

In formal writing, we abbreviate only some words that go with names, like: *Mr., Mrs., Ms., Dr., St.* (for *Saint,* not *street*), *Jr., Sr.;* degrees, like *Ph.D.* or *M.A.,;* and indications of era or time like A.D., B.C., A.M., and P.M. (We use the latter two initials only when a specific time is indicated; we speak of "4 P.M.," not "it was the P.M.") We do not abbreviate Monday or August or street or road or volume or chemistry, in ordinary writing.

Some writers use no. as an abbreviation for number, but it looks out of place in formal prose. So does *U.S.A.* instead of *the United States,* and *Penna.* or *Pa.* instead of *Pennsylvania, lb.* instead of *pound,* and *oz.* instead of *ounce.*

Some institutions are so commonly called by their initials that it is overly formal to spell them out. The *Federal Bureau of Investigation* seems a pompous way to talk about the *FBI.* On the other hand, consider your audience; many people will need to be told the first time you mention it that *SEATO* is the *South-East Asia Treaty Organization.*

In conjunction with a figure, *mph* and *rpm* are used in formal writing. We write of *50 mph* and *1,000 rpms.* But if we write without figures, we spell them out.

It is difficult to assess the speed of a space capsule, when it is told in *miles per hour.*

Titles like governor can be spelled out or shortened. Frequently, we shorten it when we give a whole name,

Gov. William Milliken

and spell it out with a last name alone,

Governor Milliken

Any abbreviation of titles is inappropriate to the most formal prose.

Capital Letters

Capitalize the names of people, cities, and countries; the titles of people, books, and plays; names of religious or national groups, languages, days of the week, months, holidays, and organizations and their abbreviations; the names of events or eras in history and important documents; and the names of specific structures like buildings and airplanes and ships. In titles of books, plays, and movies, capitalize the first word and all subsequent words *except* articles and prepositions.

John Doe	Monday
Great Britain	June
Berlin	Memorial Day
Mayor Abe Beame	General Motors
Moby-Dick	G.M.
The Importance of Being Earnest	Marathon Oil Company
	Declaration of Independence
Methodist	Empire State Building
Polish or European or Bostonian	The Winnie Mae
	the *Titanic*

Do not capitalize the seasons, or the names of college classes (*freshman, senior*), or general groups like *the lower classes* or *the jet set.* Do not capitalize school subjects or disciplines except languages:

physics
French

Adjectives are capitalized when they derive from proper nouns and still refer to them, like *Shakespearean.* Other nouns or adjectives, which derive from names but no longer refer to the person, lose their capitals:

boycott
quisling

The title that is capitalized before the proper noun

Mayor Hermann Garsich

loses its capital when it is used outside of its titling function, as a descriptive word placed after the proper noun.

Hermann Garsich, *mayor* of our town.

Sections of a country may take capitals,

the *West*
the *South*

but the same words take the lower case when they are directions.

Go *west,* young man.

Sentences begin with capitals.

Manuscript Form

Type if you can.

Double-space on one side of white 8½-by-11-inch twenty-pound bond paper. Never use erasable paper; it won't take inked corrections, it smudges, it sticks together, and it is altogether unpleasant to read. Use Ko-Rec-Type or a similar easy device for corrections.

Always make a carbon or a photocopy. The most careful graders occasionally lose a paper. The corporations providing stolen papers for rich students make off with manuscripts when they can. Keep a copy to protect yourself.

Make margins of 1 inch to 1½ inches at top, bottom, and sides.

Number pages consecutively, including notes, appendixes, and bibliography.

Put your name in the upper left-hand corner of the first page.

Type the title, capitalizing the first letter of the first word and of all other words except articles and prepositions, two or three inches down from the top of the first page. Do not underline or add a period to your title.

If quoted material is short — up to fifty words of prose, or two lines of poetry — place it within the paragraph, and use quotation marks. With lines of poetry, use a slash mark (/) to indicate line breaks, and follow the capitalization of the poem.

Of man's first disobedience, and the fruit / Of that forbidden tree. . . .

If quoted material is longer than fifty words or two lines of poetry, detach it from the text. Indent the quotation half an inch to the right of the place where you begin paragraphs, and single-space the quotation. Do not use quotation marks.

Numerals

In dealing with decimal points and highly precise or technical figures, it is wise to use numerals.

69.7 decibels

It is acceptable to print dates in numerals also.

June 14, 1971

The same goes for population figures and addresses.

> 104,000 inhabitants
> 1715 South University Avenue

Print out figures, except when they are long to the point of being ridiculous. If you can *write that a town has one hundred and four thousand inhabitants,* it is easy enough to write it out. If necessity requires precision, *104,627* will do, and *one hundred and four thousand, six hundred and twenty-seven* might look precious.

Never begin a sentence with a numeral.

> 97.6 mph showed on the speedometer.

Here you can turn it around to

> The speedometer showed 97.6 mph.
> 30 people stood up

should certainly be spelled out as

> Thirty people stood up.

It is unnecessary, unless you are a lawyer, to include both spelled-out numbers and figures. Do not write,

> The building was at least twenty (20) stories tall.

Either will do — preferably the written-out word — but both together belong only to legal or business documents.

Spelling

English spelling is irregular and irrational. There are a few rules of thumb, but the rules always have exceptions. We memorize to learn to spell. By memory we write *there* when it is fitting and *their* when it is fitting. By memory we spell *plough, although, enough,* and *slough.*

Here are some problems in spelling, and some suggestions about overcoming them.

Each of us has problems of his own, and sometimes we make up our own ways to remember the correct spelling. Suppose you have trouble with the *ite / ate* ending: *Definate* is a common mistake for *definite.* Maybe you can remember that it resembles the word *finite;* or maybe the third *i* in *infinity* will help you. Or maybe you write *infinate* by mistake. Remember the antonym *finite* and remember *sep-*

arate, as in "*separate* rooms," and not *separite.* (Not *seperate* either, for that matter.)

I / e, e / i. People mistakenly write *concieve* instead of *conceive,* and *beleive* instead of *believe.* The old recipe

> I before E
> Except after C

is useful. Examples, both ways: *achieve, niece, piece; receipt, ceiling, receive.* Exceptions: *either, seize, weird, leisure, species.*

Variant plurals. Some words change spelling in moving from singular to plural: *wife / wives* (like *knife, life, calf,* and *half*); *man / men* (like *woman, milkman,* etc.); *hero / heroes* (like *tomato, potato*).

Dropping a final -e before a vowel. Most words ending with a silent *-e* drop it when we change them to a participle or other form that begins with a vowel. We spell the verb *move,* and we spell the participle *moving.* The silent *-e* usually remains when the added form begins with a consonant. Exceptions to both generalizations occur (*argue / argument; mile / mileage*), but they are infrequent and the rule is an unusually safe one.

The final -y. When *y* is a final vowel after a consonant (*dry*) it turns to *-ie* before *-s,* and *-i* before other letters, except when the ending is *-ing,* in which case the *y* remains. *dries, drier, drying, beauty, beautiful.* When the *y* follows another vowel, it generally remains *-y,* as in *joys* and *grayer,* with occasional exceptions, as in *lay / laid.*

Doubling consonants. We double a final consonant before *-ed, -ing, -er,* or *-est* when the original verb or noun ended with a short vowel followed by a single consonant. *Hop* becomes *hopping.* When the vowel is long or a diphthong, we usually show it by a silent *-e* after the single consonant, and a single consonant with the suffix. *Hope* becomes *hoping.* Notice the difference between *plan / planning, plane / planing, slip / slipping, sleep / sleeping.*

Here are some words frequently misspelled.

accept	embarrass	professor
accommodate	exaggerate	precede

acknowledgment	explanation	proceed
advice	existence	quantity
advise	friend	quite
all right	fulfillment	receive
allusion	grammar	referred
a lot	height	separate
annual	hypocrisy	shining
argument	irritable	similar
arrangement	its	succeed
beginning	it's	surprise
believe	library	than
business	lonely	then
capital	loneliness	their
capitol	necessary	there
coming	nuclear	they're
committee	obstacle	to, two, too
complement	occurred	villain
compliment	piece	who's
decide	possession	whose
definite	principal	writing
desert	principle	written
dessert	privilege	
divide	probably	

—— EXERCISES ——————————————————————

In the following paragraph, circle every mechanical error and
correct it in the space between the lines.

During the weeks that I have spent on campus I have learned to

except the principal that definate explinations are often to exagerated

to beleive in alot. 9 out of 10 students embarass thier professers by not

realising the mayor of there towns name, or not being alright in gram-

mer, or not suceeding in reading books like "Moby Dick." Its a disg

rase.

A Glossary of Usage
and Grammatical Terms

The entries are of two kinds:

1. Words frequently misused — clichés, commonly confused pairs of words, and words or phrases that should be avoided.

2. Grammatical and rhetorical terms, and the names of figures of speech. The entry will make general comments and refer you to the pages in the text where the subject is discussed.

A, an
See **Article.**

Abbreviation
See pages 338–339.

Absolute element
An absolute element is a word or a group of words which is grammatically independent of the rest of the sentence, and which is not joined to it by a relative pronoun or a conjunction.

Come hell or high water, I'll get to Dallas by Thursday.
Neither twin was there, *to tell the truth.*

Abstract, abstraction
An abstraction is a noun referring to the idea or quality of a thing, and not to a thing itself: *redness, courage.*

We use the word *abstract* relatively, referring to more general and less particular words. *Enclosure* is more general, say, than *room* or *cage* or *zoo*.

For remarks on abstractions and prose style, see pages 88–91.

Accept, except

These words sound alike but mean different things. *Accept* means to receive something voluntarily.

I *accept* the compliment.

Except as a verb means to exclude.

I *excepted* Jones from the group I wished to congratulate.

Except as a preposition is more common.

I congratulated everyone *except* Jones.

Acronym

An acronym is an abbreviation, pronounced as a word, which is composed of the first letters of the words in the title or phrase abbreviated.

SAC (Strategic Air Command)
snafu (situation normal, all fouled up)

Use with caution.

Active voice

Verbs are in the active voice when the subject of the sentence does the action the verb describes.

Bob *hit* the spider.

When the subject is acted upon, we do not have the active voice.

The spider *was hit* by Bob.

See **Passive voice.**

Adjective

Adjectives describe or limit a noun or a noun substitute. These adjectives describe:

green onions
happiest year
The man was *old*.

These adjectives limit in a variety of ways:

indefinite:

> *Some* men walked in the road.

demonstrative:

> *Those* men walked in the road.

possessive:

> *Their* men walked in the road.

numerical:

> *Twelve* men walked in the road.

interrogative:

> *Which* men walked in the road?

relative:

> The men *who* walked in the road kept coming onward.

> Nouns can be used as adjectives.

> *university* professor

But the writer should beware of using several nouns as adjectives in a row.

For the formation of comparatives, see **Comparison of adjectives and adverbs.** For a stylistic approach to adjectives, see pages 96–106.

Adjective clause

An adjective clause is a dependent clause used as an adjective.

> The man *whose nose is purple* will stand out in a crowd.

Adjectives frequently misused

Try to avoid the adjective used vaguely. These words once meant specific things. *Terror* once inhabited *terrific;* now *terrific* can mean "unusually pleasant."

> What a *terrific* summer day!

Some other adjectives are frequently used as vague praise, vague blame, or vague intensives.

terrible	nice	cute	real
funny	unique	wonderful	fantastic
awful	interesting	incredible	

> That *terrible* man with the *cute* name was *awful* to the *nice* girl.

Adverb

Adverbs describe or limit any words except nouns and pronouns. Adverbs work with verbs, adjectives, other adverbs, verbals, and entire clauses.

Adverbs commonly show degree:

extremely hungry

or manner:

ran *slowly*

or place:

hurried *here*

or time:

she *then* left

For stylistic advice on the adverb, see pages 96–106.

Adverb clause

An adverb clause is a dependent clause used as an adverb.

I'll be gone *before she starts spraying.*

The adverb clause, *before she starts spraying,* modifies the verb *will be gone.*

Adverbs frequently misused

Most of the adjectives frequently misused become misused adverbs, with a *-ly* added. *Terrible* becomes *terribly,* as in "terribly comfortable." Strictly adverbial adjectives are misused also.

terrifically	actually	wonderfully	literally
certainly	very	rather	hopefully
absolutely	virtually	practically	really

It *certainly* was a *very* hot day and I was *practically* done at the *absolutely* last minute when *actually* a *rather* large man *virtually* beheaded me.

Advice, advise

The first word is a noun; the second, a verb.

I was *advised* to ignore your *advice.*

Affect, effect

The two words are commonly confused. These examples illustrate proper uses of them:

Bob *affected* (influenced) the writing of Wright.

Sarah *affected* (assumed) the manner of a Greek tragedian.

The harder spray was *effected* (brought about) by an adjustment of the hose's nozzle.

The *effect* (result) of the new style was unpleasant.

Agreement

The correspondence in form, or the matching of one word with another. They must correspond in number, person, and gender.

He is so evil.
They are so evil.
Tom took *his* crocodile down to the river.
Tom and Maria took *their* crocodiles down to the river.
The *car* and *its* trailer rounded the corner.

See pages 313–321.

Agree to, agree with

One *agrees to* a proposal or an action, one *agrees with* a person.

All ready, already

The words differ in meaning. To say that someone is *all ready* is to say that he is prepared; the word *already* means beforehand in time, as in

He was *already* there.

All right, alright

All right is the correct form. *Alright* means the same thing, but is a recent creation based on an analogy to the old word *already*. In formal writing, stay away from *alright*.

Along with

Avoid this wordy and useless phrase, as we use it in sentences like

Along with tennis, big game hunting is my favorite sport.

MacDowell is my candidate for the presidency, *along with* Vanderschmidt and Creelman-Carr.

Instead, say something like

Big game hunting and tennis are my favorite sports.
For the presidency, I favor MacDowell, Vanderschmidt, or Creelman-Carr.

A lot
Many people have taken to spelling *a lot*

A lot of policemen showed up.

as one word, *alot*. *A lot* is two words, like *all right*.

Although, though
Although is preferable in formal writing.

Altogether, all together
The two do not have the same meaning. *Altogether* means *wholly* or *entirely*. *All together* combines two commonly understood words.

Xavier, Abby, Frank, and Al were *all together* at the table.
Guy Woodhouse was *altogether* disgusting.

Ambiguity
Writing is ambiguous when it has more than one possible meaning or interpretation.

Amid, amidst
Avoid these words, which are not common to the American language, and which sound stuffy and bookish.

Among, amongst
Among is preferable. *Amongst* is bookish.

Among, between
Use *between* when you are dealing with two things, *among* for more than two.

between you and me
among the three of us

In highly informal writing, this distinction is often ignored.

Amoral, immoral, unmoral
Immoral is contrary to codes of morality.

Benedict Arnold was *immoral.*

Amoral means outside morality, neither moral nor immoral.

Beauty is *amoral.*

Unmoral is a near-synonym for *amoral,* and is seldom used. *Amoral* is often used when the assertion is argumentative, *unmoral* when the statement is merely factual.

> Dogs and cats are *unmoral.*

Amount, number
Amount refers to a quantity of things viewed as a whole, or to the quantity of one item; *number* describes the separate units of a group.

> The *amount* of money in his bank account was staggering.
> The *number* of dollar bills on the floor was small.
> He took a large *amount* of salt a *number* of times.

Analogy
An analogy is an extended comparison, used for illustration and argument. For examples and stylistic uses, see pages 114 115.

And / or
This legalism frequently occurs in nonlegal prose where *or* would do just as well.

> Cooking with pots *and / or* skillets requires nothing more than a hotplate.

Omit the unnecessary "*and* "

Antecedent
An antecedent is a word or group of words to which a pronoun refers.

> As *Kevin* and *Quentin* ran in, *they* dropped the gas pellets.

Kevin and *Quentin* are the antecedents of the personal pronoun *they.*

Antonym
An antonym means the opposite of another word. *Bad* is the antonym of *good.*

As there are no exact synonyms, so we must not expect antonyms to be precisely opposite.

Any, any other
Be careful to use these words properly. If you say,

> "*King Lear* is more moving than *any other* play in the English language."

you are probably saying what you intend. If you say, however, that

> "*King Lear* is more moving than *any* play in the English language."

you imply that *Lear* is not in English — or that *Lear* is better than itself, which would be nonsensical. If you say that

> "Sophia is sexier than *any* woman in Italy."

you imply that she is not in Italy.

Anybody, anyone

The words are singular, not plural. They take singular pronouns, as do *every, everyone, everybody.*

> *Everyone* charges *his* meal at Alice's.

is formally correct, and not

> *Everyone* charges *their* meal at Alice's.

But an exception to this rule could make the second example the preferable form of the sentence. When a pronoun has *anybody* (etc.) as an antecedent, and the gender of the person being discussed is unknown, we may wish to use forms of the plural *they* in order to avoid deciding between *he* and *she*, because *they* does not indicate gender.

> Did *anybody* call? What did *they* say?

Anyways

This form of *anyway* belongs to speech, not to writing.

Apostrophe

See pages 331–332.

Appositive

An appositive is a noun, or a noun substitute, which is placed next to another noun, and which explains or defines it.

> Peter, *the flying dwarf,* escorted Tarquina, his *good fairy.*

Flying dwarf is the appositive of *Peter,* and *good fairy* is the appositive of *Tarquina.*

Article

The definite article is *the,* the indefinites are *a* or *an.* They are adjectives, always indicating that a noun or a noun substitute will follow.

The names a particular:

the table
the abstraction

A and *an* name the member of a class:

a table
an abstraction

The difference in meaning is small but indispensable.

The article *a* is used before words beginning with a consonant sound (even if the letter is a vowel):

a train
a unit

An is used before words beginning with a vowel sound.

an interesting idea
an herb

As, like

As is a conjunction, *like* is a preposition. In speech we often find *like* used as a conjunction,

He smiles *like* he felt good.

but in the written language, we should avoid using *like* as a conjunction. We should use *as* instead. Instead of writing

I write *like* I talk.

we say

I write *as* I talk.

Like works as a preposition, in language written or spoken:

He talks *like* a Frenchmen.

At

Don't use the redundancy, "Where are you *at?*" *Where* means "at which place?"

Auxiliaries

Auxiliaries in verb phrases indicate distinctions in tense and person. Common auxiliaries are: *will, would, shall, should, be, have, do, can, could, may, might,* and *must.*

We *are* eating the chocolate.
You *would have* done the same.

Awful, awfully

Literally, if we are *awful,* we are "full of *awe."* We no longer use the word to mean what it means. It is a vague intensive like *terrific, wonderful,* and *horrible.*

Bad, badly

When we use the adjective *bad* after sensory verbs, in an expression like "I felt *bad* yesterday," we sometimes confuse it with the adverb *badly.* If you claim that you "felt *badly,"* your words mean that your sensory apparatus did not function correctly. This use of *bad* holds true for sensory verbs like "feel," "taste," or "sound," and also for verbs like "seem," "appear," and "look." In grammatical terms, *bad* in these circumstances is a predicate adjective.

Using *badly* instead of *bad* as a predicate adjective affects gentility but reveals ignorance. It is correct to say,

She looked *bad* when she came up to bat

and incorrect to say,

She looked *badly* when she came up to bat.

The latter sentence denigrates her vision. It is correct to say,

They seemed *bad* this morning, after the ocean voyage.

referring to the appearance of illness. Do not say,

They seemed *badly* this morning after the ocean voyage.

Other constructions require the adverb, *badly.*

She played *badly,* the first seven innings.

Here,

She played *bad* the first seven innings.

is incorrect.

Badly has another sense, which is "very much." This sense is colloquial or informal.

They wanted *badly* to be elected.
She was *badly* in need of a drink.

If you mean to employ this colloquialism, be careful of your word order. If you say, "She needed to sing very *badly,"* you say something quite different from "She needed very *badly* to sing." If in doubt, be more formal; say,

She needed *very much* to sing.

or

She needed to sing *very much*.

Balanced sentences

See pages 158–159, where I discuss balance and parallelism.

Beside, besides

Each of these words has several meanings of its own.

She stood *beside* (by the side of) the bureau.
Matt was *beside* himself (almost overwhelmed) with anger.
It's *beside* (not connected with) the point.
No one was awake *besides* (other than) him.
Besides (furthermore), it's in questionable taste.

Between

See **Among, between.**

Bibliography

See pages 281–283.

Big words

Never use a big word where a little word will do. Never say *domicile* where you could say *house*. Never say *individual* where you could say *person*. Never say *utilize* where you could say *use*.

See **Genteel words** and **-ize verbs.**

Bracket

See pages 333–334.

Can, may

Both words express possibility; *can* (or *could*) *expresses physical possibility.*

He *can* go to market because he has the car.
She *could* eat the potato salad but she doesn't want to.

May (or *might*) *implies that something is a chance, and often implies volition.*

He *may* go to Alaska (or he may not).
She *might* be the last of the clan (or she might not).

Often we can hesitate between the two, and choose the one over the other for the precise shade of meaning. "He *could* take the exam" and "He *might* take the exam" offer different possibilities.

In conversation, and in the most informal writing, *may* often disappears in favor of *can*, and a distinction disappears, which is a loss. Or instead of saying, "She *may* read Shakespeare, or Julia Child, or *Young Lust*," we substitute the wordier, "She *can* read Shakespeare, or Julia Child, or *Young Lust*, depending on what she feels like." The final clause supplies the chanciness and the volition implied in *may*.

In asking or granting permission, genteel prose uses *may*.

May I enter?
Randolph, you *may* not.

But *may* in this usage almost invariably sounds like an effort to be refined.

Cannot, can not

These arrangements are equally acceptable. *Can not* looks more formal.

Can't hardly

Because *hardly*, as Bergen Evans says, "has the force of a negation," *can't hardly* functions as a double negative, or at least as an ambiguity. Does "I *can't hardly* hear you" mean "I *can't* hear you" or "I *can* hear you well" or "I *can hardly* hear you?" Logically, the double negative should make it mean the second, but the speaker probably meant the last. We should increase the clarity of our language by saying simply, "I *can hardly* hear you." The same advice applies to *"can't scarcely."*

See **Double negative.**

Capital letters

See pages 339–340.

Case

See **Inflection.**

Cf.

We often find this abbreviation in footnotes, and sometimes in parentheses. It tells us to "compare," as in

This decision was an exception (*cf. Toothe* v. *Carey.*)

Circumlocution

Circumlocution is taking the long way to say something, using clichés, verbs combined with other parts of speech instead of simple verbs, and filler words and phrases. In

> *Notwithstanding the case of* the seamstress, it is *going to be* obvious that *in general, in a manner of speaking, we do well to remember the* observation *that a man who* is always in a hurry will lose *something or other in the long run.*

the circumlocution occurs throughout, and phrases typical in circumlocution are in italic. Notice that the last seventeen words might be rendered

Haste makes waste.

Cite, sight, site

Cite means to quote or to refer to.

They *cited* the constructive things they'd done.

A *sight* is a view,

a moving *sight*

or vision itself.

A *site* is a location.

a building *site*

Clause

A clause is a part of a sentence with a subject and a predicate. It may be principal (or main or independent) or subordinate (dependent on a main clause).

The year ended and *the year began.*

In this sentence, two whole clauses are made into a compound sentence by *and*.

The year ended *when it had just begun.*

In this sentence, the italic clause is subordinate.
See pages 125–126.

Cliché

A cliché is a much used combination of words. *Writing Well* uses and defines this word several times. See pages 3–4, for instance.

Collective noun

See **Noun.**

Colon

See page 334.

Comma
See pages 324–329.

Comma splice
See pages 310–312.

Common nouns
See **Noun.**

Compare to, compare with
To compare *to* shows similarities between things that are obviously different.

He *compared* the sparrow *to* a ten-ton truck.

(Of course by showing similarity, it reveals difference as well.) To compare *with* shows differences between things that are obviously similar.

She *compared* lunch *with* dinner.

(Of course it reveals similarities at the same time.)

Comparison of adjectives and adverbs
The comparison of adjectives and adverbs indicates relative degree. The three degrees are: positive, comparative, and superlative.

Positive	*Comparative*	*Superlative*
good	better	best
obnoxious	more obnoxious	most obnoxious
quick	quicker	quickest
quickly	more quickly	most quickly

Comparisons
For a discussion of simile, metaphor, and analogy, see pages 112–118.

Complement
A complement is one or more words that completes the meaning of a verb, or an object. A subject complement:

Phyllis is a wicked *girl.*

The predicate noun — *girl* — completes the sense of *Phyllis,* which it refers to. An object complement:

The dog chewed the bone *raw.*

Raw modifies and completes *bone.*

Complement, compliment

A *complement* makes something whole or complete.

Work is the *complement* of play.
Howard left the room *a filthy mess.*

A *compliment* is praise.

I paid you a *compliment.*

There is also an archaic meaning, in which *compliments* means something like formal politeness, and which survives in the phrase, "*compliments* of the season."

Complex sentence

A complex sentence contains a main clause and a subordinate clause. Here the subordinate (in italics) is a relative:

I whistled at the boy *who hung from the cliff.*

See pages 128–129, 135–137, 177–180.

Compound sentence

A compound sentence includes two or more main clauses and no subordinate clauses.

The moon rose at 10:35 P.M. and the stars appeared to recede into the darkness.

See pages 127–128 and 137–143.

Compound-complex sentence

This sentence type combines, as you might expect, the complex and the compound sentence. It has two main clauses, and at least one subordinate clause.

The snow stopped falling when the sun rose, but the temperature stayed below 10°.

See page 129.

Compound word

Compound words are two or more words commonly used together as a single word.

president-elect
brother-in-law

blackbird
wheelbarrow
handwriting

See a dictionary for current spelling.
See pages 336–337.

Conjugation.
See **Inflection.**

Conjunction

Conjunctions connect or coordinate (*and, but, for, or,* and occasionally *yet* or *so*), or they subordinate (*after, because, while, when, where, since*). With coordinate conjunctions be careful to preserve unity by keeping the coordinate phrases or clauses parallel (see pages 152–160). With subordinate conjunctions, remain aware of the habits of complex sentences (pages 128–129, 135–137, and 177–180). Contrary to the old rule, the best contemporary writing uses conjunctions at the beginnings of sentences.

Conjunctive adverb

A conjunctive adverb can be used to connect main clauses: *then, besides, however, therefore, otherwise.* Use a semicolon between the main clauses (before the adverb), and a comma after the adverb.

Consider . . . as

Writers frequently misuse the verb *consider* by adding an unnecessary preposition, *as.* Say

She *considered* him handsome.

not

She *considered* him *as* handsome.

Another use of the verb takes *as* appropriately. In the example above, *consider* means "believe to be." In the example below, *consider* means "think about" or "talk about":

She *considered* him *as* an administrator and *as* a scholar.

Consist in, consist of

Consist of refers to the parts that make a whole:

The government *consists of* legislative, executive, and judicial divisions.

Consist in refers to inherent qualities:

> The value of democracy *consists in* the responsibility with which it endows the citizen.

Continual, continuous

The two words have slightly different meanings. *Continual* describes an action that is repeated frequently.

> He called her *continually* throughout the day.

Continuous describes an action done without stopping.

> The bleeding was *continuous* for three hours.

Coordinates

Coordinate means equal in rank. Two infinitives are coordinate, for instance, or two main clauses, as in a compound sentence. See pages 128, 135–137, and 140–143.

Correlative conjunctions

Both . . . and, either . . . or, neither . . . nor, and *not only . . . but also* are coordinating conjunctions, and require parallel forms in the phrases or clauses they coordinate.

Could have, could of

The correct phrase is *could have. Could of* is a mistake. Don't say,

> She *could of* been a great actress.

but say,

> She *could have* been a great actress.

Counsel, council, consul

Counsel is advice, or a lawyer, or someone acting as a lawyer. Though it would be a confusing sentence, one could say,

> The court-appointed *counsel* gave his client *counsel.*

A different spelling, with the same pronunciation, gives us the word *council,* which is a legislative group.

> Harris for City *Council!*

A *consul* represents his government in another country where he keeps residence.

> The vice-*consul* was out to lunch.

Couple
In the idiomatic sense of *a few*, the word is extremely informal, and in your writing you ought to substitute *two*, or *a few*, or *several*.

Cutting words from quotations
See pages 335–336.

Dangling constructions
A phrase loosely placed in a sentence dangles. Modifiers dangle frequently, and disastrously.
See pages 319–320.

Dashes
See pages 334–335.

Data
In the most formal prose, we recognize the etymology of *data* as a Latin plural, and therefore use the word with a plural verb form. It is correct — if highly formal — to say,

> *These* data *convince* us.

rather than,

> *This* data *convinces* us.

The singular, rarely used, is *datum*.

Declension
See **Inflection.**

Deductive reasoning
In this form of thinking we apply a general truth to a specific instance. Thus, if it is true that going through a time-warp causes pain, we may *deduce* that if Quasimodo goes through a time-warp he will feel pain.

Demonstratives
Demonstratives are adjectives like *this*, *that*, *these*, and *those*, used to point the finger.

> *This* is the man who took it; *that*'s my basketball.

They can also be pronouns; when they are, they should have clear antecedents. Do not say,

> You said you couldn't read. I could not believe *that*.

See pages 317–318.

Different from, different than

Different from is usually preferable, especially in formal prose. When a clause follows, *different than* is acceptable.

This place is *different than* I expected it to be.

Direct address

A noun or pronoun used to direct a remark to a specific person, set off by commas.

I was thinking, *Ron,* that you'd like to go up in a balloon.
Irving, close that closet.
Hey, *you!*

Direct object

See **Object.**

Direct quotation

See pages 332–333.

Discreet, discrete

The two words have different meanings. *Discreet* means "prudent in one's conduct or speech."

She would never reveal it; she was exceptionally *discreet.*

Discrete means "distinct" or "separate."

The words are different; they have *discrete* meanings.

Disinterested, uninterested

These words are frequently confused. To be *uninterested* is to lack fascination about something, even to be bored by it.

I tried to arouse his enthusiasm for a game of golf, but he was *uninterested* in such a pastime.

Disinterested is the condition of being impartial or neutral, or of having no stake in an issue. Frequently the word is used positively as a precondition for fairness, as in the phrase *"disinterested* party."

The judge declared his *disinterest* in the matter.

This judge is proclaiming his ability to judge the case fairly.

Doesn't

See **Don't.**

Don't

Goes with *I, you, we,* and *they.* It doesn't go with *it, he,* or *she.* It contracts *do not.* It does not contract *does not; doesn't* does.

Double negative

A double negative occurs in a sentence that uses two negative terms when only one is needed.

He *didn't* say *nothing.*
You *shouldn't never* do that to a bird.

In earlier English such doubling was thought to give emphasis, as in "I never treacherously slew no man" (Bergen Evans's example). But today double negatives are regarded as unacceptable and illogical. If I should *not* never-do something, then by implication I should (positively) do it sometime.
See **Can't hardly.**

Doubt but

Omit *but.* Also omit *but* in *help but.*

They couldn't *doubt* but that the Racquet Club was best.

becomes

They couldn't *doubt* that the Racquet Club was best.

They couldn't *help but* know the worst.

becomes

They couldn't *help* knowing the worst.

And always avoid "They couldn't *doubt but* what...."

Due to

Never use *due to* for *because of* in adverbial phrases. "She won the race *due to* her long legs" sounds unnatural. It is probably best to reserve the word for finance. Sometimes people multiply error by writing, "due to the fact that...."

Effect, affect

See **Affect, effect.**

E.g.

This is the abbreviation for a Latin expression that means *for example.* It is usually best to use the English, but on occasion we will find these initials, often in scientific or legal prose.

The review board overlooked significant evidence, *e.g., Baxter* v. *Baxter.*

Each, every

> *Each* is a pronoun.

> *Each* went his own way.

and an adjective.

> *Each* package of bubble gum has five pieces.

Each means the individual units of a conglomerate,

> *Each* of the Boy Scouts

but *every* means the conglomerate itself.

> *Every* Boy Scout

In the Boy Scout examples, *each* is a pronoun, *every* an adjective.

When the adjective *each* modifies a singular noun, the following verb and pronouns are singular.

> *Each* player *lifts his* bat.

When *each* modifies a plural noun or pronoun, and comes before the verb, the pronoun and verb are plural.

> They *each go their* own way.

When *each* works as a pronoun, it is usually singular.

> *Each goes his* own way.

There are exceptions. In the example just above, if the pronoun referred to men and women, we might have written,

> *Each go their* own way.

When *each* refers to two or more singular words, or when a plural word comes between *each* and the verb, the number of the verb is optional. We may say,

> *Each* of the players *is*

or

> *Each* of the players *are*

We may say,

> When *Mark and Linda* speak, *each* of them *says*

or

> When *Mark and Linda* speak, *each* of them *say*

The negative of *each* is *neither*. Do not write *each* with a negative,

> *Each* did not speak.

but write,

> *Neither* spoke.

Egoism, egotism

Egoism has the connotation of a philosophy, *egotism* of a neurosis. *Egoism* is the other side of *altruism*, and is a belief in the value of self-interest. *Egotism* is the necessity to use the word *I* all the time.

Either

Either, like *each*, can be pronoun or adjective.

> *Either* Bob or Jane . . .
> *Either* of the twins . . .

When *either* means more than one, it takes a plural verb.

> *Either* of you *are* qualified.

When it means one or the other it takes the singular.

> *Either* Rick or Chris *is* lying.

Negative statements, and the pronoun *you*, make *either* take a plural verb, even if the sense is singular.

> He did not report that *either* of them *were* qualified.
> When *either* of you *are* finished, let me know.

As a correlative conjunction, *either* takes *or* and does not take *nor. Nor* belongs to *neither.*
See page 152.

Elicit, illicit

Elicit means "to bring out."

> We could *elicit* no further response from the members.

Illicit means "not permitted."

> They were having an *illicit* love affair.

Ellipses

See pages 335–336.

Eminent, immanent, imminent

Eminent means outstanding.

The *eminent* philosopher . . .

Immanent means inherent.

. . . will discuss *immanent* ideas . . .

Imminent means impending.

. . . *imminently.*

Enormity, enormousness

An *enormity* is a moral outrage. *Enormousness* is hugeness.

Etc.

This *and so forth,* from the Latin *et cetera,* is out of place in formal prose. In formal and informal prose, it often trails off the end of a sentence into vagueness, and avoids extending the brain. Stay away from it in formal prose. Think before you use it in any context. See **Foreign words and phrases.**

Etymology

Etymology is the study specializing in the origins and histories of words.

Euphemism

Euphemisms are fancy or abstract substitutes for plain words. We use them for social elevation, as when an undertaker becomes a mortician, or to avoid facing something frightening, as when we say that someone passed away, instead of saying that he died.

See pages 65–67.

Everybody, everyone

Everybody and *everyone* take a singular verb.

Everybody goes to church.

The words can take a singular pronoun, especially in a formal context,

Everyone finds his seat and waits for the minister.

or a plural pronoun, especially when it refers to men and women and we wish to avoid the prejudice of picking either *his* or *her.*

Everybody waited until *they* caught *their* breath.

See pages 315–316.

Exclamation point
> See page 324.

Expletives
> When *it* and *there* fill space in a sentence without contributing to its meaning, we call them expletives.

> *There are* thousands of people in the United States who cannot read.
> *It is* understood that the rain was falling.

These could be written:

> Thousands of people in the United States cannot read.
> Rain was falling.

Fact
> Avoid the phrase *the fact that,* which is wordy and unnecessary.

Famous, notorious
> To be *famous* is to be well known or celebrated. To be *notorious* is to be well known for something shady.

> He was a *famous* movie star, musician, and second baseman.
> He was a *notorious* pirate, extortionist, and linguist.

Farther, further
> As "distance to go" the two are interchangeable. Where *further* means "more," *farther* is not a possible alternative.

> We have no *further* use for him.

Few
> See **Less.**

Field
> Don't say, *in the field of. . . .* It is a dead metaphor, and means little.

Figure
> See **Numeral.**

Fine
> This adjective is vague and overused.

Finite verb
> A finite verb is complete, a predicate in itself.

> The house *collapses.*

Gerunds, infinitives, and participles are not finite verbs but *verbals*.

Footnote

See pages 283–286.

Foreign words and phrases

Foreign words and phrases often look pretentious in our writing. In dialog, they can be useful to characterize someone, as foreign or as pretentious. Occasionally nothing in English seems quite so apt as a foreign phrase. But look hard before you give up. If you must use one, italicize it by underlining it.

Foreword, forward

The two have different meanings. A *foreword* is a preface, the introductory statement at the beginning of a book. *Forward* is usually a direction. On occasion, *forward* means "bold" or "presumptuous."

She stuck her tongue out at him; she was very *forward*.

Fused sentence

See **Run-on sentence.**

Gender

Gender is a grammatical indication of sex. English nouns lack gender except as their own sense indicates. That is, *sister* is feminine, *brother* masculine, and *sibling* can be either. Some pronouns have gender (*he, she*) and most do not (*I, they, you, we*). In some languages, all nouns are assigned a gender. In French, *grass* is feminine, and *time* is masculine. In English both are neuter.

Genteel words

Some words act as euphemisms by seeming socially preferable to plainer alternatives. People who use them seem to be *trying* to be genteel. Avoid them unless you are making a genuine distinction. For instance:

Genteel	*Ordinary*
perspire	sweat
wealthy	rich
home	house
luncheon	lunch

Gerund

See **Verbal.**

Get

We multiply this little word in our speech; it has small place in our writing. "I went down to *get* some wallpaper" is passable but often imprecise. In writing, it would be better to *choose* or *buy* the wallpaper.

Good, well

It is common to use *good* as if it were an adverb, but it is also incorrect.

He ran *good.*

When referring to an action *well* is the right word.

He ran *well.*

Be careful with the word *feels*; to say that a person *feels good* is to say that he is in a pleasant frame of mind; to say that a person *feels well* is to say either that he feels healthy or that his sense of touch is functioning efficiently.

Grammar

Grammar describes how words function in a language.

Guerrilla, gorilla

A *guerrilla* is an irregular soldier. A *gorilla* is an animal. *Guerrilla* is also used as an adjective, and has recently been used adjectivally to indicate activity in the service of revolution: *guerrilla* theater, *guerrilla* television.

Had ought

This combination is clumsy. Instead of writing,

We knew he *had ought* to come.

write

We knew he *ought* to come.

Hanged, hung

Hanged pertains to the execution of human beings, *hung* to the suspension of objects.

Sam Hall was *hanged* in October.
We *hung* the portraits in the hall.

He, him

See **Pronoun.**

He or she

This locution is awkward and clumsy. Sometimes we wish to use it to avoid sexism.

See the note on page 148.

Help but

See **Doubt but.**

Homonym

Homonyms are words that, although pronounced the same, are spelled differently and mean different things.

| to, too, two | heir, air | blew, blue |
| through, threw | bare, bear | |

Hopefully

Hopefully is an adverb that frequently becomes a dangling modifier. We say,

Hopefully, the plane will be on time.

when we do not mean to imply that the plane is full of hope. We could say,

Hopefully, I awaited her arrival.

We come to use *hopefully* as if it meant "I hope." The first example, above, is meant to say,

I hope the plane will be on time.

Hyperbole

Hyperbole is extreme exaggeration to make a point.

That cat *weighs a ton.*

Use hyperbole with discretion; do not use it, like some writers, a thousand times on every page.

Hyphen

See pages 336–337.

I, me

See **Pronoun.**

I.e.

I.e. abbreviates the Latin *id est,* or *that is.* We use it sometimes to introduce an explanation or definition of a word or phrase.

She was nonessential, *i.e.,* they didn't need to employ her.

Usually, the expression seems overprecise, and too much like legal or scientific writing. The sentence above can omit the Latinism, and use instead a colon or a semicolon.

> She was nonessential: they didn't need to employ her.

Immigrant, emigrant

An *immigrant* is someone who enters a country; an *emigrant* leaves one. Obviously our forefathers had to emigrate before they could immigrate.

Incredible, unbelievable.

In theory, these words are synonymous. In practice, *unbelievable* holds up better.

> The charges were *unbelievable.*

states rather straightforwardly the disbelief.

> The charges were *incredible.*

suffers from the use of *incredible* as a vague intensive.

> Those hamburgers were *incredible.*

simply praises the hamburgers in hyperbole from which constant use has withdrawn the strength. *Unbelievable* undergoes some of the same diminishment:

> . . . *unbelievably* rare

and may also lose its utility in time.

Indefinite pronoun

See **Pronoun,** and pages 315–318.

Independent clause

See **Clause.**

Indirect object

See **Object.**

Indirect quotation

We use indirect quotations when we attribute a remark without claiming to use exact words, and without using quotation marks.

> The congressman from Ohio then claimed that he had heard enough.

> She said that Herbert was the nicest boy she had ever met.

When we indirectly quote information taken from a source, we should footnote it just as we would a direct quotation.

Inductive reasoning

This form of thought draws general conclusions from particular examples or evidence.

> As a result of these experiments we conclude that if water falls below 32 degrees in temperature it will freeze.

Infer, imply

We *infer* or understand from what a speaker or writer *implies* to us.

We cannot say that another person *inferred* something to us. He *implied* it, and we *inferred* a meaning in his implication.

Inferior to, inferior than

Inferior than is incorrect. Say either *inferior to* or *worse than*.

Infinitive

See **Verbal.**

Inflection

Inflection is the change in the form of a word to indicate a change in meaning or grammatical relationship. The inflection of nouns and pronouns is called *declension;* of verbs *conjugation;* and of adjectives and adverbs *comparison.*

Inflection of nouns indicates *number* and *case.*

> aardvark, aardvarks, aardvark's, aardvarks'; man, men; man's, men's

Inflection of pronouns indicates *case, person,* and *number.*

> she, her, her, hers; who, whom, whose; they, their

Inflection of verbs indicates *tense, person* and *mood.*

> bore, boring, bores, bored
> spring, sprining, springs, sprung

Inflection of modifiers indicates *comparison* and *number.*

> thin, thinner, thinnest
> this dog, that dog, these dogs, those dogs

In regard to, in regards to

In regard to is preferable, but avoid both.

Intensive pronoun
See **Pronoun.**

Intransitive verb
An intransitive verb neither has an object nor is passive in form.

I *was* at Annette's house in Santa Fe at the time.
Quaker *has been waiting* on the flagpole for hours.

Irony
Intentional irony, in our language, is the conscious statement of an untruth, intended to convey the opposite of what it seems to say. We can say that the weather is marvelous when we are standing in a downpour. Our irony is obvious. When Jonathan Swift wrote his satirical "Modest Proposal," he suggested that Irish babies be slaughtered and eaten, as a convenience to the English. He did not intend the suggestion literally. Most of his readers perceived his irony.

Irregardless
Use *regardless. Irregardless* is a redundancy, made in error on the model of *irrespective.*

Italics
See page 337.

Its, it's
It's always stands for *it is. Its* is possessive.

It's eating *its* supper.

See page 331.

-ize verbs
Avoid making new verbs ending in -ize, like "tomato-ize the spaghetti." Avoid using some recent coinages too: "utilize" (say "use"); "personalize," "finalize."

Jargon
Jargon is the argot of a profession, or a peer group, like educationists' jargon, or astronauts', or rock musicians'. Businessmen fall into a jargon frequently. Sometimes they "firm up" a deal before they "finalize" it. Sometimes two negotiators are "not in the same ballpark."
Slang makes jargon too. The hip-revolutionary talk of the late sixties was jargon.

Right on, man. Split, the pigs. Do you dig it? Heavy.

Jargon is a language by which we attempt to prove that *we are* the initiated, and to keep noninitiates in confusion and befuddlement. It is language, not to communicate, but to exclude.

Jargon has a real purpose when it is the precise shorthand of a science. But for most of us most of the time, jargon has a tendency to be considerably vaguer than the larger language we share.

Kind of

This phrase is misused, and even used properly is often not help-ful. When we say *"kind of* big" we are qualifying "big," as if we said *"rather* big." It is a misuse of the word *kind. Kind* means species.

It is a *kind* of pine tree.

This usage works, but we often slide into vague species-making.

She is a *kind of* blonde I can't stand.

The sentence cannot be rewritten; it must be rethought. What ex-actly is it that you cannot stand? Name it.

I do not like a blonde who has red eyebrows.

The same remarks apply to *sort of*.

Lay, lie

Lay / laid / laying applies to: she is *laying* an egg; you *laid* the book on the table; I *lay* my pen on this pad. *Lay* takes a direct object. The past tense is *laid*.

He *laid* the pool on the lawn.

Lie takes the past tense *lay*, which is a source of confustion. *Lie / lay / lying* applies to: I *lie* on the grass; she *lay* on the bed all day; we were *lying* in the sun. *Lie* never takes a direct object.

Lead, led

Lead is present tense, *led* is past, and *lead* — when pronounced like *led* — is the metal.

Yesterday I *led* the class.
Today I *lead* the escape.

Leave, let

Leave means "to go away"; *let* means "to allow."

> *Leave* me. (Go away from me.)
> *Let* me. (Allow me to.)
> *Leave* me out. (Don't include me.)
> *Let* me out. (Allow me to go.)

Less

This word is frequently misused where *fewer* would be correct.

> There are *less* flowers in the vase today.

should be

> There are *fewer* flowers in the vase today.

Fewer refers to actual numbers; *less* refers to quantity in general.

> The powerful nations are *fewer* than they used to be.
> Nations have *less* power.

Lie, lay

See **Lay, lie.**

Like, as

See **As, like.**

Likewise

This expression is a clumsy transition, almost always a piece of bone in the hamburger.

Linking verb

A linking verb expresses the relationship between the subject and the predicate noun or predicate adjective. The principal linking verbs are *appear, be, become, seem,* and verbs used for sensations.

> Lorca *is* magnificent.
> Rose *became* a mother.
> Joe *looks* sick.
> The steak *smells* rotten.

Literally

We often say *literally* when we mean the opposite: *figuratively.* We use a metaphor, but we realize that it is dead and we play Dr. Frankenstein to the monster by applying the cathodes of *literally* (or *literal*).

> She was *literally* as big as a house.
> He was a *literal* man of straw.
> He hit the ball *literally* a thousand miles.

The monster never walks. Use *literally* only to emphasize that you mean just what you say.

> When the police broke into the warehouse, they found the Prime Minister *literally* weeping tears of gratitude.

Literal means "according to the letter" or "as it actually appears." Never use it unless you mean it literally. When you find yourself misusing it for the purposes above, you can either omit it and settle for the corpse of your metaphor, or you can make a new metaphor. "She was as big as. . . ."

Litotes

Litotes is a figure of speech understating something by saying the negative of its opposite saying "It's not a beauty" may mean "It's ugly."

Little

Often we misuse this word — which is necessary to common speech in its literal meaning — as a vague qualifier.

> He's a *little* late.

We misuse *pretty* in the same way, without considering its meaning. James Thurber tormented his editor on *The New Yorker* by writing that something was "a little big" and "pretty ugly."

Logic

See **Deductive reasoning** and **Inductive reasoning.**

See pages 237–250 for some remarks about persuasion, and an account of some common errors in thinking.

For further reading, consult Manuel Bilsky's *Patterns of Argument.*

Loose, lose

Different spellings make different words.

> The dog is *loose.*
> I *love* the dog.
> The *loose* rope *loses* the dog.

Luxuriant, luxurious

Luxuriant means "abundant in growth"; *luxurious* means "seeking the pleasures of the senses" or providing such pleasure.

> Her *luxuriant* hair was golden red.
> It was done in a *luxurious* gold and leather edition.

Main clause

A *main clause* can stand by itself. It can be a whole, simple sentence.

They built an armadillo.

Two *main clauses* can make a compound sentence.

They built an armadillo and they traded it for a VW.

In a complex sentence, a main clause (in italics) governs a subordinate clause.

When night fell, *they built an armadillo.*

Manuscript form

See page 341.

Man who . . .

A common circumlocution uses a noun (like *man* or *woman* or *person* or *senator* or *typist*) in a relative clause when the extra words serve no function.

He was *a man who* drank half a bottle of Scotch before breakfast.
She was *a woman who* knew better.
She was *a senator who* always filibustered.

If this last sentence gave us the information that she was a senator, it would be justified.

He was *a typist who* never typed more than twenty-seven words a minute.

These sentences can become:

He drank half a bottle of Scotch before breakfast.
She knew better.
She always filibustered.
He never typed more than twenty-seven words a minute.

May, can

See **Can, may.**

Metaphor

See pages 112–113.

Mixed constructions

Avoid sentences that begin as if they would follow one form, switch forms, and become mixed and confusing. Do not say,

> Because the annual snowfall reaches eighty inches causes everybody to keep their supply of food.

This example uses a dependent clause as a subject. It could be repaired into

> Because the annual snowfall reaches eighty inches, everyone keeps a supply of food.

Here is a mixed construction in which an adverbial clause is used as a noun.

> A Fourth of July celebration is when you have fireworks and picnics.

This can be changed to,

> At a Fourth of July celebration, you have fireworks and picnics.

Modifier

Any word or group of words that describes or qualifies another word or group of words is a modifier.

For a general account of Adjectives and Adverbs and Other Modifiers, see pages 96–106. For attention to some problems common in the use of modifiers, see pages 319–321.

Momentary, momentous

Momentary has to do with time. It means something that lasts only a moment, or happens at any moment. *Momentous* means of extraordinary importance, as in the cliché, "a *momentous* occasion."

> The affliction was *momentous*.
> She looked West, awaiting his *momentary* arrival.

Mood

The mood (or mode) of the verb indicates an attitude on the part of the writer. The mood may be indicative, imperative, or subjunctive. The indicative mood states a fact or asks a question.

> Jim *lives* in here.
> *Was* Bill Walton there?

The imperative mood gives a command, gives directions, or makes a request.

> *Beware* of darkness.
> *Turn* right at Golgotha.
> *Mend* my parachute, please.

The subjunctive mood expresses uncertainty, contradiction, wishfulness, regret, or speculation.

> I would feel better if Bizarre *were* there.
> If I *had* my way, I would tear this building down.

Morale, moral

Moral is a matter of ethics, *morale* of high or low spirits.

> Their *morals* were low, but their *morale* was high.
> Murder is not a *moral* act, usually.

Ms.

A recently invented title, on the analogy of *Mr., Mrs.,* and *Miss, Ms.* reveals female gender while it conceals marital status.

N.b.

This common abbreviation means, "notice well!," and serves to draw our attention to something.

Neither

See **Either.**

Neologism

A neologism is a made-up word, often used out of laziness or affectation when an old word would do. *Finalize* is a neologism; *end* or *finish* are the old words.

None

None can be either singular or plural, depending on context and intention.

> *None* of the other guys *were* going to the game.

> *None* of his fellow senators *was* likely to take so strong a stand on the war.

Nonrestrictive modifier

A nonrestrictive modifier is a parenthetical expression that does not limit the noun or pronoun modified. It can be a nonrestrictive clause,

> The Buick, *which was a car new to my neighborhood,* was the object of fascination.

or a phrase,

> The banana, *a fruit new to our taste,* was divided evenly.

See pages 327–328.

No one, nobody

These words take a singular verb. Third person pronouns, singular and plural, can refer to them: *he, his, him, she, hers, her, they, them*. We use *they* and *them* when we feel that the gender of the pronoun would be invidious.

Not un-

Eschew the habit of writing *not un-*'s.

A *not un*distinguished gentleman, in a *not un*elegant dinner jacket, *not un*gracefully strode past the *not un*chic lady.

Noun

There are several types of nouns. *Common* nouns belong to one of a class of people, places, or things (woman, country, table). *Proper* nouns are names of specific people, places, or things (Max von Sydow, Liv Ullman, Casablanca, Ann Arbor, *The New York Times*). *Concrete* nouns name something that can be perceived by the senses (acid, trees, eggs, horses). *Abstract* nouns name a general idea or quality (terror, love, harshness, agony). *Collective* nouns refer to a group as a unit (band, team, council, league). These categories are not mutually exclusive; a word like *tree* is common and concrete.

Nouns, whatever their functions in a sentence, retain their basic form (unlike verbs), varying it only in forming the plural and the possessive. The plural in most nouns is formed by adding *-s* to the singular, the possessive by adding an apostrophe and an *-s* to the singular, or an apostrophe after the *-s* of the plural: hen, hens, hen's, hens'; house, houses, house's. Some nouns add *-es* for the plural: hero, heroes, hero's, heroes'. A few nouns change their internal spelling for the plural: man, men; woman, women; here, the possessive is formed by an apostrophe and an *-s*, in singular and in plural (man's, men's). Other nouns with an irregular plural are listed on page 343.

For stylistic advice about nouns, see pages 86–94.

Nouns commonly used as blanks

Many nouns, which are perfectly useful when spoken with care, are frequently used imprecisely, wordily, and without utility — nouns used as blanks: *aspect, case, character, factor, fact, element, effect, nature, manner, respect* and *feature*.

Some *aspects* in the *case* of Rumpelstiltskin have the *character* of *elements* that seem sinister in *nature*. The *fact* that the enraged dwarf was a *factor* in the *nature* of the King's *manner* is a *feature* with *respect* to which we can not distinguish the *effect*.

This paragraph has the consistency of mud or an annual report.

Noun substitute

A noun substitute, whether clause or phrase or pronoun, functions as a noun.

Number

See **Inflection.**

Numeral

See pages 341–342.

Object

A complete sentence needs a subject and a verb; it need not have an object.

The cat screeched.

is a complete sentence.

The cat clawed *Herbert.*

includes an object. An object is something a verb acts upon.

Objects are direct and indirect. A *direct object* is any noun (or noun substitute) that answers the questions *what?* or *whom?* after a transitive verb. Direct objects are the objects of the verb's action.

She toppled *the giant.*
He knows *what she wants.*

An *indirect object* is a noun or noun substitute which is indirectly affected by the verb's action and which tells *to whom* or *for whom* the action is done.

She gave *him* a karate chop.

Him is the indirect object, *karate chop* the direct object.

Object complement

See **Complement.**

Of

We often use *of* when we don't have to.

outside *of* the house
off *of* the ground
inside *of* the room

The phrases read more stylishly as:

outside the house
off the ground
inside the room

Keep the *of* when the extra preposition changes meaning. "Outside *of*" can mean "to the exclusion *of*," and we are correct to say, "Outside *of* scientific speculation, there is no use for such calibration." "Inside *of*" can mean "in less than." "Inside *of* an hour, he had finished the work."

One, you

Be careful not to use *one* in place of *you* so much that it sounds awkward or pretentious.

> Should *one* be careful to avoid the use of the word "one" when *one* is speaking to a woman whom *one* loves?

As suggested by this example, context is important when you consider using *one*. It is useful at times, but it has a way of seeming affected. Never use it as an obvious disguise for the word *I*.

> *One* took an amusing jaunt to Cedar Point last summer.

Finally, be careful not to mix "one" and "you" or "I" in the same sentence.

One of the most . . .

This cliché is drained of meaning.

> She is *one of the most* lovable people in the world.

> The rodeo was *one of the most* exciting experiences of my life.

If you use this phrase, cross it out and consider the particulars to which you refer. One example, showing the character *being* lovable, is worth ten thousand assertions. An exciting anecdote from the rodeo makes assertion unnecessary.

Show, don't tell.

Parallelism

See pages 152–156.

Parentheses

See pages 337–338.

Participle

See **Verbal.**

Passive voice

A verb is in the passive voice when it *acts upon* the subject.

> LeFlore *was hit* by the pitch.

See **Active voice.**

Period

See pages 323–324.

Person

In grammar, the person of a verb or a pronoun shows that someone is speaking (in *first person*), or is spoken to (*second person*), or is spoken about (*third person*). In "I see, you see, he sees," the person of the pronoun changes each time; the verb form for the first person and the second person happens to be the same, but the verb form changes to indicate the third person. With a few verbs, the form changes with each change of person (I *am*, you *are*, he *is*).

Phrase

Phrases function as a part of speech, and do not have a subject and a predicate.

An *infinitive* phrase:

I studied *to learn Greek.*

A *prepositional* phrase:

The flower grows *in the mountain.*

A *verb* phrase:

The zebra *is catching up.*

A *participle* phrase:

Sliding into second, Zarido tore a ligament.

Plagiarism

Plagiarism is using other people's work, whether it is a published source used without acknowledgment or a friend's old paper or a term paper bought from an entrepreneur.

Possessive

For the possessive of nouns, see **Noun.** For the possessive of pronouns, see **Pronoun.**

Precede, proceed

To precede is to go before or in front of.

The Pirates *preceded* the Reds onto the field.

To proceed is to continue, or to begin again.

After the game, they *proceeded* to the airport.

Predicate

A predicate is the part of the sentence *about* the subject. It includes verbs, and, on occasion, adverbs, direct objects, indirect objects, and clauses attached to the predicate.

See pages 123–124.

Predicate adjective

See **Complement.**

Predicate noun

See **Complement.**

Preposition

Prepositions show the relationship between a noun or noun equivalent and another word in the sentence. Some of the most commonly used prepositions are: *across, after, at, behind, between, by, for, from, of, on, over, to, under,* and *with.*

Tom hid *in* the attic.

The preposition *in* relates the noun *attic* to the verb *hid*

Presently

This word means "in a little while," and not "now" or "currently." Say,

He is *at present* a milkman.

not

He is *presently* a milkman.

But say,

He will come back to Chicago *presently.*

Pretty

See **Little.**

Principal, principle

Principle is a noun meaning a general truth (the *principles* of physics) or moral ideas (she had the highest *principles*). The adjective *principal* means the foremost. One could speak of the *principal principle* of a science or a philosophy. The noun *principal* means the chief officer.

Alex Emerson is the *principal* of Bob's school.

Pronoun

A pronoun is a word used in place of a noun.

Personal pronouns:

I, you, he, she, we, etc.

Relative pronouns:

who, which, that

Demonstrative pronouns:

this, that, these, those

Indefinite pronouns:

each, either, any, some, someone, all, etc.

Reciprocal pronouns:

each other, one another

Reflexive, or intensive, pronouns:

myself, yourself, etc.

Proper noun

See **Noun.**

Prophesy, prophecy

The word with the *s* is the verb, the word with the *c* the noun.

The priest *prophesied* doom.
It was an accurate *prophecy.*

Punctuation

See pages 323–338.

Quotation marks

See pages 332–333.

Rational, rationale

Rational means reasonable and sensible. It is an adjective. *Rationale* is a noun meaning the whole system of reasons behind an idea, a position, or an action.

His arguments were *rational.*
Her *rationale* for the program was easy to discern.

Real, really

Conversational usage accepts *real* as an adverb, but it will not do in writing. Write:

> The boat was *really* handsome!
> Josephine seemed to be a *really* happy girl.

Don't write:

> The boat was *real* handsome.
> Josephine seemed to be a *real* happy girl.

Real as an adjective survives.

> It was a *real* boat.

Frequently, we use *real* and *really* as weak intensifiers, and our sentences will be stronger without them.

Reason is because
Don't use this construction. If you must use "reason is," have it be *"reason is that. . . ."*

Relative clause
See **Subordinate clause.**

Relative pronoun
See **Pronoun.**

Respectfully, respectively
Respectfully is an adverb that modifies an action full of respect.

> I remain, yours *respectfully,*

Respectively pertains to each of a number, in an order.

> He swore that he saw Ted and Joan wearing a flower and a bowler, *respectively*

Therefore to end a letter "Yours *respectively*" makes little sense.

Restrictive clause or modifier
A restrictive modifier is a clause or a phrase essential to the identity of what is modified.

> Everybody *who wants* can get to the top.

See **Nonrestrictive modifier** for contrast.

Rhetoric
Rhetoric is the art of discourse, either spoken or written.

Rhetorical question
The rhetorical question is a frequent device of argument or per-

suasion. We ask a question, not to be answered, but to affect the listener or reader.

> Are we born, to suffer and to die, only to satisfy the whims of rich warmongers?

> Must we write themes forever?

Run-on sentence

A run-on sentence fuses two sentences.

> I was eight my brother was ten.

is a run-on or fused sentence. It should read:

> I was eight. My brother was ten.

Satire

Satire is a form of literature, either prose or poetry, which uses ridicule to expose and to judge behavior or ideas that the satirist finds foolish, or wicked, or both.

Seldom ever

This phrase is redundant. *Seldom* will do. Instead of,

> He *seldom ever* brushed his hair.

say

> He *seldom* brushed his hair.

Semantics

The study of the meanings and associations of words. A good book on semantics is S. I. Hayakawa, *Language in Thought and Action.*

Semicolon

See pages 330–331.

Sensual, sensuous

The two words have different meanings. *Sensual* has unfavorable connotations and means "preoccupied with or inclined to the gratification of the senses or appetites."

> He was wholly *sensual* in his priorities; his gluttony came first.

Sensuous has complimentary connotations and describes things that give pleasure to the senses.

> The passage is one of the most *sensuous* in all literature.

Sentence fragment

See pages 129–131, and 306–309.

Sentence types

See **Compound-complex sentence, Compound sentence, Complex sentence,** and **Simple sentence.**

Shall, will

In common speech and most writing, we make small distinction between the words.

Formally, *I shall* expresses a person's belief about his future.

I shall be twenty-one in December.

I will expresses his willpower, his wish.

I will get to Japan before I die!

Should, would

Should expresses obligation.

You *should* be ashamed.

It is confused with *would* when it is used in other senses.

I *should* not have reached Chicago without your loan.

When we use the past of *shall* in an indirect quotation, formal prose requires *should* instead of *would*.

I said that you *should* be ready before eight.

Would commonly expresses habitual activities.

He *would* visit the lake and fish from dawn to dusk.

When another phrase (like "every summer," if it were added to the last sentence) expresses habit, we can drop the *would* and use the past tense alone.

He visited the lake every summer, and fished from dawn to dusk.

Should have, should of

The words are *should have*, which can be pronounced *should've*. *Should of* does not make sense.

Sic

Pronounced "sick," this Latin word appears in quotations, enclosed in brackets, to signify that an error was made in the source material, not by the writer copying the quotation.

Studebaker writes, "I would rather be Thoreu [*sic*] unhappy than a contented pig."

Simile

A figure of speech in which comparison is openly made, usually by "like" or "as."

He walks like a turkey.
They play volleyball as Rome played Carthage.

Simple sentence

A simple sentence has one main clause and no subordinate clauses.

She barked at the full moon.

See pages 126–127.

So

This word is a stylistic pitfall for many beginning writers.
As a coordinating conjunction, *so* is often boring and repetitious, leading the writer into dull compound sentences.

She was tall *so* he asked her how she liked the weather up there.
She was tired of hearing that question *so* she knocked him flat.

As a vague intensive, *so* is as useless as *wonderful* and *terrible*, though it occupies less space.

The building was *so* tall.
I am *so* glad to see you!

Sort of

See **Kind of.**

Spelling

See pages 342–344.

Split infinitive

An infinitive is the form of the verb that uses *to*, as in *to run, to think, to scratch.* When we place another word (commonly an adverb) in the middle of an infinitive, we are splitting the infinitive.

to quickly run
to occasionally think
to from time to time scratch

Grammarians used to insist that the infinitive never be split. People split them anyway.

Remember *to never split* the infinitive!

Now, most grammarians consider a prohibition against split infinitives fussy. But careful writers rarely split them.

Stationary, stationery

Stationary is an adjective that means "standing still." *Stationery* means "writing materials."

Style

See Chapters I to V. See also William Strunk and E. B. White, *The Elements of Style;* and Bergen Evans, *A Dictionary of Contemporary American Usage;* and *A Dictionary of Modern English Usage* by H. W. Fowler, rev. and ed. by Sir Ernest Gowers. See also *The Modern Stylists*, ed. Donald Hall, a collection of essays and excerpts by George Orwell, Ernest Hemingway, Ezra Pound, Edmund Wilson, James Thurber, and others.

Subject

A subject is a noun, or a noun substitute, about which something is stated or questioned. The subject usually comes before the predicate. The complete subject is the subject and all the words (modifiers, etc.) that belong to it.

The grinning barbarian, his teeth clenched, looked into the barnyard.

Barbarian is the simple subject; the first six words make the complete subject.

Subjunctive

See **Mood.**

Subordinate clause

A subordinate (or dependent) clause cannot stand by itself and make a whole sentence. It depends upon a main clause.

I cannot see *who it is.*
The claws are not lethal, *because he was de-clawed.*

Substantive

A *substantive* is a word or group of words used as a noun; it may be a *noun, pronoun, phrase,* or *noun clause.*

Suppose, supposed

The past tense often disappears, and meaning disappears with it. See **Used to, use to.**

Syntax

Syntax is the way in which words are put together to form larger units, *phrases, clauses,* or *sentences.* It is also the part of grammar that describes this putting together.

Tense

The tense of a verb shows the time an action takes place in. In the last sentence, *shows* is in the present tense. In

I *showed* you.

showed is in the past tense.

I *will show* you.

uses the future tense.

Than, then

These words are different in spelling, meaning, and function. *Then* refers to time, and *than* makes a comparison.

We were nice *then.*
She was taller *than* he was.

That, which, who

We use the word *that* in a number of ways.
It is a demonstrative, as in "*that* cat."
Many writers are confused about when to use *that* and when to use *which* in introducing clauses. Nonrestrictive (nondefining) clauses take *which.*

The old car, *which* was struggling through the winter, seemed younger when spring arrived.

When the clause is restrictive or defining, we use *that* when it is possible, which is most of the time.

The old car *that* Mr. Hornback owned was struggling up the hill.

Which is possible in this last sentence, but seems overprecise or rigid, and is stylistically inferior. However, when a sentence requires several restrictive clauses in a row, *that* can become confusing, and we had better revert to *which.*

The old car *which* Mr. Hornback owned, *which* had one headlight dangling loose, and *which* smelled perpetually of gasoline, chugged struggling up the hill.

Remember that *who* applies to people, whether the clause is restrictive or nonrestrictive, and *which* never applies to people.

> The folks *which* lived next door.

is incorrect. Some writers, informally, substitute *that* for *who* on occasions when the person is seen as if from a distance.

> The man *that* stood outside the door was tall and fortyish.

Their, there, they're
See page 331.

Through, thru
Thru is incorrect, merely a labor-saving device, adopted by sign painters, advertisers, and the fabricators of headlines.

Toward, towards
Either is possible. *Toward* is more American.

Transitive verb
A transitive verb *must* have a direct object to fill out its meaning.

> He *put the book* down.

Try and
Like *take and.*

> *Try and see* if she's home.

is a long way to say,

> *See* if she's home.

Type
Type is another word to stay away from. Even used gramatically, it is usually filler.

> It was a strange *type* of animal.

boils down nicely to

> It was a strange animal.

Occasionally, as with *sort* or *kind*, we actually mean something by the word.

Never use it next to a noun, without the preposition *of* coming between. It is useless to say:

> a new *type* soft drink   their *type* business
> a long *type* Buick   that *type* handsomeness

In all these examples, an *of* would make the phrases more acceptable; but in the first three, omission of *type* would be the better solution. We save a word. In the fourth example, the idea of *type* (or *sort* or *kind*) has more meaning, but could benefit from greater specificity.

Unthinkable, inconceivable

Something that is literally *unthinkable* is probably literally unmentionable. We use *unthinkable* as hyperbole, usually to describe something that we deplore.

> His conduct was *unthinkable.*

Inconceivable means "impossible to imagine or explain."

> Her absence was *inconceivable.*

Until, till

We say *till,* but we write *until. Till* looks stilted and literary on the page.

Used to, use to

The correct form is *used to.*

> I *used to* see her every morning at 9 o'clock.

Probably because of our slovenly pronunciation, we sometimes drift into,

> I *use to* see her every morning at 9 o'clock.

when we write it down. We should use the correct form, to make temporal sense. The same is true of *supposed to.*

Verb

For advice on style and the verb, see pages 76–83. In this glossary, see **Active voice, Mood, Object, Passive voice,** and **Predicate.**

Verbal

Verbals are words derived from verbs but used as nouns or adjectives, and sometimes as adverbs. Verbals are *gerunds, participles,* and *infinitives.*

Gerunds always end in -ing and are used as nouns.

> *Flying* is fun.
> *Running* is good exercise.
> Neal and Liz have benefited from their *running.*

Participles (past and present) are used as adjectives.

This *flying* manual is essential.
His *shattered* hip was mending slowly.
"The *rising* cost of living" is a common phrase.

Infinitives are used primarily as nouns, but sometimes as adjectives or adverbs. They are composed of *to* and a verb, but in use the *to* can occasionally be omitted.

We started *to run* from Godzilla.
To fail is a pleasure he can't afford.
He dropped out *to begin* his career as a clown.
They helped [to] *eat* the submarine.

Vocative

See **Direct address.**

When

Don't use *when* as an introduction to definitions.

Loneliness is *when* you play the radio just to hear the announcer's voice.

You could say, instead:

You are lonely *when* you play the radio just to hear the announcer's voice.

or:

It is a definition of loneliness to play the radio just to hear the announcer's voice.

This usage is corny and unacceptable.

Where

See **When.** The same injunction applies.

Which, that

See **That, which, who.**

While

The word means "at the same time" or "during the time that." Sometimes writers use it in place of *although*, and it can work.

While John is large, his stomach is not excessive.

But this usage is prone to ambiguity.

Winter is warm in the southern hemisphere, *while* summer is cold.

Think about this sentence for a moment, and it is absurd.

Who, whom

Who is a subject, *whom* an object.

Who's on first?
To whom should I deliver the testimony?

In the last sentence, *whom* is the object of the preposition *to*. In formal writing, always say *whom* when it is an object — of a verb or of a preposition.

Sometimes position leads us into error. When a pronoun precedes a verb, it sounds as if it were a subject; it isn't always. We may be tempted to write,

From *who* is the noise coming?

but the phrase is *from whom*, and *the noise* (not *who*) is the subject of *is*. We should write,

From *whom* is the noise coming?

Sometimes a clause separates the subject *who* from its verb, and we misuse *whom* for *who*. We write,

Herbert, *whom* she said would be here at 6:30, strolled in at 8:00.

In this sentence the three noun-verb combinations make a box within a box within a box. "Herbert . . . strolled" is the outside box, "who . . . would be here" is the middle box, and "she said" the inside box. When *whom* comes before a preposition of which it is the object, it is correct but highly formal.

Whom am I looking at?

Here, we always write *who* in informal writing. Frequently, *whom* will sound too formal even in an essay that is mostly formal. Use your judgment. The position of the pronoun makes the problem, which comes up when it is the object of a verb as well as when it is the object of a preposition.

Whom do I see?
Who do I see?

The first is correct and the second incorrect — technically — but it would take a highly formal context to accept the "correct" form without creating a moment of stuffiness.

Whose, who's

See pages 331–332.

-wise

Stylewise, avoid this syllable in combination with words with which it has not been combined before. *Clockwise* and *otherwise* are parts of the language. Avoid literarywise, poetrywise, intelligence quotientwise. Septemberwise, costwise, Sallywise, ecologywise — and anything similar.

Woman, women

People seem to forget that the two spellings show a difference in number. *Woman* is singular, *women* plural.

Eldridge Cleaver. Quotations on pages 176, 224 from *Soul on Ice* by Eldridge Cleaver. Copyright © 1968 by Eldridge Cleaver. Reprinted by permission of McGraw-Hill Book Company.

Marvin Cohen. Quotation on pages 217–218 from *Baseball the Beautiful* by Marvin Cohen. Copyright © 1974 by Marvin Cohen. Reprinted by permission.

John Collier. Quotation on pages 225–226 from *Indians of the Americas* by John Collier. Copyright 1947, © 1975 by John Collier. Reprinted by arrangement with The New American Library, Inc., New York, N.Y.

James B. Conant. Quotation on pages 256–257 from the article "Athletics: The Poison Ivy in Our Schools," *Look Magazine,* copyright 1961, Cowles Broadcasting, Inc. Reprinted by permission of Cowles Communications, Inc.

Hart Crane. Quotation on page 275 from *The Collected Poems and Selected Letters and Prose of Hart Crane* by Hart Crane. Copyright 1933, © 1958, 1966 by Liveright Publishing Corporation. Reprinted by permission.

Joan Didion. Quotation on pages 46–47 excerpted from "On Going Home." Reprinted from *Slouching Towards Bethlehem* by Joan Didion by permission of Farrar, Straus & Giroux, Inc., and William Morris Agency, Inc., on behalf of the author. Copyright © 1967, 1968 by Joan Didion.

Annie Dillard. Quotation on page 181 from *Pilgrim at Tinker Creek,* pp. 4–5, by Annie Dillard. Copyright © 1974 by Annie Dillard. Reprinted by permission of Harper & Row, Publishers, Inc. and Blanche C. Gregory, Inc.

Robert Frost. Quotation on pages 272–273 from "Acquainted with the Night" by Robert Frost. From *The Poetry of Robert Frost,* edited by Edward Connery Lathem. Copyright 1928, © 1969 by Holt, Rinehart and Winston. Copyright © 1956 by Robert Frost. Reprinted by permission of Holt, Rinehart and Winston, Publishers, Jonathan Cape Ltd., and the Estate of Robert Frost.

Ivan Illich. Quotation on pages 257–258 from *Deschooling Society* by Ivan Illich, pp. 6–7, 76–77. Copyright © 1970, 1971 by Ivan Illich. Reprinted by permission of Harper & Row, Publishers, Inc. and Marion Boyars Ltd.

Oliver Jensen. Quotation on pages 169–170, "The Gettysburg Address in Eisenhowese" by Oliver Jensen, previously published in *The Territorial Enterprise* and *The New Republic,* June 17, 1957. Copyright © 1957 by Oliver Jensen. Reprinted by permission of the author.

R. D. Laing. Quotation on page 85 from *Self and Others* by R. D. Laing. Copyright © 1961, 1969 by R. D. Laing. Reprinted by permission of Pantheon Books, a Division of Random House, Inc.

D. H. Lawrence. Quotation on page 256 from *Pornography and Obscenity* by D. H. Lawrence. Copyright 1930 by Alfred A. Knopf, Inc. Reprinted by permission of Alfred A. Knopf, Inc., Laurence Pollinger Ltd., and the Estate of Mrs. Frieda Lawrence Ravagli.

Peter McCabe. Quotation on page 190 from "Vanity Fair" by Peter McCabe. Copyright © 1977 by *Harper's Magazine.* All rights reserved. Reprinted from the August 1977 issue by special permission.

Mary McCarthy. Quotations on pages 145–146, 184 excerpted from "America the Beautiful" in *On the Contrary* by Mary McCarthy. Copyright © 1957, 1961 by Mary McCarthy. Reprinted with the permission of Farrar, Straus & Giroux, Inc.

Antonio Machado. Quotation on page 159 from *The Sea and the Honeycomb* by Antonio Machado, translated by Robert Bly. Copyright © 1971 by Robert Bly. Reprinted by permission.

Norman Mailer. Quotation on pages 259–261 from *The Prisoner of Sex* by Norman Mailer (Boston: Little, Brown, 1971). Copyright © 1971 by Norman Mailer. Reprinted by permission of the author and the author's agent, Scott Meredith Literary Agency, 845 Third Avenue, New York, New York 10022.

James McCartney. Quotation on pages 224–225 from the *Detroit Free Press.* Reprinted by permission.

Margaret Mead. Quotation on pages 197–198 from *Male and Female* by Margaret Mead. Copyright 1949, 1955 by Margaret Mead. Reprinted by permission of William Morrow & Company, Inc., and Victor Gollancz, London. Quotations on pages 107, 258–259 from "Needed: Full Partnership for Women" by Margaret Mead, *Saturday Review,* June 14, 1975, © 1975 by Saturday Review/World, Inc. Reprinted by permission of the author.

Nancy Milford. Quotation on pages 51–52 from *Zelda* by Nancy Milford, p. 48. Copyright © 1970 by Nancy Winston Milford. Reprinted by permission of Harper & Row, Publishers, Inc. and The Bodley Head Ltd.

The New Yorker. Quotation on pages 52–53 from "Elvis!" Talk of the Town, *The New Yorker,* June 17, 1972. Reprinted by permission; © 1972 The New Yorker Magazine, Inc.

John A. Parrish. Quotations on pages 252, 254 from *12, 20 & 5: A Doctor's Year in Vietnam* by John A. Parrish, M.D. Copyright © 1972 by John A. Parrish, M.D. Reprinted by permission of the publishers, E. P. Dutton, and Gerard McCauley Agency.

Robert M. Pirsig. Quotations on pages 211–212, 223–224, 254–255 from *Zen and the Art of Motorcycle Maintenance* by Robert M. Pirsig. Copyright © 1974 by Robert M. Pirsig. Reprinted by permission of William Morrow & Company, Inc.

George Plimpton. Quotation on page 255 from "The American Tradition of Winning" by George Plimpton. Reprinted courtesy *Mainliner* Magazine carried aboard United Airlines. Copyright © 1976 East/West Network, Inc.

Ezra Pound. Quotation on page 35 from *Gaudier Brzeska,* pp. 86–87, 89, by Ezra Pound. Copyright 1926 by Ezra Pound. Copyright © 1970 by Ezra Pound. All rights reserved. Reprinted by permission of New Directions and Faber and Faber Ltd.

Tracy W. Redding. Quotation on pages 264–265 from *Hoosier Farm Boy* by Tracy Redding (Philadelphia: Dorrance, 1966). Reprinted by permission of the author's estate.

Antoine de Saint-Exupéry. Quotation on pages 221–222 from *Wind, Sand and Stars* by Antoine de Saint-Exupéry, translated by Lewis Galantiere. Copyright 1939 by Antoine de Saint-Exupéry, renewed 1967 by Lewis Galantiere. Reprinted by permission of Harcourt Brace Jovanovich, Inc., and William Heinemann Ltd.

James Thurber. Quotations on pages 39–40, 114–115, 165 from *The Years with Ross* by James Thurber, published by Atlantic-Little, Brown. Copyright © 1959 by James Thurber. Reprinted by permission of Mrs. James Thurber and Hamish Hamilton Ltd.

Dan Wakefield. Quotations on pages 96, 144 from *Island of the City* by Dan Wakefield, published by Houghton Mifflin Company. Copyright © 1957, 1958, 1959 by Dan Wakefield. Reprinted by permission of Knox Burger Associates.

Diane White. Quotation on pages 85–86 from "The Noble Asparagus," by Diane White, in *The Boston Globe,* May 26, 1977. Reprinted courtesy of *The Boston Globe.*

William Butler Yeats. Quotation on pages 64, 238 from "Ego Dominus Tuus" by William Butler Yeats. From *Collected Poems* of William Butler Yeats. Copyright 1918 by Macmillan Publishing Co., Inc., renewed 1946 by Bertha Georgie Yeats. Reprinted by permission of Macmillan Publishing Co., Inc., M.B. Yeats, and Miss Anne Yeats.

Author and
Title Index

"Second Tree from the Corner, The,"
172–173, 220
White, Theodore H.
Making of the President 1960, The, 203–
204, 204
Whitehead, A. N.
Adventures of Ideas, 40
Wiesel, Elie
Beggar in Jerusalem, A, 131
Williams, Thomas
Town Burning, 73
Wind, Sand and Stars (Antoine de Saint-
Exupéry), 221–222
Wing, George
Hardy, 274
Wolff, Cynthia Griffin
Feast of Words, A, 108

"Woodstein U." (*The Atlantic Monthly*),
23
Woolf, Virginia
"Room of One's Own, A," 120–121
Worldly Philosophers, The (Robert L.
Heilbroner), 163

Years with Ross, The (James Thurber), 39–
40, 114–115, 165

Zelda (Nancy Milford), 51–52
*Zen and the Art of Motorcycle Mainte-
nance* (Robert M. Pirsig), 211–212,
223–224, 254–255
Zen proverb, 159, 163
Zorba the Greek (Nikos Kazantzakis), 218

Subject Index

408

To the Student

   Part of our job as educational publishers is to try to improve the textbooks we publish. Thus, when revising we take into account the experience of both instructors and students with the previous edition. At some time your instructor will be asked to comment extensively on *Writing Well*, Third Edition, but right now we want to hear from you. After all, though your instructor assigned this book you are the one who paid for it.

   Please help us by completing this questionnaire and returning it to College English Developmental Group, Little, Brown and Company, 34 Beacon Street, Boston, Mass. 02106.

School: _____ Course Title:_____

Instructor's Name: _____

1. What parts of *Writing Well*, Third Edition, were most useful to you?

   Why? _____

   _____

   _____

   _____

   _____

   _____

2. What parts did you find least helpful? Why?_____

   _____

   _____

   _____

   _____

3. Did you use "A Brief Review of Grammar, Punctuation, and Mechanics?" _____

    Did you find it useful? _____

4. Did you find the Glossary helpful? _____

    _____

    _____

    _____

    _____

5. Any suggestions for improving *Writing Well?* _____

    _____

    _____

    _____

    _____

    _____

    _____

    _____

    _____

    _____

    _____

6. Will you keep this book for future reference? _____

    _____

    Date   Name

    _____

    Mailing Address

                                        Thanks for your help.